Restoring the Two Houses of Israel

by
Eddie Chumney

Restoring the Two Houses of Israel
Copyright © 1999 by Edward Chumney

ALL RIGHTS RESERVED

All Scripture references are from the Authorized King James Version of the Bible, unless otherwise marked and noted in the bibliography. Hebrew Greek Key Study Bible (King James Version) Copyright © 1984, 1991 by AMG International, Inc., Chattanooga, Tennessee 37422. Scripture quotations marked (Jewish New Testament) are taken from The Jewish New Testament, Copyright © 1979, 1989, 1990, 1991 by David H. Stern. Published by Jewish New Testament Publications. All rights reserved.

Published by:

Serenity Books
**P.O. Box 3595
Hagerstown, MD 21742-3595**

ISBN 1-884369-77-4

Printed in the United States of America
for Worldwide Distribution

Contents

Acknowledgments 5
Foreword 7

1. Who Are the Two Houses of Israel? 15
2. Who Is the Church and Who Is Israel? 23
3. G-d's Power Twins: Torah and Grace 55
4. The Sabbath: Our Rest Is in Messiah 99
5. The 7,000-Year Plan of G-d 143
6. Yeshua, Our Jewish Messiah 193
7. Is the Jewish Messiah G-d? 249
8. Israel: The Fig Tree Blossoms 293
9. The United Nations-Israel-Arab Peace Process 347
10. Jerusalem: The City of the Great King 375
11. The Judgment of the Nations 419
12. Ephraim and Judah Become One House 435

From the Author 525

Endnotes 529
Bibliography 537

Acknowledgments

I would like to give praise and thanksgiving to the L-RD G-d of Israel for blessing me with faithful and loving parents, Doyle and Lillian Chumney, who have given me much support, encouragement, care and love over the years. Dad and Mom, you are the most special parents in the entire world and I LOVE YOU !!!

This book is written exclusively for the glory of the G-d of Israel and His Kingdom *(Malkut Shamayim)*. May all blessing, glory, praise, and honor be given to the King of kings and the L-RD of lords. (Revelation 5:11-14, 7:9-12, 19:16)

The Set Time To Favor Zion

NOW is the set time to favor Zion. In Psalm *(Tehillim)* 102:13, 16-18 it is written:

> *"Thou shalt arise, and have **mercy upon Zion**: for the time to favor her, yea, the set time, is come … when the* LORD *shall **build up Zion**, he shall appear in his glory. He will regard the prayer of the destitute, and not despise their prayer. This shall be written for the generation to come: and the people which shall be created shall praise the* LORD*."*

In Isaiah *(Yeshayahu)* 62:1, 7 it is written:

> *"For **Zion's sake** will I not hold my peace, and for Jerusalem's sake I will not rest, until the righteousness thereof go forth as brightness, and the salvation thereof as a lamp that burneth. ... And give him no rest, till he establish, and till he make Jerusalem a praise in the earth."*

Blow a Trumpet in Zion

In Joel *(Yoel)* 2:1 it is written:

> *"**Blow ye the trumpet in Zion**, and sound an alarm in my holy mountain: let all the inhabitants of the land tremble: for the day of the Lord cometh, for it is nigh at hand."*

In Jeremiah *(Yermiyahu)* 31:6-7, 10 it is written:

> *"For there shall be a day, that the watchman upon the mount Ephraim shall cry, Arise ye, and **let us go up to Zion** unto the Lord our God. For thus saith the Lord, Sing with gladness for Jacob, and shout among the chief of the nations: publish ye, praise ye, and say, O Lord, save thy people, the remnant of Israel ... Hear the word of the Lord, O ye nations, and declare it in the isles afar off, and say, He that scattered Israel will gather him, and keep him, as a shepherd doth his flock."*

May the G-d of Israel arise and have mercy upon Zion speedily in our days. Amen!

Foreword

For over 2,000 years, Orthodox Jews have prayed for the Ingathering of the Exiles *(Qibbutz Galuyot)* from the four corners of the earth (Deuteronomy *[Devarim]* 30:1-5). Ever since the destruction of Jerusalem (*Yerushalayim*) and the Temple *(Beit HaMikdash)* by the Romans in 70 CE (Common Era), Orthodox Jews have prayed three times a day for this Ingathering.[1] For Orthodox Jews, the Ingathering of the Exiles is synonymous with NATIONAL Redemption.

The requests for Redemption and for the coming of the Messiah *(Mashiach)* are part of the *Amidah* prayer (known also as "The Eighteen Benedictions"). This prayer along with the *Shema* ("Hear, O Israel") is recited three times a day by Orthodox Jews and is regarded as the most important daily prayer. The *Amidah* prayer was edited by Rabban Gamaliel II soon after the destruction of the Jerusalem Temple by the Romans in 70 CE. The tenth benediction of the *Amidah* prayer is a prayer for the Ingathering of the Exiles *(Qibbutz Galuyot)*.[2] The full text of this tenth benediction reads as follows:

> "Blow the Great Shofar for our freedom, and lift up a banner to gather our exiles, and gather us from the four corners of the earth. Blessed art Thou, O Lord, who gathers the banished of thy people, Israel."

This is a prayer for **ALL 12 TRIBES** to be gathered back to the land of Israel. Closely associated with this Ingathering of the Exiles *(Qibbutz Galuyot)* is the ingathering of the Ten Lost Tribes who were exiled by the Assyrians in 721 BCE and believed to dwell beyond the mythical river Sambatyon. [3]

It is widely believed among Orthodox Jews that Elijah will precede the coming of the Messiah *(Mashiach)* and will announce the redemption to the seed of Jacob (all 12 tribes). In an Orthodox Jewish rabbinic commentary to Leviticus *(Vayikra)* 26:42 (Mid. Haser w'Yater, pp. 16, 42, and Rashi ad Leviticus 26:42) it is taught:

> "Everywhere in the Bible the name of Jacob is spelled without the [Hebrew] letter **vav**, except for five places; and everywhere the name of Elijah is spelled with a **vav**, except for five places. Why? To teach you that Elijah will come and redeem the seed of Jacob. Jacob took the **vav** from the name of Elijah as a pledge that **Elijah would come and announce the redemption** of the world to his children." [4]

In Luke 1, Zacharias was a priest of the course of Abijah (I Chronicles 24:10) who was praying the *Amidah* prayer in the Temple *(Beit HaMikdash)*. As he was praying, the angel Gabriel spoke to him and told him that his prayer had been heard and that he would have a son named John *(Yochanan)* who would be of the **SPIRIT** and power **OF ELIJAH**. In Luke 1:5-9, 11, 13, 15-17, 67-68, 72-73 it is written:

"There was in the days of Herod, the king of Judea, a certain priest named Zacharias, of the course of Abia [Abijah]: *and his wife was of the daughter of Aaron, and her name was Elisabeth* [Elisheva]. *And they were both righteous* [tzaddik] *before God, walking in all the commandments* [mitzvot] *and ordinances of the* LORD *blameless* [tamim]. *And they had no child, because that Elisabeth* [Elisheva] *was barren, and they both were now well stricken in years. And it came to pass, that while he executed the priest's office before God in the order of his course, According to the custom of the priest's office, his lot was to burn incense when he went into the temple of the* LORD *... And there appeared unto him an angel* [Gabriel] *of the* LORD *standing on the right side of the altar of incense ... the angel said unto him, Fear not, Zacharias: for thy prayer is heard; and thy wife Elisabeth* [Elisheva] *shall bear thee a son: and thou shalt call his name John* [Yochanan] *... he shall be filled with the Holy Ghost* [Ruach HaKodesh] *even from his mother's womb. And many of the children of Israel* [the seed of Jacob — Mid. Haser w'Yater, pp. 16, 42, and Rashi ad Leviticus 26:42] *shall he turn* [teshuvah] *to the* LORD *their God. And he shall go before him in the* **SPIRIT** *and power* **OF ELIJAH***, to turn the hearts of the fathers to the children* [Malachi 4:5-6] *and the disobedient to the wisdom of the just; to make ready a people prepared for the* LORD *... And his father Zacharias was filled with the Holy Ghost* [Ruach HaKodesh] *and prophesied, saying, Blessed be the* LORD *God of Israel; for he has visited and redeemed his people ... to perform the*

mercy promised to our fathers, and to remember his holy covenant; The oath which he swore to our father Abraham..."

Orthodox Jews believe that there is a suffering Messiah and a Kingly Messiah. The suffering Messiah *(Mashiach)* is known as *Messiah ben Yosef* (Joseph). The Kingly Messiah *(Mashiach)* is known as *Messiah ben David*.

Non-Jews who believe that *Yeshua*/Jesus is the Jewish Messiah *(Mashiach)* also believe in a suffering Messiah and a Kingly Messiah. However, they believe that both of these roles will be fulfilled by the Jewish Messiah *(Mashiach) Yeshua*/Jesus. In His first coming, He came to fulfill the role of the suffering Messiah (*Messiah ben Yosef* /Joseph). In His second coming, He will come to fulfill the role of the Kingly Messiah *(Messiah ben David)*.

In the first coming of the Jewish Messiah *(Mashiach) Yeshua*/Jesus, *Yochanan* the *Immerser* (John the Baptist) came in the SPIRIT OF ELIJAH (Luke 1:17). Orthodox Jews believe that Elijah will announce the redemption of the seed of Jacob to his children (Mid. Haser w'Yater, pp. 16, 42, and Rashi ad Leviticus 26:42). Is it possible that prior to the second coming of the Jewish Messiah *(Mashiach) Yeshua*/Jesus that the G-d of Israel will use the **SPIRIT OF ELIJAH** through an outpouring of the Holy Spirit *(Ruach HaKodesh)* to announce the redemption of the seed of Jacob (ALL 12 TRIBES) to the seed of Jacob *(house of Israel*/Christianity and the *house of Judah* /Judaism) and to the world?

In the first part of this book, we will examine some of the issues which have historically divided the two houses of Israel (*house of Israel*/Christianity and the *house of Judah*/Judaism). Among the issues to be discussed are:

Who is the Jewish Messiah *(Mashiach)* and is the Jewish Messiah *(Mashiach)* the G-d of Israel manifested in the flesh? What is the obligation of the non-Jew in keeping the Torah and the commandments *(mitzvot)* of the G-d of Israel? Who is the church and who is Israel? Why do we need to understand the 7,000 year plan of the G-d of Israel? What is the purpose and meaning of the Sabbath *(Shabbat)*?

In the last part of the book, we will learn how the Israel/Arab peace process is associated with the redemption, restoration and reunification of both houses of Israel (Ezekiel *[Yechezekel]* 37:15-28. As a background for understanding the Israel/Arab land conflict, we will study the modern history of the nation of Israel. We will learn that the Israel/Arab peace process is based upon UN Resolutions 242 and 338. We will understand how the G-d of Israel will judge all the nations in the earth based upon how they have treated the Jewish people *(house of Judah)* and the nation of Israel.

This book is written to communicate the soon redemption, restoration and reunification of both houses of Israel (*house of Israel*/Christianity and the *house of Judah*/Judaism) in a style that can be easily understood by both houses. Therefore, traditional Jewish terms are used and the name of the G-d of Israel is written with a hyphen (G-d, L-RD) so that this book is acceptable reading to the *house of Judah* (Jews).

There are twelve chapters in this book — one chapter in remembrance for each of the twelve tribes of Israel.

May the G-d of Israel bring redemption, restoration and reunification to both houses of Israel speedily in our days. Amen!

Hebraic Heritage Ministries International

- Teaching the Hebraic Roots of faith in Messiah

- Networking Groups who are studying the Hebraic Roots of faith in Messiah

- Standing with the Jewish people and Fighting Anti-Semitism

- Christian Zionists who have a Loving Heart for the Land of Israel

Please visit our Web Site and Join our Network ! ! !

http://www.geocities.com/Heartland/2175/index.html

OR

http://www.hebroots.org/

Mailing Address:

Hebraic Heritage Ministries International
P.O. Box 81
Strasburg, Ohio, USA 44680

Chapter 1

Who Are the Two Houses of Israel?

Who are the two houses of Israel? Historically, they were the Northern Kingdom *(house of Israel)* and the Southern Kingdom *(house of Judah)*. Today, the two houses of the G-d of Israel are known by the more common names of Christianity *(house of Israel)* and Judaism *(house of Judah)*. Both Christianity *(house of Israel)* and Judaism *(house of Judah)* worship the G-d of Israel. However, they have historically disagreed with the method of expressing true Biblical worship to the G-d of Israel. These disagreements have divided the children of the G-d of Israel into two houses of worship of the G-d of Israel. Why are the two houses of Israel *(Christianity and Judaism)* divided?

There are two MAJOR disagreements between the two houses of Israel *(Christianity and Judaism)*. These two major disagreements are the role of the Torah in true Biblical worship of the G-d of Israel and who is the Jewish Messiah *(Mashiach)*. In spite of these two disagreements, both houses of Israel have been used by the G-d of Israel to preserve the following two very important truths within the Kingdom of the G-d of Israel. Judaism *(house of Judah)* has preserved the truth that the Torah is eternal and is the *Tree of Life* given by the G-d of

Israel. Christianity *(house of Israel)* has preserved the truth that *Yeshua*/Jesus is the Jewish Messiah *(Mashiach)*.

The Family of the G-d of Israel Is Like an Olive Tree

Allegorically speaking, the family *(mishpochah)* of the G-d of Israel is likened to an olive tree. In Jeremiah *(Yermiyahu)* 11:16-17 it is written:

> *"The* LORD *called thy name. A* **green olive tree** *... For the* LORD *of hosts, that planted thee ...* **the house of Israel AND of the house of Judah**..."

The *house of Judah* (Judaism) is the root and natural branches of the olive tree of the G-d of Israel. The *house of Israel* (Christianity) is GRAFTED into this olive tree. In Romans 11:13, 17 it is written:

> *"For I speak to you Gentiles* [Christianity] *... and thou, being a wild olive tree, wast* **grafted** *in among them* [the natural root of the house of Judah]*..."*

From the viewpoint of the G-d of Israel, He only has one family *(mishpochah)* that consists of natural branches *(house of Judah/*Judaism) and wild branches *(house of Israel/*Christianity). The wild branches have been grafted into the natural root *(house of Judah/*Judaism). In Ephesians 4:3-6 it is written:

> *"Endeavoring to keep the unity of the Spirit* [Ruach] *in the bond of peace* [shalom]*. There is*

Who Are the Two Houses of Israel?

one body [kahal/congregation/ekklesia/church] ... *one* Lord*, one faith* [emunah] ... *one God and Father of all, who is above all and through all, and in you all."*

A Rejection of Replacement Theology

It may be a new revelation to many members within traditional Judaism and Christianity that the house of the G-d of Israel is divided and that Judaism represents the *house of Judah* and Christianity represents the *house of Israel*. Furthermore, there are an increasing number of people within both houses of Israel to whom the G-d of Israel is revealing this truth through the outpouring of His Holy Spirit *(Ruach HaKodesh)*.

There are various "Christian" groups who teach that there are two houses of Israel. However, some of these groups teach a *poisonous* and unbiblical doctrine of *elitism* (they are a special race of people) and *replacement theology* (they are the "new Israel") **against** the *house of Judah* (Judaism). Because of these poisonous and unbiblical doctrines, many within true Biblical Christianity *(house of Israel)* who reject the poisonous doctrines of elitism and replacement theology against the *house of Judah* (Judaism) are reluctant to accept the Biblical truth that there are two houses of Israel.

In embracing the truth of the two houses of Israel, this book **REJECTS** all forms, thought and intent of elitism and replacement theology against the *house of Judah* (Judaism). On the contrary, the purpose of this book is to promote restoration, reconciliation and unity between the *house of Judah* (Judaism) and the *house of Israel* (Christianity).

The Restoration of Both Houses of Israel

In order for restoration and reconciliation to come to both houses of Israel, they need to repent *(teshuvah)* to the G-d of Israel and to each other. The *house of Israel* (Christianity) needs to embrace the Hebraic/Jewish roots of their faith in *Yeshua*/Jesus as Messiah *(Mashiach)*. Meanwhile, the *house of Judah* (Judaism) needs to continue to follow the Torah of the G-d of Israel while maintaining and keeping their Jewish identity when accepting that *Yeshua*/Jesus is the Jewish Messiah *(Mashiach)*. The repentance, reunification, reconciliation and unity of both houses of Israel are prophesied in Ezekiel *(Yechezekel)* 37:15-27 as it is written:

> *"The word of the* Lord *came again unto me, saying, Moreover, thou son of man, take thee one stick, and write upon it, For Judah, and for the children of Israel his companions: then take another stick, and write upon it, For Joseph, the stick of Ephraim, and for all the house of Israel his companions: And join them one to another into one stick; and they shall become one in thine hand. And when the children of thy people shall speak unto thee, saying, Wilt thou not show us what thou meanest by these? Say unto them, Thus saith the* Lord *God; Behold, I will take the stick of Jo-*

Who Are the Two Houses of Israel?

seph, which is in the hand of Ephraim, and the tribes of Israel his fellows, and will put them with him, even with the stick of Judah, and make them one stick, and they shall be one in mine hand. And the sticks whereon thou writest shall be in thine hand before their eyes. And say unto them, Thus saith the LORD *God; Behold, I will take the children of Israel from among the heathen, whither they be gone, and will gather them on every side, and bring them into their own land: And I will make them one nation in the land upon the mountains of Israel; and one king shall be king to them all: and they shall be no more two nations, neither shall they be divided into two kingdoms any more at all: Neither shall they defile themselves any more with their idols, nor with their detestable things, nor with any of their transgressions: but I will save them out of all their dwelling places, wherein they have sinned, and will cleanse them: so shall they be my people, and I will be their God. And David my servant* [Messiah ben David] *shall be king over them; and they all shall have one shepherd: they shall also walk in my judgments, and observe my statutes, and do them* [follow the Torah of the G-d of Israel]. *And they shall dwell in the land that I have given unto Jacob my servant, wherein your fathers have dwelt; and they shall dwell therein, even they, and their children, and their children's children forever: and my servant David* [Messiah ben David] *shall be their prince forever. Moreover I will make a covenant of peace with them; it shall be an everlasting covenant with them; and I will place them, and multiply them, and will set my sanctuary in the midst of them forevermore* [the Messianic Age/Athid Lavo]. *My tabernacle also shall be with them: yea, I will be their God, and they shall be my people."*

May Brethren Dwell Together in Unity

When and how will the two houses be reunited? This book will examine some of the theological issues that have historically divided the two houses of Israel and when and how they will be reunited in the end of days.

The first part of the book will discuss some of the theological issues that have historically divided the two houses of Israel. Among the items that will be studied are the issues of Torah and grace, the Sabbath *(Shabbat)*, the Jewishness of the Messiah *(Mashiach)*, the deity of the Jewish Messiah *(Mashiach)*, the 7,000 year plan of the G-d of Israel and who is the church and who is Israel.

The second part of the book will focus on how and when the two houses will be reunified in the end of days. The importance of the birth of the modern day state of Israel, the city of Jerusalem *(Yerushalayim)* and the role that Israel's peace agreements with her Arab neighbors will play in the eventual reunification of both houses of Israel will be studied. By parting the land of the G-d of Israel (Joel *[Yoel]* 3:2) and the city of Jerusalem (Zechariah *[Zecharyah]* 14:2), the G-d of Israel will judge the nations. When the two houses of Israel repent

Who Are the Two Houses of Israel?

and are redeemed, restored, reconciled and dwell together in unity, the following events will occur.

1. The exile of both houses of Israel will end and they will return to the land of Israel (Ezekiel *[Yechezekel]* 37:15-27).

2. The Jewish Messiah *(Mashiach)* will dwell with His people teaching the Torah to all nations from the city of Jerusalem *(Yerushalayim)* during the Messianic Age *(Athid Lavo)* (Isaiah *[Yeshayahu]* 2:2-3).

May brethren from both houses of Israel dwell together in unity. In Psalm *(Tehillim)* 133 it is written:

"Behold, how good and how pleasant it is for brethren [from the house of Israel (Christianity) and the house of Judah (Judaism)] *to dwell together in unity! It is like the precious ointment upon the head, that ran down upon the beard, even Aaron's beard: that went down to the skirts of his garments; As the dew of Hermon, and as the dew that descended upon the mountains of Zion: for there the* LORD *commanded the blessing, even life forevermore."*

May the G-d of Israel pour out His Holy Spirit *(Ruach HaKodesh)* and bring restoration, reconciliation and unity to both the *house of Judah* (Judaism) and the *house of Israel* (Christianity) speedily in our days. Amen!

Chapter 2

Who Is the Church and Who Is Israel?

In order for full restoration to come to both the *house of Judah* (Judaism) and the *house of Israel* (Christianity), both houses of Israel need to understand the Biblical terms *"church"* and *"Israel."* In today's world, the term *"church"* is traditionally identified and associated with the *house of Israel* (Christianity) while the term *"Israel"* is traditionally identified and associated with the *house of Judah* (Jews/Judaism).

In this chapter, we will examine the Biblical terms *"church"* and *"Israel."* In doing so, we will discover that the *"church"* was **born at mount Sinai**. Furthermore, we will discover that the Biblical term *"Israel"* refers to the family *(mishpochah)* of the G-d of Israel that is likened in the Bible to an *"olive tree."* In the Biblical *"olive tree"* allegory, *"Israel"* consists of the *natural root* of the olive tree (natural born Jews). The *wild olive branches* are those who have been **grafted** (non-Jews from the nations who believe in the G-d of Israel and have accepted *Yeshua/* Jesus as the Jewish Messiah *[Mashiach]*) (Romans 11:13-26) into the natural root. As long as there is a sun, moon and stars in the heavens, the *natural root* (natural born

Jews) will remain a part of the *olive tree* of the G-d of Israel (Jeremiah *[Yermiyahu]* 31:35-37).

The Greek Word for Church Is Ekklesia

In the King James translation of the Bible, the English word *"church"* is only found in the New Testament *(Brit Hadashah)*. For this reason, the word *"church"* is most often associated with the *house of Israel* (Christianity). The English word *"church"* is the Strong's word 1577 in the Strong's Greek dictionary. It is the Greek word, *"ekklesia."* In the Strong's Greek dictionary, the Greek word, *"ekklesia"* is defined as *"a calling out, a popular meeting, a religious congregation, a Jewish synagogue or Christian community of members on earth or saints in heaven or both."*

The Hebrew Word for Church Is Kahal

In the *Thayer's Greek-English Lexicon of the New Testament* numerically coded to the *Strong's Exhaustive Concordance*, it will give a more complete and detailed definition of the Greek word, *"ekklesia."* The *Thayer's Greek-English Lexicon of the New Testament* will define the Greek word, *"ekklesia"* to mean *"an assembly"* and will explain that the corresponding equivalent word in the Septuagint (Jewish Scriptures translated into the Greek language/the Old Testament *[TeNaKh]*) as being the Hebrew word, *"kahal."* The Hebrew word *"kahal"* is the Strong's word 6951 in the Strong's Hebrew dictionary and is defined to mean, *"an assembly, congregation, company, multitude."*

Who Is the Church and Who Is Israel?

Ecclesiastes Is Derived From the Greek Word for Church

The book of the Bible named *"Ecclesiastes"* is derived from the Greek word *"ekklesia."* In the introduction to the book of *Ecclesiastes* in the *Hebrew-Greek Key Study Bible* (King James Version) by Spiros Zodhiates published by AMG publishers, the following observation is made about the title of the book, *"Ecclesiastes"*:

> "The title of this book in Hebrew, Qoheleth (6953), is the word translated as 'Preacher' in chapter one, verse one. The English title is the transliteration of the title in the Septuagint, the Greek translation of the Old Testament. The Greek word Ekklesiastes, which means 'speaker of a called out assembly,' is derived from the word ekklesia (1577) which is the New Testament word for 'church'."

The Church Was Born at Mount Sinai

I was taught within Christianity *(house of Israel)* from the time that I was a little boy that the *"church"* was born in Acts 2 with the outpouring of the Holy Spirit *(Ruach HaKodesh)* upon those who were gathered in Jerusalem *(Yerushalayim)* for the Biblical feast of Pentecost *(Shavuot)*. After being taught this, I discovered that I was told the correct **DAY** that the church was born (the Biblical feast of Pentecost/*Shavuot*), however; as I began to study the Hebraic/Jewish roots of Christianity, I discovered that the birth of the *"church"* actually happened nearly 2,000 years earlier at mount Sinai.

Restoring the Two Houses of Israel

In Stephen's sermon in Acts 7, he makes mention of Moses *(Moshe)* and the event that happened at mount Sinai in Acts 7:37-38 as it is written:

> *"This is that Moses, which said unto the children of Israel, A prophet shall the* LORD *your God raise up unto you of your brethren, like unto me; him shall you hear. This is he, that was in the* **CHURCH** *in the wilderness with the angel which spake to him in the mount Sina, and with our fathers: who received the lively oracles* [the Torah] *to give unto us."*

In Acts 7:37-38, Stephen is referring to Deuteronomy *(Devarim)* 18:15-16 as it is written:

> *"The* LORD *thy God will raise up unto thee a Prophet from the midst of thee, of thy brethren, like unto me; unto him ye shall hearken; According to all that thou desiredst of the* LORD *thy God in Horeb in the* **DAY OF THE ASSEMBLY**..."

The word in Deuteronomy *(Devarim)* 18:16 translated in the King James Bible as *"assembly"* is the Hebrew word *"kahal"* which is the Greek word *"ekklesia"* and is the English word *"church."* In the King James translation of the New Testament *(Brit Hadashah)*, the Greek word *"ekklesia"* translated into English as *"church"* in Acts 7:38 was referring to Deuteronomy *(Devarim)* 18:16 which describes the event that happened at mount Sinai *(Horeb)* as the day of the assembly/*kahal*/church/*ekklesia*.

Who Is the Church and Who Is Israel?

Three times in the book of Deuteronomy *(Devarim)*, the G-d of Israel by the pen of Moses *(Moshe)* through the inspiration of the Holy Spirit *(Ruach HaKodesh)* describes the event that happened at mount Sinai as the day of the assembly *(kahal*/church/*ekklesia)*. The occurrence in Deuteronomy *(Devarim)* 18:16 has already been quoted. The other two references are in Deuteronomy *(Devarim)* 9:10 and Deuteronomy *(Devarim)* 10:4. In Deuteronomy *(Devarim)* 9:10 it is written:

> *"And the* LORD *delivered unto me two tables of stone written with the finger of God; and on them was written according to all the words, which the* LORD *spake with you in the mount out of the midst of the fire in the* **DAY OF THE ASSEMBLY.***"*

In Deuteronomy *(Devarim)* 10:4 it is written:

> *"And he wrote on the tables, according to the first writing, the ten commandments, which the* LORD *spake unto you in the mount out of the midst of the fire in the* **DAY OF THE ASSEMBLY***: and the* LORD *gave them unto me."*

G-d's Church/Assembly Is a Mixed Multitude of People

The G-d of Israel is not a respecter of persons but considers all those who call upon His name to be members of His family *(mishpochah)*. In Acts 10:34-35 it is written:

> *"Then Peter opened his mouth, and said, Of a truth I perceive that God is no respecter of persons:*

Restoring the Two Houses of Israel

But in every nation he that feareth him, and worketh righteousness is accepted with him."

Those who were at mount Sinai when the *"church"* was first born consisted of the natural born descendents of Abraham *(Avraham)*, Isaac *(Yitzchak)* and Jacob *(Ya'acov)* and a mixed multitude who believed in the G-d of Israel and who left Egypt *(Mitzrayim)* with the children of Israel. At mount Sinai, they were called the *house of Jacob*. In Exodus *(Shemot)* 19:1-3 it is written:

> *"In the third month, when the children of Israel were gone forth out of the land of Egypt, the same day came they into the wilderness of Sinai. For they were departed from Rephidim, and were come to the desert of Sinai, and had pitched in the wilderness; and there Israel camped before the mount. And Moses went up unto God, and the* LORD *called unto him out of the mountain, saying, Thus shalt thou say to the* **HOUSE OF JACOB**, *and tell the children of Israel."*

In addition to the natural born descendents of Abraham *(Avraham)*, Isaac *(Yitzchak)* and Jacob *(Ya'acov)* who are called the *house of Jacob*, a mixed multitude who believed in the G-d of Israel and who left Egypt *(Mitzrayim)* with the children of Israel were also present at mount Sinai. In Exodus *(Shemot)* 12:29-31, 37-38 it is written:

> *"And it came to pass, that at midnight the* LORD *smote all the firstborn in the land of Egypt, from*

Who Is the Church and Who Is Israel?

> *the firstborn of Pharaoh that sat on his throne unto the firstborn of the captive that was in the dungeon; and all the firstborn of cattle. And Pharaoh rose up in the night, he, and all his servants and all the Egyptians ... and he called for Moses and Aaron by night, and said, Rise up, and get you forth from among my people, both ye and the children of Israel; and go, serve the LORD, as ye have said ... and the children of Israel journeyed from Rameses to Succoth, about six hundred thousand on foot that were men, beside children. And a* **MIXED MULTITUDE** *went up also with them; and flocks, and herds, even very much cattle."*

Therefore, the *"church"* that was **born** at mount Sinai consisted of the natural born descendents of Abraham *(Avraham)*, Isaac *(Yitzchak)* and Jacob *(Ya'acov)* called the *house of Jacob* and a mixed multitude from Egypt *(Mitzrayim)* who feared and became believers in the G-d of Israel following the plagues in the land of Egypt *(Mitzrayim)*. It was the mixed multitude who sojourned out of Egypt *(Mitzrayim)* with the *house of Jacob* and became an assembly/*kahal*/church/*ekklesia* of people unto the G-d of Israel at mount Sinai.

G-d's Spiritual Church Is a Mixed Multitude of People Who Believe in the Jewish Messiah

The spiritual (eschatological) assembly/*kahal*/church/*ekklesia* of people unto the G-d of Israel consists of both natural born Jews and non-Jews who accept the Jewish Messiah *(Mashiach) Yeshua*/Jesus as the promised Messiah *(Mashiach)* of the G-d of Israel. In Galatians 3:26, 28 it is written:

> *"For ye are all the children of God by faith in Christ Jesus* [Yeshua HaMashiach] ... *there is neither Jew nor Greek, there is neither bond nor free, there is neither male nor female: for you are all one in Christ Jesus* [Yeshua HaMashiach]*."*

In Romans 10:9-13 it is written:

> *"That if thou shalt confess with thy mouth the* LORD *Jesus, and shall believe in thine heart that God hath raised him from the dead, thou shalt be saved. For with the heart man believeth unto righteousness; and with the mouth confession is made unto salvation. For the Scripture* [TeNaKh / Old Testament] *saith,* **Whosoever** *believeth on him shall not be ashamed* [Isaiah 28:16]. *For there is* **no difference between the Jew and the Greek**; *for the same* LORD *over all is rich unto all that call upon him. For whosoever shall call upon the name of the* LORD *shall be saved.* [Joel 2:32]*"*

Who Is Israel?

What does the Biblical term Israel mean and how does it relate to the family *(mishpochah)* of the G-d of Israel and believers in *Yeshua*/Jesus as the Jewish Messiah *(Mashiach)*? In the Bible, the *house of Jacob* (consisting of the *house of Israel* and the *house of Judah*) is allegorically described as being likened to an olive tree. In Jeremiah *(Yermiyahu)* 11:1, 6, 16-17 it is written:

Who Is the Church and Who Is Israel?

> *"The word that came to Jeremiah from the* Lord, *saying ... Proclaim all these words in the cities of Judah, and in the streets of Jerusalem, saying ... The* Lord *called thy name. A green* **olive tree** *... and the* **branches of it are broken**. *For the* Lord *of hosts that planted thee ... of the* **house of Israel AND of the house of Judah***..."*

The branches of the original natural olive tree (the *house of Israel* AND the *house of Judah*) were broken. Therefore, the broken branches needed to be redeemed, restored and grafted again back into the original natural olive tree. How did this happen?

Jacob's Name Is Changed to Israel

In order to understand who is Israel *(Yisrael)*, you need to understand the origin of the name of Israel *(Yisrael)*. Israel *(Yisrael)* is the name give to Jacob *(Ya'acov)* by the G-d of Israel. In Genesis *(Bereishit)* 32:24-28 it is written:

> *"And Jacob was left alone; and there wrestled a man with him until the breaking of the day. And when he saw that he prevailed not against him, he touched the hollow of his thigh; and the hollow of Jacob's thigh was out of joint, and he wrestled with him. And he said, Let me go, for the day breaketh. And he said, I will not let thee go, except thou bless me. And he said unto him, What is thy name? And he said, Jacob. And he said,* **Thy name shall be called no more Jacob, but Israel**: *for as a prince hast thou power with God, and with men, and hast prevailed."*

Jacob Has Twelve Sons Who Become the House of Jacob

Jacob *(Ya'acov)*/Israel had twelve sons. The descendents of Jacob *(Ya'acov)*/Israel were called the children of Israel or the *house of Jacob*. The descendents of Jacob *(Ya'acov)*/Israel, the *house of Jacob*, entered into a covenant with the G-d of Israel at mount Sinai (Exodus *[Shemot]* 19. The descendents of Jacob (*Ya'acov*)/Israel, the *house of Jacob*, broke this covenant. In doing so, the **branches** of the original **olive tree** were **broken**.

The House of Jacob Is Divided Following the Reign of Solomon

Followed the reign of Solomon *(Shlomo)*, the house of Jacob *(Ya'acov)* was divided into the Northern Kingdom *(house of Israel)* and the Southern Kingdom *(house of Judah)*. This was done because the G-d of Israel judged Solomon *(Shlomo)* because he broke the Torah/covenant of the G-d of Israel by marrying foreign wives who caused the nation of Israel to worship foreign gods. In I Kings *(Melachim)* 11:1-5 it is written:

> *"But king Solomon loved many strange women, together with the daughter of Pharaoh, women of the Moabites, Ammonites, Edomites, Zidonians, and Hittites; Of the nations concerning which the* Lord *said unto the children of Israel, Ye shall not go in to them, neither shall they come in unto you: for surely they will turn away your heart after their gods* [Deuteronomy 7:1-4]: *Solomon*

Who Is the Church and Who Is Israel?

> *cleaved unto these in love. And he had seven hundred wives, princesses, and three hundred concubines: and his wives turned away his heart. For it came to pass, when Solomon was old, that his wives turned away his heart after other gods: and his heart was not perfect with the* Lord *his God, as was the heart of David his father. For Solomon went after Ashtoreth the goddess of the Zidonians, and after Milcom the abomination of the Ammonites."*

Therefore, Solomon's *(Shlomo)* kingdom *(the house of Jacob)* was divided into Northern Kingdom *(house of Israel)* and Southern Kingdom *(house of Judah)*. In I Kings *(Melachim)* 11:9-13 it is written:

> *"And the* Lord *was angry with Solomon, because his heart was turned from the* Lord *God of Israel, which had appeared unto him twice, And had commanded him concerning this thing, that he should not go after other gods: but he kept not that which the* Lord *commanded. Wherefore the* Lord *said unto Solomon, Forasmuch as this is done of thee, and thou hast not kept my covenant and my statutes, which I have commanded thee, I will surely rend the kingdom from thee, and will give it to thy servant. Notwithstanding in thy days I will not do it for David thy father's sake: but I will rend it out of the hand of thy son. Howbeit I will not rend away all the kingdom; but will give one tribe to thy son for David my servant's sake, and for Jerusalem's sake which I have chosen."*

Restoring the Two Houses of Israel

The Northern Kingdom Is Called the House of Israel

Jeroboam, Solomon's *(Shlomo)* servant, became the ruler of the Northern Kingdom who consisted of ten tribes. In I Kings *(Melachim)* 11:26, 28-32 it is written:

> *"And Jeroboam the son of Nebat, an Ephrathite of Zereda, Solomon's servant, whose mother's name was Zeruah, a widow woman, even he lifted up his hand against the king .. and the man Jeroboam was a mighty man of valor: and Solomon seeing the young man that he was industrious, he made him ruler over all the charge of the* **house of Joseph**. *And it came to pass at that time when Jeroboam went out of Jerusalem, that the prophet Ahijah the Shilonite found him in the way; and he had clad himself with a new garment; and they two were alone in the field: And Ahijah caught the new garment that was on him, and rent it in twelve pieces: And he said to Jeroboam, Take thee ten pieces: for thus saith the* LORD, *the God of Israel, Behold, I will rend the kingdom out of the hand of Solomon, and will give ten tribes to thee: (But he shall have one tribe for my servant David's sake, and for Jerusalem's sake, the city which I have chosen out of all the tribes of Israel:)"*

The Northern Kingdom was called the following names in the Bible:

1. The house of Israel (I Kings 12:21, Jeremiah 31:31)
2. The house of Joseph (I Kings 11:28)

Who Is the Church and Who Is Israel?

3. Samaria (Hosea 7:1, 8:5-6, 13:16)
4. Ephraim (Hosea 4:17, 5:3, 7:1)

The Southern Kingdom Is Called the House of Judah

Rehoboam became the leader of the Southern Kingdom. The Southern Kingdom was called the *house of Judah*. Both the Northern Kingdom *(house of Israel)* and the Southern Kingdom *(house of Judah)* broke the Torah/covenant that the G-d of Israel made with the house of Jacob *(Ya'acov)* at mount Sinai. Therefore, according to the words of the covenant, both the Northern Kingdom *(house of Israel)* and the Southern Kingdom *(house of Judah)* were dispersed into the nations of the world. In Deuteronomy *(Devarim)* 28:15, 36-37, 64 it is written:

> *"But it shall come to pass, if thou wilt not hearken unto the voice of the* Lord *thy God, to observe to do all his commandments and his statutes which I command thee this day; that all these curses shall come upon thee, and overtake thee ... The* Lord *shall bring thee, and thy king which thou shalt set over thee, unto a nation which neither thou nor thy fathers have known; and there shalt thou serve other gods, wood and stone. And thou shalt become an astonishment, a proverb, and a byword, among all nations whither the* Lord *shall lead thee ... And the* Lord *shall scatter thee among all people, from the one end of the earth even unto the other; and thou shalt serve other gods, which neither thou nor thy fathers have known, even wood and stone."*

Restoring the Two Houses of Israel

The Northern Kingdom Is Taken Captive to Assyria

The Northern Kingdom *(house of Israel)* was taken captive by the nation of Assyria (II Kings *[Melachim]* 17:7-23). In the fullness of time, they lost their identity as the *house of Israel* and became assimilated into all the nations of the world.

The Southern Kingdom Is Taken Captive to Babylon

Meanwhile, the Southern Kingdom *(house of Judah)* was initially taken captive by the Babylonians. The G-d of Israel declared through the prophet Jeremiah *(Yermiyahu)* that the duration of the Babylonian captivity was to last for 70 years (Jeremiah *[Yermiyahu]* 25:1-11). Following the 70 years of Babylonian captivity, a remnant of people from the Southern Kingdom *(house of Judah)* returned to the land of Israel during the days of Ezra and Nehemiah.

The Southern Kingdom Is the Jewish People

Those from the Southern Kingdom *(house of Judah)* who returned from Babylon with Ezra and Nehemiah were called Jews. In Ezra 2:1, 5:1 it is written:

> *"Now these are the children of the province that went up out of the captivity, of those which had*

Who Is the Church and Who Is Israel?

been carried away, whom Nebuchadnezzar the king of Babylon had carried away unto Babylon, and came again unto Jerusalem and Judah, every one unto his city ... Then the prophets, Haggai the prophet, and Zechariah the son of Iddo, prophesied unto **THE JEWS** *that were in Judah and Jerusalem in the name of the God of Israel, even unto them."*

In Nehemiah 1:1-2 it is written:

"The words of Nehemiah the son of Hachaliah. And it came to pass in the month of Chisleu, in the twentieth year, as I was in Shushan the palace, That Hanani, one of my brethren, came, he and certain **MEN OF JUDAH**; *and I asked them concerning* **THE JEWS** *that had escaped, which were left of the captivity, and concerning Jerusalem."*

The Romans Take the House of Judah into Worldwide Captivity

Following the destruction of the second Temple *(Beit HaMikdash)*, the Roman Empire took the Southern Kingdom *(house of Judah)* captive. From this captivity, the Southern Kingdom *(house of Judah)* was eventually taken captive into every nation of the world. In spite of this worldwide captivity, the Southern Kingdom *(house of Judah)* has never lost their identity of being a nation of people called Jews from the Southern Kingdom *(house of Judah)* even unto this day.

Restoring the Two Houses of Israel

Who Are Jews and Who Are Israelites?

The descendents of Jacob *(Ya'acov)*/Israel *(house of Jacob* consisting of all twelve tribes) are Israelites. The descendents of Jacob *(Ya'acov)*/Israel *(house of Jacob)* were divided into Northern Kingdom *(house of Israel)* and Southern Kingdom *(house of Judah)*. The descendents of the Northern Kingdom *(house of Israel)* lost their identity of being a nation of people from the Northern Kingdom *(house of Israel)* when they were taken captive by the nation of Assyria (around 721 BCE) and assimilated into all the nations of the world. However, the Southern Kingdom *(house of Judah)* never lost their identity of being Jews from the Southern Kingdom *(house of Judah)* during their worldwide captivity.

In a strict definition of the literal *(peshat)* Biblical word Jew, Jews are descendents from the *tribe of Judah*. However, in a broader definition of the literal *(peshat)* Biblical term Jew, those tribes from the Southern Kingdom *(house of Judah)* were also called Jews in the Biblical books of Ezra and Nehemiah. The Southern Kingdom *(house of Judah)* consisted of the tribes of Judah, Levi and a part of Benjamin.

Meanwhile, those tribes from the Northern Kingdom *(house of Israel)* are not Biblically called Jews because they are not from the Southern Kingdom *(house of Judah)*. Instead, the Northern Kingdom *(house of Israel)* is called Israelites.

Therefore, **all** Jews (those from the Southern Kingdom) are Israelites (a subset of all twelve tribes).

Who Is the Church and Who Is Israel?

However, not all Israelites (those from the Northern Kingdom) are Jews (from the Southern Kingdom).

The Northern Kingdom Is Cut-Off From the Natural Olive Tree

The judgment of the Northern Kingdom *(house of Israel)* for forsaking the Torah/covenant of the G-d of Israel at mount Sinai was that they would be cut off from the **natural olive tree**. Their judgment is given in Hosea *(Hoshea)* 1. In this chapter, the G-d of Israel told the prophet Hosea *(Hoshea)* to marry a whore named Gomer (Hosea *[Hoshea]* 1:2-3. The children born from this marriage would be a prophecy of the future judgment of the Northern Kingdom *(house of Israel)*. There are three children born from this marriage who are mentioned in Hosea *[Hoshea]* 1. The names of these three children are *Jezreel* (Hosea *[Hoshea]* 1:4, *Lo-ruhamah* Hosea *[Hoshea]* 1:6 and *Lo-ammi* Hosea *[Hoshea]* 1:9).

Jezreel is the Strong's word 3157 in the Hebrew dictionary. The Hebrew word *Jezreel* comes from two Hebrew words. These two Hebrew words are *Zarah* (2232) and *El* (410). *Zarah* means *"to sow or scatter."* *El* is the Hebrew word for G-d. Therefore, the Hebrew word *Jezreel* means *"G-d will sow or G-d will scatter."*

Lo-ruhamah is the Strong's word 3819. The Hebrew word *Lo-ruhamah* comes from two Hebrew words. These two Hebrew words are *Lo* (3808) which means *"no or not"* and *Ruhamah* which comes from the Strong's word (7355) *racham* which means *"mercy or compassion."*

Restoring the Two Houses of Israel

So, the Hebrew word *Lo-ruhamah* means *"no mercy or no compassion."*

Lo-ammi is the Strong's word 3818. The Hebrew word *Lo-ammi* comes from two Hebrew words. These two Hebrew word are *Lo* (3808) which means *"no or not"* and *ammi* which comes from the Strong's word (5971) *am* which means *"people."* So, the Hebrew word *Lo-ammi* means *"not my people."*

The forefathers of the Northern Kingdom *(house of Israel)* along with the Southern Kingdom *(house of Judah)* were called together the house of Jacob (*Ya'acov*). In Exodus *(Shemot)* 19:3, the house of Jacob *(Ya'acov)* entered into a marriage covenant (Jeremiah *[Yermiyahu]* 2:1-3) with the G-d of Israel at mount Sinai. At that time, they became a called out people unto the G-d of Israel known in Hebrew as a *kahal* (assembly) and in Greek as an *ekklesia* (church). In doing so, the rights of this covenant gave the house of Jacob (*Ya'acov*) an eternal inheritance if they were obedient in keeping the covenant (Exodus *[Shemot]* 19:5-6). However, by breaking the terms of the Torah/covenant that the G-d of Israel made with His people, the G-d of Israel is now telling the Northern Kingdom *(house of Israel)* that they are no longer His people and He will no longer have mercy upon them. In doing so, the G-d of Israel *divorced* the Northern Kingdom *(house of Israel)*. In Jeremiah *(Yermiyahu)* 3:6, 8 it is written:

> *"The* LORD *said also unto me in the days of Josiah the king, Hast thou seen that which backsliding Israel* [house of Israel] *hath done? she is gone up upon every high mountain and under every green*

Who Is the Church and Who Is Israel?

tree, and there hath played the **HARLOT** *... And I saw, when for all the causes whereby backsliding Israel* [house of Israel] *committed* **ADULTERY** [was unfaithful to the terms of the Torah/ marriage covenant at mount Sinai] *I had put her away, and given her a bill of* **DIVORCE...**"

In giving the Northern Kingdom *(house of Israel)* a divorce *(get)*, they lost the inheritance that was rightfully theirs by being a member of the family *(mishpochah)* of the G-d of Israel. The G-d of Israel declared that they would not be His people and that He would have no mercy upon them. Therefore, they were **cut off** *(karet)* (3772) from the **natural olive tree**.

The House of Judah Is an Unfaithful Wife To the G-d of Israel

Both the Northern Kingdom *(house of Israel)* and the Southern Kingdom *(house of Judah)* broke the marriage covenant that the G-d of Israel made with His called out assembly *(kahal/church/ekklesia)* at mount Sinai. In Jeremiah *(Yermiyahu)* 3:6-8, 10 it is written:

"The LORD *said also unto me in the days of Josiah the king, Hast thou seen that which backsliding Israel* [house of Israel] *hath done? she is gone up upon every high mountain and under every green tree, and there hath played the harlot ... and her treacherous sister Judah* [house of Judah] *saw it. And I saw, when for all the causes whereby backsliding Israel* [house of Israel] *committed adultery I had put her away and given her a bill of*

> divorce; yet her treacherous sister **JUDAH** feared not, but went and played the **HARLOT** also ... and yet for all this her treacherous sister Judah hath not turned unto me with her whole heart but in falsehood saith the LORD."

G-d Does Not Divorce the House of Judah

Even though the Southern Kingdom *(house of Judah)* broke the Torah/marriage covenant at mount Sinai along with the Northern Kingdom *(house of Israel)*, the G-d of Israel proclaimed that the Southern Kingdom *(house of Judah)* would be punished for their sins but that He would not remove His mercy *(chesed)* from them or divorce them because of His love for David and the city of Jerusalem *(Yerushalayim)*. In Psalm *(Tehillim)* 89:1-3, 28-37 it is written:

> "I will sing of the **MERCIES** of the LORD forever: with my mouth will I make known thy faithfulness to all generations. For I have said, Mercy shall be built up forever: thy faithfulness shalt thou establish in the very heavens. I have made a covenant with my chosen, I have sworn unto David my servant ... my **MERCY** will I **KEEP** for him forevermore, and **MY COVENANT SHALL STAND** fast with him. His seed also will I make to endure forever, and his throne as the days of heaven. If his children forsake my law [Torah], and walk not in my judgments; If they break my statutes, and keep not my commandments; Then will I visit their transgression with the rod, and their iniquity with stripes. Nevertheless my lovingkindness will I not utterly take from him,

Who Is the Church and Who Is Israel?

nor suffer my faithfulness to fail. **My covenant will I not break**, *nor alter the thing that is gone out of my lips. Once I have sworn by my holiness that I will not lie unto David.* **His seed shall endure FOREVER**, *and his throne as the sun before me. It shall be established forever as the moon, and as a faithful witness of heaven. Selah."*

The Northern Kingdom Is Promised Mercy If They Repent

The G-d of Israel is slow to anger, quick to forgive and abundant in mercy. In Psalm *(Tehillim)* 103:8-9, 17-18 it is written:

> *"The Lord is merciful and gracious, slow to anger, and plenteous in mercy. He will not always chide:* **neither will he keep his anger forever** *... But* **the mercy of the Lord is from everlasting to everlasting** *upon them that fear him, and his righteousness unto children's children; To such as keep his covenant, and to those that remember his commandments to do them."*

In Jeremiah *(Yermiyahu)* 3:5, 12-13 it is written:

> *"Will he reserve his anger forever? ... Go and proclaim these words toward the north, and say, Return, thou backsliding Israel, saith the Lord; and I will not cause mine anger to fall upon you: for* **I am merciful, saith the Lord, and I will not keep anger forever**. *Only acknowledge thine iniquity, that thou hast transgressed against*

the LORD *thy God, and hast scattered thy ways to the strangers under every green tree, and ye have not obeyed my voice, saith the* LORD."

The G-d of Israel promised that if the Northern Kingdom *(house of Israel)* would repent that they would again be called His people. In Hosea *(Hoshea)* 1:10 it is written:

"Yet the number of the children of Israel shall be as the sand of the sea, which cannot be measured nor numbered; and it shall come to pass, that in the place where it was said unto them, Ye are not my people, there it shall be said unto them, Ye are the sons of the living God."

The Northern Kingdom Becomes Future Christianity

Once again, in Hosea *(Hoshea)* 1, the G-d of Israel proclaimed that the Northern Kingdom *(house of Israel)* would not be His people *(Lo-Ammi* — Hosea 1:9) and He would have no mercy *(Lo-ruhamah* — Hosea 1:6) upon them. But, if they would repent, *(teshuvah)* (Jeremiah *[Yermiyahu]* 3:5, 12-13) they would be called again His people (Hosea *[Hoshea]* 1:10). The Apostle *(Shaliach)* Peter *(Kefa)* makes a direct link with those from among the nations who have accepted *Yeshua*/Jesus as the Jewish Messiah *(Mashiach)* with the prophecy that the G-d of Israel made to the Northern Kingdom *(house of Israel)* in Hosea *(Hoshea)* 1. In I Peter *(Kefa)* 2:5-6, 9-10 it is written:

"Ye also, as lively stones, are built up a spiritual house, a holy priesthood, to offer up spiritual sacri-

Who Is the Church and Who Is Israel?

fices, acceptable to God by Jesus Christ [Yeshua HaMashiach]. *Wherefore also it is contained in the Scripture, Behold, I lay in Zion a chief corner stone, elect, precious: and he that believeth on him shall not be confounded* [Isaiah 28:16] ... *But you are a chosen generation* [Deuteronomy 7:6], *a royal priesthood, a holy nation, a peculiar people* [Exodus 19:5-6] ... *which in time past were not a people* [**Lo-Ammi** — Hosea 1:9] *but are now the people of God* [Hosea 1:10]: *which had not obtained mercy* [**Lo-ruhamah** — Hosea 1:6], *but now have obtained mercy* [through the Jewish Messiah *(Mashiach)* Yeshua/Jesus who is of the seed of David (Revelation 5:5)]."

The Apostle *(Shaliach)* Paul *(Rav Sha'ul)* also wrote about how the G-d of Israel would pour out His mercy upon the Northern Kingdom *(house of Israel)* through the Jewish Messiah *(Mashiach)* Yeshua/Jesus. In Romans 9:23-26 it is written:

"And that he might make known the riches of his glory on the vessels of mercy [those who would accept the Jewish Messiah (Mashiach) Yeshua/Jesus], *which he had afore prepared unto glory, even us, whom he hath called, not of the Jews only, but also of the* **Gentiles** [those from the house of Israel and from the nations who previously assimilated into Gentile culture]. *As he saith also in Hosea, I will call them my people, which were not my people; and her beloved, which was not beloved* [Hosea 2:23]. *And it shall come to pass, that in the place where it was said unto them, Ye are not my people; there shall they*

be called the children of the living God [Hosea 1:10]."

The Messiah Is the Agent of G-d's Mercy Upon His People

Even though both the Northern Kingdom *(house of Israel)* and the Southern Kingdom *(house of Judah)* was an unfaithful wife to the G-d of Israel, G-d promised **MERCY/GRACE** to both houses of Israel if they would repent *(teshuvah)*. In His judgment upon His people, the G-d of Israel divorced the Northern Kingdom *(house of Israel)* but He did not divorce the Southern Kingdom *(house of Judah)*. Why did the G-d of Israel not divorce the Southern Kingdom *(house of Judah)* because of their unfaithfulness to Him? The reason is because of the G-d of Israel's love for David and for the city of Jerusalem *(Yerushalayim)*. In I Kings *(Melachim)* 11:34, 36 it is written:

> *"Howbeit, I will not take the whole kingdom out of his hand: but I will make him prince all the days of his life for David my servant's sake, whom I chose, because he kept my commandments and my statutes ... that David my servant may have a light always before me in Jerusalem* [Yerushalayim] *the city which I have chosen to put my name there."*

The G-d of Israel promised that He would ALWAYS have mercy upon the seed of David (Psalm [*Tehillim*] 89:1-3, 28-37). The Jewish Messiah *(Mashiach)* was promised to come through the seed of David. In Isaiah *(Yeshayahu)* 11:1 it is written:

Who Is the Church and Who Is Israel?

"And there shall come forth a rod out of the stem of Jesse, and a Branch [a term for the Messiah] *shall grow out of his roots."*

David was a man after the G-d of Israel's heart. In Acts 13:22-23 it is written:

"...he raised up unto them David to be their king; to whom also he gave testimony, and said, I have found David the son of Jesse, a man after mine own heart, which shall fulfill all my will. Of this man's seed hath God according to his promise raised unto Israel a Savior, Jesus [Yeshua].*"*

The Jewish Messiah (*Mashiach*) *Yeshua*/Jesus is the root and offspring of David (Revelation 22:16) and has the key of David (Revelation 3:7).

The G-d of Israel did not divorce the Southern Kingdom *(house of Judah)* because of His love and mercy for David, the city of Jerusalem *(Yerushalayim)*, and all those who believe upon the Jewish Messiah *(Mashiach) Yeshua*/Jesus for their salvation (deliverance/redemption).

The G-d of Israel made provision in the Torah that if a family member of the G-d of Israel sold his possession or inheritance (which the Northern Kingdom *[house of Israel]* did when the G-d of Israel divorced them) that one of his kin (somebody from the Southern Kingdom *[house of Judah]* — the Jewish Messiah *[Mashiach]*) could redeem a near kinsman *(go'el)*, which was sold away. In Leviticus *(Vayikra)* 25:25 it is written:

Restoring the Two Houses of Israel

> *"If thy brother be waxen poor, and hath sold away some of his possession* [Northern Kingdom (house of Israel) Hosea 1], *and if any of his kin* [Southern Kingdom (house of Judah) through the Jewish Messiah (Mashiach) Yeshua/Jesus] *come to redeem it, then shall he redeem that which his brother sold."*

The Jewish Messiah *(Mashiach) Yeshua*/Jesus is the agent of the G-d of Israel's mercy upon His people. In Luke 1:54-55, 72-73 it is written:

> *"He hath helped his servant Israel, in remembrance of his* **MERCY**; *As he spake to our fathers, to Abraham, and to his seed forever ... to perform the* **MERCY** *promised to our fathers, and to remember his holy covenant; the oath which he swore to our father Abraham"*

The House of Israel Is Grafted into the Natural Olive Tree

The physical descendents of Abraham *(Avraham)*, Isaac *(Yitzchak)* and Jacob *(Ya'acov)* are the **root** and **natural branches** of the G-d of Israel's **olive tree**. The physical descendents of Abraham *(Avraham)*, Isaac *(Yitzchak)* and Jacob *(Ya'acov)* who are members of the Southern Kingdom *(house of Judah)* will remain as a natural people as long as there is a sun, moon and stars. In Jeremiah *(Yermiyahu)* 31:35-36 it is written:

> *"Thus saith the* LORD, *which giveth the sun for a light by day, and the ordinances of the moon and of*

Who Is the Church and Who Is Israel?

> *the stars for a light by night, which divideth the sea when the waves thereof roar, The* LORD *of hosts is his name: If these ordinances depart from before me, saith the* LORD*, then the seed of Israel also shall cease from being a nation before me forever."*

Following the reign of Solomon *(Shlomo)*, the house of Jacob *(Ya'acov)* split into the Northern Kingdom *(house of Israel)* and the Southern Kingdom *(house of Judah)*. For being disobedient to the terms and conditions of the marriage contract *(ketubah)* made with the G-d of Israel at mount Sinai, the G-d of Israel divorced the Northern Kingdom *(house of Israel)*. By repenting of their sins, the G-d of Israel promised mercy to the divorced Northern Kingdom *(house of Israel)*. The agent of the mercy of the G-d of Israel is the Jewish Messiah *(Mashiach)* from the seed of David and from the Southern Kingdom *(house of Judah)*. By repenting of their sins and by putting their faith, trust and confidence *(emunah)* in the Jewish Messiah *(Mashiach) Yeshua*/Jesus for their salvation, redemption and deliverance, the assimilated Northern Kingdom *(house of Israel)* and all people from among the nations are **GRAFTED** into the **natural olive tree** and become members of the commonwealth of Israel. In Ephesians 2:11-13 it is written:

> *"Wherefore remember, that ye being in time past Gentiles in the flesh, who are called Uncircumcision by that which is called the Circumcision in the flesh made by hands; That at that time ye were without Christ* [Mashiach]*, being aliens from the commonwealth of Israel, and strangers from the covenants of promise, having no hope, and without God in the world: but now in Christ Jesus*

Restoring the Two Houses of Israel

[Yeshua HaMashiach] *ye who sometimes were far off are made nigh by the blood of Christ* [Mashiach]."

While the natural seed from the Southern Kingdom *(house of Judah)* will remain a remnant of people as long as there is a sun, moon and stars, because they have been unfaithful (Jeremiah *[Yermiyahu]* 3:6-10) in their marriage covenant (Jeremiah *[Yermiyahu]* 2:1-3) made with the G-d of Israel at mount Sinai (Exodus *[Shemot]* 19), they also need the mercy that the G-d of Israel promised David through the Jewish Messiah *(Mashiach)* *Yeshua*/Jesus.

When they accept *Yeshua*/Jesus as the Jewish Messiah *(Mashiach)*, the natural branches will be grafted into their own olive tree. The **grafting** of the **wild olive branches** (those from the nations not from the Southern Kingdom *[house of Judah]*) with the **natural root** and the **natural branches** (those from the Southern Kingdom *[house of Judah]*) into **ONE olive tree** by accepting *Yeshua*/Jesus as the Jewish Messiah *(Mashiach)* is mentioned by the Apostle *(Shaliach)* Paul *(Rav Sha'ul)* in Romans 11. In Romans 11:13, 17-19, 24, 26 it is written:

> *"For I speak to you* **Gentiles***, inasmuch as I am the apostle of the Gentiles* [the grafted Northern Kingdom/house of Israel] ... *and if some of the branches be broken off, and thou, being a* **wild olive tree***, wast* **grafted** *in among them, and with them partakest of the root and fatness of the olive tree; Boast not against the branches. But if thou boast, thou bearest not the root, but the root thee. Thou wilt say then, The branches were bro-*

Who Is the Church and Who Is Israel?

ken off, that I might be grafted in ... For if thou wast cut out of the olive tree which is wild by nature, and wast grafted contrary to nature into a good olive tree: how much more shall these, which be the **natural branches** *be* **grafted** *into their own olive tree? ... And so all Israel* [both the grafted house of Israel (wild branches) and the grafted house of Judah (natural branches)] *shall be saved: as it is written, There shall come out of Zion the Deliverer* [kinsman redeemer/go'el], *and shall turn away ungodliness in Jacob* [Isaiah 59:20]."

Who Is the Church and Who Is Israel?

In today's world, the term *"church"* is traditionally identified and associated with the *house of Israel* (Christianity) while the term *"Israel"* is traditionally identified and associated with the *house of Judah* (Jews/Judaism). In this chapter, we learned that the Biblical *"church"* was **born at mount Sinai**. It consisted of physical natural born descendents of Abraham *(Avraham)*, Isaac *(Yitzchak)* and Jacob *(Ya'acov)* and a mixed multitude from among the nations who came out of Egypt *(Mitzrayim)*.

Biblical Israel is the **olive tree** of the G-d of Israel. The physical natural born descendents of Abraham *(Avraham)*, Isaac *(Yitzchak)* and Jacob *(Ya'acov)* will remain a remnant of people and a part of the redemptive plan of the G-d of Israel as long as there is a sun, moon and stars. Biblical Israel consists of the **natural root** of Abraham *(Avraham)*, Isaac *(Yitzchak)* and Jacob *(Ya'acov)* and the **assimilated** Northern Kingdom *(house of Israel)* and all people from among the nations who are grafted into the natural olive tree by repenting *(teshuvah)* of their sins and accepting *Yeshua*/Jesus as the Jewish Messiah *(Mashiach)*. Those from the Southern Kingdom *(house of Judah)* who accept *Yeshua*/Jesus as Messiah *(Mashiach)* are natural branches grafted into their own olive tree. So, Biblical Israel consists of the physical descendents of Abraham *(Avraham)*, Isaac *(Yitzchak)* and Jacob *(Ya'acov)* and a mixed multitude from among the nations who are grafted into the natural olive tree. Therefore, the Biblical terms *"church"* and *"Israel"* are synonymous terms.

The traditional understanding of the word *"church"* (associated with Christianity) has NOT replaced *"Israel"* (associated with the traditional understanding as Jews who have not accepted *Yeshua*/Jesus as the Jewish Messiah). On the contrary, the non-Jews from among the nations who have repented *(teshuvah)* of their sins and have accepted *Yeshua*/Jesus as the Jewish Messiah *(Mashiach)* are *grafted* into the natural olive tree. While all Jews (those from the Southern Kingdom *[house of Judah]*) are Israelites, not all Israelites (those from the Northern Kingdom *[house of Israel]* and who have been grafted into the natural olive tree from among the nations) are Jews. Those grafted in from among the nations to the natural olive tree are Biblical Israelites.

In conclusion, in order for restoration to come to both the *house of Israel* (Christianity) and *the house of Judah* (Judaism), both houses of Israel need to recognize who each other are Biblically. The *house of Israel* (Christianity) needs to recognize that they have NOT replaced the natural seed of Abraham *(Avraham)*, Isaac *(Yitzchak)*

Who Is the Church and Who Is Israel?

and Jacob *(Ya'acov)* but have been *grafted* into the natural olive tree. The *house of Judah* (Judaism) needs to recognize the *house of Israel* (Christianity) as being *Messianic Israel*. Therefore, both houses of Israel need to understand that they are brethren (Psalm *[Tehillim]* 133) and members of the SAME **olive tree**. May the G-d of Israel bring redemption, restoration, reconciliation and unity to both houses of Israel speedily in our days. Amen!

Chapter 3

G-d's Power Twins: Torah and Grace

In order for full restoration to come to both the *house of Judah* (Judaism) and the *house of Israel* (Christianity), both houses of Israel need to understand that the G-d of Israel is a G-d of Torah AND a G-d of grace/mercy. Corporately speaking, the *house of Judah* (Judaism) mainly identifies with the G-d of Israel as being the giver of the Torah *(matan Torah)*. The *house of Israel* (Christianity) mainly identifies with the G-d of Israel as being a G-d of grace/mercy through the Jewish Messiah *(Mashiach) Yeshua*/Jesus.

The *house of Judah* (Judaism) needs to Biblically understand that the G-d of Israel has expressed His grace/mercy to His people through the Jewish Messiah *(Mashiach) Yeshua*/Jesus. The *house of Israel* (Christianity) needs to Biblically understand that the Torah is the Word of G-d and the Word of G-d is the Torah and that the Torah goes from Genesis *(Bereishit)* to Revelation. Furthermore, the *house of Israel* (Christianity) needs to understand that the Torah is ETERNAL and that the G-d of Israel did not do away with His Torah through the death and resurrection of the Jewish Messiah *(Mashiach) Yeshua*/Jesus. If the G-d of Israel did away with His Torah/Word, He would have to do away with

Himself because the Jewish Messiah *(Mashiach) Yeshua*/ Jesus is the Torah/Word of G-d manifested in the flesh. Heaven and earth will pass away but the Torah/Word of G-d will live and abide FOREVER (Isaiah *[Yeshayahu]* 40:8, I Peter *[Kefa]* 1:23-25).

Because the *house of Israel* (Christianity) does not understand that Biblically the Torah and the Word of G-d are synonymous terms and that G-d's Torah/Word goes from Genesis *(Bereishit)* to Revelation, they have unbiblically embraced a dispensational theology that teaches that before the Jewish Messiah *(Mashiach) Yeshua*/Jesus was the age of law and following the death and resurrection of the Jewish Messiah *(Mashiach) Yeshua*/Jesus is the age of grace. In this chapter, we will learn that the G-d of Israel has always been a G-d of Torah AND a G-d of grace/mercy and that the G-d of Israel's grace/mercy is mentioned MORE in the *TeNaKh* (Old Testament) than in the *Brit Hadashah* (New Testament). Furthermore, we will examine what the Biblical term Torah means and the purpose of the G-d of Israel's Torah. In our conclusion, we will find that the G-d of Israel is a G-d of Torah and a G-d of grace/mercy and that the Torah of the G-d of Israel and the grace/mercy of the G-d of Israel are His *Power Twins*.

Hebrew and Greek Words for Grace/Mercy

The Greek word found in the *Brit Hadashah* (New Testament) translated as *grace* in the King James Bible is *charis*. It is the Strong's number 5485 in the Greek dictionary. In the *Thayer's Greek-English Lexicon of the New Testament coded to the Strong's Concordance*, it will tell you that the Greek word *charis* (5485) corresponds to the Hebrew word *chayn*. The Hebrew word *chayn* is the Strong's word 2580 in the Strong's dictionary. It is most often translated as grace/favor in the King James Bible.

The Greek word found in the *Brit Hadashah* (New Testament) translated as *mercy* in the King James Bible is *eleos*. It is the Strong's number 1656 in the Greek dictionary. In the *Thayer's Greek-English Lexicon of the New Testament coded to the Strong's Concordance,* it will tell you that the Greek word *eleos* (1656) is related/associated/corresponds to the Hebrew word *chesed*. The Hebrew word *chesed* is the Strong's word 2617 in the Strong's dictionary. It is most often translated as mercy/lovingkindness in the King James Bible.

Therefore, the two primary Greek words for grace/mercy found in the Bible are *charis* (5485) and *eleos* (1656). The two primary Hebrew words for grace/mercy found in the Bible are *chayn* (2580) and *chesed* (2617).

The G-d of Israel Is a G-d of Grace/Mercy

The G-d of Israel is a G-d of grace/mercy. It is an attribute/characteristic of the G-d of Israel Himself. In Jeremiah *(Yermiyahu)* 9:23-24 it is written:

> *"Thus saith the LORD, Let not the wise man glory in his wisdom, neither let the mighty man glory in his might, let not the rich man glory in his riches: But let him that glorieth glory in this, that he understandeth and knoweth me, that I am the LORD*

which exercise lovingkindness [2617/chesed/mercy]..."

In Psalm *(Tehillim)* 117 it is written:

> "*O praise the* LORD, *all ye nations: praise him, all ye people. For his* **merciful kindness** [2617/chesed/mercy] *is great toward us: and the truth of the* LORD *endureth forever. Praise ye the* LORD."

The G-d of Israel's Grace/Mercy Is Eternal and Everlasting

The grace/mercy of the G-d of Israel is ETERNAL and EVERLASTING. In Psalm *(Tehillim)* 103:17-18 it is written:

> "*But the* **mercy** [2617/chesed] *of the* LORD *is from* **everlasting to everlasting** *upon them that fear him, and his righteousness unto children's children; To such as keep his covenant, and to those that remember his commandments to do them.*"

In Isaiah *(Yeshayahu)* 54:8 it is written:

> "...*with* **everlasting kindness** [2617/chesed] *will I have mercy on thee, saith the* LORD *thy Redeemer.*"

The G-d of Israel Created the Heavens and Earth by His Grace/Mercy

The G-d of Israel created the heavens and the earth by His grace/mercy. In Psalm *(Tehillim)* 136:1, 6-9 it is written:

G-d's Power Twins: Torah and Grace

"O give thanks unto the LORD*; for he is good: for his* **mercy** *[2617/chesed] endureth forever ... to him that stretched out the earth above the waters: for his* **mercy** *[2617/chesed] endureth forever. To him that made great lights: for his* **mercy** *[2617/chesed] endureth forever: The sun to rule by day: for his* **mercy** *[2617/chesed] endureth forever: The moon and stars to rule by night: for his* **mercy** *[2617/chesed] endureth forever."*

Noah Found Grace in the Eyes of G-d

Noah found grace in the eyes of the G-d of Israel. In Genesis *(Bereishit)* 6:8 it is written:

"But Noah found **grace** *[2580/chayn] in the eyes of the* LORD*."*

G-d Showed Grace/Mercy to Joseph

The G-d of Israel found grace/mercy with Joseph *(Yosef)*. In Genesis *(Bereishit)* 39:21 it is written:

"But the LORD *was with Joseph, and showed him* **mercy** *[2617/chesed] and give him* **favor** *[2580/chayn/grace] in the sight of the keeper of the prison."*

G-d Saves the Children of Israel Out of Egypt by His Grace/Mercy

The G-d of Israel saved/delivered His people out of Egypt *(Mitzrayim)* by His grace/mercy. In Exodus *(Shemot)* 3:15-16, 20-21 it is written:

Restoring the Two Houses of Israel

> "And God said moreover unto Moses ... Go, and gather the elders of Israel together, and say unto them ... And I will stretch out my hand, and smite Egypt with all my wonders which I will do in the midst thereof ... and I will give this people **favor** [2580/chayn/grace] in the sight of the Egyptians..."

In Psalm *(Tehillim)* 136:10-15 it is written:

> "To him that smote Egypt in their firstborn: for his **mercy** [2617/chesed] endureth forever: And brought out Israel from among them: for his **mercy** [2617/chesed] endureth forever: With a strong hand, and with a stretched out arm: for his **mercy** [2617/chesed] endureth forever. To him which divided the Red sea into parts: for his **mercy** [2617/chesed] endureth forever: And made Israel to pass through the midst of it: for his **mercy** [2617/chesed] endureth forever: But overthrew Pharaoh and his host in the Red sea: for his **mercy** [2617/chesed] endureth forever."

The Children of Israel are Led Through the Wilderness by the Grace/Mercy of G-d

The G-d of Israel led the children of Israel through the wilderness by His grace/mercy. In Psalm *(Tehillim)* 136:16 it is written:

> "To him which led his people through the wilderness: for his **mercy** [2617/chesed] endureth forever."

G-d's Power Twins: Torah and Grace

The "rock" which led the children of Israel through the wilderness was the Jewish Messiah *(Mashiach) Yeshua*/Jesus. In I Corinthians 10:1-4 it is written:

> *"Moreover, brethren, I would not that ye should be ignorant, how that all our fathers were under the cloud, and all passed through the sea; And were all baptized* [mikvah/immersed] *unto Moses in the cloud and in the sea; And did all eat the same spiritual meat; And did all drink the same spiritual drink: for they drank of that spiritual Rock that followed them: and that Rock was Christ."*

In Jeremiah *(Yermiyahu)* 31:2-3, it is written:

> *"Thus saith the* LORD, *The people which were left of the sword found* **grace** [2580/chayn] *in the wilderness; even Israel, when I went to cause him to rest. The* LORD *hath appeared of old unto me, saying, Yea, I have loved thee with an everlasting love: therefore with* **lovingkindness** [2617/ chesed/mercy] *have I drawn thee."*

Moses Finds Grace/Mercy in G-d's Sight

Moses *(Moshe)* found grace/mercy in the sight of the G-d of Israel. In Exodus *(Shemot)* 33:11-13, 17 it is written:

> *"And the* LORD *spake unto Moses face to face, as a man speaketh unto his friend … And Moses said unto the* LORD *… yet thou hast said, I know thee by name, and thou hast also found* **grace** [2580/ chayn] *in my sight. Now therefore, I pray thee, if I have found* **grace** [2580/chayn] *in thy sight, show me now thy way, that I may know thee, that I*

may find **grace** *[2580/chayn]* *in thy sight: and consider that this nation is thy people ...And the* LORD *said unto Moses ... for thou hast found* **grace** *[2580/chayn] in my sight, and I know thee by name."*

The Children of Israel Defeat Their Enemies and Conquer the Promised Land By the Grace/Mercy of G-d

The children of Israel defeated their enemies and conquered the Promised Land by the grace/mercy of the G-d of Israel. In Psalm *(Tehillim)* 136:1, 17-22, 24 it is written:

> *"O give thanks unto the* LORD*; for he is good: for his* **mercy** *[2617/chesed] endureth forever ... to him which smote great kings: for his* **mercy** *[2617/chesed] endureth forever: And slew famous kings: for his* **mercy** *[2617/chesed] endureth forever: Sihon king of the Amorites: for his* **mercy** *[2617/chesed] endureth forever: And Og the king of Bashan: for his* **mercy** *[2617/chesed] endureth forever: And gave their land for a heritage: for his* **mercy** *[2617/chesed] endureth forever: Even a heritage unto Israel his servant: for his* **mercy** *[2617/chesed] endureth forever ... And hath redeemed us from our enemies: for his* **mercy** *[2617/chesed] endureth forever."*

G-d Promises David's Seed Grace/Mercy

The G-d of Israel promised David that He would have grace/mercy upon His seed forever. In II Samuel *(Shmu'el)* 7:4,8, 12-16 it is written:

G-d's Power Twins: Torah and Grace

"And it came to pass that night, that the word of the Lord *came unto Nathan, saying ... Now therefore so shalt thou say unto my servant David, Thus saith the* Lord *of hosts, I took thee from the sheepcote, from following the sheep, to be ruler over my people, over Israel ... And when thy days be fulfilled, and thou shalt sleep with thy fathers, I will set up thy seed after thee, which shall proceed out of thy bowels, and I will establish his kingdom. He shall build a house for my name, and I will establish the throne of his kingdom forever. I will be his father, and he shall be my son. If he commit iniquity, I will chasten him with the rod of men, and with the stripes of the children of men: But my* **mercy** *[2617/chesed] shall not depart away from him ... and thine house and thy kingdom shall be established forever before thee: thy throne shall be established forever."*

In Psalm *(Tehillim)* 89:1-4, 24, 28-36 it is written:

"I will sing of the **mercies** *[2617/chesed] of the* Lord *forever: with my mouth will I make known thy faithfulness to all generations. For I have said,* **Mercy** *[2617/chesed] shall be built up forever: thy faithfulness shalt thou establish in the very heavens. I have made a covenant with my chosen, I have sworn unto David my servant, Thy seed will I establish forever, and build up thy throne to all generations. Selah. ... my faithfulness and my* **mercy** *shall be with him: and in my name shall his horn be exalted ... My* **mercy** *[2617/chesed] will I keep for him forevermore, and my covenant shall*

stand fast with him. His seed also will I make to endure forever, and his throne as the days of heaven. If his children forsake my law [Torah], *and walk not in my judgments; If they break my statutes, and keep not my commandments; Then will I visit their transgression with the rod, and their iniquity with stripes. Nevertheless my* **lovingkindness** [2617/chesed/mercy] *will I not utterly take from him, nor suffer my faithfulness to fail. My covenant will I not break, nor alter the thing that is gone out of my lips. Once have I sworn by my holiness that I will not lie unto David. His seed shall endure forever, and his throne as the sun before me."*

David's Sins Are Forgiven by the Grace/Mercy of G-d

David's sins were forgiven by the G-d of Israel by His grace/mercy upon David when he repented of his sins. In Psalm *(Tehillim)* 25:6-7, 51:1-2 it is written:

*"Remember, O L*ORD*, thy tender mercies and thy* **lovingkindnesses** [2617/chesed/mercy]; *for they have been ever of old. Remember not the sins of my youth, nor my transgressions: according to thy* **mercy** [2617/chesed] *remember thou me for thy goodness' sake, O L*ORD *... Have mercy upon me, O God, according to thy* **lovingkindness** [2617/chesed]: *according unto the multitude of thy tender mercies blot out my transgressions. Wash me thoroughly from mine iniquity, and cleanse me from my sin."*

G-d's Power Twins: Torah and Grace

In Psalm *(Tehillim)* 86:5 it is written:

> *"For you, LORD, art good, and ready to forgive; and plenteous in* **mercy** *[2617/chesed] unto all them that call upon thee."*

The House of Judah Was Preserved in Babylonian Captivity and Built the Temple by the Grace/Mercy of G-d

The *house of Judah* (Judaism/Southern Kingdom) was preserved in Babylonian captivity and a remnant from the *house of Judah* (Judaism/Southern Kingdom) returned to the land of Israel to rebuild the Temple *(Beit HaMikdash)* in the days of Ezra and Nehemiah because of the grace/mercy of the G-d of Israel upon His people. In Ezra 9:7-9 it is written:

> *"Since the days of our fathers have we been in a great trespass unto this day; and for our iniquities have we, our kings, and our priests, been delivered into the hand of the kings of the lands, to the sword, to captivity, and to a spoil, and to confusion of face, as it is this day. And now for a little space* **grace** *has been showed from the LORD our God, to leave us a remnant to escape, and to give us a nail in his holy place, that our God may lighten our eyes, and give us a little reviving in our bondage. For we were bondmen; yet our God hath not forsaken us in our bondage, but hath extended* **mercy** *[2617/chesed] unto us in the sight of the kings of Persia, to give us a reviving, to set up the house of our God, and to repair the desola-*

tions thereof, and to give us a wall in Judah and in Jerusalem."

The G-d of Israel Is Married to His People in Grace/Mercy

When the G-d of Israel entered into a marriage covenant with His people, He became betrothed unto them in grace/mercy. In Hosea *(Hoshea)* 2:19-20 it is written:

> *"And I will betroth* [marry] *thee unto me forever; yea, I will betroth* [marry] *thee unto me in righteousness, and in judgment, and in* **lovingkindness** [2617/chesed], *and in* **mercies**. *I will even betroth* [marry] *thee unto me in faithfulness: and thou shalt know the* Lord.*"*

G-d Will Save/Redeem the House of David Through the Messiah by His Grace/Mercy

The G-d of Israel will save/redeem the *house of David* through the Jewish Messiah *(Mashiach) Yeshua*/Jesus by His grace/mercy. In Zechariah *(Zecharyah)* 12:9-10 it is written:

> *"And it shall come to pass in that day, that I will seek to destroy all the nations that come against Jerusalem. And I will pour upon the* **house of David**, *and upon the inhabitants of Jerusalem, the* **spirit of grace** [2580/chayn] *and of supplications: and they shall look upon me* **whom they have pierced**, *and they shall mourn for him, as one mourneth for his only son, and shall be in*

G-d's Power Twins: Torah and Grace

bitterness for him, as one that is in bitterness for his firstborn."

The G-d of Israel Has Always Been a G-d of Grace/Mercy

The G-d of Israel has ALWAYS been a G-d of grace/mercy. The death and resurrection of the Jewish Messiah *(Mashiach) Yeshua*/Jesus did not usher in the age of grace. The grace/mercy of the G-d of Israel has always been from everlasting to everlasting.

Grace/mercy is an attribute/characteristic of the G-d of Israel Himself. The G-d of Israel showed grace/mercy to Noah, Joseph *(Yosef)*, Moses *(Moshe)* and David. The G-d of Israel forgave the sins of the children of Israel because of His grace/mercy toward them. The G-d of Israel forgave the sins of David because of His grace/mercy toward David. The G-d of Israel made an eternal covenant with David that His grace/mercy would be upon David's seed forever.

The G-d of Israel created the heavens and the earth because His grace/mercy endures forever. He redeemed the children of Israel from Egypt *(Mitzrayim)* because of His grace/mercy toward His people in remembrance of His covenant with Abraham *(Avraham)*. The G-d of Israel led the children of Israel in the wilderness and gave them victory over their enemies in the wilderness and in the Promised Land because of His grace/mercy toward His people.

The G-d of Israel Redeemed His People From Egypt by His Grace/Mercy

After studying in this chapter the grace/mercy of the G-d of Israel and realizing that the G-d of Israel is a

G-d of grace/mercy throughout the entire *TeNaKh* (Old Testament), it should be easy for us to understand the Biblical truth that the G-d of Israel **saved/ redeemed** the children of Israel from Egypt *(Mitzrayim)* by His **grace/mercy** and brought them to mount Sinai to show them how He wanted them to live their daily lives in obedience to the G-d of Israel AFTER they were saved/redeemed by His grace/mercy. The children of Israel were NEVER saved/redeemed/delivered from their enemies because they kept the Torah and deserved to be saved/redeemed/delivered. However, they were ALWAYS redeemed/delivered/saved because of the grace/mercy of the G-d of Israel toward His people.

The Torah is Eternal and Everlasting

Just as we have seen that the grace/mercy of the G-d of Israel is eternal and everlasting, in the last part of this chapter, we will see that the Torah of the G-d of Israel is also eternal and everlasting. We will discover that in traditional Hebraic/Jewish thought, "Torah" and the "Word of G-d" are synonymous terms. Therefore, the G-d of Israel's Torah is from Genesis *(Bereishit)* to Revelation. The age of law did not end with the death and resurrection of the Jewish Messiah *(Mashiach) Yeshua/* Jesus because the Torah/Word of G-d lives and abides forever.

Next, let us examine the meaning and purpose of the Torah of the G-d of Israel and why the Torah of the G-d of Israel should be important to every believer in *Yeshua*/Jesus as the Jewish Messiah *(Mashiach)*. By em-

G-d's Power Twins: Torah and Grace

bracing the Biblical truth that the Torah of the G-d of Israel is eternal and everlasting, the G-d of Israel can bring restoration and reconciliation to both houses of Israel.

What Is the Meaning of Torah?

Probably one of the most misunderstood words in the entire Bible to the *house of Israel* (Christianity) is the word LAW. In reality, the word LAW is a very poorly translated and misrepresented word to describe the Hebrew word, TORAH. When most believers in the Jewish Messiah *(Mashiach) Yeshua*/Jesus from the *house of Israel* (Christianity) hear the word, TORAH, they take two steps backward and put up a religious wall against any member from the *house of Israel* (Christianity) who would mention the word TORAH or who would suggest that we need to live our lives according to the *Torah* of the G-d of Israel. In fact, most members from the *house of Israel* (Christianity) view the *Torah* with the attitude, "We are not under the Law, we are New Testament believers in the Jewish Messiah *(Mashiach) Yeshua*/Jesus and under grace."

We are Saved by Grace Through Faith

It is a Biblical truth that we are NOT saved/redeemed/delivered from our sins by keeping the Torah of the G-d of Israel. We are saved/redeemed/delivered by grace (2580/*chayn*)/mercy (2617/*chesed*) through faith *(emunah)* and salvation/redemption is a FREE gift from the G-d of Israel. In Ephesians 2:8-9, it is written:

"**For by grace are ye saved through faith;** *and that not of yourselves: it is the gift of God: Not of works, lest any man should boast.*"

However, the Apostle Paul *(Rav Sha'ul)* tells us in Romans 3:28, 31 that AFTER we are saved/redeemed/delivered, we are to uphold/keep the *Torah* of the G-d of Israel as it is written:

"Therefore we conclude that **a man is justified by faith without the deeds of the law ... Do we then make void the law** *through faith? God forbid: yea,* **we establish the law [Torah].**"

Torah Means Instruction

While it is true that we are not saved/redeemed/delivered on our own merit by our own ability through keeping the Torah of the G-d of Israel, the *house of Israel* (Christianity) must know and understand WHAT the word, TORAH, means. The word Law is the Hebrew word, TORAH. It is the Strong's word 8451 in the Hebrew Concordance. The best meaning of the word, TORAH, is *"teaching or instruction."* The word TORAH does not mean salvation/redemption/deliverance but rather *"teaching or instruction."* There is a word in the Bible that means *"salvation."* The English word, Jesus, is the Hebrew word, *Yeshua*. The Hebrew word *Yeshua* means *"salvation."* This was the role of the Jewish Messiah *(Mashiach) Yeshua*/Jesus when He came to the earth at His first coming as the suffering Messiah *(Mashiach)* known as Messiah ben Joseph *(Yosef)*. In Matthew *(Mattityahu)* 1:21 it is written:

G-d's Power Twins: Torah and Grace

"And she [Mary] *shall bring forth a son, and thou shalt shall call his name JESUS* [Yeshua in Hebrew]: *for he shall SAVE his people from their sins."*

What Is the Purpose of G-d's Torah?

From this, we can understand that **YESHUA/JESUS** means **SALVATION** and **TORAH** means **INSTRUCTION**. Therefore, the Torah was NEVER meant by the G-d of Israel to be a means of salvation for His people. The G-d of Israel's only salvation for His people is by His grace/mercy *(chesed)* through the Jewish Messiah *(Mashiach) Yeshua*/Jesus!

Torah Does Not Mean Law

Because there is no proper corresponding word in Greek or English for the Hebrew word, TORAH, it is commonly translated as *"law."* Law implies a set of do's and don'ts intended to imprison people when they are broken. However, the G-d of Israel gave the Hebrew language to communicate His spiritual truths. In fact, the G-d of Israel calls Hebrew a pure language (Zephaniah 3:9). This truth is beautifully understood when we do a Biblical word study of the Hebrew word, TORAH.

The Torah Is G-d's Instruction Manual to Live Our Lives

The word *Torah*, which is the Strong's word 8451 in the Hebrew dictionary, comes from the Hebrew word,

"Yarah." The Hebrew word, *"Yarah"* is the Strong's word 3384. The meaning of the word, *"Yarah"* is *"to teach, to point out as aiming the finger, to lay a foundation."* By examining the Hebrew meaning of the word, TORAH, we can understand that the word *Torah* means, *"to instruct, to teach, to point out as aiming the finger, to lay a foundation."*

So, the Torah should be correctly seen as the G-d of Israel's INSTRUCTION tool to TEACH His people HOW to live their lives AFTER they are saved/redeemed/delivered. The TORAH should be seen as a foundation for our lives and a foundation for understanding the entire Bible. Therefore, the most basic understanding of the meaning of *Torah* is *"instruction for the purpose of teaching done by pointing out or aiming the finger."* The G-d of Israel's purpose in giving the *Torah* to His people is to *"lay a foundation"* and to communicate His spiritual truths to His people regarding the principles of the Kingdom of Heaven *(Malkut Shamayim)* and His redemptive plan for all of mankind.

While members from the *house of Judah* (Judaism) and from the *house of Israel* (Christianity) who are saved by the grace/mercy *(chesed)* of the G-d of Israel through faith *(emunah)* in the Jewish Messiah *(Mashiach) Yeshua*/Jesus without the deeds of the law will go to heaven *(olam haba)*, salvation/redemption/deliverance by the G-d of Israel by his grace/mercy *(chesed)* does not give His people the freedom to neglect the TORAH of the G-d of Israel because the TORAH is the G-d of Israel's INSTRUCTION MANUAL for members of His body to conduct and live their lives in obedience *(shema)* to the G-d of Israel AFTER they are saved/redeemed/delivered.

G-d's Power Twins: Torah and Grace

G-d's Torah Is From Genesis to Revelation

EVERYTHING in the Bible was divinely ordained by the G-d of Israel to teach or instruct His people about the spiritual truths of His Kingdom. In Romans 15:4 it is written:

> *"For whatsoever things were written aforetime were written for our **learning**, that we through patience and comfort of the Scriptures might have hope."*

ALL Scripture is divinely inspired by the G-d of Israel. In II Timothy 3:16 it is written:

> **"All Scripture is given by inspiration of God** *and is profitable for doctrine, for reproof, for correction, for instruction in righteousness."*

It should be understood that when the Apostle Paul *(Rav Sha'ul)* wrote this letter and made the statement that *"ALL Scripture is given by inspiration of God,"* he was talking about the *TeNaKh* (Old Testament) INCLUDING the TORAH. The *Brit Hadashah* (New Testament) was not yet canonized when the Apostle Paul *(Rav Sha'ul)* wrote this letter.

G-d's Torah Is the Word of G-d

The G-d of Israel's Torah is His Word. The *"Torah"* and the *"Word of G-d"* are synonymous terms in the Bible. Most members from the *house of Israel* (Christianity) view the "TORAH" as the first five books of the Bible but *"The Word of God"* as the entire Bible from

Restoring the Two Houses of Israel

Genesis *(Bereishit)* to Revelation. However, in Isaiah *(Yeshayahu)* 2:3, we see an example where the *Torah* and *the Word of God* are used interchangeably as it is written:

> *"And many people shall go and say, Come ye, and let us go up to the mountain of the* LORD*, to the house of the God of Jacob; and he will teach us of his ways, and we will walk in his paths: for out of Zion shall go forth the law* **[TORAH]***, and the* **WORD OF THE LORD** *from Jerusalem."*

In this verse, we can see an example of Hebrew parallelism. *"Out of Zion shall go forth* **the Torah***"* is the same as *"***The Word of the** LORD *from Jerusalem."* Therefore, from this example, we can see that the Torah and the Word of the L-RD are used synonymously in the Bible.

Another example where we can see the word TORAH used interchangeably with the WORD OF THE LORD is in Psalm 119. In Psalm *(Tehillim)* 119:97 it is written:

> **"O how love I thy law [Torah]!** *it is my meditation all the day."*

In Psalm *(Tehillim)* 119:105 it is written:

> **"Thy word is a lamp** *unto my feet, and a light unto my path."*

Once again, we can see from the example in Psalm *(Tehillim)* 119 that in one verse, David refers to the TORAH and in verses following he refers to the WORD OF GOD. Therefore, in a strict interpretation of the meaning of the word, TORAH, the Torah is the first five books of the Bible. However, in a broad sense, everything in the Bible from Genesis *(Bereishit)* to Revelation should be seen as the G-d of Israel's TORAH or instruction to His people.

What Was the Tree of Life in the Garden of Eden?

When the G-d of Israel created Adam and Eve *(Chavah)*, He placed them in the Garden of Eden *(Gan Eden)*. In the middle of the Garden of Eden *(Gan Eden)* was the *"Tree of Life."* (Genesis *[Bereishit]* 2:9). What was the tree of life *(etz chayim)* that the G-d of Israel planted in the middle of the Garden of Eden *(Gan Eden)*? The Tree of Life *(etz chayim)* is the Torah! In Proverbs *(Mishlei)* 3:1, 18 it is written:

> *"My son, forget not my* **law [TORAH];** *but let thine heart keep my commandments ... She is a* **tree of life** *to them that lay hold upon her: and happy is every one that retaineth her."*

The Torah Is More Desired Than Fine Gold

The G-d of Israel said that His Torah is to be more desired than fine gold. In Psalm *(Tehillim)* 19:7-8, 10 it is written:

> *"The* **law [TORAH]** *of the* Lord *is perfect, converting the soul: the testimony of the* Lord *is sure, making wise the simple. The statutes of the* Lord *are right, rejoicing the heart: the commandment of the* Lord *is pure,* **enlightening the eyes ... More**

to be desired are they than gold, *yea, than much fine gold: sweeter also than honey and the honeycomb."*

The Torah Is the Tree of Life

Those members of the family *(mishpochah)* of the G-d of Israel who delight in the TORAH of the G-d of Israel and meditate in His TORAH day and night are like a tree planted by the rivers of water. In Psalm *(Tehillim)* 1:1-3 it is written:

> "**Blessed is the man** *that walketh not in the counsel of the ungodly, nor standeth in the way of sinners, nor sitteth in the seat of the scornful. But his* **delight** *is in the* **law [TORAH] OF THE LORD;** *and in his* **law [TORAH]** *doth he* **meditate day and night.** *And he shall be like* **a tree planted by the rivers of water**, *that bringeth forth his fruit in his season; his leaf also shall not whither; and whatsoever he doeth shall prosper."*

In these verses we can see that a member of the family of the G-d of Israel who delights himself in the TORAH of the L-RD and meditates day and night in the TORAH is like a tree planted by the rivers of water. In Revelation 22:1-2, the tree planted by the rivers of water is the tree of life as it is written:

> *"And he showed me a pure river of water of life, clear as crystal, proceeding out of the throne of God and of the Lamb. In the midst of the street of it, and on either side of the river, was there the* **tree of life,** *which bare twelve manner of fruits, and*

G-d's Power Twins: Torah and Grace

yielded her fruit every month: and the **leaves of the tree** *were for the* **healing of the nations.**"

Furthermore, the Jewish Messiah *(Mashiach)* Yeshua/Jesus told the members of His body that those who DO His commandments (Torah) will have right to the tree of life. In Revelation 22:14 it is written:

> "**Blessed** *are they that* **do his commandments,** *that they may have right to the* **tree of life**, *and may enter in through the gates into the city.*"

The Pages of the Torah Scroll Are Called Leaves

In Revelation 22:2, we are told that the LEAVES of the tree of life *(Torah)* are for the healing of the nations. The *pages* of the Torah scroll are called *leaves*. An example of pages of a scroll being called leaves can be found in Jeremiah *(Yermiyahu)* 36:21, 23 it is written:

> "*So the king sent Jehudi to fetch* **the roll** ... *and it came to pass, that when Jehudi had* **read three or four leaves**..."

Therefore, from these scripture verses we can understand the following:

1. The tree of life that was planted in the Garden of Eden *(Gan Eden)* was the Torah.
2. G-d's Torah is worth far above pure gold.
3. G-d's Torah is for the healing of the nations.

4. Those who keep the Torah of the G-d of Israel have right to the tree of life.

Abraham: The Father of Our Faith

In Romans 4:16, Abraham *(Avraham)* is called the father of our faith *(emunah)*. Why did the G-d of Israel choose Abraham *(Avraham)* and why is Abraham *(Avraham)* called the father of our faith *(emunah)*? The G-d of Israel chose Abraham *(Avraham)* because G-d knew that Abraham *(Avraham)* would teach his children the Torah of the G-d of Israel. In Genesis *(Bereishit)* 18:18-19 it is written:

> *"Seeing that Abraham shall surely become a great and mighty nation, and all the nations of the earth shall be blessed in him? For I know him, that he will command his children and his household after him, and* **they shall keep the way of the Lord** [the Torah], *to do justice and judgment; that the Lord may bring upon Abraham that which he hath spoken of him."*

Abraham *(Avraham)* kept the Torah of the G-d of Israel. In Genesis *(Bereishit)* 26:5 it is written:

> *"Because that Abraham obeyed my voice, and kept my charge, my commandments, my statutes, and my* **laws [TORAH]**.*"*

What Is the Purpose of the Torah?

Listed below are seven purposes of the Torah of the G-d of Israel. They are as follows:

G-d's Power Twins: Torah and Grace

1. Teaches and reveals the Divine nature of G-d.
    a) G-d is Holy (Leviticus 19:2).
    b) G-d is Love (I John 4:7-8).
    c) G-d is Gracious, Righteous, Merciful (Psalm 116:5).
    d) G-d is Light (I John 1:5).

2. Teaches and reveals sin (Romans 3:20, Galatians 3:10, James 2:10, I John 3:4).

3. Teaches and reveals man's need to have a Messiah *(Mashiach)* (Romans 10:4). "End" in Greek means "Goal/Target."

4. Teaches and reveals the G-d of Israel's redemptive plan through the Messiah (*Mashiach*) (Psalm 40:6-7, Hebrews 10:5-7, Luke 24:36, 44).

5. Teaches and reveals that man is saved/redeemed/delivered by the grace/mercy *(chesed)* of the G-d of Israel by faith *(emunah)* and not by the deeds of the law (Romans 3:20, 24, 28, Galatians 2:16, Ephesians 2:8-9).

6. Teaches and reveals the difference between the life of the Spirit (the Torah written upon a heart of flesh) and the life of the flesh/evil inclination (the Torah written upon a heart of stone) (Romans 8:1-3, 5-9).

7. Teaches us how to grow from spiritual babies to spiritual maturity (Genesis 17:1, Psalm 19:7-8, Psalm 119:1-2, Ephesians 4:11-15, Hebrews 5:12-14).

Torah Means a Foundation

As mentioned earlier in this chapter, Torah comes from the Hebrew word, *"Yarah"* which means *"to lay a foundation."* The prophets *(Nevi'im)* and writings *(Ketuvim)* build upon that foundation. Spiritually, the Jewish Messiah *(Mashiach)* Yeshua/Jesus is the LIVING TORAH and the G-d of Israel's FIRM FOUNDATION to all that believe upon Him. In Isaiah *(Yeshayahu)* 28:16 it is written:

> *"Therefore thus saith the* Lord *God, Behold, I lay in Zion for a* **foundation a stone***, a tried stone, a precious corner stone, a* **sure foundation***; he that believeth shall not make haste."*

The firm foundation and chief cornerstone of the G-d of Israel's Kingdom is the Jewish Messiah *(Mashiach)* Yeshua/Jesus. He is the living Torah. This foundation is built upon by the prophets *(Nevi'im)* and apostles. In Ephesians 2:19-20 it is written:

> *"Now therefore ye are no more strangers and foreigners, but fellow citizens with the saints, and of the household of God; And are built upon the foundation of the apostles and prophets, Jesus Christ himself being the chief corner stone."*

What Method Did G-d Use to Communicate His Torah

The G-d of Israel gave us the understanding of the ways of His Kingdom in the form of spiritual pictures,

G-d's Power Twins: Torah and Grace

blueprints or shadows. In other words, the literal or natural world *(peshat)* was given to communicate the spiritual world *(sod)*. Therefore, the G-d of Israel spoke His Torah to His people through different mechanisms including:

1. Parables (Psalm 78:1-4, Mark 4:10-13)
2. Deep or dark sayings/mysteries *(sod)* (Proverbs 1:1-6, 1 Corinthians 2:6-10, 14)
3. Spiritual blueprints/shadows (Ezekiel 43:10-12, Colossians 2:16-17)

The Torah of the G-d of Israel was given in the form of parables, deep sayings and spiritual blueprints, so that His Word would be fulfilled concerning the righteous *(tzaddikim)* and the wicked. Those who would obey *(shema)* the greatest commandment (Deuteronomy *[Devarim]* 6:4-9, Mark 12:28-31) in Spirit and in truth (John *[Yochanan]* 4:24) would know and understand the ways of the G-d of Israel. However, the wicked would consider the things of the G-d of Israel as foolishness (I Corinthians 2:14).

The Four Levels of Understanding Torah/G-d's Word

1. Peshat — Literal
2. Ramez — One scripture tied to another scripture
3. Derash — Derived interpretation of scripture through exegesis and spiritual applications
4. Sod — Deeper spiritual meaning (dark sayings, mysteries) of the scripture not seen at its surface meaning

How Do We Grow in the Knowledge (Torah) of G-d?

The G-d of Israel supernaturally begins to reveal Himself and the principles of His Kingdom whenever we obey *(shema)* the greatest commandment to love the G-d of Israel with all our heart, mind, soul and strength. (Deuteronomy *[Devarim]* 6:4-5, Mark 12:28-31) By obeying the greatest commandment, the Holy Spirit *(Ruach HaKodesh)* will lead us so that we can grow into spiritual maturity *(tamim)*. This spiritual growth is designed by the G-d of Israel to be in a step by step fashion, building upon the foundation of the Torah. In Isaiah *(Yeshayahu)* 28:9-10, it is written:

> *"Whom shall he teach knowledge? and whom shall he make to understand doctrine? them that are weaned from the milk, and drawn from the breasts. For precept must be upon precept, precept upon precept; line upon line, line upon line; here a little, and there a little."*

It is the desire of the G-d of Israel that after we are saved/redeemed/delivered by His grace/mercy *(chesed)* through faith *(emunah)* that we grow in the knowledge *(da'at)* and understanding *(binah)* of the ways of His Kingdom *"line upon line"* and *"precept upon precept."* In doing so, the G-d of Israel desires that we grow from spiritual babies to spiritual maturity *(tamim)*. In Hebrews 5:12-14 it is written:

> *"For when for the time ye ought to be teachers* [rabbis], *ye have need that one teach you again*

G-d's Power Twins: Torah and Grace

which be the first principles of the oracles of God; and are become such as have need of milk and not of strong meat. For every one that useth milk is unskillful in the word of righteousness: for he is a babe. But strong meat belongeth to them that are of full age, even those who by reason of use have their senses exercised to discern both good and evil."

What Is the New Covenant?

Most members from the *house of Israel* (Christianity) associate the Old Testament (the Biblical name is TeNaKh - *Torah*, Prophets *[Nevi'im]*, and Writings *[Ketuvim* — Luke 24:44*]*) with the Torah, but they do not associate the New Testament *(Brit Hadashah)* with the Torah. At the same time, most members from the *house of Israel* (Christianity) fail to realize that the BIBLE tells us that the New Testament *(Brit Hadashah)* is TORAH based !!

The New Covenant Is Torah Based

The New Covenant *(Brit Hadashah)* is Torah based. In Jeremiah *(Yermiyahu)* 31:31, 33, it is written:

> *"Behold, the days come, saith the* Lord*, that I will make a* **NEW COVENANT** *with the house of Israel and with the house of Judah ...* **THIS SHALL BE THE COVENANT** *that I will make with the house of Israel; After those days, saith the* Lord*, I will put my* **law [TORAH]** *in their inward parts, and* **WRITE IT IN THEIR HEARTS**; *and will be their God, and they shall be my people."*

Restoring the Two Houses of Israel

The book of Hebrews confirms that the Holy Spirit *(Ruach HaKodesh)* is a witness that the New Covenant *(Brit Hadashah)* is the TORAH written upon our hearts. In Hebrews 10:15-16 it is written:

> *"Whereof the* **HOLY GHOST [SPIRIT]** *also* **IS A WITNESS** *to us: for after that he had said before, This is the covenant that I will make with them after those days, saith the* L<small>ORD</small>, *I will put* **my laws [TORAH]** *into their* **hearts,** *and in their minds will I write them."*

G-d Did Not Do Away with the Law

Why was the New Covenant *(Brit Hadashah)* necessary? Did the G-d of Israel find fault with His Torah? **NO** !! The G-d of Israel could not find fault with His Torah because He is the giver of the Torah. Therefore, if the G-d of Israel found fault with His Torah, He would have to find fault with Himself. So, what did the G-d of Israel need to change when He ushered in the New Covenant *(Brit Hadashah)*? The G-d of Israel didn't want to change His Torah because His Torah is a Tree of Life *(etz chayim)* and the Torah is eternal. However, the G-d of Israel desired to change the **HEARTS** of His people. We can understand this truth in Hebrews 8:7-8 as it is written:

> *"For if that first* [covenant] *had been faultless, then should no place have been sought for the second. For finding fault with* **THEM***, he saith, Behold the days come, saith the* L<small>ORD</small>*, when I will make a* **new covenant** *with the* **house of Israel AND** *with the* **house of Judah***..."*

G-d's Power Twins: Torah and Grace

Therefore, the G-d of Israel did not find fault with the Torah that HE gave at mount Sinai. However, He did find fault with the **HEARTS** of the people who received His Torah!

What Is the Difference Between the Older and Newer Covenant?

Because most members from the *house of Israel* (Christianity) believe that the G-d of Israel did away with His Torah after the death and resurrection of the Jewish Messiah *(Mashiach) Yeshua*/Jesus, they do not understand the difference between the older and newer covenant *(Brit Hadashah)*. Most members from the *house of Israel* (Christianity) believe that the G-d of Israel found fault with the TORAH given at mount Sinai and for this reason the Jewish Messiah *(Mashiach) Yeshua*/Jesus needed to come at His first coming as the suffering Messiah *(Mashiach)* known as Messiah ben Joseph *(Yosef)*.

However, as stated earlier, since the G-d of Israel was the giver of the Torah at mount Sinai, if the G-d of Israel found fault with the Torah then He would have to find fault with Himself. By understanding that BOTH the older covenant and the newer covenant *(Brit Hadashah)* is Torah based, we can understand that the G-d of Israel found fault with the **RECEIVERS** of the Torah and the **HEARTS** of the children of Israel. So, if both the older covenant and the newer covenant *(Brit Hadashah)* is Torah based, what is the difference between the two covenants?

> **a)**. The Older Covenant = Torah written upon a heart of stone
>
> **b)**. The Newer Covenant = Torah written upon a heart of flesh

The problem with the First Covenant was the **HEARTS** of the PEOPLE who RECEIVED the Torah, NOT THE TORAH!

The Older Covenant Was the Torah Written Upon a Heart of Stone

When the G-d of Israel gives His Torah/Word, the target/destination of His Torah/Word is the human heart. The older covenant was written on a *heart (tablets) of stone*. Therefore, the G-d of Israel desired to bring forth a newer (renewed) covenant *(Brit Hadashah)* so that His Torah could be written upon a *heart of flesh*. We can understand this truth in Ezekiel *(Yechezekel)* 36:26-27 as it is written:

> *"A new heart also will I give you, and a new spirit will I put within you: and I will* **take away** *the* **stony heart** *out of your flesh, and I will* **give you** *a* **heart of flesh**. *And I will put* **my spirit within you**, *and cause you to walk in my statutes, and ye shall keep my judgments, and do them."*

What Is a Stony Heart?

The Jewish Messiah *(Mashiach) Yeshua*/Jesus explained to us the characteristics of a stony heart in the

G-d's Power Twins: Torah and Grace

parable known as the parable of the sower. In Mark 4:3-6 it is written:

> *"Hearken; Behold, there went out* **a sower to sow:** *And it came to pass, as he sowed, some fell by the way side, and the fowls of the air came and devoured it up. And some fell on* **stony ground,** *where it had not much earth; and immediately it sprang up, because it had no depth of earth: But when the sun was up, it was scorched; and because it had* **no root,** *it withered away."*

In Mark 4:14-17, the Jewish Messiah *(Mashiach)* Yeshua/Jesus explains the parable and the meaning of the stony ground (heart) as it is written:

> *"The* **sower soweth the word [Torah]**. *And these are they by the way side, where the word is sown; but when they have heard, Satan cometh immediately, and taketh away the* **word [Torah]** *that was* **sown** *in their* **hearts**. *And these are they likewise which are sown on* **stony ground;** *who, when they have heard the* **word [Torah]**, *immediately receive it with gladness; And have no root in themselves, and so* **endure but for a time***: afterward, when* **affliction or persecution** *ariseth for the* **word's [Torah]** *sake, immediately they are* **offended***."*

Therefore, what are the characteristics of a stony heart according to the Jewish Messiah *(Mashiach)* Yeshua/Jesus?

1. Hears the Word
2. Receives the Word with gladness
3. No root/endures for a time
4. When affliction and persecution arises for the Torah/Word's sake they are offended and turn away

The Children of Israel Received the Torah Upon a Stony Heart

When the G-d of Israel gave His Torah to the children of Israel through Moses *(Moshe)* at mount Sinai, they heard the Torah/Word and received it with gladness (Mark 4:16). In Exodus *(Shemot)* 24:3 it is written:

> *"And Moses came and told the people all the words of the* Lord, *and all the judgments: and all* **the people answered** *with one voice, and said,* **All the words** *which* **the** Lord **hath said will we do.**"

The joy and gladness of the hearts of the children of Israel to receive and obey the Word/Torah of the G-d of Israel is seen in a greater dimension by understanding the Hebrew meaning of the phrase, *"All the words which the* Lord *has said will we do."* In Hebrew the phrase reads, *"Na'aseh v'Nishmah,"* which means, *"We agree to do even before we have heard/listened !!"*

The heart of the children of Israel was so eager to please the G-d of Israel that when the G-d of Israel said

G-d's Power Twins: Torah and Grace

"Will you ..." the people said, **YES**! even before they heard/knew what the G-d of Israel was going to request of them. This *should* be the **ATTITUDE** of every member from the *house of Israel* (Christianity) and the *house of Judah* (Judaism)!! What the children of Israel lacked was the POWER of the indwelling Holy Spirit *(Ruach HaKodesh)* to fulfill their initial conviction to love and serve the G-d of Israel with all their heart, mind, soul and strength.

In Mark 4:17, the Jewish Messiah *(Mashiach) Yeshua*/Jesus taught that a stony heart becomes offended by affliction and persecution. This is exactly what happened to the children of Israel in the wilderness. Time after time they were tempted in the wilderness and became offended by their trials and tribulations and desired to return to Egypt *(Mitzrayim)*.

When the twelve spies were sent to explore the land of Canaan, ten spies came back with an evil report that the children of Israel were not able to take the land of Canaan even though the G-d of Israel promised Abraham *(Avraham)* that He would give the descendents of Abraham *(Avraham)* the land of Canaan as their eternal inheritance. Therefore, the ten spies and those who believed their evil report became offended at the promise of the G-d of Israel to Abraham *(Avraham)* and desired to return to Egypt *(Mitzrayim)*. In Numbers *(Bamidbar)* 14:1-4 it is written:

> *"And all the congregation lifted up their voice, and cried; and the people wept that night. And all the children of Israel* **murmured** *against Moses*

> *and against Aaron: and the whole congregation said unto them,* **Would God that we had died in the land of Egypt!** *Or would God we had died in this wilderness! And wherefore hath the* LORD *brought us unto this land, to fall by the sword, that our wives and our children should be a prey?* **were it not better for us to return into Egypt?** *And they said one to another, Let us make a captain, and let us return into Egypt."*

This is the characteristic of a stony heart. The children of Israel received the Torah of the G-d of Israel with gladness (Exodus *[Shemot]* 24:3), however, when they encountered the trials and tribulations of the wilderness and they viewed with their natural eyes the giants in the land of Canaan, they became offended by the promise of the G-d of Israel to Abraham *(Avraham)* and desired to return to Egypt *(Mitzrayim)*.

A stony heart rejects the Torah/Word of the G-d of Israel. In Zechariah *(Zecharyah)* 7:11-12 it is written:

> *"But they refused to hearken, and pulled away the shoulder, and stopped their ears, that they should not hear. Yea, they made their* **hearts** *as an* **adamant stone** *lest they should hear the law [TORAH], and the WORDS which the* LORD *of hosts hath sent in his spirit by the former prophets: therefore came a great wrath from the* LORD *of hosts."*

The Ten Commandments were written on tablets (hearts) of stone (Exodus *[Shemot]* 24:12, 31:18, Deuteronomy *[Devarim]* 4:13-14, 5:22, 9:10-11).

G-d's Power Twins: Torah and Grace

A Heart of Stone Cannot Overcome the Flesh
(Sin Nature/Evil Inclination)

A stony heart exemplifies the characteristics of our sin nature *(evil inclination)* inherited from Adam and rejects the TORAH/Word of the G-d of Israel. The newer (renewed) covenant *(Brit Hadashah)* was needed because in the older covenant the heart of stone could not overcome the sin nature of the flesh *(evil inclination)*. The problem in the older covenant was not the Torah because the Torah is the tree of life! *(etz chayim)* Therefore, what the G-d of Israel wanted to do away with was a **HEART OF STONE** and NOT THE TORAH. The G-d of Israel desired to replace the Torah written upon a heart of stone with the Torah written upon a heart of flesh. The G-d of Israel wanted to do this by putting His Holy Spirit *(Ruach HaKodesh)* within us so that we would have HIS POWER to live our lives and follow our good inclinations rather than our evil inclinations. In doing this, the G-d of Israel desired to change the HEARTS of His people not His Torah because His Torah is eternal!

What Is the Difference Between a Heart of Stone and a Heart of Flesh?

The Torah given at mount Sinai was written upon a heart *(tablets)* of stone. A heart of stone does not have the power to overcome the flesh *(evil inclination)*. The newer (renewed) covenant *(Brit Hadashah)* is the Torah written upon a heart of flesh. A heart of flesh has the power to overcome the desires of the flesh and our sin nature *(evil inclination)*. The difference between a heart of stone (which cannot overcome our sin nature *[evil inclination]*) and a heart of flesh (which can overcome the desires of our sin nature *(evil inclination)* by the power of the Holy Spirit *(Ruach HaKodesh)* dwelling in our hearts) is the message that the Apostle Paul *(Rav Sha'ul)* is trying to communicate to us in Romans 8:2-10 as it is written:

> *"For the law of the Spirit of life in Christ Jesus* **[a heart of flesh]** *hath made me free from the law of sin and death* **[a heart of stone]**. *For what the law could not do, in that it was weak through the flesh* **[a heart of stone]**, *God sending his own Son in the likeness of sinful flesh, and for sin, condemned sin in the flesh* **[a heart of stone]**: *That the righteousness of the law might be fulfilled in us, who walk not after the flesh, but after the Spirit* **[a heart of flesh]**. *For they that are after the flesh do mind the things of the flesh* **[a heart of stone]**: *but they that are after the Spirit the things of the Spirit* **[a heart of flesh]**. *For to be carnally minded is death* **[a heart of stone];** *but to be spiritually minded is life and peace* **[a heart of flesh]**. *Because the carnal mind is enmity against God* **[a heart of stone]**: *for it is not subject to the law of God, neither indeed can be. So then they that are in the flesh* **[a heart of stone]** *cannot please God. But ye are not* **[have not been given a stony heart]** *in the flesh, but in the Spirit,* **[a heart of flesh]**, *if so be that the Spirit of God dwell in you* **[a heart of flesh]**. *Now if any man*

G-d's Power Twins: Torah and Grace

have not the Spirit of Christ **[a heart of flesh]**, *he is none of his. And if Christ be in you* **[a heart of flesh]**, *the body is dead because of sin* **[a heart of stone]**: *but the Spirit is life because of righteousness* **[a heart of flesh]**."

The difference between the older covenant *(which is the Torah written upon a heart of stone)* and the newer (renewed) covenant *(which is the Torah written upon a heart of flesh)* is the difference between two natures within us *(our good inclination and our evil inclination)*. The Torah written upon a heart of stone is the nature of the flesh *(evil inclination)*. The Torah written upon a heart of flesh follows after the nature of the Spirit *(Ruach HaKodesh)* of the G-d of Israel *(good inclination)*. This is the message being communicated by the Apostle Paul *(Rav Sha'ul)* in Galatians 4:22-26, 29 as it is written:

"For it is written, that Abraham had two sons, the one by a bondmaid, the other by a free woman. But he who was of the bondwoman was born after the flesh **[a heart of stone]**; *but he of the free woman was by promise* **[a heart of flesh]**. *Which things are an allegory: for these are two covenants* **[or two natures]**; *the one from the mount Sinai, which engendereth to bondage which is Agar* **[a heart of stone]**. *For this Agar is mount Sinai in Arabia, and answereth to Jerusalem which now is, and is in bondage with her children* **[a heart of stone]**. *But Jerusalem which is above is free, which is the mother of us all* **[a heart of flesh]** ... *But as then he that was born after the* flesh **[a**

heart of stone] *persecuted him that was born after the Spirit* **[a heart of flesh]**, *even so it is now."*

In Romans 7, the Apostle Paul *(Rav Sha'ul)* tells us that the Torah is holy and the commandments are holy, just, good, and spiritual. He also tells us that the Torah bears fruit after the INWARD man. In Romans 7:12,14, 22 it is written:

> *"Wherefore the* **LAW [TORAH] IS HOLY**, *and the commandment holy, and just, and good ... For we know that the* **LAW [TORAH] IS SPIRITUAL**: *but I am carnal, sold under sin ... For I delight in the* **LAW [TORAH]** *of God after the* **INWARD MAN.**"

What Is the Purpose of the Newer Covenant?

The newer (renewed) covenant is the TORAH written upon a heart of flesh (Jeremiah *[Yermiyahu]* 31:33). This would be accomplished by the G-d of Israel putting His Holy Spirit *(Ruach HaKodesh)* within us so that His Holy Spirit *(Ruach HaKodesh)* can teach G-d's people how to walk in the ways of the G-d of Israel, keep His Torah and be obedient *(shema)* to His commandments. In Ezekiel *(Yechezekel)* 11:19-20 it is written:

> *"And I will give them one heart, and I will put a* **new spirit within you**; *and I will take the stony heart out of their flesh, and will give them a* **heart of flesh**: *That they may* **walk in my statutes**, *and* **keep mine ordinances**, *and* **do them**: *and they shall be my people, and I will be their God."*

G-d's Power Twins: Torah and Grace

A stony heart brings death but a heart of flesh brings life. This is what the Apostle Paul *(Rav Sha'ul)* was talking about in 2 Corinthians 3:3, 6 as it is written:

> *"Forasmuch as ye are manifestly declared to be the epistle of Christ ministered by us, written not with ink, but with the* **Spirit of the living God**; *not in tablets of stone, but in* **fleshly tables of the heart** *... Who also hath made us able ministers of the* **new testament**; *not of the letter, but of the spirit: for the letter killeth, but the* **spirit giveth life**.*"*

What Is the Role of the Holy Spirit in the Newer Covenant?

1. The Holy Spirit *(Ruach HaKodesh)* is a witness that the Newer Covenant = Torah written upon our heart (Jeremiah 31:31, 33, Hebrews 10:15-16).

2. The Holy Spirit *(Ruach HaKodesh)* was sent into the earth to teach us the TRUTH of the ways of the G-d of Israel's Kingdom (John 14:16-17, 26, 15:26, 16:13).

3. What is the TRUTH? The G-d of Israel's Torah/Word is TRUTH. (Psalm 119:142, John 17:17).

4. The G-d of Israel wanted to write His Torah upon our heart and teach us His Torah which is called "TRUTH" (Psalm 119:142) through His Holy Spirit *(Ruach HaKodesh)* who is called "THE SPIRIT OF TRUTH" (John 14:16-17, 26, 15:26, 16:13).

5. We need the G-d of Israel's Holy Spirit *(Ruach HaKodesh)* WITHIN us for the following reasons:

   a) Have the power to overcome the sin nature *(evil inclination)* inherited by Adam.
   b) To bear spiritual fruit in our lives (Galatians 5:22-25).
   c) To understand, grow, and have a revelation of the G-d of Israel's Torah/Word and the ways of His Kingdom.

G-d's Power Twins Are His Torah and His Grace/Mercy

In this chapter, we studied the G-d of Israel's *power twins*. The G-d of Israel's *power twins* is His Torah and His grace/mercy *(chesed)*. Corporately speaking, the *house of Judah* (Judaism) mainly identifies with the G-d of Israel as being the G-d who gave the Torah *(matan Torah)* to His people. Meanwhile, the *house of Israel* (Christianity) mainly identifies with the G-d of Israel as being a G-d of grace/mercy through the Jewish Messiah *(Mashiach) Yeshua*/Jesus.

In order for restoration to come to the *house of Judah* (Judaism), they need to Biblically understand that the G-d of Israel has expressed His grace/mercy to His people through the Jewish Messiah *(Mashiach) Yeshua*/Jesus. In receiving the grace/mercy *(chesed)* expressed by the G-d of Israel through the Jewish Messiah *(Mashiach) Yeshua*/Jesus, the *house of Judah* (Judaism) needs to maintain their identity with the Torah and keep the commandments of the G-d of Israel.

G-d's Power Twins: Torah and Grace

In order for restoration to come to the *house of Israel* (Christianity), they need to realize that dispensational theology which teaches that before the death and resurrection of the Jewish Messiah *(Mashiach) Yeshua*/Jesus was the age of law and after the death and resurrection of the Jewish Messiah *(Mashiach) Yeshua*/Jesus is the age of grace is unbiblical. In this chapter, we learned that the G-d of Israel has always been a G-d of grace/mercy *(chesed)* from Genesis *(Bereishit)* to Revelation. We also learned that the New (renewed) Covenant *(Brit Hadashah)* is the Torah written upon a heart of flesh by the power of the indwelling Holy Spirit *(Ruach HaKodesh)*. Furthermore, we learned that the Torah and the Word of G-d are synonymous terms and that the G-d of Israel's Torah/Word is a tree of life and is ETERNAL. The *house of Israel* (Christianity) needs to embrace the Torah of the G-d of Israel while being led by the indwelling Holy Spirit *(Ruach HaKodah)* following the Torah in Spirit, in truth and in love.

When the *house of Judah* (Judaism) and the *house of Israel* (Christianity) embraces the Torah AND the grace/mercy *(chesed)* of the G-d of Israel expressed through the Jewish Messiah *(Mashiach) Yeshua*/Jesus, the G-d of Israel can bring redemption, restoration, reconciliation and unity to both houses of Israel through the outpouring of His Holy Spirit *(Ruach HaKodesh)* upon His people. May the G-d of Israel bring this redemption, restoration, reconciliation and unity to both houses of Israel speedily in our days. Amen!

Chapter 4

The Sabbath: Our Rest Is in Messiah

In order for full restoration to come to both the *house of Judah* (Judaism) and the *house of Israel* (Christianity), both houses of Israel need to come to a more fuller understanding and application of the weekly Sabbath *(Shabbat)* rest that the G-d of Israel ordained in the Bible that His people celebrate. The *house of Judah* (Judaism) needs to realize that the fullness of their spiritual Sabbath *(Shabbat)* rest is in the Jewish Messiah *(Mashiach) Yeshua*/Jesus. The *house of Israel* (Christianity) needs to repent *(teshuvah)* and realize that the Biblical day of rest that the G-d of Israel gave to His people is from Friday sundown to Saturday sundown. In doing so, the *house of Israel* (Christianity) needs to study the spiritual significance of the weekly Sabbath *(Shabbat)* to learn that the G-d of Israel gave His people the physical weekly Sabbath *(Shabbat)* rest as a prophetic blueprint to understand in a greater degree His redemptive plan to be accomplished through the Jewish Messiah *(Mashiach) Yeshua*/Jesus and the rule and reign of the Jewish Messiah *(Mashiach) Yeshua*/Jesus during the Messianic Age *(Athid Lavo)*.

In this chapter, we will examine these issues so that we can study, learn and understand that the G-d of Israel gave the physical weekly Sabbath *(Shabbat)* rest from Friday sundown to Saturday sundown to establish the following Biblical truths:

1) The Sabbath *(Shabbat)* is the seventh day of the week and is to be a day of rest (Genesis *[Bereishit]* 2:1-3).

2) The Sabbath *(Shabbat)* is a sanctified (set apart made holy/*kodesh*) day unto the G-d of Israel (Genesis *[Bereishit]* 2:3).

3) The Sabbath *(Shabbat)* is an eternal covenant between the G-d of Israel and His people and is to be kept forever as an everlasting ordinance (Exodus *[Shemot]* 31:16-17).

4) The Sabbath *(Shabbat)* is a festival *(mo'ed*/appointed time) of the G-d of Israel which is to be kept on a weekly basis (Leviticus *[Vayikra]* 23:1-3).

5) Spiritually, we experience Sabbath *(Shabbat)* rest when we obey the G-d of Israel, keep His commandments *(mitzvot)*, and believe the promises made by the G-d of Israel to His people in His Torah/Word of God (Leviticus *[Vayikra]* 26:1-12, Psalm *[Tehillim]* 95:6-11, Hebrews 3:7-19, 4:1-12).

6) The Sabbath *(Shabbat)* is a spiritual picture given to us by the G-d of Israel that is a shadow of the Jewish Messiah *(Mashiach) Yeshua*/Jesus (Colossians 2:16-17).

The Sabbath: Our Rest Is in Messiah

7) The Jewish Messiah *(Mashiach) Yeshua*/Jesus is the spiritual rest of the believers in the Jewish Messiah *(Mashiach) Yeshua*/Jesus (Matthew *[Mattityahu]* 11:28-30).

8) After the Jewish Messiah *(Mashiach) Yeshua*/Jesus finished the work that the G-d of Israel sent *(shaliach)* Him to do by dying on the tree/cross as the suffering Messiah *(Mashiach)* known as Messiah son of Joseph *(Yosef)*, He sat down (rested/had *Shabbat*) at the right hand of the G-d of Israel (John *[Yochanan]* 17:1,4, 19:30, Psalm *[Tehillim]* 110:1 = Hebrews 1:1-3, 10:12-13).

9) The Sabbath *(Shabbat)* is the day of the L-RD (Isaiah *[Yeshayahu]* 58:13-14).

10) The Sabbath *(Shabbat)* is personified as a bride whose bridegroom is the G-d of Israel and the Jewish Messiah *(Mashiach) Yeshua*/Jesus and is a spiritual blueprint of the Messianic Age *(Athid Lavo)* and the world to come *(Olam Haba*/eternity).

11) The Sabbath *(Shabbat)* will be kept during the time of the new heavens and the new earth and for all eternity (Isaiah *[Yeshayahu]* 66:22-23, Revelation 21:1-3).

The Sabbath Is the Seventh Day and Is a Day of Rest

In Genesis *(Bereishit)* 1:1-31, 2:1-3, we have the story of the seven days of creation. In the creation story, we learn that the Biblical day begins in the evening and ends in the morning (Genesis *[Bereishit]* 1:5, 8, 13, 19, 23, 31). Following the first six days of creation, the G-d of Israel rested on the seventh day and sanctified it. In Genesis *(Bereishit)* 2:1-3, it is written:

> *"Thus the heavens and the earth were finished, and all the host of them. And on the seventh day God ended his work which he had made; and* **he rested on the seventh day** *from all his work which he had made. And* **God blessed the seventh day, and sanctified it**: *because that in it he had rested from all his work which God created and made."*

G-d Sanctified the Sabbath and Made It Holy

When the G-d of Israel rested on the seventh day of creation, He blessed the seventh day and *sanctified* it (Genesis *[Bereishit]* 2:3). The Hebrew word for sanctified is the Strong's word (6942) in the Strong's Hebrew dictionary. It is the Hebrew word *kadesh* which comes from the Strong's word (6944) which is the Hebrew word *kodesh*. The Hebrew words *kadesh/kodesh* mean "*to make clean, consecrate, dedicate, purify, set apart, make holy.*" Therefore, when the G-d of Israel blessed the Sabbath *(Shabbat)*, He consecrated, dedicated, set apart and made holy this special day and purposed that the seventh day of the week (from Friday sundown to Saturday sundown) be a day sanctified, made holy and set apart from every other day of the week.

The Sabbath: Our Rest Is in Messiah

The Sabbath Is an Eternal Covenant Between G-d and His People

As we just stated in the previous section, when the G-d of Israel blessed the Sabbath *(Shabbat)* in Genesis *(Bereishit)* 2:3, He also *sanctified* it. The Sabbath *(Shabbat)* is personified in Jewish *(house of Judah/Judaism)* tradition as a bride whose bridegroom is Israel. [1]

The Hebrew term for the Biblical Jewish marriage ceremony *(kiddushin/*betrothal) really means "hallowing/sanctified." The Hebrew word for marriage *(kiddushin/*betrothal) comes from the three letter Hebrew root (K = Kaf, D = Dalet, SH = Shin). The Hebrew word for sanctified (6942 = *Kadesh*) which comes from the Hebrew word for holy (6944 = *Kodesh*) is also derived from the same three Hebrew root letters (K = Kaf, D = Dalet, SH = Shin). Therefore, the traditional Jewish rabbis from the *house of Judah* (Judaism), interpret the Biblical statement that "God blessed the sabbath day and *hallowed/sanctified (va-yekaddesh)* it" (Genesis *[Bereishit]* 2:3) as meaning that the G-d of Israel wedded (**kiddushin**/betrothal) the Sabbath *(Shabbat)* to His people. [2]

On the day of the wedding in the Biblical Jewish *(house of Judah/*Judaism) ceremony, the bride is seen as a queen and the groom is seen as a king. Therefore, *"queen"* and *"bride"* are two terms used to describe the weekly Sabbath day (Talmud, Shabbat 119a). Since the Sabbath *(Shabbat)* is seen as being a queen and a bride, it represents the feminine element of creation. [3]

Restoring the Two Houses of Israel

The Talmud (oral tradition of the rabbi's from the *house of Judah*/Judaism) tells us that on the eve of the Sabbath *(Sabbath)*, the famous teacher, Rabbi Hanina used to put on his best clothes and say, *"Come, let us go and welcome Queen Sabbath,"* while Rabbi Yannai used to rise and declare, *"Come, O bride; come, O bride."* From this custom, music was composed for the Sabbath *(Shabbat)* which symbolically imitated conventional marriage songs. The most famous of these is *"Lechah Dodi"* (Come my Beloved). [4]

In traditional Judaism (*house of Judah*), the rabbi's understood that the G-d of Israel entered into a marriage covenant with the *house of Jacob* (both the *house of Israel* and the *house of Judah*) at mount Sinai. In Jeremiah *(Yermiyahu)* 2:1-2, it is written:

> *"Moreover the word of the* Lord *came to me, saying, Go and cry in the ears of Jerusalem, saying, Thus saith the* Lord*; I remember thee, the kindness of thy youth, the love of thine espousals* **[betrothal/kiddushin]**, *when thou wentest after me* **[the G-d of Israel/the groom]** *in the wilderness* **[mount Sinai]**, *in a land that was not sown."*

However, in the Biblical/Jewish (*house of Judah*/Judaism) marriage ceremony, you must first be **sanctified** (consecrated/set apart/made holy) before you can get married. In Exodus *(Shemot)* 19:10-11, 14, it is written:

> *"And the* Lord *said unto Moses, Go unto the people, and* **sanctify** *[6942 = consecrate/set apart/make holy] them today and tomorrow, and let them wash their clothes, and be ready*

The Sabbath: Our Rest Is in Messiah

> *against the third day: for the third day the* LORD *will come down in the sight of all the people upon mount Sinai ... and Moses went down from the mount unto the people, and* **sanctified** [6942 = consecrate/set apart/made holy] *the people; and they washed their clothes."*

In the traditional Biblical/Jewish (*house of Judah*/Judaism) wedding ceremony, the bride becomes sanctified before the marriage by having a *mikvah* (water immersion). *Mikvah* is a Hebrew word which means *"pool or body of water." Mikvah* is the ceremonial act of purification. [5]

Every traditional Biblical/Jewish (*house of Judah*/Judaism) marriage will have two witnesses. They are called the friends of the bridegroom. Their role is to prepare the bride and escort her to meet the groom underneath the *chupah* (wedding canopy) where the marriage will occur. When the G-d of Israel entered into a marriage with the *house of Jacob* (both the *house of Israel* and the *house of Judah*) at mount Sinai, Moses *(Moshe)* was seen as being one of the friends of the bridegroom of the G-d of Israel. In Exodus *(Shemot)* 19:17, we can see Moses *(Moshe)* fulfilling the role of escorting the bride (the *house of Jacob*) to meet the G-d of Israel at mount Sinai (a type of *chupah*/wedding canopy) as it is written:

> *"And Moses brought forth the people* [the house of Jacob/escorting them] *out of the camp to meet with God; and they stood at the nether* [underneath/at the foot of] *part of the mount."*

Restoring the Two Houses of Israel

When the marriage took place between the G-d of Israel and the *house of Jacob* (both the *house of Israel* and the *house of Judah*), mount Sinai was symbolically seen as being the *chupah* (wedding canopy). [6]

When the bride and groom are married in a traditional Biblical/Jewish (*house of Judah*/Judaism) wedding ceremony, they will have a *ketubah* (marriage contract) which states the terms and the conditions of the marriage. In traditional Judaism (*house of Judah*), the rabbis saw that the *ketubah* (marriage contract) of the marriage between the G-d of Israel and the *house of Jacob* (both the *house of Israel* and the *house of Judah*) was the Torah/Word of G-d. The terms and conditions of the marriage (*ketubah*/marriage contract) between the G-d of Israel and the *house of Jacob* is given in Deuteronomy *(Devarim)* 28 and Leviticus *(Vayikra)* 26. In these two chapters, the G-d of Israel specifies the blessings to the *house of Jacob* (both the *house of Israel* and the *house of Judah*) for being faithful to the G-d of Israel in the marriage and the curses for being unfaithful to the G-d of Israel in the marriage.

The rite of betrothal is completed when the groom (the G-d of Israel) gives something of value to the bride (the *house of Jacob*) and she accepts it. The gift most often given today is the ring. The ring is a token of eternal love and remembrance of the marriage. When the groom places the ring on the bride's finger, the rite of betrothal is completed. The completed rite is known in Hebrew as *kiddushin* which means *"sanctification."*

Symbolically, the "ring" that was given to the bride (the *house of Jacob*) by the groom (the G-d of Israel) was

The Sabbath: Our Rest Is in Messiah

seen as being the Sabbath *(Shabbat)*. The keeping of the Sabbath *(Shabbat)* is seen as being a token of remembrance and eternal love between the groom (the G-d of Israel) and the bride (the *house of Jacob*).

The Sabbath *(Shabbat)* is one of the Ten Commandments given at mount Sinai to remember the marriage between the G-d of Israel and the *house of Jacob*. In Exodus *(Shemot)* 20:8, it is written:

> *"Remember the sabbath day, to keep it holy* [6942 = sanctified, consecrated, set apart].*"*

The Sabbath *(Shabbat)* is an eternal covenant between the G-d of Israel and the *house of Jacob* (both the *house of Israel* and the *house of Judah*) which is to be kept forever. In Exodus *(Shemot)* 31:12-18, it is written:

> *"And the* Lord *spake unto Moses, saying, speak thou also unto the children of Israel, saying, Verily my sabbaths ye shall keep: for it is a sign* **[a marriage ring]** *between me and you throughout your generations; that ye may know that I am the* Lord *that doth* **sanctify** [6942 = consecrate/set apart/make holy] *you. Ye shall keep* **the sabbath** *therefore;* **for it is holy** *unto you: every one that defileth it shall surely be put to death: for whosoever does any work therein, that soul shall be cut off from among his people. Six days may work be done; but in the seventh is the sabbath of rest, holy to the* Lord*: whosoever doeth any work in the sabbath day, he shall surely be put to death. Wherefore the children of Israel shall* **keep the sabbath***, to observe the sabbath throughout their*

generations, for a **perpetual covenant**. *It is a sign between me and the children of Israel forever: for in six days the* LORD *made heaven and earth, and on the seventh day he rested, and was refreshed. And he gave unto Moses, when he had made an end of communing with him upon mount Sinai, two tables of testimony, tables of stone, written with the finger of God."*

The Sabbath Is a Festival of the L-RD

The Sabbath *(Shabbat)* is a festival of the L-RD. In Leviticus *(Vayikra)* 23:1-4 it is written:

"And the LORD *spake unto Moses, saying, Speak unto the children of Israel, and say unto them, Concerning* **the feasts of the** LORD, *which ye shall proclaim to be holy convocations, even these are* **my feasts**. *Six days shall work be done: but the* **seventh day** *is the* **sabbath** *of rest,* **a holy convocation**; *ye shall do no work therein: it is the sabbath of the* LORD *in all your dwellings. These are* **the feasts of the** LORD, *even holy convocations, which ye shall proclaim in their seasons."*

What Is the Meaning of the Feast of the L-RD and Holy Convocation?

There are two important Hebrew words in Leviticus *(Vayikra)* 23:1-4 which are translated as *feasts* and *convocation* which explain to us the importance and significance of the Biblical weekly Sabbath *(Shabbat)*

The Sabbath: Our Rest Is in Messiah

from Friday sundown to Saturday sundown. In Leviticus *(Vayikra)* 23:2, the word translated as feasts is the Hebrew word *mo'ed*. The Hebrew word *mo'ed* is the Strong's word 4150 in the Hebrew dictionary and means *"an appointment, a fixed time or season, a cycle, an assembly, an appointed time, a set time or an exact time."*

In Leviticus *(Vayikra)* 23:2, the Bible tells us that the Sabbath *(Shabbat)* is not only a *mo'ed* but that it is also a *holy convocation*. The Hebrew word for holy is the Strong's word 6944 in the Hebrew dictionary and is the word *kodesh*. The Hebrew word *kodesh* means *"to consecrate, dedicate, hallow, set apart."* The Hebrew word for convocation is the Strong's word 4744 in the Strong's Hebrew dictionary and is the word *miqra*. The Hebrew word *miqra* means, *"a public meeting, an assembly, a rehearsal."*

Therefore, the G-d of Israel is telling us in His Holy Word that the Sabbath *(Shabbat)* is a *mo'ed* (an appointed time, a set time) during the week (from Friday sundown to Saturday sundown) which is a *kodesh* (holy, consecrated, dedicated and set apart) *miqra* (a public meeting, an assembly of people, a rehearsal). The Sabbath *(Shabbat)* is a commandment *(mitzvah)* which the G-d of Israel wants His people to rehearse *(miqra)* because it is an appointed time or set apart time *(mo'ed)*.

If the Sabbath *(Sabbath)* is a rehearsal *(miqra)*, what is it that the G-d of Israel wants His people to rehearse *(miqra)*? The Sabbath *(Shabbat)* is a rehearsal of all the things that the G-d of Israel gave His people regarding the Sabbath *(Shabbat)* to teach us/instruct us *(Torah)* about the ways of His Kingdom, trusting *(emunah)* in

His written Torah/Word of G-d , the redemption through the Messiah *(Mashiach)* and the Messianic Age *(Athid Lavo)*.

Who Is the L-RD?

The Sabbath *(Shabbat)* is a feast of the **L-RD.** Who is the L-RD? The Hebrew word for L-RD is the Strong's word 3068 in the Strong's Hebrew dictionary and is the Holy *(kodesh)* name (YHVH) of the G-d of Israel. The Bible tells us in Deuteronomy *(Devarim)* 6:4 that the G-d of Israel is one *(echad)*. The Hebrew word *echad* is the Strong's word 259 in the Strong's Hebrew dictionary. The Hebrew word *echad* (259) comes from the Hebrew root word *achad* which is the Strong's word 258 in the Hebrew dictionary. The Hebrew word *achad* means *"to unite, to unify."* So, the *Shema* (Deuteronomy [*Devarim*] 6:4) tells us that the G-d of Israel is *echad* which comes from the Hebrew root word *achad* which means *"to unify."* Therefore, the G-d of Israel is a compound unity. In Proverbs *(Mishlei)* 30:4 it is written:

> *"...who hath established all the ends of the earth? What is his name, and* **what is his son's name***, if thou canst tell?"*

The Jewish Messiah *(Mashiach) Yeshua*/Jesus is the G-d of Israel manifested in the flesh. The holy name (YHVH) of the G-d of Israel as spoken in Exodus *(Shemot)* 3:14 means, "I [ever] shall be [the same] that I am [today]." In Hebrews 13:8 it is written:

> *"Jesus Christ* [Yeshua HaMashiach] *the same yesterday, and today, and forever."*

The Sabbath: Our Rest Is in Messiah

In I Corinthians 12:3, it tells us that the Jewish Messiah *(Mashiach) Yeshua*/Jesus is L-RD as it is written:

> *"...no man speaking by the Spirit* [Ruach HaKodesh] *of God calls Jesus* [Yeshua] *accursed: and that no man can say that Jesus* [Yeshua] *is* LORD [YHVH] *but by the Holy Ghost* [Ruach HaKodesh]."

Philippians 2:8-11 is a *Jewish midrash* (commentary/explanation) which comes from the traditional Jewish prayer known as the *Aleinu* which is also mentioned in Isaiah *(Yeshayahu)* 45:23. In Philippians 2:8-11 it tells us that the Jewish Messiah *(Mashiach) Yeshua*/Jesus is L-RD as it is written:

> *"And being found in fashion as a man, he humbled himself, and became obedient unto death, even the death of the cross* [tree]. *Wherefore God also hath highly exalted him, and given him a name which is above every name: That at the name of Jesus* [Yeshua] *every knee should bow, of things in heaven, and things in earth, and things under the earth; And that every tongue should confess that Jesus Christ* [Yeshua HaMashiach] *is* LORD [YHVH] *to the glory of God the Father."*

The mount of Olives is known in traditional Judaism *(house of Judah)* as the mountain of the Messiah *(Mashiach)*. When the Jewish Messiah *(Mashiach) Yeshua*/Jesus ascended up into heaven *(olam haba)* following his resurrection as written in Acts 1:6-12, the angels said that the Jewish Messiah *(Mashiach) Yeshua*/Jesus would come back [in His second coming as the

Kingly Messiah *(Messiah ben David)*] in like manner (to the mount of Olives). His return to the mount of Olives as the Kingly Messiah *(Messiah ben David)* is recorded in Zechariah *(Zecharyah)* 14:3-4, 9 as it is written:

> *"Then shall the* LORD *[YHVH] go forth, and fight against those nations, as when he fought in the day of battle. And his feet [the feet of YHVH] shall stand in that day upon the mount of Olives ... and the* LORD *[YHVH] shall be king over all the earth: in that day shall there be one* LORD *[YHVH], and his name one [echad]."*

Yeshua/Jesus Is L-RD of the Sabbath

The rabbis in traditional Judaism *(house of Judah)* teach that despite all the legalistic precision to keep and observe the Sabbath *(Shabbat)* that the sages were conscious always that **the sabbath was made for man, not man for the sabbath**, and they insisted that any of the regulations might be — nay, should be — broken immediately in case of a life-and-death emergency, or of a real danger to health. In support of this relaxation, they were fond of quoting the Scriptural verse in Leviticus *(Vayikra)* 18:5 as it is written: [7]

> *"Ye shall therefore keep My statutes and Mine ordinances, which if a man do, he shall live by them."*

The Jewish Messiah *(Mashiach)* Yeshua/Jesus supported this interpretation as can be seen in Mark 2:23-28, 3:1, 4-5 as it is written:

The Sabbath: Our Rest Is in Messiah

"And it came to pass, that he [Yeshua/Jesus] *went through the corn fields on the sabbath day; and his disciples* [talmidim] *began, as they went, to pluck the ears of corn. And the Pharisees said unto him, Behold, why do they on the sabbath day that which is not lawful* [in violation of the Torah]? *And he* [Yeshua/Jesus] *said unto them, Have ye never read what David did, when he had need, and was hungry, he, and they that were with him? How he went into the house of God in the days of Abiathar the high priest, and did eat the shewbread, which is not lawful to eat but for the priests, and gave also to them which were with him? And he said unto them,* **The sabbath was made for man, and not man for the sabbath**: *Therefore, the Son of man is* LORD *also of the sabbath. And he entered again into the synagogue; and there was a man there which had a withered hand ... and he saith unto them, is it lawful to do good on the sabbath days, or to do evil? To save life, or to kill? But they held their peace. ...And he saith unto the man, Stretch forth thine hand. And he stretched it out: and his hand was restored whole as the other."*

Therefore, the Sabbath *(Sabbath)* is **a feast of the L-RD** (Leviticus *[Vayikra]* 23:2). The L-RD is the Jewish Messiah *(Mashiach) Yeshua*/Jesus). In addition, the Jewish Messiah *(Mashiach) Yeshua*/Jesus is the L-RD of the Sabbath *(Shabbat)*. So, both *the house of Israel* (Christianity) and *the house of Judah* (Judaism) need to keep and celebrate the weekly Sabbath *(Shabbat)* (from Friday sundown to Saturday sundown) that the G-d of Israel gave to His people.

Restoring the Two Houses of Israel

Our Sabbath Rest Is Believing *(Emunah)* the Written Word of G-d

Spiritually, we experience Sabbath *(Shabbat)* rest when we obey the G-d of Israel, keep His commandments *(mitzvot)*, and believe the promises made by the G-d of Israel to His people in His Torah/Word of G-d. The G-d of Israel promises **great blessings** to His people for keeping His weekly Sabbath *(Shabbat)* (from Friday sundown to Saturday sundown). In Leviticus *(Vayikra)* 26:2-12 it is written:

> *"Ye shall* **keep my sabbaths***, and reverence my sanctuary: I am the* LORD*.* **If ye walk in my statutes, and keep my commandments, and do them***; Then I will give you rain in due season, and the land shall yield her increase, and the trees of the field shall yield their fruit. And your threshing shall reach into the vintage, and the vintage shall reach unto the sowing time: and ye shall eat your bread to the full, and dwell in your land safely. And* **I will give peace** [shalom/rest] *in the land, and ye shall lie down, and none shall make you afraid: and I will rid evil beasts out of the land, neither shall the sword go through the land. And ye shall chase your enemies, and they shall fall before you by the sword. And five of you shall chase an hundred, and a hundred of you shall put ten thousand to flight: and your enemies shall fall before you by the sword. For I will have respect unto you, and make you fruitful, and multiply*

The Sabbath: Our Rest Is in Messiah

you, and **establish my covenant with you.** *And ye shall eat old store, and bring forth the old because of the new. And* **I will set my tabernacle among you:** *and my soul shall not abhor you. And* **I will walk among you, and will be your God, and ye shall be my people."**

Obedience Brings the Blessings of G-d

The G-d of Israel blesses His people when we are obedient *(shema)* to Him. In Isaiah *(Yeshayahu)* 1:19 it is written:

> *"If ye are willing and obedient* [shema], *ye shall eat the good of the land."*

In Jeremiah *(Yermiyahu)* 17:7-8 it is written:

> *"Blessed is the man that trusteth in the LORD, and whose hope the LORD is. For he shall be as a tree planted by the waters, and that spreadeth out her roots by the river, and shall not see when heat cometh, but her leaf shall be green; and shall not be careful in the year of drought, neither shall cease from yielding fruit."*

In Isaiah *(Yeshayahu)* 26:3-4 it is written:

> *"Thou wilt keep him in perfect peace* [shalom, shalom], *whose mind is stayed on thee: because he trusteth in thee. Trust ye in the LORD forever: for in the LORD Jehovah is everlasting strength."*

Restoring the Two Houses of Israel

Disobedience to G-d's Word Keeps Us From Entering into His Sabbath Rest

The Sabbath *(Shabbat)* is a day of rest. In Genesis *(Bereishit)* 2:2 it is written:

> *"And on the seventh day God ended his work which he had made; and he **rested** on the seventh day from all the work which he had made."*

In the Bible, the G-d of Israel associates entering into His rest with believing the written Torah/Word of G-d. In Isaiah *(Yeshayahu)* 28:9-13 it is written:

> *"Whom shall he teach knowledge?* [which is the Torah/Word of G-d — Hosea 4:6] *and whom shall he make to understand doctrine? them that are weaned from the milk, and drawn from the breasts. For precept must be upon precept, precept upon precept; line upon line, line upon line; here a little, and there a little: For with stammering lips and another tongue will he speak to this people. To whom he said, This is the **rest** wherewith ye may cause the weary to **rest**; and this is the refreshing: yet they would not hear* [shema]. *But the word of the* LORD *was unto them precept upon precept, precept upon precept; line upon line, line upon line; here a little, and there a little..."*

The first occurrence of the word *rest* in Isaiah *(Yeshayahu)* 28:12 is the Strong's word 4496 in the Strong's Hebrew dictionary and is the Hebrew word

The Sabbath: Our Rest Is in Messiah

menuchah. The Hebrew word *menuchah* means, *"an abode, ease, quiet, resting place, a settled spot, peace, home."*

The G-d of Israel associates believing and trusting *(emunah)* in Him and being obedient *(shema)* to His Torah/Word with entering into His *(Sabbath)* rest. In Psalm *(Tehillim)* 95:7-11, it is written:

> *"For he is our God; and we are the people of his pasture, and the sheep of his hand.* **Today if ye will hear** [shema] **his voice, harden not your heart** *as in the provocation, and as in the day of temptation in the wilderness: When your fathers tempted me, proved me, and saw my work. Forty years long was I grieved with this generation, and said, It is a people that do err in their heart, and they have not known my ways: Unto whom I sware in my wrath that they* **should not enter into my rest.***"*

In Hebrew 3:7-19, 4:1-12 it is written:

> *"Wherefore as the Holy Ghost* [Ruach HaKodesh] *saith, Today if ye will hear his voice, harden not your hearts, as in the provocation, in the day of temptation in the wilderness: When your fathers tempted me, proved me, and saw my works forty years. Wherefore I was grieved with that generation, and said, They do always err in their heart; and they have not known my ways. So I sware in my wrath, they should not enter into my rest. Take heed, brethren, lest there be in you an evil heart of unbelief, in departing from the living God. But exhort one another daily, while it is called Today;*

lest any of you be hardened through the deceitfulness of sin. For we are made partakers of Christ [Mashiach], if we hold the beginning of our confidence steadfast unto the end; While it is said, Today if ye will hear his voice, harden not your hearts, as in the provocation. For some, when they had heard, did provoke: howbeit not all that came out of Egypt by Moses. But with whom was he grieved forty years? was it not with them that had sinned, whose carcasses fell in the wilderness? **And to whom swore he that they should not enter into his rest, but to them that believed not?** *So we see that they could not enter in because of unbelief. Let us therefore fear, lest, a promise being left us of entering into his rest, any of you should seem to come short of it. For unto us was the gospel preached, as well as unto them: but the word preached did not profit them, not being mixed with faith in them that heard it.* **For we which have believed do enter into rest,** *as he said, As I have sworn in my wrath, if they shall enter into my rest: although the works were finished from the foundation of the world.* **For he spake in a certain place of the seventh day on this wise, And God did rest the seventh day** *from all his works. And in this place again, If they shall enter into my rest. Seeing therefore it remaineth that some must enter therein, and they to whom it was first preached entered not in because of unbelief: Again, he limited a certain day, saying in David, Today, after so long a time; as it is said, Today if ye will hear his voice, harden not your hearts. For if Jesus [Joshua] had given them rest, then would he not afterward have spoken of*

The Sabbath: Our Rest Is in Messiah

another day. **There remaineth therefore a rest to the people of God.** *For he that is entered into his rest, he also hath ceased from his own works, as God did from his. Let us labor therefore to enter into that rest, lest any man fall after the same example of unbelief. For* **the word of God** *is quick, and powerful, and sharper than any two-edged sword, piercing even to the dividing asunder of soul and spirit, and of the joints and marrow, and is a discerner of the thoughts and intents of the heart."*

Therefore, spiritually, we experience the Sabbath *(Shabbat)* rest of the G-d of Israel when we obey *(shema)* and believe *(emunah)* the Torah/Word of G-d and put our trust and confidence *(emunah)* in the Jewish Messiah *(Mashiach) Yeshua*/Jesus.

The Messiah Is Our Sabbath Rest

Isaiah *(Yeshayahu)* 11:1, 10 speaks about the Messiah *(Mashiach)* and the Word of G-d tells us that His rest *(menuchah)* shall be glorious *(kivod)* as it is written:

> *"And there shall come forth a rod out of the stem of Jesse, and a Branch shall grow out of his roots ... and in that day there shall be a root of Jesse, which shall stand for an ensign of the people; to it shall the Gentiles seek: and* **his rest** [menuchah] **shall be glorious** [kivod]."

In Matthew *(Mattityahu)* 11:28-30 it is written:

> *"***Come unto me***, all ye that labor and are heavy laden, and I will give you rest. Take my yoke upon*

> you, and learn of me: for I am meek and lowly of heart: and **ye shall find rest** unto your souls. For my yoke is easy, and my burden is light."

In John *(Yochanan)* 14:23 it is written:

> "Jesus answered and said unto him, If a man love me, he will keep my words: and my Father will love him, and we will come unto him, and make our abode with him."

In Matthew *(Mattityahu)* 7:24-27 it is written:

> "Therefore whosoever heareth these sayings of mine, and doeth them, I will liken him unto a wise man, which built his house upon a rock: And the rain descended, and the floods came, and the winds blew, and beat upon that house; and it fell not; for it was founded upon a rock. And every one that heareth these sayings of mine, and doeth them not, shall be likened unto a foolish man, which built his house upon the sand: And the rain descended, and the floods came, and the winds blew, and beat upon that house; and it fell: and great was the fall of it."

The Sabbath Is a Shadow/Blueprint of the Messiah

The Sabbath *(Shabbat)* is a spiritual shadow/blueprint given to us by the G-d of Israel to teach us about the Jewish Messiah *(Mashiach) Yeshua*/Jesus and the redemptive plan of the G-d of Israel for His people. In Colossians 2:16-17 it is written:

The Sabbath: Our Rest Is in Messiah

"Let no man therefore judge you in meat, or in drink, or in respect of a holy day, or of the new moon, or of **the sabbath days: which are a shadow of things to come; but the body is of Christ** [Mashiach]*."*

After the Messiah Completed His Work, He Rested

The Jewish Messiah *(Mashiach) Yeshua*/Jesus came to the earth at His first coming to be the suffering Messiah *(Messiah ben Yosef)*. He completed the work that G-d the Father sent *(shaliach)* him to do. In John *(Yochanan)* 17:1, 4, it is written:

> *"These words spake Jesus, and lifted up his eyes to heaven, and said, Father, the hour is come; glorify thy Son, that thy Son also may glorify thee ... I have glorified thee on the earth: I have finished the work which thou gavest me to do."*

After the Jewish Messiah *(Mashiach) Yeshua*/Jesus completed the work that G-d the Father sent *(shaliach)* Him to do by dying on the tree/cross and coming to the earth to fulfill the role of the suffering Messiah *(Messiah ben Yosef)*, He sat down (rested) on the right hand of G-d the Father. In Psalm *(Tehillim)* 110:1 it is written:

> *"The* Lord *said unto my* Lord, *Sit thou at my right hand, until I make thine enemies thy footstool."*

In Hebrews 1:1-3, 10:12-13 it is written:

"God, who at sundry times and in divers manners spake in time past unto the fathers by the prophets, Hath in these last days spoken unto us by his Son, whom he hath appointed heir of all things, by whom also he made the worlds; Who being the brightness of his glory, and the express image of his person, and upholding all things by the word of his power, when he had by himself purged our sins, sat down on the right hand of the Majesty on high ...But this man, **after he had offered one sacrifice for sins forever, sat down on the right hand of God**; *From henceforth expecting till his enemies be made his footstool."*

Both Jews and Non-Jews are Commanded to Keep the Sabbath

Both the *house of Judah* (Judaism) and the *house of Israel* (Christianity) are commanded by the G-d of Israel to keep His Sabbath *(Shabbat)*. In fact, the G-d of Israel promises great blessings to the non-Jew/Christianity *(house of Israel)* who keeps His Sabbath *(Shabbat)* and all those who are grafted into the family of the G-d of Israel. In Isaiah *(Yeshayahu)* 56:1-8 it is written:

"Thus saith the Lord, *Keep ye judgment, and do justice: for my salvation is near to come, and my righteousness to be revealed.* **Blessed is the man** *that doeth this, and the son of man that layeth hold on it:* **that keepeth the sabbath** *from polluting it, and keepeth his hand from doing any evil. Neither let the son of the stranger, that hath joined himself to the* Lord, *speak, saying, The* Lord *hath*

The Sabbath: Our Rest Is in Messiah

> *utterly separated me from his people: neither let the eunuch say, Behold, I am a dry tree. For thus saith the* LORD *unto* **the eunuchs that keep my sabbaths**, *and choose the things that please me, and take hold of my covenant; Even unto them will I give in mine house and within my walls a place and a name better than of sons and of daughters: I will give them an everlasting name, that shall not be cut off. Also the sons of the stranger, that* **join themselves to the** LORD, *to serve him, and to love the name of the* LORD, *to be his servants*, **every one that keepeth the sabbath** *from polluting it, and taketh hold of my covenant; Even them will I bring to my holy mountain, and make them joyful in my house of prayer: their burnt offerings and their sacrifices shall be accepted upon mine altar; for* **mine house shall be called a house of prayer for all people**. *The* LORD *God which gathereth the outcasts of Israel saith, Yet will I gather others to him, beside those that are gathered unto him."*

The Sabbath Is Personified as a Bride

Earlier in this chapter, it was seen that the Sabbath (*Shabbat*) is personified in Jewish tradition *(house of Judah)* as a bride. The G-d of Israel and the Jewish Messiah *(Mashiach) Yeshua*/Jesus is the bridegroom of the *house of Judah* (Judaism) and the *house of Israel* (Christianity). Once again, the Hebrew term for the Biblical / Jewish marriage ceremony (*kiddushin*/betrothal) really means "*hallowing/sanctified.*" The Hebrew word for marriage (*kiddushin*/betrothal) comes from the three letter Hebrew root (K = Kaf, D = Dalet, SH = Shin). The Hebrew word for sanctified (6942 = *Kadesh*) which comes from the Hebrew word for holy (6944 = *Kodesh*) is also derived from the same three Hebrew root letters (K = Kaf, D = Dalet, SH = Shin). Therefore, the traditional Jewish rabbis from the *house of Judah* (Judaism), interpret the Biblical statement that "God blessed the sabbath day and *hallowed/sanctified* (va-ye**kaddesh**) it" (Genesis *[Bereishit]* 2:3 as meaning that the G-d of Israel wedded (***kiddushin***/betrothal) the Sabbath *(Shabbat)* to His people.

On the day of the wedding in the Biblical Jewish *(house of Judah*/Judaism) ceremony, the bride is seen as a queen and the groom is seen as a king. Therefore, *"queen"* and *"bride"* are two terms used to describe the weekly Sabbath day (Talmud, Shabbat 119a). Since the Sabbath *(Shabbat)* is seen as being a queen and a bride, it represents the feminine element of creation.

In traditional Judaism *(house of Judah)* the Sabbath *(Shabbat)* is welcomed by the woman of the house when she lights two Sabbath *(Shabbat)* candles. [8] When she lights the candles, she pronounces the blessing:

> "Blessed are you, O L-RD our G-d, King of the Universe, who has hallowed [sanctified/ consecrated/set apart] us by your commandments [mitzvot] and commanded us to kindle the lamp." [9]

Even as it is traditional to light two Sabbath *(Shabbat)* candles, the traditional Jewish *(house of Judah)* wedding

The Sabbath: Our Rest Is in Messiah

ceremony will have two witnesses.[10] These two witnesses are called the friends of the bridegroom. The two candles which are lit are called the two witnesses.

There are various interpretations of the meaning of lighting two candles. In one interpretation, one candle will represent the Torah and the other candle will represent the Prophets. Moses *(Moshe)* is personified by the Torah and Elijah *(Eliyahu)* is personified by the Prophets. Obedience *(shema)* to the Torah and the Prophets will sanctify (consecrate, dedicated, set apart) and prepare the family of the G-d of Israel to enter into the second stage of the traditional Jewish *(house of Judah)* wedding ceremony when the marriage will be consummated between the bridegroom (the G-d of Israel) and members from the *house of Judah* (Judaism) and the *house of Israel* (Christianity) who believe in the Jewish Messiah *(Mashiach) Yeshua*/Jesus and have prepared themselves for the wedding by being sanctified unto the G-d of Israel by keeping His commandments *(mitzvot)*. The Jewish Messiah *(Mashiach) Yeshua*/Jesus declared that the Torah and the Prophets were written to speak of Him. In Luke 24:27, 44-47 it is written:

> *"And beginning at Moses and all the prophets, he* [Yeshua / Jesus] *expounded unto them in all the Scriptures* [TeNaKh] *the things concerning himself ... and he said unto them, These are the words which I spake unto you, while I was yet with you, that all things must be fulfilled, which were written in the law of Moses, and in the prophets, and in the Psalms, concerning me. Then opened he their understanding, that they might understand the Scriptures, and said unto them, Thus it is*

written, and thus it behooved Christ to suffer, and to rise from the dead the third day: and that repentance [teshuvah] *and remission of sins should be preached in his name among all nations, beginning at Jerusalem."*

The Jewish Messiah *(Mashiach) Yeshua*/Jesus prayed that the family of the G-d of Israel would be sanctified (consecrated, dedicated, set apart) by keeping His commandments *(mitzvot)* and the Torah of the G-d of Israel. In John *(Yochanan)* 14:15, 17:1-4, 17 it is written:

> **"If ye love me, keep my commandments** [mitzvot] ... *These words spake Jesus, and lifted up his eyes to heaven, and said, Father, the hour is come; glorify thy Son, that thy Son also may glorify thee: As thou hast given him power over all flesh, that he should give eternal life to as many as thou hast given him.* **And this is life eternal, that they might know thee the only true God, and Jesus Christ,** *whom thou hast sent* [shaliach]*. I have glorified thee on the earth:* **I have finished the work** *which thou gavest me to do ...* **sanctify them** *through thy truth: thy word is truth."*

When the Jewish Messiah *(Mashiach) Yeshua*/Jesus prayed in John *(Yochanan)* 17:17 that the family of the G-d of Israel would be sanctified through the Word of G-d which He called truth, the Jewish Messiah *(Mashiach) Yeshua*/Jesus was quoting Psalm *(Tehillim)* 119:142 as it is written:

> *"Thy righteousness is an everlasting righteousness, and thy law* **[TORAH]** *is* **THE TRUTH."**

The Sabbath: Our Rest Is in Messiah

Therefore, the two candles which are lit on the Sabbath *(Shabbat)* by the woman of the house represents the Torah and the Prophets which speak about the Jewish Messiah *(Mashiach) Yeshua*/Jesus. Because the Sabbath *(Shabbat)* is personified in traditional Jewish *(house of Judah)* interpretation as being personified as a bride, the two candles spiritually represent both the Jewish Messiah *(Mashiach) Yeshua*/Jesus and the marriage of the bride of the Messiah to Himself. In Revelation 19:7-9 it is written:

> *"Let us be glad and rejoice, and give honor to him: for the marriage of the Lamb is come, and his wife hath made herself ready. And to her was granted that she should be arrayed in fine linen, clean and white: for the fine linen is the righteousness* [righteous acts/keeping of the commandments/mitzvot and sanctification] *of saints* [the righteous/tzaddik]."

The Candle Is the Lamp of G-d

The *candles* which are lit on the Sabbath *(Shabbat)* by the woman of the house are called *lamps*. When the woman pronounces the blessing over the candles she says:

> "Blessed are you, O L-RD our G-d ... who has commanded us to kindle the **lamp**."

The Hebrew word for candle/lamp is the Strong's word 5216 in the Hebrew dictionary and is the Hebrew word, *"Ner/Nerah."* Candle/lamp/light are very important spiritual pictures in the Bible of the Torah/Word of

G-d, keeping the commandments *(mitzvot)*, the Gospel *(basar/*good news), the spirit of man, the Messiah *(Mashiach)*, the believers in the Messiah *(Mashiach)*, marriage and being wedded to the Messiah *(Mashiach)*.

The Torah/Word of G-d is likened unto a candle/lamp. Psalm *(Tehillim)* 119:105 it is written:

> *"Thy word is a lamp* [5216] *unto my feet, and a light unto my path."*

Keeping the Torah and the commandments *(mitzvot)* of the G-d of Israel is likened unto a candle/lamp/light. In Proverbs *(Mishlei)* 6:23 it is written:

> *"For the* **commandment is a lamp** *[5216] and the law* **[Torah] is light**; *and reproofs of instruction are the way of life."*

The Gospel *(basar/*good news) of the Jewish Messiah *(Mashiach) Yeshua/*Jesus is light. In II Corinthians 4:3-4, 6 it is written:

> *"But if our gospel* [basar/good news] *be hid, it is hid to them that are lost* [have no light/candle/lamp]: *in whom the god of this world* [HaSatan/Satan/Lucifer who is called the angel of light — II Corinthians 11:14] *hath blinded the minds of them which believe not, lest the light* [ner] *of the glorious* [kivod] *gospel* [basar/good news] *of Christ* [Mashiach], *who is the image of God, should shine unto them ... For God, who commanded the light* [ner] *to shine out*

The Sabbath: Our Rest Is in Messiah

of darkness, hath shined in our hearts, to give the light [ner] *of the knowledge* [da'at] *of the glory* [kivod] *of God in the face of Jesus Christ* [Yeshua HaMashiach]."

The spirit (heart) of man is the candle/lamp of the G-d of Israel. In Proverbs *(Mishlei)* 20:27 it is written:

> *"The* **spirit of man is the candle** [5216] *of the* LORD, *searching all the inward parts of the belly."*

The Jewish Messiah *(Mashiach) Yeshua*/Jesus is the light of the world. In John *(Yochanan)* 8:12, 12:35-36, 46 it is written:

> *"Then spake Jesus again unto them, saying,* **I am the light of the world**: *he that followeth me shall not walk in darkness, but shall have the light of life … Then Jesus said unto them, Yet a little while is the light with you. Walk while ye have the light, lest darkness come upon you: for he that walketh in darkness knoweth not whither he goeth. While ye have light,* **believe in the light, that ye may be the children of light** *… I am come a light into the world, that whosoever believeth on me should not abide in darkness."*

The lives of the believers in the Jewish Messiah *(Mashiach) Yeshua*/Jesus are to shine as a candle. In Matthew *(Mattityahu)* 5:14-16 it is written:

> *"***Ye are the light of the world***: A city that is set on a hill cannot be hid. Neither do men light a*

candle, and put it under a bushel, but on a candlestick; and it giveth light unto all that are in the house. **Let your light so shine before men,** *that they may see your good works* [mitzvot], *and glorify your Father which is in heaven."*

The candle/lamp is associated with the Jewish *(house of Judah)* marriage. In Jeremiah *(Yermiyahu)* 25:10 it is written:

"Moreover I will take from them the voice of mirth, and the voice of gladness, **the voice of the bridegroom, and the voice of the bride***, the sound of the millstones, and* **the light of the candle** *[5216]."*

In Matthew *(Mattityahu)* 25:1-13, the Jewish Messiah *(Mashiach) Yeshua*/Jesus compared His wedding to His bride like unto ten virgins who took lamps to their wedding. In Matthew *(Mattityahu)* 25:1, it is written:

"Then shall the kingdom of heaven [malkut shamayim] *be likened unto* **ten virgins which took their lamps, and went forth to meet the bridegroom.***"*

In traditional Jewish *(house of Judah)* thought, the city of Jerusalem *(Yerushalayim)* is seen as the city of the bride. In Revelation 21:2, 9-11, 23 it is written:

"And I John saw **the holy city, new Jerusalem** [Yerushalayim]*, coming down from God out of*

The Sabbath: Our Rest Is in Messiah

heaven [olam haba], **prepared as a bride adorned for her husband** ... *and there came unto me one of the seven angels ... saying, come hither,* **I will show thee the bride, the Lamb's wife**. *And he carried me away in the spirit to a great and high mountain, and showed me that great city, the holy Jerusalem* [Yerushalayim], *descending out of heaven* [olam haba] *from God, having the glory* [kivod] *of God: and* **her light** [ner] *was like unto a stone most precious, even like a jasper stone, clear as crystal ... and the city had no need of the sun, neither of the moon, to shine in it: for the glory* [kivod] *of God did lighten it, and* **the Lamb is the light** *thereof."*

The Two Candles Represent Ephraim and Judah and Their Reuniting

In another interpretation of the symbolic meaning of lighting the two candles for Sabbath *(Shabbat)*, the one candle represents Judah, the *house of Judah* (Judaism) and the other candle represents Ephraim, the *house of Israel*, (Christianity) and the marriage/reunification/ restoration and reuniting that is prophesied to take place in Ezekiel *(Yechezekel)* 37:15-16, 19 as it is written:

> *"The word of the* LORD *came again unto me, saying, Moreover, thou son of man, take thee one stick, and write upon it, For Judah, and for the children of Israel his companions: then take another stick, and write upon it, For Joseph, the stick*

of Ephraim, and for all the house of Israel his companions ... Say unto them, thus saith the LORD *God; Behold, I will take the stick of Joseph, which is in the hand of Ephraim, and the tribes of Israel his fellows, and will put them with him, even with the stick of Judah, and make them one stick, and they shall be one in mine hand."*

In the traditional Jewish *(house of Judah)* prayers on the Sabbath *(Shabbat)*, prayers are said for the G-d of Israel to reunite and restore the *house of Judah* with the *house of Israel*. The *house of Judah* (Judaism) and the *house of Israel* (Christianity) are the G-d of Israel's two witnesses upon the earth.

The Sabbath Is a Blueprint of the Messianic Age and the World to Come

In traditional Jewish *(house of Judah)* thought, the Sabbath *(Shabbat)* is a blueprint of the Messianic Age *(Athid Lavo)*. It is also a foretaste of the world to come *(Olam Haba)* (Genesis R. xvii; Ber, 57b). The Sabbath *(Shabbat)* is a day which points toward the future. It is a day of hope and anticipation of the Messianic fulfillment which the Talmud describes as *"Yom shekulo Shabbat,"* a time of eternal Shabbat.[11] (Mishnah Tamid 7.4, Talmud Rosh HaShanah 31a)

The Sabbath Is the Day of the L-RD

The Sabbath *(Shabbat)* is the *day of the* L-RD. In Isaiah *(Yeshayahu)* 58:13-14 it is written:

The Sabbath: Our Rest Is in Messiah

"If thou turn away thy foot from the **sabbath***, from doing thy pleasure on* **my holy day***; and call the sabbath a delight,* **the holy of the** L<small>ORD</small>**,** *honorable; and shalt honor him, not doing thine own ways, nor finding thine own pleasure, nor speaking thine own words: Then shalt thou delight thyself in the* L<small>ORD</small>*; and I will cause thee to ride upon the high places of the earth, and feed thee with the heritage of Jacob your father: for the mouth of the* L<small>ORD</small> *hath spoken it."*

The Day of the L-<small>RD</small> Is a Title for the Messianic Age

The *day of the* L-<small>RD</small> is a major theme in the Bible especially in the writings of the prophets. The subject of the *day of the* L-<small>RD</small> in the writings of the prophets mostly concerns the advent of the coming of the Messiah *(Mashiach)*, the judgment of the nations, the tribulation period *(Chevlai shel Mashiach/Ya'acov's trouble)* and the Messianic age *(Athid Lavo)*. Because the Sabbath *(Shabbat)* is called the *day of the* L-<small>RD</small> (Isaiah *[Yeshayahu]* 58:13-14), it is therefore a foreshadowing of the Messianic Age *(Athid Lavo)*.

The term, *day of the* L-<small>RD</small>, can be found in the following Scripture verses (Isaiah *[Yeshayahu]* 2:12, 13:6, 9, Ezekiel *[Yechezekel]* 13:5, 30:3, Joel *[Yo'el]* 1:15, 2:1, 11, 3:14, Amos 5: 18, 20, Obadiah 1:15, Zephaniah 1:7, 14, Zechariah 14:1, Malachi 4:5, I Thessalonians 5:2, II Peter 3:10).

"In that Day" Is a Jewish Idiom
For the Day of the L-RD

The *day of the* L-RD is often referred to in the writings of the prophets with the shortened code form of *"in that day."* Actually, *in that day* is a Jewish idiom for *the day of the* L-RD. In fact, a major subject and theme of the book of Isaiah (*Yeshayahu*) are the events that will be taking place during the time period known as *the day of the* L-RD. In his writings, the prophet Isaiah (*Yeshayahu*) most often uses the term *"in that day"* to refer to the day of the L-RD. The term *"in that day"* can be found in the following verses (Isaiah [*Yeshayahu*] 2:11, 17, 20, 3:7, 18, 4:1-2, 5:30, 7:18, 21, 23, 10:20, 27, 11:10-11, 16, 12:1, 4, 17:4, 9, 19:16, 18-19, 21, 23-24, 20:6, 22:8, 12, 20, 25, 23:15, 24:21, 25:9, 26:1, 27:1-2, 12-13, 28:5, 29:18, 30:23, 25-26, 31:7, 52:6).

"At that Time" Is a Jewish Idiom
For the Day of the L-RD

There is another Jewish idiom which refers to the day of the L-RD. The phrase *"at that time"* is another code word (Jewish idiom) for *the day of the* L-RD. The term, *"at that time"* can be found in the following verses (Isaiah [*Yeshayahu*] 18:7, Jeremiah [*Yerushalayim*] 3:17, 4:11, 8:1, 31:1, 50:4, 20, Daniel 12:1, Joel (*Yo'el*) 3:1, Zephaniah 1:12, 3:20).

The Biblical Day Begins
in the Evening and Ends in the Morning

The Biblical day begins in the evening and ends in the morning (Genesis [*Bereishit*] 1:1,5,8,13,19,23,31). Like-

The Sabbath: Our Rest Is in Messiah

wise, the Sabbath *(Shabbat)* begins in the evening and ends in the morning. Each of the seven days of creation is a spiritual picture of 1,000 years of time. In Psalm *(Tehillim)* 90:4 it is written:

> *"For a thousand years in thy sight are but as yesterday when it is past, and as a watch in the night."*

The seventh day of creation, the Sabbath *(Shabbat)*, is a spiritual picture of the 1,000-year Messianic Age *(Athid Lavo)*. The Apostle *(Shaliach)* Peter *(Kefa)* associates the day of the L-RD to the coming of the Messiah *(Mashiach)* and the Messianic Age *(Athid Lavo)* in II Peter 3:7-10 it is written:

> *"But the heavens and the earth, which are now, by the same word are kept in store, reserved unto fire against the day of judgment and perdition of ungodly men. But, beloved,* **be not ignorant** *of this one thing,* **that one day is with the** L ORD **as a thousand years, and a thousand years as one day**. *The* L ORD *is not slack concerning his promise, as some men count slackness; but is longsuffering to us-ward, not willing that any should perish, but that all should come to repentance. But* **the day of the** L ORD *will come as a thief in the night; in the which the heavens shall pass away with a great noise, and the elements shall melt with fervent heat, the earth also and the works that are therein shall be burned up."*

Restoring the Two Houses of Israel

The Sabbath and Biblical Prophecy

The Sabbath *(Shabbat)* was given to us by the G-d of Israel to understand end-time Bible prophecy because the Sabbath *(Shabbat)* is a foreshadowing of the time known as the *day of the* L-RD or the Messianic Age *(Athid Lavo)*. Furthermore, the Biblical day begins in the EVENING (a time of darkness) and ends in the MORNING (a time of light). Therefore, is it possible that the *day of the* L-RD or the 1,000-year Messianic Age *(Athid Lavo)* also begins in the EVENING (the time of the seven year tribulation or birth pangs of the Messiah (*Chevlai shel Mashiach*/Ya'acov's trouble) and ends in the MORNING (a time of light) or the remaining 993 years ???

In my book, *The Seven Festivals of the Messiah*, I explain that one of the themes of Rosh HaShanah (the Feast of Trumpets — Leviticus *(Vayikra)* 23:23-25) is *HaMelech* (the king). This is the Biblical appointed time when the Jewish Messiah *(Mashiach) Yeshua*/Jesus will be crowned King *(Messiah ben David)*. Psalm *(Tehillim)* 47 is a coronation psalm. This event happens in Revelation 4-5.

After the Jewish Messiah *(Mashiach) Yeshua*/Jesus has His coronation ceremony, the events of the tribulation (*Chevlai shel Mashiach*/Ya'acov's trouble) and the judgment of the nations are described in Revelation 6-18. The return of the Jewish Messiah *(Mashiach) Yeshua*/Jesus as the Kingly Messiah known as *Messiah ben David* when He sets His feet down upon the mount of Olives (Zechariah 14:4) happens also in Revelation 19. Because

The Sabbath: Our Rest Is in Messiah

traditional corporate Christianity *(house of Israel)* has not understood that the Sabbath *(Shabbat)* was given by the G-d of Israel as a prophetic foreshadowing of the Messianic Age *(Athid Lavo)* and by corporately rejecting that the Biblical Sabbath *(Shabbat)* is the seventh day of the week and goes from Friday sundown to Saturday sundown, is it possible that this has darkened the understanding of traditional corporate Christianity *(house of Israel)* regarding correctly interpreting the events surrounding the coming of the Jewish Messiah *(Mashiach)* Yeshua/Jesus as the Kingly Messiah *(Messiah ben David)*, the tribulation *(Chevlai shel Mashiach/*Ya'acov's trouble) and the Messianic Age *(Athid Lavo)*???

Titles for the Day of the L-RD

There are many titles for the *day of the* L-RD. Some of these titles will indicate a time of trial, trouble, tribulation and darkness (EVENING = a time of darkness) while other titles will indicate a time of peace and tranquility (MORNING = a time of light). Some of the titles of the *day of the* L-RD that indicate trial, trouble, tribulation, wrath and darkness are:

1) A day of visitation and desolation (Isaiah 10:3)
2) A day of fierce anger (Isaiah 13:13)
3) The day of grief and desperate sorrow (Isaiah 17:11)
4) The day of trouble (Isaiah 22:5, Jeremiah 51:2, Zephaniah 1:14-15)
5) The day of the great slaughter (Isaiah 30:25)
6) The day of the Lord's vengeance (Isaiah 34:8, 61:2, 63:4)

Restoring the Two Houses of Israel

7) The day of His wrath (Zephaniah 1:15,18)
8) The day of darkness and gloominess (Joel 2:1-2, Zephaniah 1:14-15)
9) The day of clouds and thick darkness (Joel 2:1-2, Zephaniah 1:14-15)
10) The great and terrible day of the LORD (Joel 2:31, Malachi 4:5)
11) The day of battle (Zechariah 14:3)
12) The day of Jacob's trouble (Jeremiah 30:7, Daniel 12:1)
13) A day of desolation (Zephaniah 1:15)
14) A day of trumpet and alarm (Zephaniah 1:16)
15) The day of judgment and perdition of ungodly men (II Peter 3:7)

There are other titles for the *day of the* L-RD which seem to indicate a time of peace, rest, comfort, tranquility and victory. Some of the these titles are:

1) A day the LORD gives you rest (Isaiah 14:3)
2) The day of the EAST wind (Isaiah 27:8)
3) The day of salvation (Isaiah 49:8)
4) A day of clouds (clouds refer to believers) — (Ezekiel 30:3, Hebrews 12:1)
5) The day that I am glorified (Ezekiel 39:13)
6) The day of His preparation (Nahum 2:3)
7) The day when the Son of Man is revealed (Luke 17:30)
8) The day of our LORD Jesus (I Corinthians 1:8, II Corinthians 1:14, Philippians 1:6)
9) The day of redemption (Ephesians 4:30)
10) The day of Christ (Philippians 1:10, 2:16)
11) The day of G-d (II Peter 3:12)

The Sabbath: Our Rest Is in Messiah

After the Jewish Messiah *(Mashiach) Yeshua*/Jesus returns to the earth at His second coming as the Kingly Messiah *(Messiah ben David)*, there will be perpetual peace and harmony on the earth during the Messianic Age *(Athid Lavo)*. Some of the Scriptures which speak of this time of peace *(shalom)* are:

1) The animals will be at peace with each other and with mankind (Isaiah 11:6-8).
2) The farmland will be prosperous (Ezekiel 34:24-27).
3) G-d's people shall dwell safely and peacefully (Ezekiel 34:25, 28).
4) The whole world will be filled with the knowledge of G-d (Isaiah 11:9, Jeremiah 31:33-34).
5) There will be peace and no wars (Isaiah 2:3-4, Micah 4:3).
6) The Torah will be taught from Jerusalem (Isaiah 2:2-3, Micah 4:1-2).
7) There will be continual light on the earth (Zechariah 14:6-8).
8) The Jewish Messiah *(Mashiach) Yeshua*/Jesus will be King over all the earth (Daniel 7:13-14,18,27, Zechariah 14:9, Revelation 2:27, 11:15, 12:5, 19:15-16).

So, the *day of the* L-RD is described as being a time of trial, trouble, tribulation, wrath and darkness and ends with a time of peace, prosperity, dwelling safely, no wars, universal knowledge of the Torah and the Messiah *(Mashiach)* and light. There is no contradiction that the *day of the* L-RD is both darkness and light if we understand the Sabbath *(Shabbat)* is a term for the *day of the*

L-RD and that each Biblical day begins in the evening and ends in the morning.

Therefore, it seems quite possible that the evening part of the *day of the* L-RD and the first seven years of the 1,000-year Messianic Age *(Athid Lavo)* is the tribulation or birth pangs of the Messiah *(Chevlai shel Mashiach/* Ya'acov's trouble) and the morning part of *the day of the* L-RD is the last 993 years of the 1,000-year Messianic Age *(Athid Lavo)* when the Jewish Messiah *(Mashiach) Yeshua*/Jesus who is called the day star (II Peter *[Kefa]* 1:19) and the bright and morning star (Revelation 22:16) returns to the earth at His second coming as the Kingly Messiah *(Messiah ben David)* and sets His feet down on the mount of Olives (Zechariah 14:4).

The Sabbath Will Be Kept for All Eternity

When the G-d of Israel gave the Sabbath *(Shabbat)* to His people, He proclaimed that it was to be an ETERNAL/EVERLASTING ordinance. In Exodus *(Shemot)* 31:15-17 it is written:

> *"Six days may work be done; but in the seventh is the sabbath of rest, holy to the* LORD: *whosoever doeth any work in the sabbath day, he shall surely be put to death. Wherefore the children of Israel shall keep the sabbath, to* **observe the sabbath** *throughout their generations, for a* **perpetual covenant**. *It is a sign between me and the children of Israel* **forever**: *for in six days the* LORD

The Sabbath: Our Rest Is in Messiah

made heaven and earth, and on the seventh day he rested, and was refreshed."

The Sabbath (*Shabbat*) will be kept during the days of the new heaven and the new earth. In Revelation 21:1 it is written:

"And I saw a new heaven and a new earth: for the first heaven and the first earth were passed away; and there was no more sea."

During the days of the new heaven and the new earth, the G-d of Israel will REQUIRE that ALL FLESH keep the Sabbath *(Shabbat)*. In Isaiah *(Yeshayahu)* 66:22-23 it is written:

"For as the new heavens and the new earth, which I will make, shall remain before me, saith the L<small>ORD</small>, *so shall your seed and your name remain. And it shall come to pass, that from one new moon to another, and* **from one sabbath to another**, *shall* **all flesh** *come to worship before me, saith the* L<small>ORD</small>*."*

In conclusion, in order for full restoration to come to both the *house of Judah* (Judaism) and the *house of Israel* (Christianity), both houses of Israel need to come to a more fuller understanding and application of the Biblical Sabbath *(Shabbat)* that the G-d of Israel gave His people to celebrate on the seventh day of the week from Friday sundown to Saturday sundown. For the *house of Judah* (Judaism), they need to realize that the fullness of their Sabbath *(Shabbat)* rest is in the Jewish Messiah *(Mashiach) Yeshua*/Jesus. For the *house of Israel* (Christianity), they need to understand that the Biblical Sabbath *(Shabbat)* day is from Friday sundown to Saturday sundown and that the G-d of Israel gave the Sabbath *(Shabbat)* as an eternal covenant that is to be kept by His people forever.

Furthermore, the *house of Israel* (Christianity) needs to understand that the G-d of Israel gave the Sabbath *(Shabbat)* to His people to more fully reveal His redemptive plan through the Jewish Messiah *(Mashiach)* Yeshua/Jesus including the marriage of His bride, the prophetic events regarding the second coming of the Jewish Messiah *(Mashiach)* Yeshua/Jesus as the Kingly Messiah *(Messiah ben David)* and the events surrounding His rule and reign during the Messianic Age *(Athid Lavo)*.

May the Jewish Messiah *(Mashiach) Yeshua*/Jesus come speedily in our days and set up His Messianic Kingdom bringing eternal peace *(shalom)* and teaching the Torah to all nations from the city of Jerusalem *(Yerushalayim)* so that both houses of Israel can abide forever in the Sabbath *(Shabbat)* rest of the G-d of Israel. Amen !!!

Chapter 5

The 7,000-Year Plan of G-d

In order for full restoration to come to both the *house of Israel* (Christianity) and the *house of Judah* (Judaism), both houses of Israel need to understand and embrace the 7,000-year redemptive plan of the G-d of Israel. The *house of Israel* (Christianity) needs to embrace the 7,000-year redemptive plan of the G-d of Israel rather than dispensational theology. The *house of Judah* (Judaism) needs to understand that the Jewish Messiah *(Mashiach) Yeshua*/Jesus came to the earth as the suffering Messiah known as *Messiah be Yosef* (Joseph) after 4,000 years since the creation of Adam and Eve in the Garden of Eden *(Gan Eden)* exactly as expected by the ancient rabbi's *(Sanhedrin 97/98)*.

It was explained to the *house of Israel* (Christianity) in chapter 3 that before the death of the Jewish Messiah *(Mashiach) Yeshua*/Jesus was NOT the *"age of law"* because the Torah and the Word of G-d are synonymous terms and the Torah/Word of G-d lives and abides forever (Isaiah *[Yeshayahu]* 40:8, I Peter *[Kefa]* 1:25). Furthermore, it was explained that the G-d of Israel has ALWAYS redeemed/saved His people by His grace/mercy.

In the last chapter, we learned that the *"day of the* L<small>ORD</small>*"* is the Sabbath *(Shabbat)* and the Sabbath is a foreshadowing of the 1,000-year Messianic Age *(Athid Lavo)*. The 1,000-year Messianic Age *(Athid Lavo)* is the last 1,000 years of the 7,000-year redemptive plan of the G-d of Israel.

Each day in the Bible begins in the *"evening"* and ends in the *"morning"* (Genesis *[Bereishit]* 1). The *"evening"* part of the *"day of the* L-<small>RD</small>*"* (the Messianic Age/*Athid Lavo*) is the tribulation/birth pangs of the Messiah *(Chevlai shel Mashiach)*. The Jewish Messiah *(Mashiach)* Yeshua/Jesus will return to the earth at His second coming as the Kingly Messiah known as *Messiah ben David* at the *"break of the morning."* He is the *"star that comes out of Jacob"* (Numbers *[Bamidbar]* 24:17) and the *"bright and morning star"* (Revelation 22:16). In the *"morning"* part of the *"day of the* L<small>ORD</small>*"* (Messianic Age/*Athid Lavo*), the Jewish Messiah *(Mashiach)* will teach the Torah to the nations from the city of Jerusalem *(Yerushalayim)* (Isaiah *[Yeshayahu]* 2:2-3).

The Ages of the 7,000-Year Plan of G-d

When the G-d of Israel created Adam and Eve in the Garden of Eden *(Gan Eden)*, He ordained that from the creation of Adam and Eve to the end of the Messianic Age *(Athid Lavo)* would be 7,000 years of time. Before the creation of Adam and Eve in the Garden of Eden *(Gan Eden)* was eternity past. After the Messianic Age *(Athid Lavo)* is eternity future. Future eternity *(Olam Haba)* will be a return to the paradise of eternity past

The 7,000-Year Plan of G-d

(represented by the Garden of Eden *[Gan Eden]* before the sin of Adam). Time is going forward to the past. That which was (Garden of Eden before the sin of Adam) is that which shall be (eternity future/*Olam Habah*/Heaven). In Ecclesiastes *(Kohelet)* 1:9 it is written:

> *"The thing that hath been, it is that which shall be; and that which is done is that which shall be done: and there is no new thing under the sun."*

Traditional Judaism *(house of Judah)* understands that the first 6,000 years is known as the present age/world *(Olam Hazeh)*. These first 6,000 years are divided into three 2,000-year periods of time or ages. The first 2,000 years from the creation of Adam to the time of Abraham *(Avraham)* is known as the period/age of desolation *(Tohu)*. The next two thousand years from the time of Abraham to the expected arrival of the Jewish Messiah *(Mashiach)* is known as the period/age of *Torah*. The final 2,000 years of time within the 6,000 years of the present/age world *(Olam Hazeh)* is known as the days of the Messiah *(Yemot Mashiach)*. The last 1,000 years is known as the Messianic era or the future age/coming *(Athid Lavo)*. The 7,000-year redemptive plan of the G-d of Israel can be seen in the following chart.

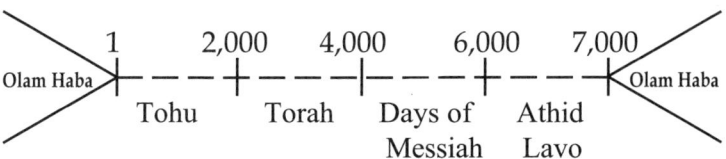

Restoring the Two Houses of Israel

The Seven Days of Creation Is a Blueprint for the 7,000 years of Time

The 7,000-year plan of the G-d of Israel is a major concept and foundational truth in understanding Bible prophecy and eschatology *(study of the last things)*. The rabbis of traditional Judaism *(house of Judah)* understand that the G-d of Israel gave the seven days of creation in the book of Genesis as *Torah*/instruction to teach His people that there are 7,000 years of time from the creation of Adam and Eve in the Garden of Eden *(Gan Eden)* to the end of the Messianic Age *(Athid Lavo)*. Each day in creation represents 1,000 years in time. This is based upon connecting Psalm *(Tehillim)* 90:4 to the seven days of creation. In Psalm *(Tehillim)* 90:4 it is written:

> *"For a thousand years in thy sight are but as yesterday when it is past, and as a watch in the night."*

In rabbinic literature, it is also taught that each day in creation represents 1,000 years of time. In the *Talmud* in *Sanhedrin 97* it is written:

> "It has been taught in accordance with R. Kattina: Just as the seventh year is one year of release in seven, so is the world: one thousand years out of seven shall be fallow, as it is written. And the LORD alone shall be exalted in that day; [Isaiah 2:11] and it is further said, A Psalm and song for the sabbath day; [Psalm 92] meaning the day that is altogether Sabbath [i.e. the period of complete desolation] and it is also said, For a thousand years in thy

The 7,000-Year Plan of G-d

sight are but as yesterday when it is past. [Psalm 90:4: thus 'day' in the preceding verses means a thousand years]."

In an article entitled, *"The Coming of Messiah"* written in *The Jewish Press* newspaper (Brooklyn, New York) by Rabbi Sholom Klass, he explains the traditional Jewish view *(house of Judah)* of each day in creation representing 1,000 years of time based upon Psalm *(Tehillim)* 90:4 as explained by the respected Orthodox Jewish rabbi, Moses Ben Nachman (1194-1270). He is known in Jewish tradition by the acronym RaMBaN. The articles reads:

> "The Ramban explains that in the creation of the world which is itemized in Genesis, G-d left a blue print for the future. Each day of creation represents 1,000 years of the total existence of the world — 6,000 years. The first day was null and void, no one knew the Torah. G-d created light, Adam, whose light shone from one end of the earth to the other. In this thousand years no one worshiped idols. In the second day, G-d created the heaven which divided the waters, representing Noah who was divided from the evil people who perished in the waters. In the third day (third millennium) came the grass and fruit representing Abraham, as the Psalm says, 'A Tzadik [righteous] grows as the grass,' and out of him came the fruit of Torah and mitzvohs [commandments] when his children accepted the Torah on Mount Sinai. On the fourth day (fourth millennium) came the planets and the stars representing the two Botei Hamikdosh (Holy Temples) whence came forth the light to protect the world. On

the fifth day came the animals, fish and fowl, signifying that after the destruction of the Temples, man would spread over the earth and a new sect would multiply as the fish of the sea, but they would be as cruel as the animals and the people would not seek to embrace G-d as the Torah commands. On the sixth day G-d created man, symbolizing the present era when man would reach his highest peak in knowledge and Messiah ben David [the Kingly Messiah] will come. The seventh day, Shabbos [Sabbath] represents the 'Olam Habah,' the future world which will follow the Messianic era. May G-d protect us and hasten these glorious days for all of us (Rambam, Bereishes Genesis 2)."

The traditional Jewish view *(house of Judah)* of linking each of the seven days of creation to 1,000 years of time based upon Psalm *(Tehillim)* 90:4 is restated in the extra-biblical book of *Barnabas* Chapter 13, verses 3-6 as it is written:

> "And even in the beginning of the creation he makes mention of the sabbath. And God made in six days the works of his hands; and he finished them on the seventh day, and he rested the seventh day, and sanctified it. Consider, my children, what that signifies, he finished them in six days. The meaning of it is this; that in six thousand years the LORD God will bring all things to an end. For with him one day is a thousand years; as himself testifieth, saying, Behold this day shall be as a thousand years. Therefore, children, in six

The 7,000-Year Plan of G-d

days, that is, in six thousand years, shall all things be accomplished. And what is it that he saith, And he rested the seventh day: he meaneth this; that when his Son shall come, and abolish the season of the Wicked One, and judge the ungodly; and shall change the sun and the moon, and the stars; then he shall gloriously rest in that seventh day."

The traditional Jewish view *(house of Judah)* of each day of creation representing 1,000 years of time is expressed in the New Testament *(Brit Hadashah)* in II Peter *(Kefa)* 3:8-10 as it is written:

"But, beloved, **be not ignorant** *of this one thing, that* **one day** *is* **with the** L<small>ORD</small> *as* **a thousand years**, *and a thousand years as one day. The* L<small>ORD</small> *is not slack concerning his promise, as some men count slackness; but is longsuffering to us-ward, not willing that any should perish, but that all should come to repentance. But the day of the* L<small>ORD</small> *will come as a thief in the night; in the which the heavens shall pass away with a great noise, and the elements shall melt with fervent heat, the earth also and the works that are therein shall be burned up."*

What Is the Current Jewish Year?

The current year in the Jewish calendar is 57xx. In the book, *Gates of the Seasons* by the Central Conference of American Rabbis in an article written by Alexander Guttmann on pages 7-10, he explains the origin and understanding of the present Jewish calendar.

Restoring the Two Houses of Israel

"The main purpose of the Jewish calendar is, and always has been, to set the dates of the festivals. Our present calendar has its roots in the Torah, but it has been modified by Jewish religious authorities through the ages. The principal rules were established by the Sages and Rabbis of antiquity and were supplemented by medieval scholars. In Talmudic times the regulation of the calendar was the exclusive right of the Jewish leadership in the Land of Israel, particularly that of the Nasi (Patriach). Since that time, such regulation has been regarded as a task of crucial importance for the observance of Judaism...

In the Bible, the Hebrew months are lunar (i.e. each month begins with the "birth" of the new moon). However, since festivals such as Passover and Sukkot had to occur in the proper agricultural season (i.e. according to the solar year), it is obvious that the Jewish calendar must be lunar-solar. This means that the lunar year (approximately 354 days) and the solar year (approximately 365 days) had to be harmonized and adjusted to each other, a complex process that was meticulously refined by the ancient and medieval Rabbis.

The Jewish day has twenty-four hours and starts in the evening. The length of the lunar month is traditionally calculated as 29 days, 12 hours, and 793 parts of an hour (divided into 1080 parts). This is the time span between one new moon and the next. Since it is impractical to start a new month at varying hours of the day, the Sages of antiquity ordained that the

The 7,000-Year Plan of G-d

length of the month should alternate between 29 and 30 days. Since the lunar month is somewhat longer than 29 days and 12 hours, the remainder is taken care of by making the months of Cheshvan and Kislev flexible, i.e. they can both have either 29 or 30 days.

The introduction of a permanent Jewish calendar became increasingly urgent after Jews began to spread throughout the world. As Jewry dispersed, regular contacts with the Jewish leadership in the Land of Israel, which had the sole privilege of regulating the calendar, became more and more difficult. The most important step in this process of permanent calendar reform was the adoption in the eighth century CE of a nineteen-year cycle of "intercalation" (i.e. harmonization of the solar and lunar calendars). The adoption of this cycle made the actual physical observation of the new moon and the signs of approaching spring unnecessary. This cycle of nineteen years adjusts the lunar year to the solar year by inserting into it seven leap years (i.e. the additional 30-day month of Adar) in the following order: every third, sixth, eighth, eleventh, fourteenth, seventeenth, and nineteenth year.

In the Bible the months are most frequently designated by ordinal numbers. However, there are references both to such ancient names as Ziv, Ethanim, and Aviv and to some of the now customary names of Kislev, Tevet, Adar, Nisan, Sivan, and Elul, which are of Babylonian origin. But, it is only since the first century that the Hebrew calendar has employed the now traditional names of Nisan, Iyar, Sivan, Tamuz, Av, Elul, Tishri, Cheshvan, Kislev, Tevet, Shevat, and Adar.

The Jewish tradition of counting years since the creation of the world has it roots in early Talmudic times, but it was not adopted authoritatively until several centuries later. In Biblical times, dates were referred to as being "two years before the earthquake," the year of the death of King Uzziah," etc. In Talmudic times, we find instances of dating from the creation of the world, but this was adopted as **the** Jewish method only much later as a response to Christian dating.

It was in the eighth century that Christians began to date their documents generally as AD (Anno Domini, the year of the Lord), and so it is hardly a coincidence that in the eighth and ninth centuries we find more and more Jewish documents dated "since the creation of the world" (sometimes referred to as AM, Anno Mundi, the year of the world). Obviously, calculating dates based on the Christian theological principles were not acceptable to Jews; nevertheless, it was not until the twelfth century that dating "since the creation" was accepted by Jews universally.

Only a minority of Jews today would take the traditional Jewish date as being literally "since the creation of the world" ... Jewish texts will often use such designations as BCE (Before the Common, or Christian Era) or CE in order to avoid any dating related to Chris-

The 7,000-Year Plan of G-d

tianity. In order to determine the Jewish year for a given civil year, the number 3760 is added; conversely, in order to find the civil year for a given Jewish year, 3760 is subtracted. Of course, since the Jewish year changes with Rosh HaShanah, the number to work with from Rosh HaShanah to December 31 is 3761.

The greatest change which the Rabbis made in the festival calendar was the addition of a day to each of the holidays ordained in the Torah, except Yom Kippur. This was done in the early Talmudic period (i.e. first century). Compelling circumstances at that time forced the Rabbis to make this change.

Not only was the confirmation and sanctification of the new moon — and therefore the new month — the duty of the Palestinian authorities, but theirs was also the task of communicating the dates of the new moon to every Jewish community. This was a task of vital importance, as the new moon determines the dates of the festivals. At an earlier time, the new moon (i.e. the first of the month) was communicated to all the Jews in Palestine and the Diaspora by kindling flares on hilltops. However, after the Samaritans kindled flares at the wrong time to confuse the Jews, the news about the New Moon had to be communicated by messengers. The change was introduced by Judah Hanasi (c. 135-200 CE).

Since it often happened that the messengers did not arrive in time at the places of their destination outside of Palestine because of road hazards, wars, or political upheavals, a second day was added to the holidays for the Jews in the Diaspora. This assured that one of the two days on which they celebrated the festival was indeed the proper holy day. In Palestine the addition of these "second days" to the festivals was not necessary because the news about the sighting of the new moon, proclaimed in Palestine, reached every part of that land in due time, i.e. prior to the dates of the festivals. The exception was Rosh HaShanah, which falls on the first day of the month of Tishri, making timely communication about this New Moon, even in Palestine, impossible.

During the Talmudic period a stable, scientifically determined calendar was adopted, and so the pragmatic need for "second days" disappeared. But the Palestinian authorities did not abolish these extra days of observance for Diaspora Jews (nor the second day of Rosh HaShanah for Palestinian Jews) because of the Rabbinic principle that we "may not change the custom of [our] forefathers."

Because it was mostly in response to more and more Christians *(house of Israel)* beginning to date their documents around the eighth century as AD (*Anno Domini*, in the year of our Lord) and because it was not until the twelfth century that the present way of Jewish dating of time was accepted by Jews *(house of Judah)* universally, it can be concluded that the modern Jewish calendar is not literally *"since the creation of the world."* When the Jewish people *(house of Judah)*, recalculated time *"since*

The 7,000-Year Plan of G-d

the beginning of the world", they did not recalculate all of the years when they were taken captive in Babylon *(Judaism in the 1st Century Christian Era)* Volume I, Chapter 1 by George Foote Moore. However, Biblically, the G-d of Israel did ordain that there would be 6,000 years of time from the creation of Adam to the beginning of the Messianic Age *(Athid Lavo)*. Therefore, only the G-d of Israel knows for sure how close we are to the conclusion of 6,000 years of time and the beginning of the Messianic Age *(Athid Lavo)*.

The 6,000-Year Present Era in Genesis 1:1

In the audio tape series, *America's Biblical Blueprint* by Orthodox Jewish Rabbi Daniel Lapin, Volume 1, he explains the allusion to the first 6,000 years of the 7,000-year plan of the G-d of Israel in Genesis *(Bereishit)* 1:1 by examining the text of the verse in Hebrew. In English, Genesis *(Bereishit)* 1:1 reads:

> *"In the beginning God created the heavens and the earth"*

In Hebrew, Genesis *(Bereishit)* 1:1 reads:

> *"Bereishit b'rah elohim et hashamayim v'et ha'eretz."*

As Orthodox Jewish Rabbi Daniel Lapin explains in the tape series, in Genesis *(Bereishit)* 1:1, the first letter of the Hebrew alphabet, *Alef,* appears 6 times in a very improbable sequence. The Hebrew letter, *Alef,* is the **third letter** of the first two Hebrew words, *Bereishit* and *B'rah*. The Hebrew letter, *Alef,* is the **first letter** in the next two Hebrew words, *elohim* and *et*. The Hebrew letter, *Alef,* is the **second letter** in the last two Hebrew words, *v'et* and *ha'eretz*.

Restoring the Two Houses of Israel

The Wisdom of Keeping the Torah and the Hebrew *Alef*

In traditional Jewish *(house of Judah)* thought, the Hebrew letter, *Alef*, represents wisdom. In the Bible, wisdom is associated and linked with keeping the Torah of the G-d of Israel. In Deuteronomy *(Devarim)* 4:1, 5-8 it is written:

> *"Now therefore hearken, O Israel, unto the statutes and unto the judgments, which I teach you, for to do them ... Behold, I have taught you statutes and judgments, even as the* Lord *my God commanded me, that ye should do so in the land whither ye go to possess it.* **Keep** *therefore and* **do** *them; for this is your* **wisdom** *and your understanding in the sight of the nations, which shall hear all these statutes, and say, Surely this great nation is a* **wise** *and* **understanding people***. For what nation is there so great, who hath God so nigh unto them, as the* Lord *our God is in all things that we call upon him for? And what nation is there so great, that hath statutes and judgments so righteous as all this law* **[TORAH]**, *which I set before you this day?"*

So, in this Scripture, keeping the Torah of the G-d of Israel is associated with wisdom and understanding. In traditional Jewish thought, the Hebrew letter, *Alef*, is also associated with wisdom. Therefore, it is logical to conclude that the G-d of Israel would choose the Hebrew letter, *Alef*, in Genesis *(Bereishit)* 1:1, to represent the wisdom of keeping His Torah during the first 6,000

The 7,000-Year Plan of G-d

years of time known as the *Olam Hazeh* (the present world/age).

How is the *Alef* (which represents wisdom) and the wisdom of keeping the Torah of the G-d of Israel linked to an allusion of 6,000 years of time in Genesis 1:1? As Orthodox Jewish Rabbi Daniel Lapin explains in his tape series, in Genesis *(Bereishit)* 1:1, the Hebrew letter, *Alef*, appears 6 times in a very improbable sequence. The Hebrew letter, *Alef*, is the **third letter** in the first two Hebrew words, *Bereishit*, and *B'rah*. These first two occurrences of the Hebrew letter, *Alef*, as the **third letter** in each of the first two Hebrew words, *Bereishit* and *B'rah* represents the first 2,000 years of time known as *Tohu* when there was the least amount of knowledge of the Torah/Word of the G-d of Israel among the earth's people.

The Hebrew letter, *Alef*, is the **first letter** in the next two Hebrew words, *elohim* and *et*. These next two occurrences of the Hebrew letter, *Alef*, as the **first letter** in each of the next two Hebrew words, *elohim* and *et* represents the next 2,000 years of time known as *Torah* when the knowledge and understanding of the Torah/Word of the G-d of Israel and following it would be at its greatest within the first 6,000 years of time.

The Hebrew letter, *Alef*, is the **second letter** in the last two Hebrew words in Genesis *(Bereishit)* 1:1, *v'et* and *ha'eretz*. These last two occurrences of the Hebrew letter, *Alef*, as the **second letter** in each of the next two Hebrew words, *v'et* and *ha'eretz* represents the last 2,000 years of time known as the days of the Messiah (*Yemot Mashiach*) of the first 6,000 years. This signifies that during this time there would be a great religious/secular debate among the people of the earth regarding whether or not they should follow the Torah/Word of the G-d of Israel.

When Is the End of the 6,000-Year Present Era?

The greatest 1,000-year period of the 7,000 years of time will be during the days of the Messianic Age *(Athid Lavo)*. This period of time follows the first 6,000 years of time known as the *Olam Hazeh* (the present world/age). As we have just studied, the last 2,000 years of the *Olam Hazeh* (the present world/age) known as the days of the Messiah *(Yemot Mashiach)* would be a period of time when there would be an ideological struggle among the people of the world whether they should follow the Torah/Word of the G-d of Israel or live according to the values of a secular society.

Being Jewish, the disciples *(talmidim)* of the Jewish Messiah *(Mashiach) Yeshua*/Jesus had an understanding of the 7,000-year redemptive plan of the G-d of Israel and knew that they were living in the *Olam Hazeh* (the present world/age). By knowing that the *Olam Hazeh* (the present world/age) is followed by the Messianic Age *(Athid Lavo)* and by knowing that they were speaking to the Jewish Messiah *(Mashiach) Yeshua*/Jesus Himself, they decided to ask Him what signs that His people should expect to see so that they would know

The 7,000-Year Plan of G-d

when the present world/age *(Olam Hazeh)* was concluding and the Messianic Age *(Athid Lavo)* was about to arrive. In Matthew *(Mattityahu)* 24:3 it is written:

> *"When he was sitting on the Mount of Olives, the talmidim [disciples] came to him privately. 'Tell us,' they said, 'when will these things happen? And what will be the sign that you are coming and that the* **'olam hazeh'** *is ending?' "* (The Complete Jewish Bible version by David Stern)

The Jewish *(house of Judah)* disciples of the Jewish Messiah *(Mashiach)* Yeshua/Jesus had no concept, no knowledge and no understanding of the 7,000-year redemptive plan of the G-d of Israel through the eyes of modern traditional Christian *(house of Israel)* dispensational theology *(the age of law and the age of grace)*. Furthermore, we should notice that the Jewish Messiah *(Mashiach)* Yeshua/Jesus did not rebuke His disciples *(talmidim)* for understanding that the first 6,000 years of time were known as the *Olam Hazeh* (the present world/age). However, the Jewish Messiah *(Mashiach)* Yeshua/Jesus did acknowledge the premise of their question and gave a detailed answer in the rest of Matthew *(Mattityahu)* 24 known within Christianity *(house of Israel)* as the Olivet discourse.

The Jewish Messiah Will Come After 4,000 Years of Time

It is traditional Jewish *(house of Judah)* understanding that the Jewish Messiah *(Mashiach)* would come 4,000 years after the creation of Adam and Eve. In the *Talmud* in *Sanhedrin 97* it is written:

> "The Tanna debe Eliyyahu teaches: The world is to exist six thousand years. In the first two thousand there was desolation; [i.e. no Torah. It is a tradition that Abraham was fifty-two years old when he began to convert men to the worship of the true God; from Adam until then, two thousand years elapsed] two thousand years the Torah flourished; and the next two thousand years is the Messianic era, [i.e. Messiah will come within that period] but through our many iniquities all these years have been lost. [He should have come at the beginning of the last two thousand years; the delay is due to our sins.]"

Therefore, as recorded in the *Talmud* in *Sanhedrin 97*, there was an expectation that the Jewish Messiah *(Mashiach)* would come after 4,000 years of time. In an article in the *Jewish Press* newspaper (Brooklyn, New York) by Rabbi Sholom Klass entitled, *The Coming of the Messiah*, he explains that there was a high expectation among the Jewish people for a Jewish Messiah *(Mashiach)* during the first century. In his article, Rabbi Sholom Klass writes:

> "The belief in a personal Messiah reached its highest tension during that period of the first century when Rome sent her despotic procurators to rule over Judea. The yoke was most oppressive and the Jews awaited a leader whom G-d would send to articulate their latent spirit of rebellion and free them from the Roman tyranny."

The 7,000-Year Plan of G-d

4,000 Years From the Creation of Adam to the Jewish Messiah

Next, we will examine the Biblical chronology of time to understand that the Jewish Messiah *(Mashiach) Yeshua*/Jesus came to the earth 4,000 years from the creation of Adam and Eve in the Garden of Eden *(Gan Eden)*. This matches exactly the period of time when the Messiah was expected to come to the earth according to traditional Jewish expectation. The purpose of this chronology is NOT to Biblically justify EXACTLY the entire 4,000 year period of time from the creation of Adam to the coming of the Jewish Messiah *(Mashiach) Yeshua*/Jesus in the first century. However, it is given to establish a Biblical basis for the credibility of making such a hypothesis.

From Adam to Abraham

Adam to Seth	130 years (Genesis 5:3)
Seth to Enos	105 years (Genesis 5:6)
Enos to Cainan	90 years (Genesis 5:9)
Cainan to Mahalaleel	70 years (Genesis 5:12)
Mahalaleel to Jared	65 years (Genesis 5:15)
Jared to Enoch	162 years (Genesis 5:18)
Enoch to Methuselah	65 years (Genesis 5:21)
Methuselah to Lamech	187 years (Genesis 5:25)
Lamech to Noah	182 years (Genesis 5:28-29)
Noah to the Flood	600 years (Genesis 7:6)
Flood to Arphaxad	2 years (Genesis 11:10)
Arphaxad to Salah	35 years (Genesis 11:12)
Salah to Eber	30 years (Genesis 11:14)
Eber to Peleg	34 years (Genesis 11:16)
Peleg to Reu	30 years (Genesis 11:18)

Reu to Serug .... 32 years (Genesis 11:20)
Serug to Nahor .... 30 years (Genesis 11:22)
Nahor to Terah .... 29 years (Genesis 11:24)
Terah to Abraham .... 70 years (Genesis 11:26)

Adam to Abraham .... 1948 years

It is interesting to note that from Adam to Abraham *(Avraham)* was 1948 years. The birth of the modern day state of Israel happened on the Gregorian calendar in 1948.

From Abraham to Egypt

Abraham to Isaac .... 100 years (Genesis 21:5)
Isaac to Jacob .... 60 years (Genesis 25:26)
Jacob to Egypt .... 130 years (Genesis 47:28)

Abraham to Egypt .... 290 years

From Egypt to the Exodus

From Egypt to the Exodus .... X years

— Jacob and his family went to Egypt

Jacob went to Egypt .... (Genesis 46:8,11)
Levi went to Egypt (Jacob's son) .... (Genesis 46:8,11)
Kohath went to Egypt (Levi's son) ... (Genesis 46:8,11)

Kohath had a son named Amram ..... (Exodus 6:18)
Amram had a son named Moses .... (Exodus 6:20)
Moses to the Exodus — 80 years .... (Exodus 7:7)

The 7,000-Year Plan of G-d

From Egypt to the Exodus:

X = (Kohath to Amram to Moses + 80)

From the Wilderness to Joshua's Death

In the Wilderness .... 40 years (Numbers 32:13)
Wilderness to death Joshua ... 30 years (Joshua 14:7, 24:29)

Exodus to death Joshua ...... 70 years

The Period of the Judges

Under King Cushanrishathaim .. 8 years (Judges 3:8)
Under Othniel .... 40 years (Judges 3:10-11)
Under King Eglon .... 18 years (Judges 3:14)
Under Ehud .... 80 years (Judges 3:15,30)
Under King Jabin .... 20 years (Judges 4:1-3)
Under Deborah .... 40 years (Judges 4:4, 5:31)
Under Midianites .... 7 years (Judges 6:1)
Under Gideon .... 40 years (Judges 6:7, 8:28)
Under Abimelech .... 3 years (Judges 8:32, 9:22)
Under Tola .... 23 years (Judges 10:1-2)
Under Jair .... 22 years (Judges 10:3)
Under Ammonites .... 18 years (Judges 10:5-8)
Under Jephthah .... 6 years (Judges 12:7)
Under Ibzan .... 7 years (Judges 12:8-9)
Under Elon .... 10 years (Judges 12:11)
Under Abdon .... 8 years (Judges 12:13-14)
Under Philistines .... 40 years (Judges 13:1)
Under Samson .... 20 years (Judges 16:30-31)
Under Eli/Samuel .... 40 years (I Samuel 4:15,18)

Judges to Samuel .... 450 years (Acts 13:20)

Restoring the Two Houses of Israel

The Kings of Judah

Under King Saul	40 years (Acts 13:21)
Under King David	40 years (I Chron 29:26-27)
Under King Solomon	40 years (I Kings 11:42-43)
Under King Rehoboam	17 years (I Kings 14:21)
Under King Abijam	3 years (I Kings 15:1-2)
Under King Asa	41 years (I Kings 15:8-10)
Under King Jehoshaphat	25 years (I Kings 22:41-42)
Under King Jehoram	8 years (II Chron 21:5)
Under King Ahaziah	1 year (II Chron 22:1-2)
Under Queen Athaliah	6 years (II Chron 22:12)
Under King Joash	40 years (II Chron 24:1)
Under King Amaziah	29 years (II Chron 25:1)
Under Uzziah	52 years (II Chron 26:3)
Under Jotham	16 years (II Chron 27:1)
Under Ahaz	16 years (II Chron 28:1)
Under Hezekiah	29 years (II Chron 29:1)
Under Manasseh	55 years (II Chron 33:1)
Under Amon	2 years (II Chron 33:21)
Under King Josiah	31 years (II Chron 34:1)
Under King Jehoahaz	3 months (II Chron 36:2)
Under King Jehoiakim	11 years (II Chron 36:3-7)
Under King Jehoiachin	3 months (II Chron 36:9)
Under King Zedekiah	11 years (II Chron 36:11)

KINGS OF JUDAH	513 years

History tells us that the Jews *(house of Judah)* were taken captive to Babylon in 586 BCE.

The 7,000-Year Plan of G-d

Summary of the Time From Adam to *Yeshua*/Jesus

Adam to Abraham	1948 years
Abraham to Egypt	290 years
From Egypt to Moses	X years

The Bible does not explicitly give us this time but Kohath went to Egypt and Moses *(Moshe)* is the grandson of Kohath. So, this is an arbitrary number.

Let X = 63 years
X = (Kohath to Amram to Moses)

Moses to the Exodus	80 years
Exodus to death Joshua	70 years
Judges to Samuel	450 years
Kings of Judah	513 years
Babylonian Captivity	586 years (BCE)
From Adam to *Yeshua*/Jesus	4000 years

Therefore, we can conclude that there is credible Biblical evidence to prove that the Jewish Messiah *(Mashiach) Yeshua*/Jesus came to the earth around 4,000 years from the creation of Adam in the Garden of Eden *(Gan Eden)* exactly according to the traditional Jewish *(house of Judah)* expectation from the *Talmud Sanhedrin 97* that the Jewish Messiah *(Mashiach)* would come to the earth after 4,000 years of time at the beginning of the last 2,000-year period of time known as the days of the Messiah *(Yemot Mashiach)* within the 6,000-year period of time known as the *Olam Hazeh* (the present world/age).

Restoring the Two Houses of Israel

The Coming of the Messiah After 4,000 Years in Genesis 1:1

Earlier in this chapter, we studied the allusion to the 6,000 years of time of the *Olam Hazeh* (the present world/age) from Genesis *(Bereishit)* 1:1 by analyzing the six occurrences of the Hebrew letter, *Alef*, and relating these occurrences to each of the three 2,000 years of time within the 6,000-year period of the *Olam Hazeh* (the present world/age) by looking at this verse in the Hebrew language. Next, we will examine Genesis *(Bereishit)* 1:1 in Hebrew, once again, to see the allusion of the coming of the Jewish Messiah *(Mashiach) Yeshua*/Jesus after 4,000 years of time following the creation of Adam in the Garden of Eden *(Gan Eden)*. In Hebrew, Genesis *(Bereishit)* 1:1 is written:

> *"Bereishit b'rah elohim et hashamayim v'et ha'eretz."*

There are seven Hebrew words in Genesis *(Bereishit)* 1:1. If each word represents 1,000 years of time, the fourth word would represent 4,000 years of time. The fourth Hebrew word in Genesis *(Bereishit)* 1:1 is *"et."* The Hebrew word *"et"* is spelled with the first letter of the Hebrew alphabet, *Alef*, and the last letter of the Hebrew alphabet, *Tav*. In Revelation 1:5, 7-8 it is written:

> *"And from Jesus Christ, who is the faithful witness, and the first begotten of the dead, and the prince of the kings of the earth. Unto him that loved us, and washed us from our sins in his own blood ... behold he cometh with clouds; and every*

The 7,000-Year Plan of G-d

eye shall see him, and they also which pierced him: and all kindreds of the earth shall wail because of him. Even so, Amen. **I am Alpha and Omega,** *the beginning and the ending, saith the* LORD, *which is, and which was, and which is to come, the Almighty."*

Alpha and *Omega* are the first and last letters in the Greek alphabet. Being born in the land of Israel and being a Jew, the Jewish Messiah *(Mashiach) Yeshua*/Jesus would have spoken Hebrew. Translating Revelation 1:8 from Greek to Hebrew, the Jewish Messiah *(Mashiach) Yeshua*/Jesus said that He is the **Alef** and the **Tav**. In a literal *(Peshat)* sense, the Hebrew word *"et"* in Genesis *(Bereishit)* signifies a direct object in the grammar of the Hebrew language. However, since the Jewish Messiah *(Mashiach) Yeshua*/Jesus Himself told us in Revelation 1:8 that He is the **Alef** and the **Tav**, we can translate Genesis *(Bereishit)* 1:1 to read as follows:

> *"In the beginning* [Bereishit] *God created* [b'ray elohim] *et* [alef, tav ... the Jewish Messiah (Yeshua/Jesus)]..."

In traditional Jewish *(house of Judah)* thought, the Messiah was one of the seven things created before the **foundation of the world** *(Talmud, Pesachim 54)*. In Revelation 13:8, it is written:

> *"...the Lamb* [Yeshua/Jesus ... John 1:29] *slain from the* **foundation of the world**.*"*

In Zechariah 12:10, the Hebrew word *"et"* *(alef, tav)* appears, once again, in reference to the Jewish Messiah *(Mashiach) Yeshua*/Jesus as it is written:

"...and they shall look upon me **[et] [alef, tav]** *whom they have pierced, and they shall mourn for him, as one mourneth for his only son, and shall be in bitterness for him, as one that is in bitterness for his firstborn."*

The Timing of the Coming of the Jewish Messiah

The Jews *(house of Judah)* were taken captive to Babylon in three stages.

The first deportation took place in the fourth year of King Jehoiakim. This was the first year of the reign of King Nebuchadnezzar of Babylon (II Chronicles 36:5-7, Jeremiah *[Yermiyahu]* 25:1). This event happened around 605 BCE.

The second deportation took place in the seventh year of the reign of King Nebuchadnezzar of Babylon (Jeremiah *[Yermiyahu]* 52:28). At this time, 3,023 people were taken to Babylon. In the eighth year of the reign of King Nebuchadnezzar, Jerusalem *(Yerushalayim)* was besieged (II Kings *[Melachim]* 24:10-12) and 10,000 people were taken captive to Babylon (II Kings *[Melachim]* 24:14) along with King Jehoiachin. This event is in II Kings *[Melachim]* 24:8-14. It happened around 597 BCE. The city of Jerusalem *(Yerushalayim)* was besieged until the eleventh year of King Zedekiah's reign (II Kings *[Melachim]* 25:1-2).

The third deportation occurred in the nineteenth year of the reign of King Nebuchadnezzar. This would have

The 7,000-Year Plan of G-d

been in the eleventh year of King Zedekiah's reign. Jerusalem *(Yerushalayim)* and the Temple *(Beit HaMikdash)* were destroyed at this time (II Kings *[Melachim]* 25:8-11). This event happened in 586 BCE.

The G-d of Israel told the prophet Jeremiah *(Yermiyahu)* that the captivity in Babylon was for 70 years (Jeremiah *[Yermiyahu]* 25:1, 11). The 70 years of exile was due to Israel not keeping the seventh year sabbatical for the land (Leviticus *[Vayikra]* 25:1-4, II Chronicles 36:20-21).

At the end of 70 years of captivity in Babylon, Cyrus, King of Persia, will defeat Babylon and allow the Jews *(house of Judah)* to return to Jerusalem *(Yerushalayim)* to rebuild the Temple *(Beit HaMikdash)* (II Chronicles 36:22-23, Ezra 1:1-3, 5:13-14, Jeremiah *(Yermiyahu)* 29:10, Daniel 9:2).

Cyrus made the decree in 538 BCE. The building of the Temple began two years later (Ezra 3:8) in 536 BCE.

The Jews *(house of Judah)* did not return to the land of Israel as a corporate people after the 70 year Babylonian captivity. Only a remnant returned. Those Jews *(house of Judah)* who did return from the exile in Babylon did so in three stages.

The first stage was under Cyrus, King of Persia. This is found in Ezra chapters 1-6. The leaders of Israel were Zerubbabel and Jeshua (Ezra 3:2). But they had difficulties (Ezra 4:3-5, 5:2). The Temple *(Beit HaMikdash)* was rebuilt after a period of time (Ezra 6:14-15). Herod enlarged and beautified this Temple (John *[Yochanan]* 2:18-20).

Restoring the Two Houses of Israel

From the first deportation to the beginning of the rebuilding of the Temple *(Beit HaMikdash)* was 70 years (605 BCE - 536 BCE). The Temple *(Beit HaMikdash)* was destroyed in 586 BCE. The Temple *(Beit HaMikdash)* was completed in the sixth year of the reign of Darius, King of Persia (Ezra 6:14-15). This would make the completion taking place in 516 BCE. From the time the Temple *(Beit HaMikdash)* was destroyed to the time the Temple *(Beit HaMikdash)* was rebuilt was 70 years.

The second stage of return from captivity is in Ezra 7. This happened in the seventh year of the reign of Artaxerxes, King of Persia (Ezra 7:1-7). This would be in 458 BCE. As many as wished could go back from Babylon based upon the decree of King Artaxerxes in Ezra 7:11-13. The number who returned were 1,758 (Ezra 8:1-20).

The third stage of return from captivity is in the book of Nehemiah. The Jews *(house of Judah)* began to come back in the twentieth year of the reign of King Artaxerxes (Nehemiah 2:1). This would be in 444 BCE. Those people who returned are listed in Nehemiah 7. A decree given by King Artaxerxes to rebuild the Temple in the twentieth year is found in Nehemiah 2:1-8, 5:14.

From the commandment to restore and rebuild the Temple (Nehemiah 2:1-8, 5:14) which was 444 BCE until the death of the Jewish Messiah *(Mashiach) Yeshua/* Jesus was prophesied to be 69 weeks or 483 years. This prophecy was given to Daniel in Daniel 9:1-4, 20-26 as it is written:

> *"In the first year of Darius the son of Ahasuerus, of the seed of the Medes, which was made king over*

The 7,000-Year Plan of G-d

the realm of the Chaldeans; In the first year of his reign I Daniel understood by books the number of the years, whereof the word of the L<small>ORD</small> *came to Jeremiah the prophet, that he would accomplish seventy years in the desolations of Jerusalem. And I set my face unto the* L<small>ORD</small> *God, to seek by prayer and supplications, with fasting, and sackcloth, and ashes: And I prayed unto the* L<small>ORD</small> *my God, and made my confession, and said, O* L<small>ORD</small>*, the great and dreadful God, keeping the covenant and mercy to them that love him, and to them that keep his commandments ... And while I was speaking, and praying, and confessing my sin and the sin of my people Israel, and presenting my supplication before the* L<small>ORD</small> *my God for the holy mountain of my God; Yea, while I was speaking in prayer, even the man Gabriel, whom I had seen in the vision at the beginning, being caused to fly swiftly, touched me about the time of the evening oblation. And he informed me, and talked with me, and said, O Daniel, I am now come forth to give thee skill and understanding. At the beginning of thy supplications the commandment came forth, and I am come to show thee: for thou art greatly beloved: therefore understand the matter, and consider the vision. Seventy weeks* [490 years] *are determined upon thy people and upon thy holy city, to finish the transgression, and to make an end of sins, and to make reconciliation for iniquity, and to bring in everlasting righteousness, and to seal up the vision and prophecy, and to anoint the most Holy. Know therefore and understand, that* **from** *the going forth of* **the commandment to restore and to build Jerusalem unto the Messiah the**

Prince *shall be* **seven weeks, and threescore and two weeks [69 weeks]:** *the street shall be built again, and the wall, even in troublous times.* **And after threescore and two weeks shall Messiah be cut off**, *but not for himself: and the people of the prince that shall come shall destroy the city and the sanctuary; and the end thereof shall be with a flood, and unto the end of the war desolations are determined."*

The Jewish Messiah *(Mashiach) Yeshua*/Jesus was crucified and hung on a tree 69 weeks from the commandments to restore and rebuild Jerusalem *(Yerushalayim)* exactly according to the prophecy that was given to Daniel. When the Jewish Messiah *(Mashiach) Yeshua*/Jesus entered into the city of Jerusalem *(Yerushalayim)* during the final week of His life, He wept over the city because they did not know the *"day of their visitation."* In Luke 19:37-38, 41-44, it is written:

> *"And when he was come nigh, even now at the descent of the mount of Olives, the whole multitude of the disciples began to rejoice and praise God with a loud voice for all the mighty works that they had seen; Saying, Blessed be the King that cometh in the name of the* LORD*: peace in heaven, and glory in the highest ... And when he was come near, he beheld the city, and wept over it, Saying, If thou hadst known, even thou, at least in this thy day, the things which belong unto thy peace! but now they are hid from thine eyes. For the days shall come upon thee, that thine enemies shall cast a trench about thee, and compass thee round, and keep thee in on every side, and shall lay thee even*

with the ground, and thy children within thee; and they shall not leave in thee one stone upon another; because thou knewest not **the time of your visitation.***"*

Pictures of 6,000 and 7,000 Years In the Bible

The G-d of Israel has given us many spiritual pictures of His 7,000-year redemptive plan in the Bible. In this section of the chapter, we will examine some of these spiritual pictures that the G-d of Israel gave His people to understand the 6,000 years of the present age (*Olam Hazeh*) as well as the entire 7,000 years of His redemptive plan.

Noah and the Flood

Noah was **600 years old** when the flood (judgment) came upon the earth. In Genesis *(Bereishit)* 7:11-12, it is written:

> *"In the* **six hundredth year** *of Noah's life, in the second month, the seventeenth day of the month, the same day were all the fountains of the great deep broken up, and the windows of heaven were opened. And the rain was upon the earth forty days and forty nights."*

This is a spiritual picture/blueprint given to us by the G-d of Israel that after 6,000 years (the end of the *Olam Hazeh*), judgment (the tribulation/birth pangs of the Messiah/*Chevlai shel Mashiach*) will come upon the earth.

Restoring the Two Houses of Israel

Moses and Mount Sinai

After **six days**, Moses *(Moshe)* was called up to mount Sinai to be in the presence *(kivod)* of the G-d of Israel in the midst of the cloud. In Exodus *(Shemot)* 24:13-18 it is written:

> "…and Moses went up into the mount of God … and Moses went up into the mount, and a cloud covered the mount. And the glory of the LORD abode upon mount Sinai, and the cloud covered it **six days**: and the seventh day he called unto Moses out of the midst of the cloud … And Moses went into the midst of the cloud, and gat him up into the mount: and Moses was in the mount forty days and forty nights."

This is a spiritual picture/blueprint given to us by the G-d of Israel that after 6,000 years (the end of the *Olam Hazeh*), the glory *(kivod)* of the G-d of Israel will be upon the Bride of the Jewish Messiah *(Mashiach) Yeshua*/Jesus and she will be caught up in the clouds to be in the presence of the G-d of Israel (Daniel 7:13, Matthew 24:30, Hebrews 12:1, Revelation 1:5,7).

In I Thessalonians 4:16-17 it is written:

> "For the LORD himself shall descend from heaven with a shout, with the voice of the archangel, and with the trump [shofar] of God; and the dead in Christ shall rise first: Then we which are alive and remain shall be caught up together with them in the clouds to meet the LORD in the air: and so shall we ever be with the LORD."

The 7,000-Year Plan of G-d

It is traditional Jewish thought *(house of Judah)* that two themes associated with the Feast of Trumpets *(Rosh HaShanah)* is the resurrection of the dead and the blowing of the last trump. Therefore, I Thessalonians 4:16-17 is an allusion to the resurrection of the dead which will take place after 6,000 years of time on the Feast of Trumpets *(Rosh HaShanah)*. For a more detailed study of the Biblical Festivals and how the G-d of Israel gave the Biblical Festivals in Leviticus *(Vayikra)* 23 to teach about the first and second coming of the Jewish Messiah *(Mashiach)* Yeshua/Jesus and our personal relationship *(halacha)* with Him, I would encourage you to read my book, *The Seven Festivals of the Messiah*.

The Disciples and the Transfiguration

After **six days**, the Jewish Messiah *(Mashiach)* Yeshua/Jesus took Peter *(Kefa)*, James *(Ya'acov)*, and John *(Yochanan)* up into a high mountain and was transfigured before them. In Matthew *(Mattityahu)* 17:1-4, it is written:

> *"And after* **six days** *Jesus taketh Peter, James, and John his brother, and bringeth them up into a high mountain apart, and was transfigured before them: and his face did shine as the sun, and his raiment was white as the light. And, behold, there appeared unto them Moses and Elijah talking with him. Then answered Peter, and said unto Jesus,* LORD *it is good for us to be here: if thou wilt, let us make here three tabernacles; one for thee, and one for Moses, and one for Elijah."*

Restoring the Two Houses of Israel

Once again, this is a spiritual picture/blueprint given to us by the G-d of Israel that after 6,000 years (the end of the *Olam Hazeh*), there will be the resurrection of the dead and the Bride of the Jewish Messiah *(Mashiach) Yeshua*/Jesus will rule and reign with Him during the Messianic Age *(Athid Lavo)*. The Feast of Tabernacles *(Sukkot)* is associated with the Messianic Age. In Revelation 5:10, it is written:

> *"And hast made us unto our God kings and priests: and we shall reign on the earth."*

The Resurrection of Lazarus

The resurrection of Lazarus in John *(Yochanan)* 11 took place over **six days**.

1. Lazarus is sick for two days (John 11:1-6).
2. Lazarus is dead for four days (John 11:14, 39).
3. *Yeshua*/Jesus resurrects Lazarus after these six days (John 11:40-44).

One again, this is a spiritual picture/blueprint given to us by the G-d of Israel that after 6,000 years (the end of the *Olam Hazeh*), there will be the resurrection of the dead. This last 1,000-year period is the *"final day"* (Psalm 90:4, II Peter 3:8) of the 7,000-year plan of the G-d of Israel. Martha, the sister of Lazarus, spoke to the Jewish Messiah *(Mashiach) Yeshua*/Jesus stating that she knew that the resurrection of the dead would take place in the *"last day."* In John *(Yochanan)* 11:21-27 it is written:

> *"Then said Martha unto Jesus,* Lord, *if thou hadst been here, my brother had not died. But I know,*

The 7,000-Year Plan of G-d

that even now, whatsoever thou wilt ask of God, God will give it thee. Jesus saith unto her, Thy brother shall rise again. Martha saith unto him, I know that he shall **rise again** *in the* **resurrection at the last day***. Jesus said unto her, I am the resurrection, and the life: he that believeth in me, though he were dead, yet shall he live: And whosoever liveths and believeth in me shall never die. Believest thou this? She saith unto him, Yea,* LORD*: I believe that thou art the Christ, the Son of God, which should come into the world."*

Slaves Worked for Six Years

The G-d of Israel declared in the Torah that a Hebrew servant was to work for **six years** and on the seventh year he was to be freed. In Exodus *(Shemot)* 21:2, it is written:

"If thou buy a Hebrew servant, six years he shall serve: and in the seventh he shall go out free for nothing."

This is a spiritual picture/blueprint given to us by the G-d of Israel that He ordained that the punishment for Adam's sin in the Garden of Eden *(Gan Eden)* was that man would be a slave to the earth for 6,000 years (until the end of the *Olam Hazeh*). Afterward, man would be freed from his bondage to the earth and would enjoy the peace *(shalom)* of the Messianic Age *(Athid Lavo)*. Adam's bondage to the earth as punishment by the G-d of Israel because of his sin in the Garden of Eden *(Gan Eden)* is given to us in Genesis *(Bereishit)* 3:17-19 as it is written:

"And unto Adam he said, Because thou hast hearkened unto the voice of thy wife, and hast eaten of

> the tree, of which I commanded thee, saying, thou shalt not eat of it: cursed is the ground for thy sake; in sorrow shalt thou eat of it all the days of thy life; Thorns also and thistles shall it bring forth to thee; and thou shalt eat the herb of the field; In the sweat of thy face shalt thou eat bread, till thou return unto the ground; for out of it wast thou taken: for dust thou art, and unto dust shalt thou return."

This is also a spiritual picture/blueprint of mankind being under the bondage of sin (John 8:34, Romans 6:16) and the slavery of Satan's kingdom for 6,000 years because Adam sinned and yielded to the temptation of the serpent (*Nachash*) in the Garden of Eden *(Gan Eden)*. Afterward, man would be free from the slavery of Satan's kingdom (but not sin) during the Messianic Age *(Athid Lavo)* when Satan would be bound (Revelation 20:2) and the Jewish Messiah *(Mashiach) Yeshua*/Jesus would rule and reign for 1,000 years (Revelation 20:4) teaching the Torah to the nations from Jerusalem *(Yerushalayim)*. (Isaiah *[Yeshayahu]* 2:2-4).

The Hiding of King Joash

King Joash was hidden in the Temple *(Beit HaMikdash)* for **six years**. At the beginning of the seventh year, King Joash was crowned King over Israel. In II Kings *(Melachim)* 11:1-4, 21 it is written:

> "And when Athaliah the mother of Ahaziah saw that her son was dead, she arose and destroyed all the seed royal. But Jehosheba, the daughter of king Joram, sister of Ahaziah, took Joash the son of

The 7,000-Year Plan of G-d

Ahaziah, and stole him from among the king's sons which were slain; and they hid him, even him and his nurse, in the bedchamber from Athaliah, so that he was not slain. And he was with her **hid in the house of the** LORD **six years***. And Athaliah did reign over the land. And the seventh year Jehoiada sent and fetched the rulers over hundreds, with the captains and the guard, and brought them to him into the house of the* LORD*, and made a covenant with them, and took an oath of them in the house of the* LORD*, and showed them the king's son ... seven years old was Jehoash when he began to reign."*

In this story, King Joash is a type of the Jewish Messiah *(Mashiach) Yeshua*/Jesus. In traditional Jewish thought *(house of Judah)*, the Messiah *(Mashiach)* is one of the seven things created before the creation of the world and the timing of his coming or the redemption is also one of the seven things which are hidden from man *(Talmud, Pesachim 54)*. Therefore, King Joash is a spiritual picture / blueprint given to us by the G-d of Israel to teach us that the Jewish Messiah *(Mashiach) Yeshua*/Jesus would be hid from ruling and reigning on the earth (physically) as King (Zechariah 14:9) for 6,000 years (the end of the *Olam Hazeh*).

At the end of 6,000 years *(Olam Hazeh)*, the Jewish Messiah *(Mashiach) Yeshua*/Jesus will be crowned King on the Feast of Trumpets (*Rosh HaShanah*). In traditional Jewish thought *(house of Judah)*, this is the coronation day of the King. The coronation of the Jewish Messiah *(Mashiach) Yeshua*/Jesus on the Feast of Trumpets *(Rosh*

HaShanah) to rule and reign in righteousness as King over all the earth is revealed to us in Revelation 5. In Revelation 5:1-5 it is written:

> *"And I saw in the right hand of him that sat on the throne a book written within and on the backside, sealed with seven seals. And I saw a strong angel proclaiming with a loud voice, Who is worthy to open the book, and to loose the seals thereof? And no man in heaven nor in earth, neither under the earth, was able to open the book, neither to look thereon. And I wept much, because no man was found worthy to open and to read the book, neither to look thereon. And one of the elders saith unto me, Weep not: behold,* **the Lion of the tribe of Juda, the Root of David***, hath prevailed to open the book, and to loose the seven seals thereof."*

The Jewish Messiah *(Mashiach) Yeshua*/Jesus is the King of kings and the L-RD of lords (Zechariah 14:9, Philippians 2:9-11, Revelation 19:11-16).

The Steps to King Solomon's Throne

King Soloman *(Shlomo)* had **six steps** to his throne and the seventh step was his throne. In II Chronicles 9:18 it is written:

> *"And there were* **six steps** *to the throne, with a footstool of gold, which were fastened to the throne, and stays on each side of the sitting place, and two lions standing by the stays."*

The 7,000-Year Plan of G-d

This is a spiritual picture/blueprint given to us by the G-d of Israel that mankind is climbing a stairway of six steps (6,000 years of time known as the *Olam Hazeh*) until we reach that seventh step (the Messianic Age/*Athid Lavo*) when the Jewish Messiah *(Mashiach) Yeshua*/Jesus will be crowned King of kings and L-RD of lords (Zechariah 14:9, Revelation 19:11-16).

King Solomon Is a Type of the Messiah

King Solomon is a type of the Jewish Messiah *(Mashiach) Yeshua*/Jesus.

1. Solomon *(Shlomo)* sat upon the throne of his father David (I Kings *[Melachim]* 2:12) and was given the throne of his father David (I Kings *[Melachim]* 3:6-7).

   The Jewish Messiah *(Mashiach) Yeshua*/Jesus sat upon the throne of His father David and He was given the throne of His father David (Luke 1:30-32, Acts 2:29-30).

2. Solomon's *(Shlomo)* kingdom was established greatly (I Kings *[Melachim]* 2:12) and the throne of David shall be established before the L-RD forever (I Kings *[Melachim]* 2:45).

   The Jewish Messiah *(Mashiach) Yeshua*/Jesus' kingdom shall have no end (Isaiah *[Yeshayahu]* 9:6-7, Luke 1:33).

3. Solomon reigned over all the kingdoms and they served Solomon all the days of his life (I Kings *[Melachim]* 4:21).

Restoring the Two Houses of Israel

The Jewish Messiah *(Mashiach) Yeshua*/Jesus will rule over all the kingdoms and they shall serve Him forever (Daniel 2:44, 7:14, 27).

4. Solomon *(Shlomo)* is the Strong's word 8010 in the Hebrew Concordance which means *"Peaceful."* Solomon *(Shlomo)* which is the Strong's word 8010 comes from the Strong's word 7965 which is the Hebrew word *shalom* which means *"peace."*

The Jewish Messiah *(Mashiach) Yeshua*/Jesus is called the *"Prince of Peace"* (Isaiah *[Yeshayahu]* 9:6).

5. Solomon *(Shlomo)* was king in the midst of his people (I Kings *[Melachim]* 3:7-8).

The Jewish Messiah *(Mashiach) Yeshua*/Jesus will be King in the midst of His people (Isaiah *[Yeshayahu]* 12:6 = Psalm *[Tehillim]* 89:18, Zechariah 2:10-11).

6. Solomon *(Shlomo)* was the wisest of earthly kings (I Kings *[Melachim]* 3:5, 9-13, 4:29-31, 10:23, II Chronicles 9:22-23).

The Jewish Messiah *(Mashiach) Yeshua*/Jesus is the wisdom of the G-d of Israel (I Corinthians 1:24, Colossians 2:2-3).

7. Solomon *(Shlomo)* built the Temple *(Beit HaMikdash)* and he had rest on every side (I Kings *[Melachim]* 5:2-4, 6:9, 14).

The 7,000-Year Plan of G-d

The Jewish Messiah *(Mashiach) Yeshua*/Jesus will build the Temple *(Beit HaMikdash)* of the Messianic Age *(Athid Lavo)* and will have rest on every side (Zechariah 6:12-13). The Branch (Zechariah 6:12) is a term for the Jewish Messiah *(Mashiach) Yeshua*/Jesus (Isaiah *[Yeshayahu]* 11:1, 10).

8. Solomon *(Shlomo)* was given wisdom and understanding to righteously judge good and evil. (I Kings *(Melachim)* 3:9-13).

The Jewish Messiah *(Mashiach) Yeshua*/Jesus has wisdom and understanding to righteously judge good and evil. (Isaiah *[Yeshayahu]* 11:1-6).

9. The whole earth sought Solomon *(Shlomo)* to hear his wisdom (I Kings *[Melachim]* 10:24).

The whole earth will speak of the wisdom of the Jewish Messiah *(Mashiach) Yeshua*/Jesus during the Messianic Age. (Psalm *[Tehillim]* 145:1, 11-13).

10. During the reign of Solomon *(Shlomo)*, every man was *"under his vine and fig tree"* (I Kings *[Melachim]* 4:25).

"Under his vine and under his fig tree" is a Jewish *"idiom"* for the 1,000-year Messianic Age *(Athid Lavo)*.

During the reign of the Jewish Messiah *(Mashiach) Yeshua*/Jesus during the Messianic Age *(Athid Lavo)* every man will sit *"under his vine and under his fig tree"* (Micah 4:3-4, John 1:47-49).

Restoring the Two Houses of Israel

The Marriage in Cana of Galilee

The book of John *(Yochanan)* beginning in John 1:19 through John 2:1 will outline events which will happen over seven days of time.

1. John 1:19 = Day 1
2. John 1:29 = Day 2
3. John 1:35 = Day 3
4. John 1:43 = Day 4

   After the fourth day, the Jewish Messiah *(Mashiach) Yeshua*/Jesus will go forth into Galilee. Galilee is the Strong's word 1551 in the Hebrew dictionary. The word Galilee in Hebrew means *"a circle."* A circle is a synonym for heaven. These four days are a spiritual picture/blueprint given to us by the G-d of Israel that the Jewish Messiah *(Mashiach) Yeshua*/Jesus would come to the earth after being in heaven/circle *(Olam Haba)* 4,000 years from the creation of Adam in the Garden of Eden *(Gan Eden)*.

5. John 2:1 describes a marriage in Cana of Galilee on the third day. This third day (after the four previous days) is the seventh day. On this day, there is a wedding.

   This is a spiritual picture/blueprint given to us by the G-d of Israel that after 6,000 years of time (the end of the *Olam Hazeh*) He will enter into the fullness of the marriage with His people when the Jewish Messiah *(Mashiach) Yeshua*/Jesus will rule and reign with His Bride during the Messianic Age *(Athid Lavo)*. In traditional Jewish thought *(house of Judah)*, the Feast of Trumpets *(Rosh HaShanah)* is the day of the fullness of the wedding of the G-d of Israel with His people.

The 7,000-Year Plan of G-d
Joshua Crossing the Jordan River

The crossing of the Jordan river by the children of Israel is a spiritual picture/blueprint of the first 6,000 years of time known as the *Olam Hazeh* (the present age).

1. Joshua 3:1 = Day 1
2. Joshua 3:2 = After three days (Day 4), the children of Israel cross the Jordan river.

   In this Scripture passage, Joshua *(Yehoshua)* is a type of the Jewish Messiah *(Mashiach) Yeshua*/Jesus. Joshua is the Strong's word 3091 in the Hebrew dictionary. Jesus is the Strong's word 2424 in the Greek dictionary of the New Testament *(Brit Hadashah)* and corresponds to the Hebrew name Joshua *(Yehoshua)*.

   Joshua became the leader of the children of Israel after the death of Moses *(Moshe)* and led G-d's chosen people into the Promised Land. These four days are a spiritual picture/blueprint given to us by the G-d of Israel of the Jewish Messiah *(Mashiach) Yeshua*/Jesus coming to the earth 4,000 years after the creation of Adam in the Garden of Eden *(Gan Eden)* to lead all those who would put their faith, trust and confidence *(emunah)* in Him into the Promised Land of the Messianic Kingdom.

3. Joshua 3:3-4. There is a space of 2,000 cubits between the ark of the covenant and the children of Israel.

   These 2,000 cubits are a spiritual picture/blueprint given to us by the G-d of Israel that the

Restoring the Two Houses of Israel

Jewish nation *(house of Judah)* as a corporate people would remove themselves from the G-d of Israel's spiritual ark of the covenant (the Jewish Messiah *[Mashiach] Yeshua*/Jesus) for 2,000 years following the first coming of *Yeshua*/Jesus as the suffering Messiah *(Mashiach)* known as *Messiah ben Yosef* (Joseph). At the end of 6,000 years of time *(Olam Hazeh)*, the Jewish people as a corporate nation will accept *Yeshua*/Jesus as their Messiah *(Mashiach)*. In Hosea *(Hoshea)* 5:15, 6:1-3 it is written:

> *"I will go and return to my place, till they acknowledge their offense, and seek my face: in their affliction they will seek me early. Come and let us return unto the* LORD*: for he hath torn, and he will heal us; he hath smitten, and he will bind us up. After two days* [2,000 years from the Messiah's first coming] *will he revive us: in the third day* [the Messianic Age/Athid Lavo] *he will raise us up, and we shall live in his sight. Then shall we know, if we follow on to know the* LORD*: his going forth is prepared as the morning; and he shall come unto us as the rain, as the latter and former rain unto the earth."*

4. Joshua 3:5. Sanctify yourselves for TOMORROW the L-RD will do wonders among you.

Joshua 3:7. The LORD said to Joshua, THIS DAY will I begin to magnify thee in the sight of all of Israel.

The TOMORROW and the THIS DAY = Four days + 2,000 cubits or 6,000 years.

The 7,000-Year Plan of G-d

After 6,000 years (*Olam Hazeh* / the present age), the L-RD will magnify the sight of the Jewish Messiah *(Mashiach) Yeshua*/Jesus in the sight of all of Israel during the time of Jacob's *(Ya'acov's* trouble — Jeremiah *[Yermiyahu]* 30:7) tribulation/birth pangs of the Messiah *(Chevlai shel Mashiach)*.

The Birth of Jacob

The birth of Jacob *(Ya'acov)* is a spiritual picture/blueprint of 6,000 years *(Olam Hazeh)*. Jacob *(Ya'acov)* is Israel (Genesis *[Bereishit]* 32:27-28)

1. Isaac *(Yitzchak)* is 40 years old when he marries Rebekah *(Rivkah)* (Genesis *[Bereishit]* 25:20).

   Isaac *(Yitzchak)* is a type of the Jewish Messiah *(Mashiach) Yeshua*/Jesus. These 40 years are a spiritual picture/blueprint that the Jewish Messiah *(Mashiach) Yeshua*/Jesus will come to the earth at His first coming as the suffering Messiah *(Mashiach)* known as *Messiah ben Yosef* (Joseph).

2. Rebekah *(Rivkah)* will be barren for 20 years before Jacob (Israel) is born (Genesis *[Bereishit]* 25:21,26).

   After 20 years (2,000 years), Rebekah *(Rivkah)* bears Jacob *(Ya'acov)*. This is a spiritual picture/blueprint given to us by the G-d of Israel that 2,000 years following the first coming of the Jewish Messiah *(Mashiach) Yeshua*/Jesus as the suffering Messiah known to the Jewish people *(house of Judah)* as *Messiah ben Yosef* (Joseph), the

Restoring the Two Houses of Israel

Jewish people *(house of Judah)* as a corporate nation will accept the Jewish Messiah *(Mashiach) Yeshua*/Jesus as their Messiah.

The Children of Jacob by Leah

In Genesis *(Bereishit)* 29, Leah has seven children. This is a spiritual picture/blueprint given to us by the G-d of Israel of His 7,000-year redemptive plan from the creation of Adam in the Garden of Eden *(Gan Eden)* to the end of the Messianic Age *(Athid Lavo)*.

1. The first son is Reuben (Genesis *[Bereishit]* 29:32). Reuben is the Strong's word 7205 which comes from two Hebrew words. These two Hebrew words are the Strong's word 7200 which means *"to see"* and the Strong's word 1121 which means *"a son."* So, Reuben means *"to see a son."*

2. The second son is Simeon (Genesis *[Bereishit]* 29:33). Simeon is the Strong's word 8095 in the Hebrew dictionary and comes from the Strong's word 8085 which is the Hebrew word *"Shema"* which means *"to hear."* So, the name Simeon means *"hearing."*

3. The third son is Levi (Genesis *[Bereishit]* 29:34). Levi is the Strong's word 3878 in the Hebrew dictionary and comes from the Strong's word 3867 which is the Hebrew word *"Lavah"* which means *"to join."* So, the name Levi means *"to join."*

4. The fourth son is Judah (Genesis *[Bereishit]* 29:35). Judah is the Strong's word 3063 which is the Hebrew word *"Yehudah"* which means *"to praise."*

The 7,000-Year Plan of G-d

Judah *(Yehudah)* is the fourth son of Leah. It was prophesied by the G-d of Israel though Jacob *(Ya'acov)* that the scepter (authority to rule and reign) would not depart from Judah and that the Jewish Messiah *(Mashiach)* would be from the tribe of Judah. In Genesis *(Bereishit)* 49:10 it is written:

> *"The scepter shall not depart from Judah, nor a lawgiver from between his feet, until Shiloh* [a term for the Jewish Messiah] *come; and unto him shall the gathering of the people be."*

Even as Judah *(Yehudah)* was the fourth son of Leah, the Jewish Messiah *(Mashiach) Yeshua*/Jesus came to the earth 4,000 years from the creation of Adam in the Garden of Eden *(Gan Eden)* and was born from the *tribe of Judah* (Hebrews 7:14, Revelation 5:5). After four children, Leah's womb stops (Genesis *[Bereishit]* 29:35). This is a spiritual picture/blueprint given to us by the G-d of Israel that the Jewish people *(house of Judah)* would not receive the Jewish Messiah *(Mashiach) Yeshua*/Jesus as a corporate nation during His first coming as the suffering Messiah known as *Messiah ben Yosef* (Joseph) following the creation of Adam in the Garden of Eden *(Gan Eden)*.

5. The fifth son is Issachar (Genesis *[Bereishit]* 30:18). Issachar is the Strong's word 3485 in the Hebrew dictionary. Issachar comes from the Strong's word 7939 which means *"hire or wages."* So, Issachar means *"my hiring or my wages."*

This is a spiritual picture/blueprint given to us by the G-d of Israel that following the first coming of the Jewish Messiah *(Mashiach) Yeshua/* Jesus as the suffering Messiah known as *Messiah ben Yosef* (Joseph) and the destruction of the Temple *(Beit HaMikdash)* that the Jewish people *(house of Judah)* would be scattered among the nations as a *"hired"* people.

6. The sixth son is Zebulun (Genesis *[Bereishit]* 30:19-20). Zebulun is the Strong's word 2074 in the Hebrew dictionary. Zebulun comes from the Strong's word 2082 which means *"to dwell."* So, Zebulun means *"dwelling."*

This is a spiritual prophetic/blueprint given to us by the G-d of Israel that after 6,000 years of time *(Olam Hazeh/*the present age) He will dwell with His people through the Jewish Messiah *(Mashiach) Yeshua/*Jesus during the Messianic Age *(Athid Lavo).*

7. The seventh child is a daughter named Dinah (Genesis *[Bereishit]* 30:21). Dinah is the Strong's word 1783. It is related to the Strong's word 1779 which is *"Din"* which means *"to judge."* So, Dinah means *"judge."*

Dinah (female) is a spiritual picture/blueprint given to us by the G-d of Israel that after 6,000 years of time *(Olam Hazeh)* the Jewish Messiah *(Mashiach) Yeshua/*Jesus will live and dwell with His Bride (female) during the Messianic Age *(Athid Lavo)* ruling and reigning with her judging the nations. In I Corinthians 6:2-3 it is written:

The 7,000-Year Plan of G-d

"Do ye not know that the saints shall judge the world? ... know ye not that we shall judge angels? how much more things that pertain to this life?"

In Revelation 5:10 it is written:

"And hast made us unto our God kings and priests: and we shall reign on the earth."

In Revelation 20:4 it is written:

"And I saw thrones, and they sat upon them, and judgment was given unto them: and I saw the souls of them that were beheaded for the witness of Jesus, and for the word of God, and which had not worshiped the beast, neither his image, neither had received his mark upon their foreheads, or in their hands; and they lived and reigned with Christ a thousand years."

Chapter Summary

In this chapter, we studied the 7,000-year redemptive plan of the G-d of Israel. In doing so, we were able to understand that the G-d of Israel gave the seven days of creation in the book of Genesis *(Bereishit)* as a prophetic foreshadowing of His 7,000-year plan for man following the creation of Adam in the Garden of Eden *(Gan Eden)*. Each day in creation represents 1,000 years of time. The seventh day of creation *(Sabbath)* is a prophetic picture/blueprint of the 1,000-year Messianic Age *(Athid Lavo)*.

These 7,000 years of time were outlined for us in Genesis *(Bereishit)* 1:1 with the six occurrences of the Hebrew letter, *Alef*. The fourth word in Hebrew in Genesis *(Bereishit)* 1:1 is the Hebrew word *(Alef, Tav)* which spiritually represents the Jewish Messiah *(Mashiach) Yeshu*a/Jesus. This fourth letter is also a spiritual picture/blueprint given to us by the G-d of Israel that the Jewish Messiah *(Mashiach) Yeshua*/Jesus would come to the earth as the suffering Messiah known as *Messiah ben Yosef* (Joseph) 4,000 years after the creation of Adam and Eve.

We examined the Biblical evidence through genealogy and chronology that the Jewish Messiah *(Mashiach) Yeshua*/Jesus came to the earth around 4,000 years following the creation of Adam in the Garden of Eden *(Gan Eden)*. Finally, we studied Biblical pictures/blueprints *(sod*/deeper meaning) of the 7,000-year prophetic plan of the G-d of Israel using various examples in Scripture.

In order for full restoration to come to both the *house of Judah* (Judaism) and the *house of Israel* (Christianity), Christianity *(house of Israel)* must begin to replace their traditional prophetic understanding of time based upon dispensationalism *(age of law/age of grace)* with the 7,000-year redemptive plan of the G-d of Israel. Meanwhile, the *house of Judah* (Judaism) needs to realize that the Jewish Messiah *(Mashiach) Yeshua*/Jesus came to the earth 4,000 years following the creation of Adam in the Garden of Eden *(Gan Eden)* as the suffering Messiah known as *Messiah ben Yosef* (Joseph) at the exact time when they were expecting the G-d of Israel to send the Jewish Messiah *(Mashiach)*.

May the G-d of Israel bring redemption, restoration, reconciliation and unity to both houses of Israel speedily in our days. Amen !!

Chapter 6

Yeshua, Our Jewish Messiah

Yeshua/Jesus was/is a Jew. He was born a Jew, He lived as a Jew and He died a Jew. While most members from the *house of Israel* (Christianity) recognize that *Yeshua*/Jesus was Jewish, they do not worship the G-d of Israel by identifying with the Jewishness of the Messiah. The roots of faith *(emunah)* in *Yeshua*/Jesus as the Jewish Messiah is biblical Judaism. In fact, the early believers in *Yeshua*/Jesus as Messiah *(Mashiach)* were considered a sect of Judaism *(house of Judah)* (Acts 28:22). On the other hand, many members from the *house of Judah* (Judaism) do not recognize *Yeshua*/Jesus as being a Jew. For those Jews *(house of Judah)* who do recognize that *Yeshua*/Jesus was Jewish, they do not realize that *Yeshua*/Jesus was a Torah observant Jew. Therefore, both houses of Israel need to identify in a greater measure with the Jewishness of the Jewish Messiah *(Mashiach) Yeshua*/Jesus.

In this chapter, we will examine the Jewishness of *Yeshua*/Jesus. We will discover that *Yeshua*/Jesus was born a Jew, He lived His life as a Torah observant Jew and He died a Jew. Furthermore, when He returns to the earth to rule and reign for 1,000 years during the Messianic Age *(Athid Lavo)*, He will do so as a Torah observant Jew teaching the Torah of the G-d of Israel to the nations of the world (Isaiah *[Yeshayahu]* 2:2-4). In this chapter, we will study the Jewishness of the life of *Yeshua*/Jesus. We will be mainly focusing on His life as recorded for us in the New Testament *(Brit Hadashah)* books of Matthew *(Mattityahu)*, Mark, Luke and John *(Yochanan)*. In doing so, may both houses of Israel (Judaism and Christianity) recognize and identify with the Jewishness of *Yeshua*/Jesus and realize that He is our **JEWISH** Messiah *(Mashiach)*.

Our Jewish Messiah: Yeshua/Jesus Was Born a Jew

Yeshua/Jesus was born a Jew. He was born of the seed of David and in the city of David which is called Bethlehem. When *Yeshua*/Jesus was born, His parents were betrothed to each other. Betrothal is the first of two stages of a biblical Jewish marriage. *Yeshua*/Jesus was circumcised the eighth day *(brit milah)* as is the custom for the birth of a Jewish boy. The name of Jesus in Hebrew is *Yeshua*. *Yeshua* is the Hebrew word which means salvation. *Yeshua*/Jesus was born a Jew. *Yeshua*/Jesus was born to be the Savior of the world and the Messiah *(Mashiach)* of both houses of Israel (Judaism and Christianity).

Yeshua/Jesus Was Born a Jew From the Seed of David

Yeshua/Jesus was born a Jew. Traditional Judaism *(house of Judah)* believes that the Jewish Messiah *(Mashiach)* will be born from the seed of David. The

Yeshua, Our Jewish Messiah

house of Israel (Christianity) also believes that the Jewish Messiah *(Mashiach)* will be born from the seed of David. In I Chronicles 17:7-14 it is written:

> *"Now therefore thus shalt thou say unto my servant David, Thus saith the L*ORD *of hosts, I took thee from the sheepcote, even from following the sheep, that thou shouldest be ruler over my people Israel: And I have been with thee whithersoever thou hast walked, and have cut off all thine enemies from before thee, and have made thee a name like the name of the great men that are in the earth. Also I will ordain a place for my people Israel, and will plant them, and they shall dwell in their place, and shall be moved no more: neither shall the children of wickedness waste them any more, as at the beginning, And since the time that I commanded judges to be over my people Israel. Moreover I will subdue all thine enemies. Furthermore I tell thee that the L*ORD *will build thee an house. And it shall come to pass, when thy days be expired that thou must go to be with thy fathers, that I will raise up thy seed after thee, which shall be of thy sons; and I will establish his kingdom. He shall build me an house, and I will establish his throne forever. I will be his father, and he shall be my son: and I will not take my mercy away from him, as I took it from him that was before thee: But I will settle him in mine house and in my kingdom forever: and his throne shall be established forevermore."*

The G-d of Israel's promise to David is repeated in Psalm *(Tehillim)* 89:20, 34-37 as it is written:

Restoring the Two Houses of Israel

"I have found David my servant; with my holy oil have I anointed him ... my covenant will I not break, nor alter the thing that is gone out of my lips. Once have I sworn by my holiness that I will not lie unto David. His seed shall endure forever, and his throne as the sun before me. It shall be established forever as the moon, and as a faithful witness in heaven. Selah."

The Jewish Messiah *(Mashiach) Yeshua*/Jesus was born of the seed of David according to the flesh. In Romans 1:3, it is written:

"Concerning his Son **Jesus Christ our** L<small>ORD</small>*, which was made of the* **seed of David** *according to the flesh"*

In Hebrew 7:14 it is written:

"For it is evident that our L<small>ORD</small> *sprang out of Judah..."*

In Revelation 5:5, it is written:

"And one of the elders saith unto me, Weep not: behold, the **Lion of the tribe of Juda***, the* **Root of David***, hath prevailed to open the book..."*

When *Yeshua*/Jesus was born, the angel Gabriel spoke to Mary *(Miryam)*, the Jewish mother of *Yeshua*/Jesus and said in Luke 1:30-33 as it is written:

"And the angel said unto her, Fear not, **Mary***: for thou hast found favor with God. And, behold, thou*

Yeshua, Our Jewish Messiah

shalt conceive in thy womb, and **bring forth a son,** *and shalt call his name* **JESUS.** *He shall be great, and shall be called the Son of the Highest:* **and the** L<small>ORD</small> **God shall give unto him the throne of his father David:** *And he shall reign over the house of Jacob forever; and of his kingdom there shall be no end."*

Jesus in Hebrew Means Salvation

In Luke 1:31, the angel Gabriel told Mary *(Miryam)* that the Messiah's name would be Jesus. The name Jesus in Hebrew is *Yeshua* which means salvation. In Hebrew thought, a name is given to a person to represent a person's character, identity, purpose or destiny. A name represents who a person is to be. One of the roles of the Jewish Messiah *(Mashiach)* is to redeem the *house of Jacob* and save the world from their sins. Therefore, the Jewish Messiah *(Mashiach)* was named *Yeshua* which means in Hebrew *"salvation"* because the Messiah would save His people from their sins. In Matthew *(Mattityahu)* 1:21 it is written:

> *"And she shall bring forth a son, and thou shalt call his name JESUS* **[Yeshua]***: for he shall* **save** *his people from their sins"*

The Importance of a Name in Hebraic Thought

A Hebrew name is important because a name in Hebrew thought represents a person's character, identity, purpose or destiny. The angel Gabriel gave instructions to Mary *(Miryam)* to name the Jewish Messiah, *Yeshua/* salvation because his character, identity, purpose and destiny in the heart of the G-d of Israel is to save His people from their sins. Next, we will examine the names of the patriarch's, Abraham *(Avraham)*, Isaac *(Yitzchak)* and Jacob *(Ya'acov)* to understand in a greater way how a name in Hebraic thought represents a person's character, identity, purpose or destiny.

Abraham in Hebrew Means Father of a Multitude

Abram is the Strong's word 87 in the *Strong's Hebrew Concordance*. It is the Hebrew word *Avram*. *Avram* (Abram) in Hebrew means *"exalted Father."* When the G-d of Israel made a covenant with Abram *(Avram)*, He changed Abram's name to Abraham *(Avraham)*. Abraham is the Strong's word 85 which in Hebrew means *"father of a multitude."* When He changed Abraham's name, the G-d of Israel added the Hebrew letter, *hay* ("h"), to Abraham's name. The Hebrew letter, *hay* ("h"), represents the *breath and life* of the G-d of Israel.

By making a covenant with Abraham *(Avraham)* and changing his name, the G-d of Israel was communicating to Abraham *(Avraham)* that He was going to change the character, identity, purpose and destiny of Abraham and his descendents. The G-d of Israel was going to do this by adding His *breath and life* (the Hebrew letter, *hay*, ["h"]) to the life of Abraham *(Avraham)* and make him a *"father of a multitude."* In Genesis *(Bereishit)* 17:1-7 it is written:

Yeshua, Our Jewish Messiah

"And when Abram was ninety years old and nine, the LORD *appeared to Abram, and said unto him, I am the Almighty God; walk before me, and be thou perfect. And I will make my covenant between me and thee, and will multiply thee exceedingly ... As for me, behold, my covenant is with thee, and thou shalt be* **a father of many nations** [Avraham in Hebrew]. *Neither shall thy name any more be called Abram* [which means 'exalted father' in Hebrew] *but thy name shall be Abraham;* [which means 'father of a multitude' in Hebrew] for **a father of many nations** *have I made thee. And I will make thee exceedingly fruitful, and I will make nations of thee, and kings shall come out of thee. And I will establish my covenant between me and thee and thy seed after thee in their generations for an everlasting covenant, to be a God unto thee and to thy seed after thee."*

Isaac in Hebrew Means Laughter

Isaac *(Yitzchak)* is the son of Abraham *(Avraham)* and Sarah. Isaac is the Strong's word 3327 and is the Hebrew word *Yitzchak* which means *"laughter."* When the G-d of Israel told Abraham that Sarah was going to have a child in her old age when she was past child bearing age, Sarah *"laughed."* (Genesis [*Bereishit*] 18:9-14). Therefore, Abraham and Sarah named their child Isaac *(Yitzchak)* or *"laughter."* When Isaac *(Yitzchak)* was born, Sarah said that the G-d of Israel has made her to *"laugh"* (which has a deeper spiritual meaning of rejoicing with great joy) so that all that hear (SHEMA in Hebrew which means to hear, do and obey) will *"laugh"* (have great joy in the L-RD) with me. Therefore, Abraham and Sarah named their child, Isaac *(Yitzchak)*, because the name Isaac (laughter) represented a prophetic event that the G-d of Israel performed in their lives. In Genesis *(Bereishit)* 18:9-14 it is written:

> *"And they said unto him* [Abraham], *Where is Sarah thy wife? And he said, Behold in the tent. And he said, I will certainly return unto thee according to the time of life; and, lo, Sarah thy wife shall have a son. And Sarah heard it in the tent door, which was behind him. Now* **Abraham and Sarah were old** *and well stricken in age; and* **it ceased to be with Sarah after the manner of women.** *Therefore* **Sarah laughed** *within herself, saying, After I am waxed old shall I have pleasure, my lord being old also? And the* LORD *said unto Abraham, Wherefore did* **Sarah laugh**, *saying, Shall I of a surety bear a child, which am old? Is anything too hard for the* LORD*? At the time appointed I will return unto thee, according to the time of life, and Sarah shall have a son."*

When Isaac was born, Abraham *(Avraham)* and Sarah named him *Yitzchak* in Hebrew which means *"laughter."* In Genesis *(Bereishit)* 21:1-3, 6 it is written:

> *"And the* LORD *visited Sarah as he had said, and the* LORD *did unto Sarah as he had spoken. For Sarah conceived, and bare Abraham a son in his old age, at the set time of which God had spoken to him. And* **Abraham called the name of his son** *that was born unto him, whom Sarah bare to him,* **Isaac** *... And Sarah said, God hath made me to*

Yeshua, Our Jewish Messiah

laugh *so that all that* **hear** [which is the Hebrew word SHEMA which means hear, do and obey and is the Strong's word 8085] **will laugh** *with me."*

Jacob in Hebrew Means Supplanter

Jacob is the Strong's word 3290 in the Strong's Hebrew Concordance. Jacob is the Hebrew word *Ya'acov* which means *"supplanter, deceiver, kiniver, heel catcher."* The meaning of the name of Jacob *(Ya'acov)* was prophetic of the life of Jacob *(Ya'acov)* until the G-d of Israel changed his name to Israel. Israel is the Strong's word 3478 which means *"to rule and have power as a prince with God."* Jacob *(Ya'acov)* was given the name *"heel catcher"* because when he was born, he *"caught the heel"* of his older brother Esau. Therefore, his name was called Jacob *(Ya'acov)* which means a *"heel catcher."*

During his life, Jacob *(Ya'acov)* greatly desired to inherit the covenant blessing that the G-d of Israel made with Abraham *(Avraham)*. While Jacob's heart was honorable in desiring the covenant blessing that the G-d of Israel promised Abraham *(Avraham)* and the G-d of Israel honored the heart of Jacob *(Ya'acov)* for desiring this blessing, the method that Jacob *(Ya'acov)* used to obtain this blessing is best characterized as being a *"supplanter, deceiver or kiniver."* This is the meaning of the name Jacob *(Ya'acov)* in Hebrew.

Esau and Jacob *(Ya'acov)* were twin sons of Isaac *(Yitzchak)* and Rebekah *(Rivkah)*. Because Esau was the firstborn, the family inheritance legally belonged to him. However, Jacob *(Ya'acov)* purposed in his heart that he would obtain the blessing of the firstborn. Because Jacob desired the covenant blessing that the G-d of Israel made with Abraham *(Avraham)* so greatly, Jacob *(Ya'acov)* asked his brother Esau to sell him the birthright of Esau when Esau was hungry and needed food to eat.

Esau represents the carnal (earthly) believer in *Yeshua*/Jesus as Messiah *(Mashiach)*. Esau's heart was more preoccupied with meeting his TEMPORARY fleshly, earthly needs than inheriting the ETERNAL covenant promises that the G-d of Israel made with Abraham *(Avraham)*. Therefore, Esau sold his *"birthright"* to satisfy his temporary earthly desire of food for his body. However, Jacob *(Ya'acov)* was more concerned with the eternal covenant blessing that the G-d of Israel promised to the descendents of Abraham *(Avraham)*.

Jacob *(Ya'acov)* had a *"wrestling"* in his life between his carnal nature *(evil inclination)* being a *"supplanter, deceiver, kiniver"* with his brother Esau and his spiritual nature *(good inclination)* which desired the blessing of the G-d of Israel. When Jacob *(Ya'acov)* had a *"wrestling"* match with the G-d of Israel toward the end of his life, this was prophetic of his life. In the *"wrestling"* match, Jacob *(Ya'acov)* prevailed. Even though Jacob's method of obtaining the blessing of the firstborn was carnal, fleshly and earthly *(evil inclination)*, the G-d of Israel honored the spiritual nature *(good inclination)* of Jacob's heart to desire the covenant blessing that He made with Abraham *(Avraham)*.

Yeshua, Our Jewish Messiah

When Jacob *(Ya'acov)* prevailed in his *"wrestling"* match with the G-d of Israel, G-d changed Jacob's name to Israel. Israel is the Strong's word 3478 which means *"to rule and have power as a prince with G-d."* The changing of the name of Jacob *(Ya'acov)* to Israel represented a change in the character, identity, purpose and destiny of Jacob's *(Ya'acov)* life.

When Jacob *(Ya'acov)* was born, he grabbed the heel of his twin brother Esau who came out of the womb of their mother Rebekah *(Rivkah)* first. In Genesis *(Bereishit)* 25:21-26 it is written:

> *"And Isaac entreated the* Lord *for his wife, because she was barren: and the* Lord *was entreated of him, and Rebekah his wife conceived. And the children struggled together within her; and she said, If it be so, why am I thus? And she went to inquire of the* Lord. *And the* Lord *said unto her, Two nations are in thy womb, and two manner of people* [Esau after the flesh and Jacob after the Spirit] *shall be separated from thy bowels; and the one people shall be stronger than the other people; and the elder* [Esau, the flesh] *shall serve the younger* [Jacob, the Spirit]. *And when her days to be delivered were fulfilled, behold, there were twins in her womb. And the first came out red, all over like a hairy garment; and they called his name Esau. And after that came his brother out, and* **his hand took hold on Esau's heel**; *and his name was called* **Jacob**: *and Isaac was threescore years old when she bare them.*

Restoring the Two Houses of Israel

Jacob Supplants the Birthright of Esau

In Genesis *(Bereishit)* 25:28-34, Esau sells his birthright to Jacob *(Ya'acov)* when Esau was hungry for food as it is written:

> *"And Isaac loved Esau, because he did eat of his venison: but Rebekah loved Jacob. And Jacob sod pottage: and Esau came from the field, and he was faint: And Esau said to Jacob, Feed me, I pray thee, with that same red pottage; for I am faint: therefore was his named was called Edom. And Jacob said, Sell me this day thy birthright. And* **Esau said***, Behold, I am at the point to die: and* **what profit shall this birthright do to me?** *And Jacob said, Swear to me this day; and he sware unto him: and* **he sold his birthright unto Jacob***. Then Jacob gave Esau bread and pottage of lentils; and he did eat and drink, and rose up, and went his way: thus* **Esau despised his birthright.***"*

Jacob Supplants Isaac's Blessing to Esau

In Genesis *(Bereishit)* 27:1-36, Jacob *(Ya'acov) supplants* the blessing of his father Isaac *(Yitzchak)* to Esau with the help of his mother Rebekah *(Rivkah)* as it is written:

> *"And it came to pass, that when Isaac was old, and his eyes were dim, so that he could not see, he called Esau his eldest son, and said unto him, My son: and he said unto him, Behold, here am I. And he said, Behold now, I am old, I know not the day of my death: Now therefore take, I pray thee, thy*

weapons, thy quiver and thy bow, and go out to the field, and take me some venison; And make me savory meat, such as I love, and bring it to me, that I may eat; that my soul may bless thee before I die. And Rebekah heard when Isaac spake to Esau his son. And Esau went to the field to hunt for venison and to bring it. And Rebekah spake unto Jacob her son, saying, Behold, I heard thy father speak unto Esau thy brother, saying, Bring me venison, and make me savory meat, that I may eat, and bless thee before the L<small>ORD</small> *before my death. Now therefore, my son, obey my voice according to that which I command thee. Go now to the flock, and fetch me from thence two good kids of the goats; and I will make them savory meat for thy father, such as he loveth: And thou shalt bring it to thy father, that he may eat, and that he may bless thee before his death. And Jacob said to Rebekah his mother, Behold, Esau my brother is a hairy man, and I am a smooth man: My father peradventure will feel me, and I shall seem to him as a* **DECEIVER**; *and I shall bring a curse upon me, and not a blessing. And his mother said unto him, Upon me be thy curse, my son: only obey my voice, and go fetch me them. And he went, and fetched, and brought them to his mother: and his mother made savory meat, such as his father loved. And Rebekah took goodly raiment of her eldest son Esau, which were with her in the house, and put them upon Jacob her younger son: And she put the skins of the kids of the goats upon his hands, and upon the smooth of his neck: And she gave the savory meat and the bread, which she had prepared, into the hand of her son Jacob. And he came* *unto his father, and said, My father: and he said, Here am I; who art thou, my son? And Jacob said unto his father, I am Esau thy firstborn; I have done according as thou badest me: arise, I pray thee, sit and eat of my venison, that thy soul may bless me. And Isaac said unto his son, How is it that thou hast found it so quickly, my son? And he said, Because the* LORD *thy God brought it to me. And Isaac said unto Jacob, Come near, I pray thee, that I may feel thee, my son, whether thou be my very son Esau or not. And Jacob went near unto Isaac his father; and he felt him, and said, The voice is Jacob's voice, but the hands are the hands of Esau. And he discerned him not, because his hands were hairy, as his brother Esau's hands: so he blessed him. And he said, Art thou my very son Esau? And he said, I am. And he said, Bring it near to me, and I will eat of my son's venison, that my soul may bless thee. And he brought it near to him, and he did eat: and he brought him wine, and he drank. And his father Isaac said unto him, Come near now, and kiss me, my son. And he came near and kissed him: and he smelled the smell of his raiment, and blessed him, and said, See, the smell of my son is as the smell of a field which the* LORD *hath blessed: Therefore God give thee of the dew of heaven, and the fatness of the earth, and plenty of corn and wine: Let people serve thee, and nations bow down to thee: be lord over thy brethren, and let thy mother's sons bow down to thee: cursed be every one that curseth thee, and blessed be he that blesseth thee. And it came to pass, as soon as Isaac had made an end of blessing Jacob, and Jacob was yet scarce gone out from the pres-*

ence of Isaac his father, that Esau his brother came in from his hunting. And he also had made savory meat, and brought it unto his father, and said unto his father, Let my father arise, and eat of his son's venison, that thy soul may bless me. And Isaac his father said unto him, Who art thou? And he said, I am thy son, thy firstborn Esau. And Isaac trembled very exceedingly, and said, Who? Where is he that hath taken venison, and brought it me, and I have eaten of all before thou camest and have blessed him? Yea, and he shall be blessed. And when Esau heard the words of his father, he cried with a great and exceeding bitter cry, and said unto his father, Bless me, even me also, O my father. And he said, **Thy brother came with subtlety** *and hath taken away thy blessing. And he said,* **Is not he rightly named Jacob?** *for he hath* **supplanted** *me these two times: he took away my birthright; and, behold, now he hath taken away my blessing..."*

The Spiritual Meaning of Jacob and Esau

Jacob *(Ya'acov)* is a spiritual type and picture of the children of the Promise who walk according to the Spirit *(good inclination)* and not according to the carnal nature of the flesh *(evil inclination)*. Esau is a spiritual type and picture of those who walk according to the carnal nature of the flesh and not after the Spirit. The G-d of Israel loves those whose heart is toward Him and His promises *(Jacob)* and hates those who are more concerned with pleasing the desires of their flesh *(Esau)* above loving the G-d of Israel with all their heart, mind, soul and strength and living for the eternal Kingdom of

G-d. This is explained for us in Romans 9:8-13 as it is written:

> "...They which are the children of the flesh, these are not the children of God [Esau]: but the children of the promise are counted for the seed [Jacob]. For this is the word of promise, At this time will I come, and Sarah shall have a son. And not only this; but when Rebecca also had conceived by one, even by our father Isaac; (For the children being not yet born, neither having done any good or evil, that the purpose of God according to election might stand, not of works, but of him that calleth;) It was said unto her, the elder shall serve the younger. As it is written, Jacob have I loved, but Esau have I hated."

Jacob Wrestles with G-d and Prevails

In Genesis *(Bereishit)* 32:24-30, Jacob *(Ya'acov)* has a wrestling match with the G-d of Israel and prevails. Jacob *(Ya'acov)* would not leave Him depart until the G-d of Israel blessed Jacob. In Genesis *(Bereishit)* 32:24-30 it is written:

> "And Jacob was left alone; and there wrestled a man with him until the breaking of the day. And when he saw that he prevailed not against him, he touched the hollow of his thigh; and the hollow of Jacob's thigh was out of joint, as he wrestled with him. And he said, Let me go, for the day breaketh. And he said, I will not let thee go, except thou bless me. And he said unto him, **What is thy name?** And he said, **Jacob.** And he said, **Thy name**

Yeshua, Our Jewish Messiah

> shall be called no more Jacob, but Israel: for as a prince hast thou power with God and with men, and hast prevailed. *And Jacob asked him, and said, Tell me, I pray thee, thy name. And he said, Wherefore is it that thou dost ask after my name? And he blessed him there. And Jacob called the name of the place Peniel: for I have seen God face to face, and my life is preserved."*

How did the G-d of Israel bless Jacob *(Ya'acov)*? He blessed him by changing his name from Jacob *(Ya'acov)* which means a *"supplanter, deceiver, kiniver"* (which was characteristic of Jacob's *[Ya'acov's]* life) to Israel which means **"to rule and have power as a prince with God."**

Therefore, we can see from the lives of Abraham *(Avraham)*, Isaac *(Yitzchak)* and Jacob *(Ya'acov)* that their names represented their character, identity, purpose and destiny in G-d. In Hebraic thought, a name is prophetic of your character and your destiny. For this reason, the Jewish Messiah is named *Yeshua*. His name represents His character, destiny and purpose as the Jewish Messiah *(Mashiach)* to both houses of Israel (Judaism and Christianity). He is our Savior and He was sent by the G-d of Israel as the Jewish Messiah *(Mashiach)* to save His people from their sins (Matthew *[Mattityahu]* 1:21).

Miryam Was Betrothed to Yosef

Mary *(Miryam)* the Jewish mother of *Yeshua*/Jesus was betrothed to Joseph *(Yosef)* when Mary *(Miryam)* was pregnant with the Jewish Messiah *(Mashiach)*

Restoring the Two Houses of Israel

Yeshua/Jesus. In the ancient biblical Jewish wedding ceremony, there are two stages to the wedding process. The first stage is called betrothal. During betrothal, you are legally married to your spouse but you do not physically dwell with your spouse. By understanding the Hebrew language, we can see how betrothal is legally binding. The word for betrothal in Hebrew is *erusin* which comes from the Hebrew root word *aras*. *Aras* is related to the Hebrew word *asar* which means *"to bind."* By this, we can see that the Hebrew language teaches us that betrothal is legally binding.

According to the ancient biblical Jewish wedding customs, once you are betrothed, the only way that you can get out of the marriage is through a divorce. A divorce is known as a *"get"* to the *house of Judah* (Judaism). The second stage of marriage is called in Hebrew *nesu'in*. It is during the second stage of marriage that the bride and groom physically come together and consummate the marriage. In Matthew *(Mattityahu)* 1:18-20, we can understand that the Jewish parents of the Jewish Messiah *(Mashiach) Yeshua*/Jesus were wedded according to the ancient biblical Jewish wedding customs as it is written:

> *"Now the birth of Jesus Christ was on this wise: When as his mother Mary was espoused* [betrothed] *to Joseph,* **before they came together** [the first of two stages of the ancient Jewish wedding ceremony], *she was found with child of the Holy Ghost* [Ruach HaKodesh]. *Then Joseph her husband, being a just man* [tzaddik], *and not willing to make her a public example,* **was minded to put her away** *privily* [get/divorce]. *But*

Yeshua, Our Jewish Messiah

while he thought on these things, behold, the angel of the L*ord* *appeared unto him in a dream, saying, Joseph, thou son of David, fear not to take unto thee Mary thy wife; for that which is conceived in her is of the Holy Ghost* [Ruach HaKodesh]."

Therefore, the Jewish parents of the Jewish Messiah *(Mashiach) Yeshua*/Jesus were wedded in accordance with the ancient Jewish wedding customs.

The Spiritual Meaning of Betrothal

What is the spiritual *(sod/*deeper meaning) understanding of the ancient Jewish wedding ceremony to Jewish and non-Jewish believers in *Yeshua*/Jesus as the Jewish Messiah? The Messiah *(Mashiach)* is the groom and the Jewish and non-Jewish believers in Messiah are His Bride. When the Jewish Messiah *(Mashiach) Yeshua*/Jesus came to the earth nearly 2,000 years ago, He came so that whosoever would put their faith and confidence *(emunah)* in Him would be wedded to Him forever. At His first coming, the Jewish Messiah *(Mashiach) Yeshua*/Jesus came as the suffering Messiah known as *Messiah ben Yosef* (Joseph). Following His resurrection, He ascended to Heaven *(olam haba)* to be with G-d the Father until He returns at His second coming to be the Kingly Messiah known as *Messiah ben David*.

Today, the Jewish Messiah *(Mashiach) Yeshua*/Jesus does not physically dwell with those who trust in Him. Therefore, the believers in the Jewish Messiah *(Mashiach) Yeshua*/Jesus are currently betrothed to Him. We will enter the fullness of the marriage and physically dwell with the Messiah during the Messianic Age known as the *Millennium* to the *house of Israel* (Christianity) or the *Athid Lavo* to the *house of Judah* (Judaism).

Circumcision Is a Sign of the Covenant

It is a commandment in the Torah that every Jewish boy be circumcised the eighth day. Circumcision is the physical sign of the covenant between the G-d of Israel and His people. The G-d of Israel gave instruction to Abraham *(Avraham)* in Genesis *(Bereishit)* 17:9-14 that the physical offspring of Abraham *(Avraham)* were to be circumcised as it is written:

> *"And God said unto Abraham, Thou shalt keep my covenant therefore, thou, and thy seed after thee in their generations. This is my covenant, which ye shall keep, between me and you and thy seed after thee; Every man child among you shall be circumcised. And ye shall circumcise the flesh of your foreskin; and it shall be a token of the covenant between me and you. And he that is* **eight days** *old shall be* **circumcised** *among you, every man child in your generations, he that is born in the house, or bought with money of any stranger, which is not of thy seed. He that is born in thy house, and he that is bought with thy money, must needs be circumcised: and my covenant shall be in your flesh for an* **everlasting covenant**. *And the uncircumcised man child whose flesh of his foreskin is not circumcised, that soul shall be cut off from his people; he hath broken my covenant."*

Yeshua, Our Jewish Messiah

Yeshua/Jesus Was Circumcised the Eighth Day

In accordance with the G-d of Israel's commandment to Abraham *(Avraham)* that every Jewish boy be circumcised the eighth day, the earthly Jewish parents of the Jewish Messiah *(Mashiach)* Yeshua/Jesus circumcised Him on the eighth day. In Luke 2:22-24 it is written:

> *"And when the days of her purification according to the law* [Torah] *of Moses were accomplished, they brought him to Jerusalem, to present him to the* LORD*; (As it is written in the law* [Torah] *of the* LORD*, Every male that openeth the womb shall be called holy to the* LORD*;) And to offer a sacrifice according to that which is said in the law* [Torah] *of the* LORD*, A pair of turtledoves, or two young pigeons."*

This instruction is given in the Torah of the G-d of Israel in Leviticus *(Vayikra)* 12:1-3,6,8 as it is written:

> *"And the* LORD *spake unto Moses, saying, Speak unto the children of Israel, saying, If a woman have conceived seed, and born a man child: then she shall be unclean seven days; according to the days of the separation for her infirmity shall she be unclean. And in the* **eighth day** *the flesh of his foreskin shall be* **circumcised** *… And when the days of her purifying are fulfilled, for a son, or for a daughter, she shall bring a lamb of the first year for a burnt offering, and a young pigeon, or a turtledove, for a sin offering unto the door of the tabernacle of the congregation, unto the priest …*

And if she be not able to bring a lamb, then she shall **bring two turtles, or two young pigeons**; *the one for the burnt offering, and the other for a sin offering: and the priest shall make an atonement for her, and she shall be clean."*

Yeshua/Jesus Was Born in Bethlehem

The Jewish Messiah *(Mashiach)* Yeshua/Jesus was born in Bethlehem. In Matthew *(Mattityahu)* 2:1, 4-6 it is written:

"Now when **Jesus was born in Bethlehem** *of Judea in the days of Herod the king, behold, there came wise men from the east to Jerusalem ... And when he* [Herod] *had gathered all the chief priests and scribes of the people together, he demanded of them where Christ* [Messiah/Mashiach] *should be born. And they said unto him, In Bethlehem of Judea: for thus it is written by the prophet, And thou Bethlehem, in the land of Juda, are you not least among the princes of Juda: for out of thee shall come a Governor, that shall rule my people Israel."*

The prophecy that the Jewish Messiah *(Mashiach)* would be born in Bethlehem of Judah is in Micah 5:2 as it is written:

"But thou, **Bethlehem** *Ephratah, though thou be little among the thousands of Judah, yet out of thee shall he come forth unto me that is to be* **ruler in Israel**; *whose goings forth have been from of old,* **from everlasting***."*

Yeshua, Our Jewish Messiah

The ruler in Israel who has been from everlasting and who was born in Bethlehem is the Jewish Messiah *(Mashiach) Yeshua*/Jesus.

The Hebrew Meaning of the Word Bethlehem

Bethlehem is the Strong's word 1035 in the Hebrew Concordance. It comes from two Hebrew words, *Beit* and *Lechem*. Beit is the Strong's word 1004 which means *"House."* Lechem is the Strong's word 3899 which means *"Bread."* So, Bethlehem means in Hebrew, *"House of Bread."* In John *(Yochanan)* 6:33-35, the Jewish Messiah *(Mashiach) Yeshua*/Jesus said that He was the Bread *(manna)* that the G-d of Israel sent from Heaven *(Malkut Shamayim)* as it is written:

> *"For the* **bread of God** *is he which cometh down from heaven, and* **giveth life unto the world***. Then said they unto him,* LORD*, evermore give us this bread. And* **Jesus** *said unto them,* **I am the bread of life***: he that cometh to me shall never hunger; and he that believeth on me shall never thirst."*

The evening before the Jewish Messiah *(Mashiach) Yeshua*/Jesus was crucified on the tree (I Corinthians 11:23), He had a Passover *(Pesach)* Seder meal (Luke 22:15). During the Seder meal, bread known as *matzah* is eaten. In Luke 22:15, 19, *Yeshua*/Jesus said that this *matzah* bread represented His body as it is written:

> *"And he* [Yeshua/Jesus] *said unto them, With desire I have desired to eat this* **passover** *with you*

> *before I suffer ... and* **he took bread**, *and gave thanks, and broke it, and gave unto them, saying,* **This is my body** *which is given for you: this do in remembrance of me."*

The blessing that is said over the bread is called *HaMotzi*. In Hebrew, the blessing is: "*Baruch Atah Adonai Eloheynu Melech Ha Olam Ha Motzi Lechem Min Ha Aretz*" which means in English, "Blessed are you O L-RD our G-d King of the Universe who brings forth the bread from the earth."

Spiritually (*sod*/deeper meaning), the *HaMotzi* is a prayer of thanks to the G-d of Israel for the resurrection of the Jewish Messiah *(Mashiach) Yeshua*/Jesus who was *"brought forth"* (resurrected) from the earth. Furthermore, the Jewish Messiah *(Mashiach) Yeshua*/Jesus was born at a place called Bethlehem *(Beit Lechem)* which means *"House of Bread"* in Hebrew.

The Earthly Father of Yeshua/Jesus Was Joseph

The earthly father of the Jewish Messiah *(Mashiach) Yeshua*/Jesus was Joseph *(Yosef)*. In Matthew *(Mattityahu)* 1:16, it is written:

> "*And Jacob begat Joseph the husband of Mary, of whom was born Jesus, who is called Christ.*"

It is traditional Jewish thought that the Jewish Messiah *(Mashiach)* has two primary roles to fulfill in the redemption. The Jewish Messiah *(Mashiach)* is seen as

Yeshua, Our Jewish Messiah

being a suffering Messiah and a Kingly Messiah. The suffering Messiah is given the name *Messiah ben Yosef* (Joseph). The Kingly Messiah is given the name *Messiah ben David*. Both Jewish and non-Jewish believers in *Yeshua*/Jesus as the Jewish Messiah *(Mashiach)* know that He came to the earth at His first coming as the suffering Messiah *(Messiah ben Yosef)* and will return in His second coming as the Kingly Messiah *(Messiah ben David)*.

The earthly father of the Jewish Messiah *(Mashiach) Yeshua*/Jesus was named Joseph *(Yosef)*. Therefore, *Yeshua*/Jesus was the *son of Joseph*. This has a double meaning. In the literal *(peshat)*, *Yeshua*/Jesus was the earthly son of Joseph *(Yosef)*. Spiritually *(sod*/deeper meaning), the son of Joseph is an allusion to *Yeshua*/Jesus being *Messiah ben Yosef* (Messiah son of Joseph). In John *(Yochanan)* 1:45, Philip recognized that *Yeshua*/Jesus was the son of Joseph *(Messiah ben Yosef)* as it is written:

> *"Philip findeth Nathanael, and saith unto him, We have found him, of whom Moses in the law* [Torah]*, and the prophets did write,* **Jesus** *of Nazareth,* **the son of Joseph.***"*

Therefore, from these things, we can understand that the Jewish Messiah *(Mashiach) Yeshua*/Jesus was born a Jew.

Yeshua/Jesus Was Raised a Jew

In Luke 2:40, we are told that the Jewish Messiah *(Mashiach) Yeshua*/Jesus grew both physically and spiritually as it is written:

"And the child grew, and waxed strong in spirit, filled with wisdom [chokmah]: *and the grace* [chesed] *of God was upon him."*

Yeshua/Jesus Is a Son of the Commandment

At the age of 12/13, a Jewish child is considered an adult. At this age, a Jewish child is responsible for knowing, studying and walking in the commandments of the G-d of Israel. Today, there is a special remembrance for this event in the life of a Jewish child. It is known as a *"Bar Mitzvah."* Bar Mitzvah means *"son of the commandment."*

The Torah is the commandments of the G-d of Israel. Those who know the Torah of the G-d of Israel and walk in the instructions of the Torah are known as the *"sons"* of G-d. The Jewish Messiah *(Mashiach) Yeshua/*Jesus showed his superior knowledge of the Torah of the G-d of Israel at the *Bar Mitzvah* age of 12 years old. In Luke 2:42, 46-47 it is written:

> *"And when he was* **twelve years old**, *they went up to Jerusalem after the custom of the feast … And it came to pass, that after three days they found him in the temple,* **sitting in the midst of the doctors** [rabbi's of the Torah] *both hearing them, and asking them questions.* **And all that heard him were astonished at his understanding and answers.***"*

Our Jewish Messiah: His Life, Ministry and Teachings

So far, we have studied how the Jewish Messiah *(Mashiach) Yeshua/*Jesus was born a Jew and was raised

Yeshua, Our Jewish Messiah

a Jew. Next, we will examine the Jewishness of his adult life, ministry and teachings.

Yeshua/Jesus Was a Carpenter

The earthly occupation of the Jewish Messiah *(Mashiach) Yeshua*/Jesus was a carpenter. In Mark 6:2-3, it is written:

> *"And when the sabbath day was come, he began to teach in the synagogue: and many hearing him were astonished, saying ... Is not this the* **carpenter**, *the son of Mary..."*

Yeshua/Jesus Is a Builder of G-d's House

Just as there is a double meaning that the Jewish Messiah *(Mashiach) Yeshua*/Jesus was the son of Joseph, the occupation of *Yeshua*/Jesus also has a double meaning. In the literal *(peshat)*, *Yeshua*/Jesus was a carpenter and built houses. Spiritually *(sod*/deeper meaning), the Jewish Messiah *(Mashiach) Yeshua*/Jesus was faithful to *"build the house"* of the G-d of Israel. In Hebrews 3:1-6 it is written:

> *"Wherefore, holy brethren, partakers of the heavenly calling, consider the Apostle* [Shaliach] *and High Priest* [Cohen HaGadol] *of our profession, Christ Jesus: Who was faithful to him that appointed him, as also Moses* [Moshe] *was faithful in all his house. For this man was counted worthy of more glory than Moses* [Moshe], *inasmuch as he who hath builded the house hath more honor*

than the house. For every house is builded by some man; but he that built all things is God. And Moses [Moshe] *verily was faithful in all his house, as a servant, for a testimony of those things which were to be spoken after; But Christ as a son over his own house; whose house are we, if we hold fast the confidence and the rejoicing of the hope firm unto the end."*

The Jewish Messiah *(Mashiach) Yeshua*/Jesus was faithful in building the spiritual house of G-d.

Having a Son Is Building a House

In traditional Jewish thinking, having a son is associated with building a household and raising up the family name. In Psalm *(Tehillim)* 2:6-7, the Jewish Kingly Messiah *(Machiach)* is called the Son of G-d as it is written:

> *"Yet have I set* **my king** *upon my holy hill of Zion. I will declare the decree:* [one of the steps of the enthroning ceremony of a Jewish king] *the* LORD *hath said unto me, Thou art* **my Son**; *this day have I begotten thee."*

In Acts 13:33, it confirms that Psalm *(Tehillim)* 2:6-7 is speaking about the Jewish Messiah *(Mashiach) Yeshua*/Jesus as it is written:

> *"God hath fulfilled the same unto us their children, in that he hath raised up Jesus again; as it is also written in the second psalm, Thou art my Son, this day have I begotten thee."*

Yeshua, Our Jewish Messiah

At the *Mikvah* (immersion/baptism) of the Jewish Messiah *(Mashiach) Yeshua*/Jesus, a voice *(kol)* from heaven spoke to *Yeshua*/Jesus and called Him the Son of G-d. In Matthew *(Mattityahu)* 3:13, 16-17 it is written:

> *"Then cometh* **Jesus** *from Galilee to Jordan unto John* [Yochanan the Immerser], *to be baptized* [mikvah/immersed] *of him ... And Jesus, when he was baptized* [mikvah/immersed], *went up straightway out of the water: and, lo, the heavens were opened unto him, and he saw the Spirit of God* [Ruach HaKodesh] *descending like a dove, and lighting upon him: And lo a voice from heaven, saying, This is* **my beloved Son** [Psalm 2:7], *in whom I am well pleased."*

Once again, in traditional Jewish thought, having a son is associated with building a house. This truth can be understood from the Hebrew language itself. The word for son in Hebrew is *"ben."* It is the Strong's word 1121 in the Hebrew Concordance. Son or *ben* in Hebrew means *"a son or builder of a family name."* Son or *ben* in Hebrew comes from the Strong's word 1129 which is the Hebrew word *"Banah"* which means *"to build."* The Hebrew word for house is *beit*. It is the Strong's word 1004. The Hebrew word for house, *beit*, also comes from the Hebrew word *"banah"* which means *"to build."* Therefore, the Hebrew language communicates to us that having a son is associated with building a house or raising up the family name. This spiritual truth can be seen in the Torah in the book of Deuteronomy *(Devarim)* 25:5-9 as it is written:

> *"If brethren dwell together, and one of them die, and have no child, the wife of the dead shall not*

marry without unto a stranger: her husband's brother shall go in unto her, and take her to him to wife, and perform the duty of a husband's brother unto her. And it shall be, that the firstborn which she beareth shall succeed in the name of the brother which is dead, that his name be not put out of Israel. And if the man like not to take his brother's wife ... Then the elders of his city shall call him, and speak unto him: and if he stand to it, and say, I like not to take her; Then shall his brother's wife come unto him in the presence of the elders, and loose his shoe from off his foot, and spit in his face, and shall answer and say, So shall it be done unto **that man that will not build up his brother's house**."

It can also be seen in Ruth 4:11 that having a son is associated with building a house. The two earthly mothers of the two houses of Israel, Rachel and Leah, had a competition between them about having sons to build up the *house of Jacob*. In Ruth 4:11 it is written:

"And all the people that were in the gate, and the elders, said, We are witnesses. The LORD make the woman that is come into thine house like Rachel and like Leah, which two did **build the house of Israel**: and do thou worthily in Ephratah, and be famous in Bethlehem."

The Spiritual Family of G-d Is Named After the Messiah

Because the Jewish Messiah *(Mashiach) Yeshua*/Jesus was faithful in His task to build the spiritual house of

Yeshua, Our Jewish Messiah

G-d, the spiritual family of the G-d of Israel is named after the Jewish Messiah *(Mashiach) Yeshua/*Jesus. In Ephesians 3:14-15 it is written:

> *"For this cause I bow my knees unto the Father of our* Lord **Jesus Christ**, *of whom the* **whole family** *in heaven and earth* **is named**.*"*

The Jewish Messiah *(Mashiach) Yeshua/*Jesus came to rule over both houses of Israel known as the *house of Jacob*. In Luke 1:31-33 it is written:

> *"And, behold, thou shalt conceive in thy womb, and bring forth a son, and shalt call his name Jesus* [Yeshua]. *He shall be great, and shall be called the* **Son of the Highest**: *and the* Lord *God shall give unto him the throne of his father David: And he shall* **reign** *over the* **house of Jacob forever**, *and of his kingdom there shall be no end."*

Yeshua/Jesus Is Our High Priest

The Jewish Messiah *(Mashiach) Yeshua/*Jesus began his public ministry at 30 years of age. In Luke 3:21-23 it is written:

> *"Now when all the people were baptized* [mikvah/immersed] *it came to pass, that Jesus also being baptized* [mikvah/immersed] *and praying, the heaven was opened, And the Holy Ghost* [Ruach HaKodesh] *descended in a bodily shape like a dove upon him, and a voice came from heaven, which said, Thou art my beloved Son; in thee I am*

well pleased. And Jesus himself began to be about **thirty years of age**..."

Spiritually (*sod*/deeper meaning), by starting His public ministry at thirty years of age, the G-d of Israel is communicating to us that the Jewish Messiah *(Mashiach) Yeshua*/Jesus had a priestly ministry. In the Torah, it tells us that a priest could not perform his duties in the tabernacle until he was thirty years of age. In Numbers *(Bamidbar)* 4:1-3 it is written:

> *"And the* LORD *spake unto Moses and unto Aaron, saying, Take the sum of the sons of Kohath from among the sons of Levi, after their families, by the house of their fathers, From* **thirty years old** *and upward even until fifty years old, all that enter into the host, to do the work in the tabernacle of the congregation."*

The Jewish Messiah *(Mashiach) Yeshua*/Jesus is our great High Priest *(Cohen HaGadol)*. In Hebrew 3:1, 4:14-16 it is written:

> *"Wherefore, holy brethren, partakers of the heavenly calling, consider the Apostle* [shaliach] *and* **High Priest** [Cohen HaGadol] *of our profession, Christ Jesus ... Seeing then that we have a great high priest, that is passed into the heavens,* **Jesus the Son of God***, let us hold fast to our profession. For we have not an high priest which cannot be touched with the feelings of our infirmities; but was in all points tempted like as we are, yet without sin.* **Let us therefore come boldly unto the throne of grace***, that we may obtain mercy, and find grace to help in time of need."*

Yeshua, Our Jewish Messiah

The Jewish Messiah *(Mashiach) Yeshua*/Jesus is our great High Priest *(Cohen HaGadol)* after the order of Melchisedec. In Hebrews 7:15,17,21 it is written:

> *"And it is yet far more evident: for that after the similitude of Melchisedec there ariseth another priest ... For he testifieth, Thou art a priest forever after the order of Melchisedec* [Psalm 110:4] *...* **The** LORD **swore** *and will not repent,* **Thou** [Yeshua/Jesus] **art a priest forever after the order of Melchisedec.**"

Yeshua/Jesus Was a Jewish Rabbi

The Jewish Messiah *(Mashiach) Yeshua*/Jesus was a rabbi. A *rabbi* in Hebrew means *"a teacher."* In John *(Yochanan)* 1:38, *Yeshua*/Jesus is called rabbi as it is written:

> *"Then* **Jesus** *turned, and saw them following, and saith unto them, What seek ye? They said unto him,* **Rabbi**, *(which is to say, being interpreted, Master* [teacher]*) where dwellest thou?"*

The Jewish Messiah *(Mashiach) Yeshua*/Jesus is also called *rabbi* in John *(Yochanan)* 3:1-2 as it is written:

> *"There was a man of the Pharisees* [P'rushim], *named Nicodemus* [Nakdimon], *a ruler of the Jews: The same came to* **Jesus** *by night, and said unto him,* **Rabbi**, *we know that thou art a* **teacher** *come from God: for no man can do these miracles that thou doest, except God be with him."*

Restoring the Two Houses of Israel

In Jewish thought, another name for the Messiah (*Mashiach*) is the teacher of righteousness. In Hosea (*Hoshea*) 6:3 it is written:

> *"Then shall we know, if we follow on to know the* LORD: **his going forth** *is prepared as the morning; and he shall come unto us* **as the rain,** *as* **the latter and former rain** *unto the earth."*

In Joel *(Yoel)* 2:23 it is written:

> *"Be glad then, ye children of Zion, and rejoice in the* LORD *your God: for he hath given you the* **former rain moderately,** *and he will cause to come down for you the rain, the former rain, and the latter rain in the first month."*

Hosea *(Hoshea)* 6:3 is talking about the coming of the Jewish Messiah *(Mashiach)*. If we cross-reference Hosea *(Hoshea)* 6:3 with Joel *(Yoel)* 2:23, we can see that the *former rain* is the Hebrew word *moreh* which means *"teacher"* and the word *moderately* in Joel *(Yoel)* 2:23 is the Hebrew word *tzedakah* which means *"righteousness."* Rabbi's are teachers of the Torah. In Jewish thought, rain is a type of the Torah. Therefore, the Jewish Messiah *(Mashiach)* Yeshua/Jesus was a rabbi who was a teacher of righteousness (the Torah).

The Jewish Rabbi Yeshua/Jesus Had Students of His Teachings

In Jewish thought, a *rabbi* (which means teacher) has students/disciples *(talmidim)*. A disciple is a student.

Yeshua, Our Jewish Messiah

The closest students of the Jewish Messiah *(Mashiach)* Yeshua/Jesus were called his disciples *(talmidim)*. Yeshua/Jesus had twelve disciples *(talmidim)*. These twelve disciples *(talmidim)* are listed in Matthew *(Mattityahu)* 10:1-4 as it is written:

> *"And when he had called unto him his twelve disciples* [talmidim], *he gave them power against unclean spirits, to cast them out, and to heal all manner of sickness and all manner of disease. Now the names of the twelve apostles are these; The first, Simon, who is called Peter, and Andrew his brother; James the son of Zebedee, and John his brother; Philip, and Bartholomew; Thomas, and Matthew the publican; James the son of Alphaeus, and Lebbaeus whose surname was Thaddaeus; Simon the Canaanite, and Judas Iscariot, who also betrayed him."*

Yeshua/Jesus Taught As a Rabbi in Parables

The Jewish Messiah *(Mashiach)* Yeshua/Jesus taught in parables. Parables are a rabbinic style of teaching the Torah. In the first century, most rabbi's were *aggadic* rabbi's. *Aggadah* is a Jewish style of teaching the Torah using parables and illustrated stories to communicate a spiritual message. Today in the *house of Judah* (traditional Judaism) most rabbi's are *halachic* rabbi's. *Halacha* is the way one walks or follows the commandments of the G-d of Israel. *Halachic* rabbi's give instruction on how to follow the Torah of the G-d of Israel that has been handed down from generation to generation. It was prophesied that the Jewish Messiah *(Mashiach)* would teach the Torah of the G-d of Israel in parables. In Psalm *(Tehillim)* 78:1-3 it is written:

> *"Give* **ear***, O* **my people, to my law [Torah]***: incline your ears to the words of my mouth.* **I will open my mouth in a parable***: I will utter dark sayings of old: Which we have heard and known, and our fathers have told us."*

In Matthew *(Mattityahu)* 13:34-35 it is told to us that the Jewish Messiah *(Mashiach)* Yeshua/Jesus spoke in parables as it is written:

> *"All these things* **spake Jesus** *unto the multitude* **in parables***; and without a parable spake he not unto them: That it might be fulfilled which was spoken by the prophet, saying, I will open my mouth in parables; I will utter things which have been kept secret from the foundation of the world."*

Yeshua/Jesus Taught From the Jewish Scriptures (Tenakh)

The Jewish Messiah *(Mashiach)* Yeshua/Jesus taught from the Jewish scriptures. The Jewish Scriptures are known as the *TeNaKh*. The Jewish Scriptures are divided into three sections. The first section is known as the *Torah*. The next section is known as the prophets *(Nevi'im)*. The last section is known as the writings *(Ketuvim)*. The Psalms *(Tehillim)* are located in the section of the Jewish Scriptures known as the writings

Yeshua, Our Jewish Messiah

(Ketuvim). *TeNaKh* is an acronym in Hebrew consisting of the first letter of each of the three sections of the Jewish scriptures.

It is traditional Jewish thought that all scriptures in the *TeNaKh* (Old Testament) are written about the Jewish Messiah *(Mashiach)*. In Psalm *(Tehillim)* 40:7-8 it is written:

> *"Then said I, Lo, I come: in the volume of the book it is written of me* [the Jewish Messiah], *I delight to do thy will, O my God: yea, thy law* [Torah] *is within my heart."*

In Luke 24:44, the Jewish Messiah *(Mashiach) Yeshua*/Jesus referred to the order of the three sections of the Jewish scriptures *(TeNaKh)* and proclaimed that the Jewish scriptures speak of Him as it is written:

> *"And he said unto them, These are the words which I spake unto you, while I was yet with you, that all things must be fulfilled, which were written in the law* [Torah] *of Moses* [first section of the Jewish scriptures], *and in the prophets* [the second section of the Jewish scriptures] *and in the Psalms* [the third section of the Jewish scriptures] *concerning me* [Psalm 40:7-8]."

Yeshua/Jesus Was a Torah Observant Jew

Earlier in the chapter, we saw that *Yeshua*/Jesus was a Jewish rabbi. He had students/disciples *(talmidim)* which learned His teachings. His teachings came from the Jewish scriptures (*TeNaKh*). As a Jewish rabbi, *Yeshua*/Jesus taught the Torah of the G-d of Israel. He taught the Torah as an *Aggadic rabbi* in parables. The Jewish Messiah *(Mashiach) Yeshua*/Jesus was a Torah observant Jew and He taught His followers to be Torah observant. Sin is the transgression of the Torah. In I John *(Yochanan)* 3:4 it is written:

> *"Whosoever committeth sin transgresseth also the law* [Torah]: *for* **sin is the transgression of the law [Torah]**.*"*

The Jewish Messiah *(Mashiach) Yeshua*/Jesus was SINLESS. Therefore, He NEVER transgressed the Torah of the G-d of Israel. In I Peter *(Kefa)* 2:21-22 it is written:

> *"For even hereunto were ye called: because* **Christ** [Mashiach] *also suffered for us, leaving an example, that ye should follow his steps: Who* **did no sin, neither was guile found in his mouth**.*"*

The prophet Isaiah *(Yeshayahu)* also tells that the Jewish Messiah *(Mashiach)* would live a life without sin. In Isaiah *(Yeshayahu)* 53:1-6, 9-10 it is written:

> *"Who hath believed our report? And to whom is* **the arm [zeroa] of the** Lord *revealed? ...* **He** *is despised and rejected of men; a man of sorrows, and acquainted with grief: and we hid as it were our faces from him; he was despised, and we esteemed him not. Surely he hath borne our griefs, and carried our sorrows: yet we did esteem him stricken, smitten of God, and afflicted. But he was*

Yeshua, Our Jewish Messiah

wounded for our transgressions [sin is the transgression of the Torah – I John 3:4], *he was bruised for our iniquities: the chastisement of our peace was upon him; and with his stripes we are healed. All we like sheep have gone astray; we have turned every one to his own way; and the* LORD *hath laid on him the iniquity of us all ... And he made his grave with the wicked, and with the rich in his death; because* **he had done no violence, neither was any deceit in his mouth**. *Yet it pleased the* LORD *to bruise him; he hath put him to grief: when thou shalt make his soul an offering for sin, he shall see his seed, he shall prolong his days, and the pleasure of the* LORD *shall prosper in his hand."*

In II Corinthians 5:19, 21 is it written:

"To wit, that God was in **Christ** [Mashiach], *reconciling the world unto himself, not imputing their trespasses unto them; and hath committed unto us the word of reconciliation ... for he hath made him to be sin for us,* **who knew no sin**; *that we might be made the righteousness of God in him."*

The Jewish Messiah *(Mashiach) Yeshua*/Jesus was sinless. Since sin is the transgression of the Torah, the Jewish Messiah *(Mashiach) Yeshua*/Jesus never transgressed the Torah. The Jewish Messiah *(Mashiach) Yeshua*/Jesus was a Torah observant Jew. Like any Torah observant Jewish rabbi, He taught His students *(talmidim)* to be Torah observant. In fact, *Yeshua*/Jesus taught that those who believed in Him as Messiah *(Mashiach)* and were Torah observant would be blessed above those who believed in Him as Messiah *(Mashiach)* and were not Torah observant. In Matthew *(Mattityahu)* 5:17-19, *Yeshua*/Jesus taught these words as it is written:

> "**THINK NOT that I am come to destroy the law [Torah]**, *or the prophets* [Nevi'im]: *I am not come to destroy* [to incorrectly interpret and teach the Torah], *but to fulfill* [to correctly interpret and teach the Torah]. *For verily I say unto you, Till heaven and earth pass, one jot* [yud which is the smallest letter in the Hebrew alphabet] *or one tittle* [taggim which is the decoration crowns which are put on various Hebrew letters] *shall in no wise pass from the law* [Torah], *till all be fulfilled. Whosoever therefore shall* **break** *one of* **these least commandments**, *and shall teach men so, he shall be* **called the least** *in the kingdom of heaven* [malkut shamayim]: *but whosoever shall* **do and teach them**, *the same shall be* **called great** *in the kingdom of heaven* [malkut shamayim]."

In these verses, the Jewish Messiah *(Mashiach) Yeshua*/Jesus taught that He did not come to destroy the Torah but to fulfill the Torah. *"Destroying the Torah"* and *"fulfilling the Torah"* are Jewish idioms. An *idiom* is a slang expression that is understood in the culture of its day. *"Destroying the Torah"* is a Jewish idiom that means to **incorrectly** interpret and **teach the Torah**. *"Fulfilling the Torah"* is a Jewish idiom that means to **correctly** interpret and **teach the Torah**. Therefore, we can understand from these things that the Jewish Messiah *(Mashiach) Yeshua*/Jesus was a

Yeshua, Our Jewish Messiah

Torah observant Jew and He taught His students *(talmidim)* to be Torah observant.

The Torah Is Truth and Light

The Torah of the G-d of Israel is called truth. In Psalm *(Tehillim)* 119:142 it is written:

> *"Thy righteousness is an everlasting righteousness, and thy* **law [Torah] is the truth**.*"*

The Torah is also called truth in Malachi 2:1, 6-7 as it is written:

> *"And now, O ye priests, this commandment is for you ... The* **law [Torah] of truth** *was in his mouth, and iniquity was not found in his lips ... for the priest's lips should keep knowledge, and they should seek the law* [Torah] *at his mouth: for he is the messenger of the* LORD *of hosts."*

In these scriptures, we see that the G-d of Israel calls His Torah truth and it is the priests who are commanded to teach the Torah of the G-d of Israel to His people. The Jewish Messiah *(Mashiach) Yeshua*/Jesus is the great High Priest *(Cohen HaGadol)* of the G-d of Israel (Hebrews 3:1, 4:14). Being a Torah observant Jew, a Jewish rabbi and the great High Priest of the G-d of Israel, the Jewish Messiah *(Mashiach) Yeshua*/Jesus taught His students/disciples *(talmidim)* to walk *(halacha)* in the truth which is the Torah (Psalm 119:142). In John *(Yochanan)* 8:31-32, *Yeshua*/Jesus taught His students/disciples *(talmidim)* these words as it is written:

Restoring the Two Houses of Israel

> *"Then said Jesus to those Jews which believed on him, If ye continue in my word* [in Jewish thought, Torah is synonymous with the Word of G-d], *then are ye my disciples* [talmidim] *indeed; And ye shall know the truth* [which is the Torah – Psalm 119:142], *and the truth* [Torah] *shall make you free."*

In John *(Yochanan)* 17:17, the Jewish Messiah *(Mashiach) Yeshua*/Jesus prayed that his students/disciples *(talmidim)* would be sanctified (which means to be holy and set apart) by following the truth (which is the Torah – Psalm 119:142) as it is written:

> *"Sanctify* [be holy and set apart] *them through thy truth: thy word* [Torah] *is truth* [Psalm 119:142]*."*

The Holy Spirit *(Ruach HaKodesh)* came to dwell inside the hearts of both Jewish *(house of Judah)* and non-Jewish *(house of Israel)* believers in *Yeshua*/Jesus as Messiah *(Mashiach)* and to write the Torah of the G-d of Israel upon the hearts of His people. In Hebrews 10:15-16 it is written:

> *"Whereof the* **Holy Ghost** [Ruach HaKodesh] *also is a* **witness** *to us: for after that he had said before, This is the covenant that I will make with them after those days, saith the* Lord, *I will put* **my laws [Torah]** *into their* **hearts**, *and in their* **minds** *will I write them."*

The Holy Spirit *(Ruach HaKodesh)* is called the Spirit of truth (which is the Torah – Psalm 119:142). It is His

Yeshua, Our Jewish Messiah

responsibility to guide the followers of *Yeshua*/Jesus as Messiah *(Mashiach)* in following the Torah of the G-d of Israel and to testify that *Yeshua*/Jesus in the Jewish Messiah *(Mashiach)*. In John *(Yochanan)* 15:26, 16:13, it is written:

> *"But when the Comforter is come, whom I will send unto you from the Father, even the* **Spirit of truth***, which proceedeth from the Father, he* **shall testify of me** *... Howbeit when he, the* **Spirit of Truth***, is come, he will* **guide you into all truth***: for he shall not speak of himself; but whatsoever he shall hear, that shall he speak: and he will show you things to come."*

The Torah is also called a lamp and a light. In Proverbs *(Mishlei)* 6:23 it is written:

> *"For the commandment is a lamp; and the* **law [Torah] is light***; and reproofs of instruction are the way of life."*

In Psalm *(Tehillim)* 119:97, 105, David writes that he loves the Torah because it is a light to him as it is written:

> *"O how love I thy* **law [Torah]***! It is my meditation all the day ... thy word is a* **lamp** *unto my feet, and a* **light** *unto my path."*

The Jewish Messiah *(Mashiach) Yeshua*/Jesus taught that those who keep the Torah of the G-d of Israel (which is light) become a light to the world. In Matthew *(Mattityahu)* 5:14-16 it is written:

> "**Ye** are the **light of the world**. *A city that is set on a hill cannot be hid. Neither do men light a candle, and put it under a bushel, but on a candlestick; and it giveth light unto all that are in the house.* **Let your light so shine** *before men, that they may see your good works, and glorify your Father which is in heaven.*"

The followers of the Jewish Messiah *(Mashiach)* Yeshua/Jesus are called to be children of light (which is the Torah). In Ephesians 5:8 it is written:

> *"For ye were sometimes darkness, but now are ye light in the* LORD*:* **walk [halacha] as children of light.**"

Yeshua/Jesus Taught the Shema

The Jewish Messiah *(Mashiach)* Yeshua/Jesus taught his students/disciples *(talmidim)* that the greatest commandment in the Torah is the SHEMA. The Hebrew word SHEMA is the Strong's word 8085 in the Hebrew concordance and means *"to hear, do and obey."* It is the first word in Deuteronomy *(Devarim)* 6:4. In Deuteronomy *(Devarim)* 6:4-5 it is written:

> *"Hear, O Israel: The* LORD *our God is one* LORD*: And thou shalt love the* LORD *thy God with all thine heart, and with all thy soul, and with all thy might."*

The G-d of Israel also commanded His people in the Torah to love your neighbor as yourself. In Leviticus *(Vayikra)* 19:18 it is written:

Yeshua, Our Jewish Messiah

"Thou shalt not avenge, nor bear any grudge against the children of thy people, but thou **shalt love thy neighbor as thyself***: I am the* L<small>ORD</small>*."*

The Jewish Messiah *(Mashiach) Yeshua*/Jesus taught that the SHEMA is the greatest commandment in the Torah and loving your neighbor as yourself is the second greatest commandment in the Torah. In Mark 12:28-31 it is written:

"And one of the scribes came, and having heard them reasoning together, and perceiving that he had answered them well, asked him, Which is the first [greatest] *commandment* [in the Torah] *of all? And Jesus answered him, The first of all the commandments is, Hear, O Israel; The* L<small>ORD</small> *our God is one* L<small>ORD</small>*: And thou shalt love the* L<small>ORD</small> *thy God with all thy heart, and with all thy soul, and with all thy mind, and with all thy strength:* [Deuteronomy 6:4-5] *this is the first commandment. And the second is like, namely this, Thou shalt love thy neighbor as thyself* [Leviticus 19:18]. *There is none other commandment greater than these."*

Yeshua/Jesus Worshipped in the Synagogue on the Sabbath

Being a Torah observant Jew, the Jewish Messiah *(Mashiach) Yeshua*/Jesus worshipped in a Jewish synagogue every *Sabbath*. In Luke 4:14-16 it is written:

> *"And **Jesus** returned in the power of the Spirit into Galilee: and there went out a fame of him through all the region round about. And he **taught** in their **synagogues**, being glorified of all. And he came to Nazareth, where he had been brought up: and, as his custom was, he went into the synagogue on the **sabbath** day, and stood up for to read."*

It is a Jewish custom to call a reader to read the *parasha* (weekly reading) every *Sabbath* from a raised podium *(bema)*. When he comes, the reader is regarded as making an *aliyah* (which means to go up or to ascend). It is a tremendous blessing for the reader to be able to read the Jewish Scriptures of the G-d of Israel. In Luke 4:17, the Jewish Messiah *(Mashiach) Yeshua*/Jesus followed this Jewish custom. In Luke 4:17 it is written:

> *"And there was delivered unto him* [he made an aliyah] *the book of the prophet Isaiah..."*

Because the Jewish Messiah *(Mashiach) Yeshua*/Jesus was a Torah observant Jew, He worshipped weekly in the Jewish synagogue on the *Sabbath*.

Yeshua/Jesus Kept the Biblical Festivals

The Jewish Messiah *(Mashiach) Yeshua*/Jesus and His parents kept the Biblical Festivals found in Leviticus *(Vayikra)* 23. In Luke 2:41-42, *Yeshua*/Jesus and His parents kept the Biblical festival of Passover *(Pesach)* as it is written:

> *"Now* **his parents went to Jerusalem every year at the feast of the passover.** *And when he*

Yeshua, Our Jewish Messiah

was twelve years old, they went up to Jerusalem after the custom of the feast."

In fact, the last meal that the Jewish Messiah *(Mashiach) Yeshua*/Jesus had was a Passover *(Pesach)* Seder meal. In Luke 22:14-15 it is written:

"And when the hour was come, he sat down, and the twelve apostles with him. And he said unto them, With desire I have desired to **eat this passover** *with you before I suffer* [be crucified on the tree]."

The Jewish Messiah *(Mashiach) Yeshua*/Jesus kept *Sukkot* (the Feast of Tabernacles). The last day of *Sukkot* is a special day known as *Hoshana Rabbah* which means *"the great salvation."* In the first century, a special ceremony took place in the Temple *(Beit HaMikdash)* on *Hoshana Rabbah* where there was a circling of the altar seven times. While circling the altar seven times, special *hoshanah* prayers were recited. These prayers include the words, *"Save us now; we implore you!"*

Water is a very important aspect of the celebration of *Sukkot* (Feast of Tabernacles). During the first century, there was a very important water pouring ceremony that took place every day during the seven days of *Sukkot* (Feast of Tabernacles) except the first day. This ceremony was known as the *Simchat Beit HaShoevah* (the rejoicing at the house of the water-drawing) (Talmud, Sukkot 5). It was with this setting that the Jewish Messiah *(Mashiach) Yeshua*/Jesus was attending *Sukkot* (Feast of Tabernacles) on the last day known as *Hoshana Rabbah*. In John *(Yochanan)* 7:2, 37-38 it is written:

Restoring the Two Houses of Israel

"Now the Jews' **feast of tabernacles** *was at hand* **...In the last day, that great day of the feast** [Hoshana Rabbah], *Jesus stood and cried, saying, If any man thirst, let him come unto me, and drink. He that believeth on me, as the Scripture hath said, out of his belly shall flow rivers of living water."*

The Feast of Tabernacles *(Sukkot)* is known as the *"season of our joy"* by the *house of Judah* (Judaism). During the celebration of *Sukkot* (Feast of Tabernacles), Isaiah *(Yeshayahu)* 12:3 is often quoted as it is written:

"Therefore with **joy** *shall ye* **draw water** *out of the* **wells of salvation.**"

Yeshua/Jesus in Hebrew means *"salvation."* He is the Jewish Messiah *(Mashiach)* and the salvation *(Yeshua)* of both the *house of Judah* (Judaism) and the *house of Israel* (Christianity).

For a more detailed study of Messiah and the Biblical Festivals, I would encourage you to read my book, *"The Seven Festivals of the Messiah."* In this book, I teach how the G-d of Israel gave the Biblical Festivals in Leviticus *(Vayikra)* 23 to teach about the first and second coming of the Jewish Messiah *(Mashiach)* Yeshua/Jesus and our personal relationship with the G-d of Israel.

Yeshua/Jesus Lived as a Jew

In this section of this chapter of the book, we showed that the Jewish Messiah *(Mashiach)* Yeshua/Jesus lived as a Jew. He was a Jewish rabbi. He taught His followers to be Torah observant. The followers of His teachings were known as students/disciples *(talmidim)*. The Jewish Messiah *(Mashiach) Yeshua*/Jesus taught His followers in parables as an *aggadic rabbi*. He taught that the greatest commandment in the Torah is the SHEMA (Deuteronomy *[Devarim]* 6:4-5).

The Jewish Messiah *(Mashiach) Yeshua*/Jesus was a Torah observant Jew. He worshipped in the Jewish synagogue on the Sabbath. He kept the Biblical Festivals found in Leviticus *(Vayikra)* 23. In His adult life, ministry and teachings, *Yeshua*/Jesus lived a Jewish lifestyle as a Torah observant Jew.

In the final sections of this chapter, we will show how the Jewish Messiah *(Mashiach) Yeshua*/Jesus died a Jew and will return to rule and reign in the Messianic Age *(Athid Lavo)* teaching the Torah of the G-d of Israel to all nations during that time.

Yeshua/Jesus Died a Jew

The Jewish Messiah *(Mashiach) Yeshua*/Jesus died a Jew. He had a Jewish burial. In John *(Yochanan)* 19:40, it is written:

> *"Then took they the* **body of Jesus***, and wound it in linen clothes with the spices,* **as the manner of the Jews is to bury***."*

Belief in the Resurrection of the Dead Is Jewish

In traditional Judaism, there are thirteen articles to Jewish faith. One of these articles is a belief in the resurrection of the dead. The Apostle Paul *(Rav Sha'ul)* was a Jew and an Israelite from the tribe of Benjamin (Philippians 3:5). He took a Nazarite vow (Numbers 6:1-21) in Acts 21:20-26 as a witness and to testify that he taught Jewish believers *(house of Judah)* in *Yeshua*/Jesus as Messiah *(Mashiach)* to be Torah observant. In I Corinthians 15:1, 3-4, 14, 20, 23 the Apostle Paul *(Rav Sha'ul)* writes:

> *"Moreover, brethren, I declare unto you the gospel which I preached unto you, which also ye have received, and wherein ye stand ... For I delivered unto you first of all that which I also received, how that Christ died for our sins according to the* [Jewish] *Scriptures; And that he was buried* [as a Jew], *and that he rose again the third day according to the* [Jewish] *Scriptures ... And if Christ be not risen, then is our preaching vain, and your faith is also vain ... But now is Christ risen from the dead, and become the firstfruits of them that slept ... But every man in his own order: Christ the firstfruits; afterward they that are Christ's at his coming."*

The Jewish Messiah *(Mashiach) Yeshua*/Jesus was resurrected from the dead in accordance with the traditional Jewish belief in the resurrection of the dead.

Yeshua Will Return at His Second Coming on the Mount of Olives

It is Jewish tradition that the Mount of Olives is called the *"mountain of the Messiah."* When the Jewish Messiah

Yeshua, Our Jewish Messiah

(Mashiach) Yeshua/Jesus ascended into heaven following His resurrection from the dead, He did so from the Mount of Olives. In Acts 1:9-12 it is written:

> *"And when he had spoken these things, while they beheld, he was taken up; and a cloud received him out of their sight. And while they looked steadfastly toward heaven as he went up, behold, two men stood by them in white apparel; Which also said, Ye men of Galilee, why stand ye gazing up into heaven? this same Jesus, which is taken up from you into heaven, shall so come in like manner as ye have seen him go into heaven. Then returned they unto Jerusalem from the mount called Olivet* [Olives]*…"*

When the Jewish Messiah *(Mashiach) Yeshua*/Jesus returns to the earth at His second coming as the Kingly Messiah *(Messiah ben David)*, He will do so by setting His feet on the mount of Olives. In Zechariah 14:3-4, it is written:

> *"Then shall* **the** L<small>ORD</small> *go forth, and fight against those nations, as when he fought in the day of battle. And* **his feet shall stand in that day upon the mount of Olives***, which is before Jerusalem on the east …"*

Yeshua Will Teach the Torah to the Nations During the Messianic Age

After the Jewish Messiah *(Mashiach) Yeshua*/Jesus returns to the earth at His second coming as the Kingly

Restoring the Two Houses of Israel

Messiah *(Messiah ben David)* following setting His feet upon the mount of Olives (Acts 1:9-12, Zechariah 14:3-4), He will rule and reign over all nations teaching them the Torah during the Messianic age *(Athid Lavo)* from the city of Jerusalem *(Yerushalayim)*. In Isaiah *(Yeshayahu)* 2:2-3, it is written:

> *"And it shall come to pass in the last days, that the mountain of the Lord's house shall be established in the top of the mountains, and shall be exalted above the hills; and all nations shall flow unto it. And many people shall go and say, Come ye, and let us go up to the mountain of the* LORD*, to the house of the God of Jacob; and he will teach us of his ways, and we will walk in his paths: for out of Zion shall go forth the law* [Torah]*, and the word of the* LORD *from Jerusalem."*

When the Torah is taught to all the nations during the Messianic Age *(Athid Lavo)* then the great commission of the Jewish Messiah *(Mashiach) Yeshua*/Jesus will be fulfilled. The great commission of *Yeshua*/Jesus is a commandment for His followers to make students/disciples *(talmidim)* of all nations teaching them to observe all things (the Torah) that He commanded them. In Matthew *(Mattityahu)* 28:18-20, it is written:

> *"And Jesus came and spake unto them, saying, All power is given unto me in heaven and in earth. Go ye therefore, and teach all nations* [the Torah]*, baptizing* [mikvah/immersion] *them in the name of the Father, and of the Son, and of the Holy Ghost* [Ruach HaKodesh]*: Teaching them to observe all things whatsoever I have commanded you*

Yeshua, Our Jewish Messiah

[the Torah]: *and, lo, I am with you always, even unto the end of the world."*

During the Messianic age *(Athid Lavo)*, there will be a Temple *(Beit HaMikdash)* in Jerusalem *(Yerushalayim)*. We are told this in Ezekiel *(Yechezekel)* chapters 40-48. In these chapters, it also tells us that during the Messianic Age *(Athid Lavo)*, all the nations will be keeping the Sabbath, the biblical festivals and the new moon. In Ezekiel *(Yechezekel)* 41:1, 42:1, 43:5, 44:1, 46:1, 3, the Sabbath and new moon will be observed as it is written:

> *"Afterward he brought me to the* **temple** *... Then he brought me forth into the* **utter court** *... So the spirit took me up, and brought me into the* **inner court***; and, behold, the glory of the* LORD *filled the house ...Then he brought me back the way of the gate of the outward sanctuary which looketh toward the east; and it was shut ... Thus saith the* LORD *God; The gate of the inner court that looketh toward the east shall be shut the six working days; but on the sabbath it shall be opened, and in the day of the new moon it shall be opened ....* **Likewise the people of the land shall worship** *at the door of this gate before the* LORD *in* **the sabbaths** *and in the* **new moons.***"*

The worship of the G-d of Israel on the Sabbath and new moon will also be done during the times of the new heavens and the new earth. In Isaiah *(Yeshayahu)* 66:22-23 it is written:

> *"For as the* **new heavens and the new earth,** *which I will make, shall remain before me, saith*

> *the* LORD, *so shall your seed and your name remain. And it shall come to pass, that from one* **new moon** *to another, and from one* **sabbath** *to another, shall* **all flesh** *come to* **worship** *before me, saith the* LORD."

During the Messianic Age *(Athid Lavo)*, the Jewish Messiah *(Mashiach) Yeshua*/Jesus will instruct all nations to keep the biblical festivals. In Ezekiel *(Yechezekel)* 45:21, Passover *(Pesach)* and Unleavened Bread *(Hag HaMatzah)* will be observed as it is written:

> *"In the first month, in the fourteenth day of the month, ye shall have the* **passover**, *a feast of seven days;* **unleavened bread** *shall be eaten."*

In addition, during the Messianic Age *(Athid Lavo)*, the G-d of Israel will require all nations to keep the feast of tabernacles *(Sukkot)*. In Zechariah 14:16-17 it is written:

> *"And it shall come to pass, that every one that is left of* **all the nations** *which came against Jerusalem shall even go up from* **year to year to worship the King**, *the* LORD *of hosts, and to* **keep the feast of tabernacles**. *And it shall be, that whoso will not come up of all the families of the earth unto Jerusalem to worship the King, the* LORD *of hosts, even upon them shall be no rain."*

Therefore, from these scriptures, we can understand that the Jewish Messiah *(Mashiach) Yeshua*/Jesus will be teaching the nations to follow the Torah during the Messianic Age.

Yeshua, Our Jewish Messiah

Yeshua/Jesus Is Our Jewish Messiah

In this chapter, we learned that the Jewish Messiah *(Mashiach) Yeshua* / Jesus is the Messiah *(Mashiach)* of both houses of Israel (Judaism and Christianity). *Yeshua* / Jesus was born a Jew. He was raised by Jewish parents in a Jewish home. He lived a Torah observant Jewish lifestyle. He was a Jewish rabbi and He taught His students/disciples *(talmidim)* to live a Torah observant lifestyle. *Yeshua*/Jesus died a Jew. When He returns at His second coming to be the Kingly Messiah known as *Messiah ben David*, He will teach the Torah to the nations from the city of Jerusalem *(Yerushalayim)*.

In order to be fully restored to the G-d of Israel, the *house of Judah* (Judaism) and the *house of Israel* (Christianity) need to recognize that *Yeshua*/Jesus is our **JEWISH** Messiah *(Mashiach)* and need to identify with His Jewishness. The *house of Judah* (Judaism) needs to accept that *Yeshua*/Jesus is the promised Messiah *(Mashiach)* as foretold in the Jewish scriptures. The *house of Israel* (Christianity) needs to more fully identify with the Jewishness of *Yeshua*/Jesus and embrace the Jewish roots of faith in Messiah. When these things are done, the G-d of Israel will bring full restoration to both houses of Israel. May it be done speedily in our days. Amen.

Chapter 7

Is the Jewish Messiah G-d?

Over the past 2,000 years, there has been a major division between the *house of Judah* (Judaism) and the *house of Israel* (Christianity) about who is the Jewish Messiah *(Mashiach)*. Furthermore, there has also been a major disagreement between the two houses of Israel over whether the Jewish Messiah *(Mashiach)* is just an earthly man who is anointed by the G-d of Israel and fulfills the expected functions of his office of ministry or whether the Jewish Messiah *(Mashiach)* is the G-d of Israel manifested in the flesh.

In the last chapter, we learned that the Jewish Messiah *(Mashiach) Yeshua*/Jesus was born a Jew, lived a Jew and died a Jew. In this chapter, using Scriptures from the *TeNaKh* (Old Testament) and the *Brit Hadashah* (New Testament) along with Rabbinic and other Jewish literature, we will examine the issue of whether the Jewish Messiah *(Mashiach) Yeshua*/Jesus is the G-d of Israel manifested in the flesh. We will learn that the entire Bible along with selected Rabbinic and other Jewish literature teaches us that the Jewish Messiah *(Mashiach) Yeshua*/Jesus is the G-d of Israel *(YHVH)* manifested in the flesh.

Furthermore, we will cross-reference Rabbinic and other Jewish literature with Scripture passages from the *Brit Hadashah* (New Testament) to further clarify that the WORD OF YHVH as mentioned in Jewish literature is the Jewish Messiah *(Mashiach) Yeshua*/Jesus. Once the *house of Judah* (Judaism) and the *house of Israel* (Christianity) recognize that *Yeshua*/Jesus is the G-d of Israel *(YHVH)* manifested in the flesh and is the promised Jewish Messiah *(Mashiach)*, full restoration can come to both houses of Israel.

The G-d of Israel Is YHVH

The G-d of Israel is *YHVH*. YHVH is also known as the *tetragrammaton*. In respect to the holiness of the name of the G-d of Israel *(YHVH)*, the *house of Judah* (Judaism) refers to *YHVH* as *Adonai*. In English, we pronounce the name of G-d *(YHVH)* as Jehovah. In our English Bibles, *YHVH* is mostly translated as LORD. In respect to the holiness and the sanctity of the name of the G-d of Israel, when referring to the G-d of Israel in written form, the *house of Judah* (Judaism) will write the name of God as G-d rather than God and write L-RD rather than LORD.

The G-d of Israel and the Jewish Messiah are Echad

To the *house of Judah* (Judaism), the most important verse in the Torah is found in Deuteronomy *(Devarim)* 6:4. This scripture passage is known as the *Shema*. In Hebrew, this verse reads transliterated into English as:

"*Shema Yisrael YHVH Eloheynu YHVH Echad.*"

Is the Jewish Messiah G-d?

In mystical Jewish literature, it is explained that this verse declares that the G-d of Israel is YHVH and is a COMPOUND UNITY. In the (*Zohar*, Volume 2, page 43) it is written:

> "The prescribed daily form of prayer (a confession of the **unity of the Godhead**), has for its object, that you shall know and comprehend it. We have said in many places that this daily form of prayer is one of those passages concerning the unity, which is taught in the Scriptures. In Deuteronomy 6:4, we read first YHVH, then ELOHEYNU and again YHVH, which together make **one unity**. But how can three names be one? Are they truly one because we call them one? How three can be one can only be known through the revelation of the Holy Spirit, and, in fact, with closed eyes. This is also the mystery of the voice. The voice is heard only as one sound, yet it consists of three substances, fire, wind, and water, but all three are one, as indicated through the mystery of the voice. Thus are YHVH; ELOHEYNU; YHVH but **one unity**, three substantive beings which are one; and this is indicated by the voice which a person uses in reading the words, "Hear, O Israel," thereby comprehending with the understanding the most perfect unity of EYN SOF (the boundless one); because all three are read with one voice, which indicates a trinity. And this is the daily confession of faith of the **unity**, which is **revealed by the Holy Spirit** in a mystery. Although there are so many persons united in the unity, yet each person is a true-one; **what one does, the other does.**" [1]

Restoring the Two Houses of Israel

The Jewish Messiah *(Mashiach) Yeshua*/Jesus confirmed the above belief as written in the *Zohar* that He is a compound unity with the limitless one (Eyn Sof) as taught in the *Shema*. In John *(Yochanan)* 10:30 it is written:

> *"I and my Father* [Eyn Sof] *are one* [Echad].*"*

In John *(Yochanan)* 17:11, 21-23 it is written:

> *"And now I am no more in the world, but these are in the world, and I come to thee. Holy Father, keep through thine own name those whom thou hast given me, that* **they may be one, as we are** ... *That they all may be* **one; as thou, Father, are in me**, *and* **I in thee**, *that they also may be one in us: that the world may believe that thou hast sent me. And the glory which thou gavest me I have given them; that they may be one,* **even as we are one**: *I in them,* **and thou in me**, *that they may be made perfect in one; and that the world may know that thou hast sent me, and hast loved them as thou hast loved me."*

The Word of YHVH Is the Jewish Messiah

The *Targumim* are a Jewish commentary on the Scripture passages in the Torah and the Prophets. The *Targumim* were considered to be authoritative Aramaic paraphrases of the books of the *TeNaKh* in the first century and were read in the synagogues along with the Hebrew of the Torah and Haftorah readings. [2]

Is the Jewish Messiah G-d?

In various Scripture passages in the Torah and the Prophets, the *Targumim* interpret YHVH as being the WORD OF YHVH. In some of these Scripture passages, it is explained that various individuals trusted *(emunah)* in the WORD OF YHVH and prayed in the name of the WORD OF YHVH. The Word of YHVH is also seen as being the Creator, the covenant maker and the mediator between the G-d of Israel and mankind. Furthermore, Israel and the *house of Jacob* are also seen being saved by the Word of YHVH. In Jewish mystical writings, the Word of YHVH is known as *Meditron* who is explained to be the *Son of Yah*.

In the *Brit Hadashah* (New Testament), the Jewish Messiah *(Mashiach) Yeshua*/Jesus is seen riding on a white horse, known as the Word of G-d (YHVH) and is the King of kings and the L-RD of lords. In Revelation 19:11, 13, 16 it is written:

> *"And I saw heaven opened, and behold a white horse; and he that sat upon him was called Faithful and True ... and his name is called the* WORD *of* GOD [YHVH] *... and on his thigh a name written,* KING OF KINGS, *and* LORD OF LORDS."

We will now examine some of the *Targumim* which speak of the WORD OF YHVH being YHVH.

Abraham and Jacob Trusted in the Word of YHVH

Abraham *(Avraham)* trusted in the WORD OF YHVH. According to *Targum Onkelos*, Genesis 15:6 it is written:

> *"And Abraham trusted* [emunah] *in the* WORD OF YHVH, *and He counted it to him for righteousness."* (*Targum Onkelos*, Genesis 15:6) [3]

According to the *Brit Hadashah* (New Testament), the WORD OF YHVH that Abraham *(Avraham)* trusted in was the Jewish Messiah *(Mashiach) Yeshua*/Jesus. In Galatians 3:7-9, 14 it is written:

> *"Know ye therefore that they which are of faith, the same are the children of Abraham. And the Scripture, foreseeing that God would justify the heathen through faith* [emunah], *preached before the gospel unto Abraham, saying, In thee shall all nations be blessed. So then they which be of* **faith** [emunah] *are blessed with faithful Abraham ... That the* **blessing of Abraham** *might come on the Gentiles* **through Jesus Christ;** *that we might* **receive the promise** *of the Spirit* **through faith** [emunah]*."*

According to *Targum Onkelos* Genesis 28:20-21, Jacob *(Ya'acov)* trusted in the WORD OF YHVH and the WORD OF YHVH was His G-d as it is written:

> *"And Jacob vowed a vow, saying, If the* WORD OF YHVH *will be my support, and will keep me in the way that I go, and will give me bread to eat, and raiment to put on, so that I come again to my father's house in peace; then shall the* WORD OF YHVH *be my* GOD.*"* (*Targum Onkelos*, Genesis 28:20-21) [4]

Is the Jewish Messiah G-d?

According to the *Targum* of Psalm 62, King David urged Israel to trust in the WORD OF YAH at all times. In Psalm *(Tehillim)* 62:9 (Jewish version) it is written:

> *"Trust in the* WORD OF YAH *at all times, O people of the house of Israel! Pour out before Him the sighings of your heart; Say, God is our trust forever." (Targum,* Psalm 62:9) [5]

Abraham Prayed in the Name of YHVH

According to the *Jerusalem Targum* of Genesis 22:14, Abraham PRAYED in the NAME of the WORD OF YHVH as it is written:

> *"And Abraham worshipped and* **prayed** in **the name** *of the WORD OF YHVH, and said, You are YHVH who does see, but You cannot be seen." (Jerusalem Targum* Genesis 22:14) [6]

In the *Brit Hadashah* (New Testament), the Jewish Messiah *(Mashiach) Yeshua* / Jesus instructed His followers to pray to G-d the Father [Eyn Sof] in His name. In John *(Yochanan)* 15:16 it is written:

> *"...whatsoever ye shall* **ask of the Father in my name**, *he may give it you."*

The Word of YHVH Is the Creator

According to the *Targumim*, the WORD OF YHVH is the Creator. According to *Targum Jonathan* Genesis 1:27 it is written:

Restoring the Two Houses of Israel

> *"And the* WORD OF YHVH *created man in his likeness, in the likeness of* YHVH, YHVH *created, male and female created He them. (Targum Jonathan, Genesis 1:27)* [7]

In Exodus *(Shemot)* 3:13-15, the G-d of Israel revealed to the children of Israel that His name is YHVH as it is written:

> *"And Moses said unto God, Behold, when I come unto the children of Israel, and shall say unto them, The God of your fathers hath sent me unto you; and they shall say to me,* **What is his name?** *What shall I say unto them? And* **God said** *unto Moses,* **I AM THAT I AM**: *and he said, Thus shalt thou say unto the children of Israel,* **I AM** *hath sent me unto you. And God said moreover unto Moses, Thus shalt thou say unto the children of Israel, the* Lord *God of your fathers, the God of Abraham, the God of Isaac, and the God of Jacob, hath sent me unto you:* **this is my name forever**, *and this is my memorial unto all generations."*

In the *Jerusalem Targum* to Exodus *(Shemot)* 3:14 it is written:

> *"And the* WORD OF YHVH *said to Moses: 'I am He who said unto the world, 'Be!' and it was: and who in the future shall say to it 'Be!' and it shall be.' And He said, 'Thus you shall say to the children of Israel: 'I AM' has sent me unto you."* (Jerusalem Targum, Exodus 3:14) [8]

Is the Jewish Messiah G-d?

YHVH Means to Eternally Exist

The name of the G-d of Israel (YHVH) means in Hebrew "to eternally exist." In the *Gesenius's Hebrew-Chaldee Lexicon to the Old Testament*, by H.W.F. Gesenius, printed by Baker Book House Company, on page 337 in the explanation of the phrase "I AM THAT I AM," in Exodus *(Shemot)* 3:14, Gesenius writes:

> "To this origin, allusion is made Exodus 3:14; (of the Hebrew), **'I (ever) shall be (the same) that I am (today)'**; compare Apoc 1:4,8: the name YHVH being derived from the (Hebrew) verb HVH (which means) to be, was considered to signify **God as eternal and immutable**, who will never be other than the same."

Therefore, the name of the G-d of Israel (YHVH) fully translated into English expresses that G-d is eternal and immutable and that His name means, *"I (ever) shall be (the same) that I am (today)."* In other words, the name of the G-d of Israel (YHVH) means that He eternally exists and that He is the same yesterday, today and forever. This is the name of the Jewish Messiah *(Mashiach)* Yeshua/Jesus in Hebrews 13:8 as it is written:

> *"Jesus Christ* (Yeshua HaMashiach) *the same yesterday, and today, and forever."*

The Jewish Messiah *(Mashiach) Yeshua*/Jesus confirmed the words of the *Jerusalem Targum* to Exodus 3:14 when He declared to the Jews that questioned Him that He was the I AM (YHVH) spoken of in Exodus *(Shemot)* 3:14.

Restoring the Two Houses of Israel

In John *(Yochanan)* 8:56-58 it is written:

> *"Your father Abraham rejoiced to see my day: and he saw it, and was glad. Then said the Jews unto him, Thou art not yet fifty years old, and hast thou seen Abraham? Jesus said unto them, Verily, verily, I say unto you, Before Abraham was,* **I am**.*"*

The Messiah Is the I AM (YHVH) of the G-d of Israel

The Jewish Messiah *(Mashiach) Yeshua*/Jesus referred to Himself many times as I AM in the following scripture passages:

1) **I AM** the bread of life (John 6:35).
2) **I AM** the light of the world (John 8:12).
3) **I AM** the door (John 10:9).
4) **I AM** the good shepherd (John 10:11).
5) **I AM** the resurrection and the life (John 11:25).
6) **I AM** the way, truth and the life (John 14:6).
7) **I AM** the true vine (John 15:1).

In the *Targum* to Psalm *(Tehillim)* 33:6 we are told that the WORD OF YHVH was the Creator as it is written:

> *"By the* WORD OF YHVH *were the heavens made, and all the hosts of them by the Spirit of His mouth."*

The *Brit Hadashah* (New Testament) confirms what was written in the *Targumim* that the Word of YHVH is the Creator. However, in the *Brit Hadashah* (New Testament), the WORD OF YHVH is known as the Jewish

Is the Jewish Messiah G-d?

Messiah *(Mashiach) Yeshua*/Jesus. In Colossians 1:15-17 it is written:

> "[Jesus] *Who is the image of the invisible God, the firstborn of every creature: For* **by him were all things created**, *that are in heaven, and that are in earth, visible and invisible, whether they be thrones, or dominions, or principalities, or powers: all things were created by him, and for him: And he is before all things, and* **by him all things consist**."

The Word of YHVH Is the Covenant Maker

According to *Targum Onkelos* the WORD OF YHVH made the Noahide Covenant in Genesis 9:17 as it is written:

> "*And* YHVH *said to Noah, 'This is the token of the covenant which I have established between* MY WORD *and between all flesh that is upon the earth.*" (*Targum Onkelos* Genesis 9:17) [9]

Also according to *Targum Onkelos*, it was the WORD OF YHVH who made the covenant with Abraham in Genesis 17:7 as it is written:

> "*And I will establish my covenant between* MY WORD *and between you…*" (*Targum Onkelos* Genesis 17:7) [10]

The *Brit Hadashah* (New Testament) confirms what was written in *Targum Onkelos* that the WORD OF

YHVH made a covenant with Abraham *(Avraham)*. However, in the *Brit Hadashah* (New Testament), the WORD OF YHVH is known as the Jewish Messiah *(Mashiach) Yeshua*/Jesus. In Galatians 3:16 it is written:

> *"Now to* **Abraham** *and* **his seed** *were the* **promises** [Covenant] **made**. *He saith not, And to seeds, as of many; but as of one, And to thy seed,* **which is Christ.***"*

The Word of YHVH Is Meditron

According to the Babylonian *Talmud* in *Sanhedrin 38b*, another name for the WORD OF YHVH is *Meditron* as it is written:

> "Once a Min [Nazarene] said to R. Idith: It is written: And unto Moses He [YHVH] said, 'Come up unto YHVH...' [Exodus 24:1] But surely it should have stated: ... 'Come up unto Me!' It was METATRON [who was speaking] he replied, 'Whose name is similar to that of his Master, for it is written: For my name is in him.' [Exodus 23:21]" (*Babylonian Talmud,* Sanhedrin 38b) [11]

According to the writings of Jewish mysticism, *Meditron* is the *"Middle Pillar of the Godhead"* and this *"Middle Pillar"* is the *"Son of Yah"* as it is written:

> "The **Middle Pillar** [of the Godhead] is **Metatron**, who has accomplished peace above, according to the glorious state there."

Is the Jewish Messiah G-d?

(*Zohar, Volume 3, Ra'aya Mehaimna*, page 227, Amsterdam Edition)

"Better is a neighbor that is near, than a brother far off. This neighbor is the **Middle Pillar in the Godhead**, which is the **Son of Yah**." (*Zohar, Volume 2, Ra'aya Mehaimna*, page 115, Amsterdam Edition) [12]

The *Brit Hadashah* (New Testament) confirms what was written in the *Zohar* that the WORD OF YHVH otherwise known as *Meditron* is the Middle Pillar of the Godhead and the Son of Yah. However, in the *Brit Hadashah* (New Testament), the WORD OF YHVH otherwise known as *Meditron* and the Son of Yah is the Jewish Messiah (*Mashiach*) *Yeshua*/Jesus. In Colossians 1:15, 19, 2:6, 9 it is written:

"[Jesus] *Who is the image of the invisible God … For it pleased the Father that in him should all fullness dwell … As ye have therefore received* **Christ Jesus the** L<small>ORD</small>, *so walk ye in him … For in him* **dwelleth** *all the* **fullness of the Godhead bodily.**"

The Word Of YHVH Is the First Begotten of All the Creatures of G-d

According to the writings of Jewish mysticism, the WORD OF YHVH is not only *Meditron* and the Son of Yah but He is also the *"first begotten of all the creatures of God"* as it is written:

"And Abraham said to his oldest servant of his house ... [Genesis 24:2] Who is this of whom it said 'his servant?' In what sense must this be understood? Who is this servant? R. Nehori answered: 'It is in no other sense to be understood than expressed in the word, 'His servant,' His servant, the servant of God, the chief in His service. And **who is he? Metratron,** as said, His is appointed to glorify the bodies which are in the grave. This is the meaning of the words, 'Abraham said to His servant' that is to the servant of God. The servant is **Meditron,** the eldest of His [YHVH's] House**, who is the first-begotten of all creatures of God**, who is the ruler of all He has; because God has committed to Him the government over all His hosts." (*Zohar, Genesis; Midrash HaNe'elam;* Page 126, Amsterdam Edition) [13]

The *Brit Hadashah* (New Testament) confirms what was written in the *Zohar* that the WORD OF YHVH otherwise known as *Meditron* is the first begotten of all the creatures of G-d. However, in the *Brit Hadashah* (New Testament), the WORD OF YHVH otherwise known as the first begotten of all the creatures of G-d is the Jewish Messiah *(Mashiach) Yeshua*/Jesus. In John *(Yochanan)* 1:1, 14, 3:16 it is written:

> *"In the beginning was the Word* [of YHVH]*, and the Word* [of YHVH] *was with God, and the Word* [of YHVH] *was God* [a compound unity with Eyn Sof] ... *And the Word* [of YHVH] *was made flesh and dwelt* [shakan] *among us (and we*

Is the Jewish Messiah G-d?

beheld his glory, the glory as of the only [first] *begotten of the Father) ... For God so loved the world that he gave his only* [first] *begotten Son* [the Son of Yah] *that whosoever believeth in him should not perish, but have everlasting life."*

In I John *(Yochanan)* 5:1, Revelation 1:5, 7 it is written:

"Whosoever believeth that **Jesus** *is the Christ is born of God: and every one that loveth him that begat loveth him also that is* [first] **begotten** *of him ... And from Jesus Christ, who is the faithful witness, and the* **first begotten** *of the dead ... Behold, he cometh with clouds; and every eye shall see him, and they also which pierced him: and all kindreds of the earth shall wail because of him* [Zechariah 12:10,12 — *Babylonian Talmud,* Sukkot 52a]. *Even so, Amen."*

The Word of YHVH Is the Way to the Tree of Life and the Heavenly City of Jerusalem

According to the writings of Jewish mysticism, the WORD OF YHVH is not only *Meditron,* the Son of Yah and the first begotten of all the creatures of God but He is also the way to the tree of life and the heavenly city of Jerusalem.

"To keep the way of the tree of life. [Genesis 3:24] **Who is the way to the tree of life?** It is the great **Metatron**, for he is the way to that great tree, to that mighty tree of life. Thus it is written, 'The Angel of God, which went before the camp of Israel, removed and went behind them.' [Exodus 14:19] And Meditron is called the Angel of God. Come and see, thus says R. Simeon. The holy One, blessed Be He, has prepared for Himself a holy Temple above in the heavens, a holy city, a city in the heavens, and called it Jerusalem, the holy city..." (*Zohar, Volume 2, Exodus,* page 51, Amsterdam Edition) [14]

The *Brit Hadashah* (New Testament) confirms what was written in the *Zohar* that the WORD OF YHVH otherwise known as *Meditron* is the way to the tree of life and the heavenly city of Jerusalem. However, in the *Brit Hadashah* (New Testament), the WORD OF YHVH otherwise known as the way to the tree of life and the heavenly city of Jerusalem is the Jewish Messiah *(Mashiach) Yeshua*/Jesus. In Revelation 21:10, 22:12, 14 it is written:

> *"And he carried me away in the spirit to a great and high mountain, and showed me that great city,* **the holy Jerusalem***, descending out of heaven from God ... And, behold, I* [Yeshua/Jesus] *come quickly; and my reward is with me, to give every man according as his work shall be ... Blessed are they that do his commandments, that they may have right to the* **tree of life** *and may* **enter in through the gates of the city.***"*

The Word of YHVH Is the only Mediator Between G-d and Man

According to the writings of Jewish mysticism, the WORD OF YHVH is not only *Meditron*, the Son of Yah,

Is the Jewish Messiah G-d?

first begotten of all the creatures of God, the way to the tree of life and the heavenly Jerusalem but He is also the only mediator between the G-d of Israel and man as it is written:

> "...**Every petition sent to the King must be through Metatron.** Every message and petition from here below, must first go to Meditron, and from thence to the king. **Medatron is the Mediator** of all that comes from heaven down to the earth, or from the earth up to heaven. And because he is the mediator of all, it is written 'And the Angel of God, which went before the camp of Israel, removed; that is, before Israel which is above. [Exodus 14:19] This Angel of God is the same of whom it is written, 'And YHVH went before them...' [Exodus 13:21] to go by day and by night as the ancients have expounded it. Whoever will speak to me [says God] shall not be able to do so, till he has made it known to Metatron, thus the holy One, blessed be He, on account of the great love to and mercy with which He has over the Assembly of Israel, commits her [the Assembly] to Metratron's care. What shall I do Him [Metatron]? I will commit my Whole house into His hand, etc. Henceforth be you a Keeper As it is written, 'The Keeper of Israel' [Psalm 121:4]" (*Zohar, Volume 2, Exodus,* page 51, Amsterdam Edition) [15]

The *Brit Hadashah* (New Testament) confirms what was written in the *Zohar* that the WORD OF YHVH otherwise known as *Meditron* is the only mediator between the G-d of Israel and mankind. However, in the *Brit*

Hadashah (New Testament), the WORD OF YHVH otherwise known as the only mediator between the G-d of Israel and mankind is the Jewish Messiah *(Mashiach) Yeshua*/Jesus. In I Timothy 2:5 and Hebrews 9:15 it is written:

> *"For there is one God, and* **one mediator between God and men, the man Christ Jesus** ... *And for this cause he is the mediator of the new testament, that by means of death, for the redemption of the transgressions that were under the first* [original] *testament, they which are called might receive the promise of eternal inheritance."*

The Word Of YHVH Is the Savior and Salvation of the House of Jacob

According to the *Targumim*, the WORD OF YHVH is the Savior and Salvation of the *house of Jacob* as it is written:

> *"Our father Jacob said: My soul does not wait for salvation such as that wrought by Gideon, the son of Joush, for that was but temporal; neither for a salvation like that of Samson, which wus only transitory; but for that* **SALVATION** *which you have promised to come,* **THROUGH YOUR WORD** *unto Your people, the children of Israel; for your salvation my soul hopes."* (*Targum Jonathan*, Genesis 49:18) [16]

> *"But Israel shall be saved by the* WORD OF YHVH *with an everlasting salvation ... By the*

Is the Jewish Messiah G-d?

WORD OF YHVH *shall all the seed of Israel be justified ..." (Targum Jonathan,* Isaiah 45:17, 25) [17]

"But I will have mercy upon the house of Judah, and I will save them by the WORD OF YHVH, *their God." (Targum Jonathan,* Hosea 1:7) [18]

Many Scripture passages in the *TeNaKh* (Old Testament) and the *Brit Hadashah* (New Testament) confirms what was written in the *Targumim* that the WORD OF YHVH is both the Savior and the Salvation of the G-d of Israel for the entire *house of Jacob* (Judaism and Christianity).

The G-d Of Israel Is Our Savior

The Jewish Scriptures (*TeNaKh*) teach us that the G-d of Israel ALONE is our salvation. In Isaiah (*Yeshayahu*) 43:1, 3, 11 it is written:

> *"But now thus saith the* LORD *that created thee, O Jacob* [house of Israel and house of Judah], *and he that formed thee, O Israel, Fear not: for I have redeemed thee, I have called thee by thy name; thou art mine ... For I am the* LORD **[YHVH]** *thy God* [Elohim], *the Holy One of Israel,* **thy Savior [Yeshua]** *... I, even I, am the* LORD **[YHVH];** *and* **beside me there is no savior.**"

In Isaiah *(Yeshayahu)* 45:21-22 it is written:

> *"Tell ye, and bring them near; yea, let them take counsel together: who hath declared this from an-*

cient time? who hath told it from that time? have not **I the** L{\scriptsize ORD}? *And there is no God else beside me; a just God and a* **Savior**; *there is* **none beside me**. *Look unto me, and be ye saved, all the ends of the earth: for I am God, and there is none else."*

In Isaiah *(Yeshayahu)* 63:7-8, it is written:

"I will mention the **lovingkindnesses of the** L{\scriptsize ORD}, *and the praises of the* L{\scriptsize ORD}, *according to all that the* L{\scriptsize ORD} *hath bestowed on us, and the great goodness toward the house of Israel, which he hath bestowed on them according to his mercies, and according to the multitude of his lovingkindnesses. For he said, Surely they are my people ... so* **he was their Savior**.

In Hosea *(Hoshea)* 13:4, it is written:

"Yet I am **the** L{\scriptsize ORD} **thy God** *from the land of Egypt, and thou shalt know no god but me: for* **there is no savior beside me**.*"*

In Luke 1:46-47, it is written:

"And Mary said, My soul doth magnify the L{\scriptsize ORD}, *And my spirit hath rejoiced in* **God my Savior**.*"*

Therefore, it is the G-d of Israel alone who is our Savior.

Yeshua Is Our Savior

The Hebrew word for savior is the Strong's word 3467 in the Strong's Concordance. It is the Hebrew

Is the Jewish Messiah G-d?

word *Yasha* which means *"salvation, save, savior, preserve, rescue or bring deliverance."*

The Hebrew word for the English word Jesus is *Yeshua*. It is related to the Hebrew word *Yasha*. As we studied in the last chapter, the Hebrew name of the Jewish Messiah *(Mashiach)*, *Yeshua*, communicates to us in Hebrew thought that He is the Savior of both the *house of Judah* (Judaism) and the *house of Israel* (Christianity).

The Jewish Messiah *(Mashiach) Yeshua*/Jesus is the Savior of the G-d of Israel for the *house of Jacob*. In Luke 2:10-11, it is written:

> *"And the angel said unto them, Fear not: for, behold, I bring you good tidings of great joy, which shall be to all people. For unto you is born this day in the city of David* **a Savior, which is Christ the** Lord.*"*

In John *(Yochanan)* 4:25-26, 41-42, it is written:

> *"The woman saith unto him, I know that the Messias cometh, which is called Christ: when he is come, he will tell us all things. Jesus saith unto her, I that speak unto thee am he ... And many more believed because of his own word; And said unto the woman, Now we believe, not because of thy saying: for we have heard him ourselves, and know that this is indeed the* **Christ, the Savior** *of the world."*

Restoring the Two Houses of Israel

In Acts 5:30-32, it is written:

> *"The God of our fathers raised up* **Jesus**, *whom ye slew and hanged on a tree. Him hath God exalted with his right hand to be a Prince and* **a Savior**, *for to give repentance to Israel, and forgiveness of sins. And we are his witnesses of these things; and so is also the Holy Ghost* [Ruach HaKodesh] *whom God hath given to them that obey him."*

In Acts 13:22-23, it is written:

> *"And when he had removed him, he raised up unto them David to be their king; to whom also he gave testimony, and said, I have found David the son of Jesse, a man after mine own heart, which shall fulfill all my will. Of this man's seed hath God according to his promise raised unto Israel* **a Savior, Jesus**.*"*

Since the G-d of Israel alone is our Savior and the Jewish Messiah *(Mashiach) Yeshua*/Jesus is our Savior, *Yeshua*/Jesus is the G-d of Israel manifested in the flesh.

The G-d of Israel Is Our Salvation

The Bible not only tells us that the G-d of Israel is our Savior *(yasha)* but He is also our salvation *(yeshua)*. In Exodus *(Shemot)* 15:2, it is written:

> *"***The** LORD **is** *my strength and song, and he is become* **my salvation** [yeshua]: *he is my God,*

Is the Jewish Messiah G-d?

and I will prepare him a habitation; my father's God, and I will exalt him."

In Psalm *(Tehillim)* 62:1-2, it is written:

"Truly my soul waiteth upon **God**: *from him cometh* **my salvation**. **He** *alone* **is** *my rock and* **my salvation**; *he is my defense; I shall not be greatly moved."*

In Isaiah *(Yeshayahu)* 12:2 it is written:

"Behold, **God is my salvation**; *I will trust, and not be afraid: for the* LORD *Jehovah is my strength and my song; he also is become my salvation."*

Therefore, it is the G-d of Israel who is the salvation of His people.

Yeshua Is Our Salvation

The Hebrew word for salvation is the Strong's word 3444 in the Strong's Concordance. It is the Hebrew word *Yeshooah* which means *"salvation, save, victory or bring deliverance."*

The Hebrew word for the English word Jesus is *Yeshua*. It is related to the Hebrew word *Yeshooah*. The Hebrew word for the English word Jesus communicates to us that He is the Salvation of both the *house of Judah* (Judaism) and the *house of Israel* (Christianity).

The Jewish Messiah *(Mashiach) Yeshua*/Jesus is the Salvation of the G-d of Israel unto the *house of Jacob*. In Acts 4:8, 10-12 it is written:

Restoring the Two Houses of Israel

> *"Then Peter [Kefa], filled with the Holy Ghost [Ruach HaKodesh], said unto them, Ye rulers of the people, and elders of Israel ... Be it known unto you all, and to all the people of Israel, that by* **the name of Jesus Christ** *of Nazareth, whom ye crucified, whom God raised from the dead, even by him doth this man stand here before you whole. This is the stone which was set at naught of you builders, which is become the head of the corner.* **Neither is there salvation in any other**: *for there is none other name under heaven given among men, whereby we must be saved."*

In Romans 10:9-12, it is written:

> *"That if thou shalt confess with thy mouth the* LORD **Jesus**, *and shalt* **believe in thine heart** *that God hath raised him from the dead,* **thou shalt be saved**. *For with the heart man believeth unto righteousness; and with the mouth confession is made unto salvation. For the Scripture saith, Whosoever believeth on him shall not be ashamed. For there is no difference between the Jew and the Greek: for the same* LORD *over all is rich unto all that call upon him."*

In I Thessalonians 5:9, it is written:

> *"For God hath not appointed us to wrath, but to obtain* **salvation by our** LORD **Jesus Christ**.*"*

The Hand and Arm of G-d Brings Salvation

The word hand is the Strong's number 3027 in the Hebrew Concordance. It is the Hebrew word 3027

Is the Jewish Messiah G-d?

which is *yad*. The Hebrew word *yad* means *"hand indicating power, strength or to draw from strength."* The word for arm is the Strong's number 2220 in the Hebrew Concordance. It is the Hebrew word *zeroah*. The Hebrew word *zeroah* means *"arm (as stretched out), mighty, power, strength."*

In Jewish thought, the hand and arm is associated with salvation, strength and victory. It is the G-d of Israel who stretches out his hand and arm to save His people. In Isaiah *(Yeshayahu)* 59:1 it is written:

> *"Behold, the* **Lord's hand** *is not shortened, that it cannot* **save** *…"*

In Exodus (*Shemot*) 6:6, it is written:

> *"Wherefore say unto the children of Israel,* **I am the** L ORD, *and I will bring you out from under the burdens of the Egyptians, and I will rid you out of their bondage,* **and I will redeem you with a stretched out arm**, *and with great judgments."*

In Deuteronomy *(Devarim)* 4:32, 34 it is written:

> *"For ask now of the days that are past, which were before thee, since the day that God created man upon the earth, and ask from the one side of heaven unto the other, whether there hath been any such thing as this great thing is, or hath been heard like it? … Or hath God attempted to go and take him a nation from the midst of another nation, by temp-*

tations, by signs, and by wonders, and by war, and **by a mighty hand, and by a stretched out arm**, and by great terrors, according to all that the LORD your God did for you in Egypt before your eyes?"

In Psalm (*Tehillim*) 136:1, 10-12 it is written:

"O give thanks unto the LORD; *for he is good: for his mercy endureth forever ... To him that smote Egypt in their firstborn: for his mercy endureth forever: And* **brought out Israel** *from among them: for his mercy endureth forever:* **With a strong hand, and with a stretched out arm**: *for his mercy endureth forever."*

In Isaiah *(Yeshayahu)* 52:10, it is written:

"The LORD *hath made bare* **his holy arm** *in the eyes of all the nations; and all the ends of the earth shall see* **the salvation of our God.**"

In Luke 1:46-47, 51 it is written:

"And Mary said, My soul doth magnify the LORD, *And my spirit hath rejoiced in* **God my Savior** *... He hath showed* **strength with his arm**..."

The Arm of the G-d of Israel Is the Messiah

The arm of the G-d of Israel is the Jewish Messiah *(Mashiach) Yeshua*/Jesus. In Isaiah *(Yeshayahu)* 59:1-2, 12, 15-16 it is written:

Is the Jewish Messiah G-d?

"Behold, the Lord's hand is not shortened, that it cannot save; neither his ear heavy, that it cannot hear: But **your iniquities have separated between you and your God**, *and your sins have hid his face from you, that he will not hear ... For our transgressions are multiplied before thee, and our sins testify against us: for our transgressions are with us; and as for our iniquities, we know them .. Yea, truth faileth; and he that departeth from evil maketh himself a prey: and* **the Lord saw it**, *and it displeased him that there was no judgment. And he saw that there was no man, and wondered that there was no intercessor: therefore* **his arm brought salvation unto him**; *and his righteousness, it sustained him."*

The arm of the L-RD was wounded for the sins of G-d's people. In Isaiah *(Yeshayahu)* 53:1, 5-6 it is written:

"Who hath believed our report? and to whom is **the arm of the Lord revealed?** *... But he was wounded for our transgressions, he was bruised for our iniquities ...* **the Lord hath laid on him the iniquity of us all**.*"*

The Jewish Messiah *(Mashiach) Yeshua*/Jesus was born to save His people from their sins. In Matthew *(Mattityahu)* 1:21 it is written:

"And she [Mary/Miryam] *shall bring forth a son, and thou shalt call his name* JESUS [Yeshua]: **for he shall save his people from their sins**.*"*

The Right Hand and Arm of G-d Brings Salvation

In Jewish thought, it is specifically the *right* hand and arm which brings forth victory and salvation. In Exodus *(Shemot)* 15:2, 6 it is written:

> *"The LORD is my strength and song, and he is become* **my salvation** *... Thy* **right hand***, O LORD, is become glorious in* **power***: thy right hand, O LORD, hath dashed in pieces the enemy."*

In Psalm *(Tehillim)* 17:7 it is written:

> *"Show thy marvelous lovingkindness, O thou* **that savest by thy right hand** *them which put their trust in thee from those that rise up against them."*

In Psalm *(Tehillim)* 89:13 it is written:

> *"Thou hast a mighty arm:* **strong** *is thy hand, and* **high** *is thy* **right hand***."*

In Psalm *(Tehillim)* 98:1 it is written:

> *"O sing unto the LORD a new song, for he hath done marvelous things: his* **right hand***, and his holy arm, hath gotten him* **the victory***."*

The Right Hand of the G-d of Israel Is the Messiah

The right hand of the G-d of Israel is the Jewish Messiah *(Mashiach) Yeshua*/Jesus. In Mark 14:61-62 it is written:

Is the Jewish Messiah G-d?

"...Again the high priest [Cohen HaGadol] *asked him, and said unto him,* **Art thou the Christ** [Mashiach]*, the Son of the Blessed? And* **Jesus said, I am***: and ye shall see the Son of man sitting on the* **right hand of power,** *and coming in the clouds of heaven."*

In Luke 22:66-69 it is written:

"And as soon as it was day, the elders of the people and the chief priests and the scribes came together, and led him into their council, saying, **Art thou the Christ** [Mashiach]*? tell us. And he said unto them ... Hereafter shall the Son of man sit on* **the right hand of the power** *of God."*

In Acts 2:29-36 it is written:

"Men and brethren, let me freely speak unto you of the patriarch David, that he is both dead and buried, and his sepulcher is with us unto this day. Therefore being a prophet, and knowing that God has sworn with an oath to him, that of the fruit of his loins, according to the flesh [II Samuel 7:12-13]*, he would raise up Christ to sit on his throne; He seeing this before spake of the resurrection of Christ, that his soul was not left in hell, neither his flesh did see corruption* [Psalm 16:10]*. This* **Jesus** *hath God raised up, whereof we all are witnesses. Therefore being by* **the right hand of God exalted***, and having received of the Father the promise of the Holy Ghost* [Ruach HaKodesh]*, he hath shed forth this, which ye now see and hear. For David is not ascended into the heavens: but he*

saith himself, The LORD *said unto my* LORD, **Sit thou on my right hand**, *Until I make thy foes thy footstool* [Psalm 110:1]. *Therefore let all the house of Israel know assuredly, that God hath made that same Jesus, whom ye have crucified, both* LORD *and Christ."*

In Hebrews 1:1-5, 13 it is written:

"**God** *who at sundry times and in divers manners spake in time past unto the fathers by the prophets, Hath in these last days spoken unto us by* **his Son**, *whom he hath appointed heir of all things, by whom also he made the worlds; Who being the brightness of his glory, and the* **express image of his person**, *and upholding all things by the word of his power, when he had by himself purged our sins,* **sat down on the right hand** *of the Majesty on high; Being made so much better than the angels, and he hath by inheritance obtained a more excellent name than they. For unto which of the angels said he at any time, Thou art my son, this day have I begotten thee?* [Psalm 2:7] *And again, I will be to him a Father, and he shall be to me a Son?* [II Samuel 7:14] ... *But to which of the angels said he at any time,* **Sit on my right hand**, *until I make thine enemies thy footstool* [Psalm 110:1]."

We Must Trust in the Arm of the Messiah and Not Our Own Strength

Both the *house of Judah* (Judaism) and the *house of Israel* (Christianity) must trust in the arm of the Messiah

Is the Jewish Messiah G-d?

(Mashiach) to be our salvation and not trust in our own arm and strength. In Jeremiah *(Yermiyahu)* 17:5, 7 it is written:

> *"Thus saith the* Lord: **Cursed be the man** *that trusteth in man and* **maketh flesh his arm**, *and whose heart departeth from the* Lord ... **Blessed is the man** *that* **trusteth in the** Lord, *and whose hope the* Lord *is."*

The G-d of Israel Is the First and Last

The G-d of Israel is the first and the last. In Isaiah *(Yeshayahu)* 41:4 it is written:

> *"Who hath wrought and done it, calling the generations from the beginning? I am the* Lord, *the* **first**, *and with the* **last**, *I am he."*

The G-d of Israel is the first and the last. He is the King of Israel and the redeemer of His people. In Isaiah *(Yeshayahu)* 44:6, it is written:

> *"Thus saith the* Lord *the* **King of Israel**, *and his redeemer the* Lord *of hosts: I am the* **first,** *and I am the* **last**; *and beside me there is no God."*

The way that you would express the phrase first and the last using the Hebrew alphabet is with the Hebrew letters *Alef* and *Tav*. *Alef* is the first letter in the Hebrew alphabet and *Tav* is the last letter in the Hebrew alphabet. The first and last letters in the Greek alphabet are *Alpha* and *Omega* respectively.

The Messiah Is the First and the Last

The Jewish Messiah *(Mashiach) Yeshua*/Jesus is the first and the last, the beginning and the end. He is the *Alef* and the *Tav*, the *Alpha* and *Omega*. In Revelation 1:5, 7-8 it is written:

> *"And from* **Jesus Christ**, *who is the faithful witness, and the first begotten of the dead, and the prince of the kings of the earth. Unto him that loved us, and washed us from our sins in his own blood .. Behold, he cometh with clouds: and every eye shall see him, and they also which pierced him: and all kindreds of the earth shall wail because of him. Even so, Amen. I am Alpha and Omega* [Alef and Tav in Hebrew], **the beginning** *and* **the ending***, saith the* Lord, **which is**, *and* **which was**, *and* **which is to come**, *the Almighty."*

The way that you would say *"which is, and which was and which is to come"* in Hebrew is YHVH. The Jewish Messiah *(Mashiach) Yeshua*/Jesus is YHVH, the beginning and the end, the *Alef* and the *Tav*. In Revelation 2:8 it is written:

> *"And unto the angel of the church in Smyrna write: These things saith* **the first and the last**, *which was dead and is alive."*

In Revelation 21:5-6 it is written:

> *"And he that sat upon the throne said, Behold, I make all things new. And he said unto me, Write: for these words are true and faithful. And he said unto me, It is done.* **I am Alpha and Omega**

Is the Jewish Messiah G-d?

[Alef and Tav in Hebrew], **the beginning and the end**. *I will give unto him that is athirst of the fountain of the water of life freely."*

In Revelation 22:12-13 it is written:

"And, behold, **I come quickly**; *and my reward is with me, to give every man according as his work shall be. I am Alpha and Omega,* **the beginning and the end, the first and the last**.*"*

The Messiah in Isaiah 52/53 in Jewish Literature

In various Jewish commentaries in Jewish literature when referring to the Scripture passages in Isaiah *(Yeshayahu)* 52/53, it will be said that these verses in Isaiah 52/53 speak about the Jewish Messiah *(Mashiach)*. We will examine of few of these references in this section of the chapter. On Isaiah 52:7 it is written:

"Rabbi Jose the Galilean says: Great is peace — for at the hour the **King Messiah** reveals himself unto Israel, he will begin in no other way than with 'peace' as it is written: *How beautiful upon the mountains are the feet of the messenger of good news, that announces peace* [Isaiah 52:7]." (Numbers Rabbah XI, 16-20) [19]

On Isaiah 52:13 it is written:

"Behold, **My servant the Messiah** *shall prosper, he shall be exalted and great and very powerful."* (*Targum Jonathan,* Isaiah 52:13) [20]

Restoring the Two Houses of Israel

On Isaiah 52:15-53:2 it is written:

> "Regarding the mission by which **Messiah** will present himself ... Isaiah states, *He grew like a tender plant and as a root out of dry land ... At him will kings shut their mouths, for what had not been told unto them shall they see, and what they never heard shall they understand.*" *(Maimonides)* [21]

On Isaiah 53:3 it is written:

> *"Man"* in the passage [Isaiah 53:3] ... **refers to the Messiah, the Son of David** ... (*Midrash Thanhumi*, Rabbi Nahman) [22]

On Isaiah 53:4-5 it is written:

> "The Rabanan say that the **Messiah's name** is the Suffering Scholar of Rabbi's House (or the Leper Scholar) for it is written, *'Surely he has born our grief and carried our sorrows, yet we did esteem him stricken, smitten of God and afflicted.'* " [Isaiah 53:4] (*Babylonian Talmud*, Sanhedrin 98a) [23]

> "**The Messiah — what is his name?** ... The House of Rabbi Judah the Holy One says: **The Sick One** ... *Surely he has born our sicknesses* [Isaiah 53:4] (*Babylonian Talmud*, Sanhedrin 98b) [24]

> *"The Holy One gave* **Messiah** *the opportunity to save souls but to be severely chastised ...* **Messiah**

Is the Jewish Messiah G-d?

accepted the chastisement of love … *'He was oppressed, and he was afflicted.'* And when Israel is sinful, the Messiah seeks mercy on them … *'By his stripes we were healed and He carried the sins of many'* …" (Rabbi Moshe Hadershan; *Midrash Rabbah;* Bereshit Rabbah) [25]

The Messiah Will Set His Feet Upon the Mount of Olives

In traditional Judaism and in Rabbinic literature, the mount of Olives is called the mountain of the Messiah *(Mashiach)*. After the Jewish Messiah *(Mashiach) Yeshua/* Jesus was resurrected, He left the earth to return to Heaven *(Olam Haba)* to sit at the right hand of the Father from the Mount of Olives. In Acts 1:9-12 it is written:

> *"And when he had spoken these things, while they beheld,* **he** [Jesus] **was taken up;** *and a cloud received him out of their sight. And while they looked steadfastly toward heaven as he went up, behold, two men stood by them in white apparel; Which also said, Ye men of Galilee, why stand ye gazing up into heaven?* **this same Jesus**, *which is taken up from you into heaven,* **shall so come in like manner** *as ye have seen him go into heaven. Then returned they unto Jerusalem* **from the mount called Olivet [Olives]**, *which is from Jerusalem a sabbath day's journey."*

When the Jewish Messiah *(Mashiach) Yeshua/*Jesus returns at His second coming as the Kingly Messiah *(Messiah* *ben David)*, He will set His feet upon the mount of Olives. In Zechariah 14:3-4, 9 it is written:

> *"Then shall the* LORD *go forth ... and* **his feet shall stand in that day upon the mount of Olives** *... and the* LORD *shall be* **king over all the earth**: *in that day shall there be one* LORD, *and his name one."*

The person's feet who stands upon the mount of Olives in Zechariah 14:4 is the L-RD in Zechariah 14:3. The word translated as LORD in Zechariah 14:3 is the Hebrew word YHVH. The feet of YHVH will stand upon the mount of Olives. This is the feet of the Jewish Messiah *(Mashiach) Yeshua*/Jesus (Acts 1:9-12).

The Messiah Is King of Kings and L-RD of Lords

There is an ancient Jewish prayer known as the *Aleinu* which is prayed regularly in Jewish synagogue services around the world. The *Aleinu* prayer is an affirmation that the G-d of Israel is King over all the earth. In reciting this prayer, Isaiah *(Yeshayahu)* 45:23 is quoted as it is written:

> *"...That unto me every knee shall bow, every tongue shall swear."*

In the preceding verse in Isaiah *(Yeshayahu)* 45:22, it tells us that the one to whom every knee shall bow, and every tongue shall swear is the G-d of Israel as it is written:

Is the Jewish Messiah G-d?

"**Look unto me, and be ye saved**, *all the ends of the earth: for* **I am God**, *and there is none else.*"

Every knee will bow to the Jewish Messiah *(Mashiach) Yeshua*/Jesus, the Kingly Messiah *(Messiah ben David)*. In Philippians 2:5-11 it is written:

> *"Let this mind be in you, which was also in* **Christ Jesus: Who, being in the form of God, thought it not robbery to be equal with God**: *But made himself of no reputation, and took upon him the form of a servant, and was made in the likeness of men: And being found in fashion as a man, he humbled himself, and became obedient unto death, even the death of the cross. Wherefore* **God also hath highly exalted him**, *and given him a name which is above every name: That* **at the name of Jesus every knee should bow**, *of things in heaven, and things in earth, and things under the earth: And that* **every tongue should confess that Jesus Christ is** L<small>ORD</small>, *to the glory of God the Father."*

The Jewish Messiah *(Mashiach) Yeshua*/Jesus is the King of kings and the L-<small>RD</small> of lords. In Revelation 19:11, 13, 15-16 it is written:

> *"And I saw heaven opened, and behold a white horse* [symbolic of the Kingly Messiah in Jewish thought]: *and he that sat upon him was called Faithful and True, and in righteousness he doth judge and make war ... and he was clothed with a vesture dipped in blood: and* **his name is called The Word of God** *... and out of his mouth goeth*

a sharp sword, that with it he should smite the nations: and he shall rule them with a rod of iron: and he treadeth the winepress of the fierceness and wrath of Almighty God. And he hath on his vesture and on his thigh a name written, **King of kings and** Lord **of lords.**"

The Messiah as YHVH in the Talmud

In the days that the G-d of Israel restores the *house of Judah* (Judaism) with the *house of Israel* (Christianity), the *house of Judah* (Judaism) will mourn and weep for the Jewish Messiah *(Mashiach) Yeshua*/Jesus whom they have pierced. In Zechariah 12:9-10 it is written:

"And it shall come to pass in that day, that I will seek to destroy all the nations that come against Jerusalem. And I will pour upon the house of David, and upon the inhabitants of Jerusalem, the spirit of grace and of supplications: and **they shall look upon me whom they have pierced**, *and* **they shall mourn for him**, *as one mourneth for his only son, and shall be in bitterness for him,* **as one that is in bitterness for his firstborn.**"

When the Jewish Messiah *(Mashiach) Yeshua*/Jesus returns at His second coming as the Kingly Messiah known as *Messiah ben David*, the *Babylonian Talmud* explains in *Sukkot 52a* that they will mourn because of the slaying of the suffering Messiah known as *Messiah be Yosef* as it is written:

"**What is the cause of the mourning** [of Zechariah 12:12] ... it is well according to him

Is the Jewish Messiah G-d?

> who explains that the cause is the **slaying of Messiah the son of Joseph**, since that well agrees with the scripture verse: *'And they shall look upon Me whom they have pierced, and they shall mourn for him as one mourns for his only son.'* [Zechariah 12:10]" (*Babylonian Talmud, Sukkot 52a*) [26]

While the Babylonian *Talmud* in *Sukkot* 52a does not recognize that the one being slain is the Jewish Messiah (*Mashiach*) *Yeshua*/Jesus, the one who is said to be slain in Zechariah 12:10 in the Hebrew text is YHVH when read in the context of Zechariah 12:7-12. *Sukkot 52a* in the *Talmud* interprets YHVH in Zechariah 12:7-12 as the suffering Messiah known as *Messiah ben Yosef*.

In Isaiah *(Yeshayahu)* 8:13-14 it is written:

> *"Sanctify the* LORD *[YHVH] of hosts ... And he [YHVH] shall be a sanctuary; but for a stone of stumbling and for a rock of offense to* **both the houses of Israel**..."

While the text in Israel 8:13-14 speaks of YHVH being a sanctuary and a stone of stumbling to both houses of Israel, the Babylonian *Talmud* in *Sanhedrin* 38a interprets YHVH in these verses to be the Messiah as it is written:

> "The **son of David** [the Messiah] cannot appear ere the two ruling Houses of Israel shall have come to an end ... And he [Messiah/YHVH] will become **a sanctuary**, but to both the houses of Israel..." (*Babylonian Talmud, Sanhedrin 38a*) [27]

The Messiah Is the G-d of Israel (YHVH) Manifested in the Flesh

The Jewish Messiah *(Mashiach) Yeshua*/Jesus is the G-d of Israel manifested in the flesh. In I Timothy 3:16 it is written:

> *"And without controversy great is the mystery* [sod/deeper meaning] *of godliness:* **God was manifest in the flesh**, *justified in the Spirit, seen of angels, preached unto the Gentiles, believed on in the world, received up into glory."*

Whom Do Men Say That the Messiah Is?

Historically, the *house of Judah* (Judaism) and the *house of Israel* (Christianity) have had a difference of viewpoint regarding who is the Jewish Messiah *(Mashiach)*? Is the Jewish Messiah *(Mashiach) Yeshua*/Jesus or should we expect another? Whom do the people of the earth say that the Messiah *(Mashiach)* is? This is the question that every person on the earth must ask and answer for himself including the *house of Judah* (Judaism) and the *house of Israel* (Christianity). This is the question that the Jewish Messiah *(Mashiach) Yeshua*/Jesus asked His disciples *(talmidim)* in Matthew *(Mattityahu)* 16:13-17 as it is written:

> *"When* **Jesus** *came into the coasts of Caesarea Philippi, he* **asked his disciples**, *saying,* **Whom do men say that I the Son of man am?** *And they said, Some say that thou art John* [Yochanan] *the Baptist* [Immerser]: *some, Elijah* [Eliyahu]; *and*

Is the Jewish Messiah G-d?

> *others, Jeremiah* [Yermiyahu], *or one of the prophets. He saith unto them, But whom say ye that I am? And Simon* [Shimon] *Peter* [Kefa] *answered and said,* **Thou art the Christ [Mashiach], the Son of the Living God***. And Jesus answered and said unto him, Blessed art thou, Simon* [Shimon] *Bar-jona: for flesh and blood* [natural human reasoning and understanding] *hath not revealed it unto thee, but my Father which is in heaven."*

It is G-d the Father through His Holy Spirit *(Ruach HaKodesh)* who reveals unto men that *Yeshua*/Jesus is the Jewish Messiah *(Mashiach)*. In I Corinthians 12:3 it is written:

> *"Wherefore I give you to understand, that no man speaking by the Spirit of God calleth Jesus accursed: and that* **no man can say that Jesus is the** Lord**, but by the Holy Ghost** [Ruach HaKodesh]*."*

Yeshua/Jesus Is the Jewish Messiah

When the Jewish Messiah *(Mashiach) Yeshua*/Jesus came at His first coming as the suffering Messiah *(Mashiach)* known as the Messiah son of Joseph *(Messiah ben Yosef)*, He claimed to be the Jewish Messiah. In Luke 24:36, 44-46 it is written:

> *"And as they thus spake,* **Jesus** *himself stood in the midst of them, and saith unto them, Peace be unto you* [Shalom Alechem] *... And he* **said** *unto them, These are the words which I spake unto*

you, while I was yet with you, that **all things must be fulfilled, which were written in the law [Torah] of Moses,** *and* **in the prophets,** *and* **in the Psalms, concerning me.** *Then opened he their understanding, that they might understand the Scriptures, and said unto them, Thus it is written, and thus it behooved Christ* [Mashiach] *to suffer, and to rise from the dead the third day."*

The Jewish Messiah *(Mashiach) Yeshua*/Jesus testified to the leaders of the *house of Judah* (Judaism) in His day that He was the Messiah *(Mashiach)*. In Luke 22:66-67, 69-71 it is written:

"And as soon as it was day, the elders of the people and the chief priests and the scribes came together, and led him into their council, saying, Art thou the Christ [Mashiach]? *tell us. And he said unto them ... Hereafter shall the Son of man sit on the right hand of the power of God. Then said they all, Art thou then the Son of God? And he said unto them, Ye say that I am. And they said, What need we any further witness? For we ourselves have heard of his own mouth."*

The Messiah Is the G-d of Israel

In this chapter, we examined the question that has been a MAJOR disagreement between the *house of Judah* (Judaism) and the *house of Israel* (Christianity) for nearly 2,000 years. Is the Jewish Messiah *(Mashiach)* the G-d of Israel manifested in the flesh or is the Jewish Messiah *(Mashiach)* just an ordinary human being who is

Is the Jewish Messiah G-d?

anointed by the G-d of Israel to perform a divine mission?

The name of the G-d of Israel is YHVH. We learned by examining Rabbinic and other Jewish literature that when the Biblical text speaks of YHVH that the Jewish commentaries often viewed the text to read the WORD OF YHVH. In various places in Jewish literature, it was explained that various individuals trusted *(emunah)* in the WORD OF YHVH and prayed in the name of the WORD OF YHVH. The Word of YHVH is also seen as being the Creator, the Covenant maker and the Mediator between the G-d of Israel and mankind. Furthermore, Israel and the *house of Jacob* are seen being saved by the WORD OF YHVH. In Jewish mystical writings, the WORD OF YHVH is known as *Meditron* who is explained to be the Son of Yah. From this, we were able to discover that all the references which we examined in Jewish literature that mentions the WORD OF YHVH actually speaks of the Jewish Messiah *(Mashiach) Yeshua*/Jesus in the *Brit Hadashah* (New Testament).

Furthermore, by comparing the *TeNaKh* (Old Testament) with the *Brit Hadashah* (New Testament), we were able to understand that the G-d of Israel is our Savior and our salvation. He saves by the strength of His right hand and arm. He is the beginning and the end, the first and the last, the *Alef* and the *Tav*, the King of kings and the L-RD of lords. Finally, we were able to understand that all of these characteristics and attributes of the G-d of Israel are associated with the Jewish Messiah *(Mashiach) Yeshua*/Jesus. Through this extensive study, we were able to understand that the

Restoring the Two Houses of Israel

Jewish Messiah *(Mashiach) Yeshua*/Jesus is the G-d of Israel *(YHVH)* manifested in the flesh.

When the *house of Judah* (Judaism) recognizes that the Jewish Messiah *(Mashiach) Yeshua*/Jesus is the G-d of Israel manifested in the flesh, restoration can come to both houses of Israel. May the G-d of Israel pour out His Holy Spirit *(Ruach HaKodesh)* speedily in our days so that redemption, restoration, reconciliation, and unity can come to both houses of Israel. Amen.

Chapter 8

Israel: The Fig Tree Blossoms

After over two thousand years of exile in the nations of the world, the birth and blossoming of the modern day nation of Israel is a major end-time prophetic event given to us by the G-d of Israel. It is a sign to the Jewish people *(house of Judah)* and the nations of the world of the soon return of the Jewish Messiah *(Mashiach) Yeshua*/Jesus to the earth as the Kingly Messiah *(Mashiach)* known as *Messiah ben David* to usher in the Messianic Age *(Athid Lavo)*. The prophets *(nevi'im)* of Israel in the *TeNaKh* (Old Testament) wrote how the birth of the nation of Israel, the return of the *house of Israel* **and** the *house of Judah* from worldwide exile to the land of Israel, and the nations of the world gathering against the city of Jerusalem *(Yerushalayim)* would precede the coming of the Messiah *(Mashiach)*.

Israel is the fig tree of the G-d of Israel. In Hosea *(Hoshea)* 9:10 it is written:

> "I found **Israel** like grapes in the wilderness; I saw your fathers as the firstripe in the **fig tree**..."

When the Jewish Messiah *(Mashiach) Yeshua*/Jesus was asked by His disciples *(talmidim)* the signs that His followers could watch so that they would understand when the present age *(Olam Hazeh)* was concluding and the Messianic Age *(Athid Lavo)* was at hand, He prophetically made mention of the birth of the modern day state of Israel. In Matthew *(Mattityahu)* 24:3, 32-33 it is written:

> *"When he was sitting on the Mount of Olives, the talmidim* [disciples] *came to him privately. Tell us, they said, when will these things happen? And what will be the sign that you are coming, and the* **'olam hazeh'** [end of the age] *is ending?* [Complete Jewish Bible version by David Stern] ... *Now learn a parable of the* **fig tree**; *When his branch is yet tender, and putteth forth leaves, ye know that summer is nigh: So likewise ye, when ye shall see all these things, know that it is near even at the doors."*

A Heart To Be Redeemed from Exile

Redemption from exile has always been the heart and desire of the Jewish people *(house of Judah)*. The redemption from their first exile in Egypt *(Mitzrayim)* and the receiving of the Torah of the G-d of Israel at mount Sinai has been the central event that has helped to preserve the identity of the Jewish people *(house of Judah)* through later exiles to Babylon and eventually into all the nations of the world *(Diaspora)*. While being in exile, the prayers of the Jewish people *(house of Judah)* have always been to return to the land of Israel, end the exile and live in the Messianic Age *(Athid Lavo)*. This dream of restoration, the end of the exile and the return

Israel: The Fig Tree Blossoms

to the land of Israel is expressed in Psalm *(Tehillim)* 137:1 as it is written:

> *"By the rivers of Babylon, there we sat down, yea, we wept, when we remembered Zion."*

The Desire for a Political Messiah

In the first century, the Jewish people *(house of Judah)* longed for a political Messiah *(Mashiach)* who would free them from the oppression of Rome. Because of this desire, various Jewish groups rose up in opposition against Rome. Major wars were fought by the Jewish people *(house of Judah)* against Rome in 70 CE (Common Era) and in 135 CE. In 135 CE, a Jewish military leader named Simon Bar Kochba led a revolt against Rome. At this time, one of the most respected rabbi's of the period, Rabbi Akiva, proclaimed Bar Kochba as the political Jewish Messiah *(Mashiach)* who would free the Jewish people *(house of Judah)* from the oppression of Rome. During this time, Rome was successful in winning every war against the Jewish people *(house of Judah)*. As a result, Rome began to sell the Jewish people *(house of Judah)* into slavery and initiated the exile of the Jewish people *(house of Judah)* into all the nations of the world.

Passive Resistance to Oppression

Because of the hardship brought to the Jewish people *(house of Judah)* in fighting against Rome, losing the wars, being sold into slavery and being exiled into the nations of the world, the Jewish people *(house of Judah)* began to embrace the ideology of passive resistance against their oppressors from that time forward. This mindset continued to be prevalent in the late 1800s. In fact, many Orthodox Jews have long insisted that any return to the Holy Land would be carried out by the Messiah and that to take matters into one's own hands would be blasphemous.[1] However, anti-Jewish sentiment in Europe in the late 1800s began to change this mindset among secular Jews. This change in mindset and the desire for secular Jews *(house of Judah)* to return to the land of Israel to escape oppression and anti-Semitism without waiting for these matters to be carried out through the rise of a political Jewish Messiah *(Mashiach)* became known as the Zionist movement.

The Rise of Zionism in Europe

"Zionism" comes from the biblical word *"Zion."* It is often used as a synonym for Jerusalem *(Yerushalayim)* and the Land of Israel *(Eretz Yisrael)*. Zionism is an ideology that expresses the yearning of Jews all over the world for their historical homeland of Zion, the Land of Israel. The foundation of Zionism is rooted in the belief that the Land of Israel is the historical birthplace of the Jewish people *(house of Judah)* and that Jewish life anywhere else in the world is a life of exile.

The emergence of Zionism in Europe in the late 1800s was a crucial turning point in Jewish history. Through this movement, ancient hopes and dreams of the Jewish people *(house of Judah)* to end the exile and return to the land of Israel was resurrected. Zionism rejects the idea that assimilation of the Jewish people *(house of Judah)* into the nations of the world is the best way to ensure Jewish survival.

In the late 1800s, a grass-roots youth movement contributed to this Jewish awakening in Eastern Europe.[2] At this time in history, a large number of Jews lived in the Polish and Russian pales. Czarist policy aimed at restricting the Jews prompted "thousands of idealistic young Russian Jews" to organize themselves "into a political and cultural group called the "lovers of Zion."[3] These youngsters held their first convention in Constantinople in 1882, boldly issuing a manifesto declaring their need for a Jewish homeland and their God-given right to Zion.[4]

Theodor Herzl: The Father of Modern Zionism

Theodor Herzl is the man credited with being the founder of modern Zionism. He was born in Budapest, Hungary, in 1860. His parents, though Jewish, had no religious sentiment and young Herzl was educated in the spirit of the German-Jewish "Enlightenment" of the time. Theodor Herzl studied law at the University of Vienna. After graduating in 1884 with a doctorate in law, he left law and became the Paris correspondent for the Vienna Free Press, a liberal newspaper. During this time, Herzl became sensitive toward the Jewish problem of anti-Semitism.

In 1892, the famous Dreyfus trial began in Paris, France. Here, an assimilated Jew named Alfred Dreyfus on the French General Staff was wrongly accused and

Restoring the Two Houses of Israel

imprisoned. Herzl witnessed the riotous behavior of French mobs and the public humiliation of the Jewish officer, Dreyfus, when they taunted the French Jewish army captain with shouts of "death to the Jews." These events impacted Herzl so strongly that he became consumed with the desire for all Jews to have a national homeland to free them from social injustice and anti-Semitism. For Herzl, this meant a sovereign Jewish State. For the first time in his life, Herzl began attending Jewish religious services. [5]

In 1896, Herzl began to communicate his dream by publishing *Der Judenstaat* (The Jewish State). More than any other single factor, Herzl's book was most responsible for galvanizing the support of world Jewry for political Zionism. His solution called for individual Jews to immigrate to Palestine, buy land from the Turks, cultivate it into productivity, build a Jewish majority in the land, and thus reestablish the Jewish homeland. [6]

In 1897, Theodor Herzl called the first Zionist Congress at Basle, Switzerland. It opened on August 29th, 1897 and was attended by some 204 participants from seventeen countries. At this time, the World Zionist Organization was established and Herzl became its first president. Here he officially launched the Zionist movement with a specific statement of purpose: "The object of Zionism is to establish for the Jewish people a publicly and legally assured home in Palestine." [7]

Initially, when Herzl began to expound his ideas of having a central world organization so that Jews worldwide could move in mass to some yet unknown

Israel: The Fig Tree Blossoms

territory, he was met with stiff opposition from eastern European Jews who dismissed the idea and thought that Herzl was crazy. Both Orthodox and Reform rabbis branded Herzl and his ideas as visionary and impractical. Nevertheless, Herzl continued to pursue his dream and spread his ideas.

Herzl's greatest desire was for the Jewish people *(house of Judah)* to have a national homeland to shelter them from the anti-Semitism that they have historically experienced in the nations of the world where they have lived over the centuries. Therefore, it did not matter to Herzl which country or territory was given to the Jewish people. Herzl's energies seemed boundless as he assumed the role of roving ambassador for the Jews in the highest echelons of government. No confrontation fazed him. He fearlessly challenged opulent financiers; held audiences with the kaiser, the Turkish sultan, the king of Italy, and the pope; and approached leading officials of Russia and Great Britain. With his unique, polished demeanor he became a diplomat *par excellence* for the Zionist cause.[8]

Herzl worked hard to find a territory for the Jews. At first, Sinai and Cyprus were two territories under consideration. In 1903, the British offered Herzl the area called Uganda. Because pogroms and oppression in Russia was increasing for the Jews during this period, Herzl felt that a homeland in Uganda was a credible proposal. Therefore, Herzl submitted the Uganda plan to the sixth Zionist Congress. However, this proposal met strong opposition and was rejected. The eastern European Jews regarded it as a betrayal of the dream of settling in the land of Israel. So strong and hostile was the opposition to the Uganda plan that Herzl wrote a written commitment to abandon it.

In 1904, Herzl died of a heart attack at the age of forty-four. For his efforts, Theordor Herzl became a living legend and became known as the father of modern Zionism.[9]

Chaim Weizmann and the Balfour Declaration

After Herzl's death, the new leader of Zionism became Chaim Weizmann. Born in Motol, Russia in 1874, Weizmann attended college at German and Swiss universities. In 1904, he began teaching at Manchester, England. Unlike Herzl, Weizmann believed that a homeland in the ancient land of Israel was the only practical solution for the Jewish people. His reasons were not religious but were derived from his perceived political realities.

Just as Herzl's journalism caused him to be in the right place at the divinely appointed time, Weizmann's chemistry talents caused the same thing to happen to him. Because of World War I, Britain had a need that Weizmann was able to meet. When the allies' supply of acetone to produce munitions began to run out (previously imported from Germany), the British staff called on Weizmann to find some substitute. Following a two-year project, his team developed a superior synthetic that made a considerable contribution to the Allied war effort.[10]

Israel: The Fig Tree Blossoms

Weizmann's contacts with the Manchester society and his supervision of mass production of synthetic acetone for the Allies war effort gave him visibility and opened doors for him to make contact with high ranking British government officials. These contacts included Prime Minister Lloyd George, First Lord of the Admiralty Winston Churchill, and Foreign Secretary Arthur Balfour. Weizmann made personal appeals to these individuals to help him find a homeland in the ancient land of Israel for the Jewish people to further the cause of Zionism. [11]

Weizmann's success in developing synthetic acetone for the Allied war effort so elated the British cabinet that LORD Balfour exclaimed to Weizmann, "You know that after the war you may get your Jerusalem." [12]

The major result of Weizmann's diplomacy was the Balfour Declaration. It granted the Jewish people *(house of Judah)* an international right to a homeland in Palestine with the help of Great Britain. The substance of the Declaration was given in a letter to Lord Rothschild by the British Foreign Secretary Arthur Balfour on November 2, 1917. The declarations reads:

> His Majesty's Government view with favour the establishment in Palestine of a national home for the Jewish people, and will use their best endeavours to facilitate the achievement of this object, it being clearly understood that nothing shall be done which may prejudice the civil and religious rights of the existing non-Jewish communities in Palestine, or the rights and political status enjoyed by Jews in any other country.

Restoring the Two Houses of Israel

WWI and the Fall of the Ottoman Empire

One of the significant events that contributed to the possibility of the Jewish people returning to their ancient homeland was the defeat of the Ottoman Empire in WWI. Because of this, control of the Middle East came under the rule of Great Britain.

During World War I, Turkey was on the side of Germany. The British through the leadership of Sir Edward Allenby defeated the Turks and ended four hundred years of Turkish rule over Palestine and six hundred years of Muslim dominance in the area. The Palestine armistice was signed on October 31, 1918. This was eleven days before the World War I armistice was signed.[13] This coincidence prompted Lord Balfour later to declare that "the founding of the Jewish National Home was the most significant outcome of the First World War."[14]

Oscar Janowsky has summarized this relationship between Zionism and World War I as follows:[15]

> The First World War proved decisive in the history of Zionism. On November 2, 1917, the British government issued the Balfour Declaration, pledging to facilitate "the establishment in Palestine of a national home for the Jewish people." Soon thereafter the British conquered the country and, when the war was over, Palestine was administered as a Mandate under the League of Nations, with the United Kingdom as Mandatory or trustee. The Balfour pledge was incorporated in the

Israel: The Fig Tree Blossoms

terms of the Mandate, which recognized "the historical connection of the Jewish people with Palestine" and the right to reconstitute "their national home in that country." Britain was to encourage the immigration and close settlement of the Jews on the land; Hebrew (as well as English and Arabic) was to be an official language; and a "Jewish Agency" was to assist and cooperate with the British in the building of the Jewish National Home.

The British Mandate was given international approval by the Council of the League of Nations on June 28, 1919. The following map shows the land area in the Middle East governed by the British Mandate.

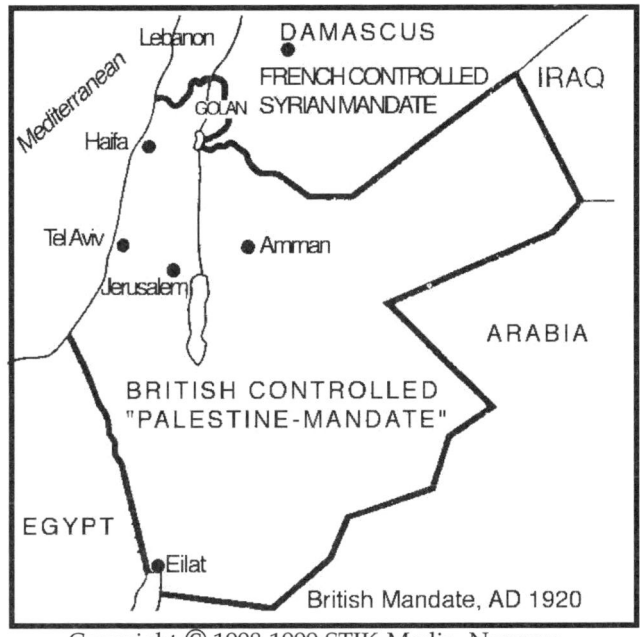

Copyright © 1998-1999 STIK-Media, Norway

Restoring the Two Houses of Israel

However, before its final sanction on September 29, 1922, the homeland projected for the Jews had been reduced to exclude Transjordan when Great Britain created the state of Transjordan under the kingship of Abdullah ibn Hussein.[16] The following map shows how the land of the Middle East looked after Great Britain gave the land that was originally projected to be a national homeland for the Jewish people to Transjordan. In order to satisfy the Arabs, "land was given for peace."

Copyright © 1998-1999 STIK-Media, Norway

What Theodor Herzl invigorated in the Jewish people for a national homeland with the writing of his book, *Der Judenstaat* (The Jewish State), Chaim Weizmann continued with the Balfour Declaration. With the defeat of the

Israel: The Fig Tree Blossoms

Ottoman Empire in WWI and British control over the land of Palestine, the fire of Zionism became a blaze in the hearts of the Jewish people. Jews in the Diaspora became encouraged that they would once again be able to live in the land of their forefathers.

David Ben-Gurion and the "Yishuv"

While Weizmann furthered the cause of Zion through his diplomatic contacts in the West, David Ben-Gurion became a pioneer for Zionism among the people in the land of Palestine *(Yishuv)*. David Ben-Gurion was born in Poland in 1886. He migrated to the land of Israel in 1906. In the land, he became the most active Zionist during this time. He became involved in the creation of the first agricultural workers' commune (which evolved into the *Kvutzah* and finally the *Kibbutz*). He also helped establish the Jewish self-defense group, *"Hashomer"* (The Watchman).

In the land, Ben-Gurion was a founder of the trade unions, and in particular, the national federation, the *Histadrut*, which he dominated from the early 1920s. He also served as the *Histadrut's* representative in the World Zionist Organization and Jewish Agency and was elected chairman of both organizations in 1935. He led the Jewish Legion against the Turks in World War I. After leading the struggle to establish the State of Israel in May 1948, Ben-Gurion became Prime Minister and Defense Minister when Israel became a nation.

Ben Yehuda and the Hebrew Language

With the rise of Zionism and the return of the Jewish people to their ancient homeland, Hebrew became the common language that all immigrants were required to learn. With the dispersion of the Jewish people into the nations of the world, Hebrew had practically become a "dead" language.

It was the dream of Eliezer Ben-Yehuda that when the Jewish people returned to their ancient homeland that they would speak their ancient tongue of Hebrew. Ben-Yehuda was most responsible for this becoming a reality. Therefore, he is remembered as being the creator of the modern Hebrew language.

Ben-Yehuda, was born Eliezer Yitzhak Perelman, in the Lithuanian village of Luzhky on January 7, 1858. He learned Hebrew at a young age as a part of his religious upbringing. Though migrating from Russia with tuberculosis in 1881, he devoted his life to rejuvenating the language for modern use, even producing a Hebrew dictionary. In spite of much ridicule, he and his wife "took a vow that no words would ever again pass their lips except in Hebrew, a vow that proved to be one of the turning points in the history of Palestine." [17]

Arab Response to Jewish Immigration

In the decade following the international approval of the Balfour Declaration, many Jews made *aliyah* and returned to the land of Palestine. During these years, they came mostly from Russia and Eastern Europe. In the eight years since the Balfour Declaration, the Jewish population had doubled from 55,000 to 103,000. Zionism had finally caught the imagination of the Jewish people, and as oppression increased in Europe, thou-

Israel: The Fig Tree Blossoms

sands of Jews fled to Palestine and the sanctuary of a Jewish national homeland during the decade of the 1920's. [18]

However, all of this was greeted with stiff Arab rejection of Jewish immigration *(house of Judah)* to the land of Israel. The main source of agitation was the Grand Mufti of Jerusalem, Haj Amin al-Husseini. The British had sought to control the country through two leading families of Palestine with large land holdings, the Husseinis and the Nashashibis. [19] Haj Amin was appointed president of the Supreme Muslim Counsel in 1922, giving him immense political, economic, and religious clout. [20] During World War II, he defected to the Nazis, moving to Rome and Berlin. In the twenties and thirties, he missed no opportunity to stir antagonism and wage war against the Jewish families settling in Palestine.

Despite Arab opposition, a flood of 150,000 Jewish immigrants entered Palestine from 1931 to 1935. [21] While the Jewish community was trying to persuade the British to allow increased Jewish immigration, the Arabs were threatening to cut off access to Middle Eastern oil supplies if immigration was increased. [22] However, when European Jews needed the refuge of immigration the most, it was cut off from them. The ominous year was 1939.

On May 17, 1939, the British government of Prime Minister Neville Chamberlain issued a paper known as the "*MacDonald White Paper*" (after Malcolm MacDonald, the Colonial Secretary), which cut the immigration of Jews to Palestine almost to nothing. [23]

Restoring the Two Houses of Israel

The 1939 White Paper specified three guidelines for Palestine:

(1) Jewish immigration would be slowed, then halted;
(2) Jews would only be allowed to buy land in areas where they were already the majority population;
(3) Britain would support an independent Palestinian state, controlled by the Arabs, after the war.

Winston Churchill called it a "gross breach of faith." [24] It was the virtual surrender to the demands of Arab terrorists. Yet the Grand Mufti even rejected this paper, demanding "the immediate setting up of an independent Arab state in Palestine and no further Jewish immigration." [25]

What happened to the Balfour agreement? It fell victim to the Chamberlain government's policies of "appeasement." Just as Czechoslavakia was offered to appease the führer in Europe, so the Balfour guarantee was sacrificed to stroke the Mufti in Palestine.

This restrictive British policy appears to have received an immediate frown from heaven. Four months after issuing this White Paper (May 1939), Britain was reluctantly drawn into World War II (September 1, 1939).

One year later Chamberlain was forced to resign when Germany invaded Norway and threatened the British Isles. Nevertheless, the Chamberlain policy on immigration continued throughout the war. Although thousands did escape Hitler's clutches, they were halted as they approached Palestine. Many were turned back at gunpoint when coming ashore; many more died at sea. [26]

Adolf Hitler and Word War II

As the Second World War erupted, Jewish emigration to Palestine came to a virtual halt. Visas from Europe were cut off by Adolf Hitler and entrance into Palestine was shut off by the British. [27]

Adolf Hitler had a demonic desire to destroy and eliminate the Jewish people from existence. His desire could be seen in five progressive stages. [28]

1) The first stage began immediately when he took office and purposed to destroy all Jewish businesses in Germany.

2) The second stage came in 1935 when the Nuremburg laws were passed, depriving all Jews of citizenship.

3) The third stage began with a mass arrest of Jews in September 1939 at the outbreak of war. Jews were put in concentration camps and required to wear the "Badge of Shame" (Yellow Star of David) to distinguish them from non-Jews. For those still allowed to migrate, the ransom price was surrender of all possessions. By 1939, only 200,000 of the 500,000 Jews living in Germany six years earlier still remained.

Restoring the Two Houses of Israel

4) The fourth stage came in 1940 when all Jews were incarcerated in concentration camps. This roundup was later extended to all parts of German-occupied Europe. Nazis hauled Jews in from Austria, Czechoslavakia, Hungary, Poland, Rumania, France, Holland, Switzerland, Belgium, Northern Italy, Yugoslavia, Denmark, and Norway, with only several outstanding exceptions.

5) The fifth and final stage of this madness was called the "final solution" and was initiated by Nazi leadership in 1942. The purpose of the concentration camps changed from detention to extermination, and murder became a full-time German occupation. [29]

The main death camps were located in Germany, Poland, Austria, and Czechoslovakia. The memorial at Yad Vashem has listed twenty-two of the largest camps, names known in infamy: Auschwitz, Buchenwald, Dachau, Mauthausen, and Treblinka. The largest was Auschwitz in Poland where over three million were murdered. [30]

So, important was this carnage to Nazi leaders that it was given an even higher priority than that of the war effort itself. [31] Although the Nazi cause was clearly lost in early 1945, the gas chambers and furnaces were kept running full blast. As Finkelstein remarks, "The actual annihilation of the Jewish population was one of the main ideological and military objectives of the German Nazified war machine. And this objective was to a large extent achieved." [32]

Israel: The Fig Tree Blossoms

The following figures on Jewish casualties during the Holocaust have been taken and are compiled by *Judaica Encyclopedia*.

Distribution of Jewish Victims of the Holocaust

Austria	65,000
Hungary	402,000
Belgium	24,000
Italy	7,500
Czechoslavakia	277,000
Luxembourg	700
France	83,000
Norway	760
Germany	125,000
Poland-Soviet	4,565,000
Greece	65,000
Rumania	40,000
Holland	106,000
Yugoslavia	60,000
Total Jewish Victims	**5,820,000**

World Outrage Demands a Zionist State

When international teams of investigators confirmed the horrors of the Holocaust, most of the Western world agreed that immediate measures should be taken to open the door to Palestine. Even the British Labour Party agreed.[33] With "regard to the unspeakable horrors that have been perpetrated upon the Jews in Germany and other occupied countries in Europe," it said, "it is morally wrong and politically indefensible to impose obstacles to the entry into Palestine now of Jews who desire to go there..." [34] It furthermore proposed that the Americans, Soviet, and British governments should "see whether we cannot get that common support for a policy which will give us a happy, free, and a prosperous State in Palestine." [35]

Post WWII Politics in England

Even before the war ended, a significant shift occurred through the British elections of July 1945. Britain still had the League of Nations' Mandate to control Palestine. During the war, Prime Minister Churchill had been strongly supportive of Zionism and gave Weizmann his word that a State of Israel would be set up in Palestine after the war with three to four million Jews. [36] That was the view of both the Labour and Tory parties in their electioneering campaigns.

But in 1945, Churchill's coalition was voted out of office in a landslide. [37] Britain's severe economic setbacks during the war and its shrinking world empire led to the dissatisfaction that produced this ouster. The Labour party of Clement Atlee took over with high expectations from everyone — including the Zionists.

Despite candidate Atlee's pro-Zionist stance, however, his administration soon reversed itself on the Palestine issue. Ernest Bevin was made Foreign Secretary and thus became Czar of the Mideast and its problems. Though a sharp statesman and keenly perceptive of growing Soviet power, he did not share the

Israel: The Fig Tree Blossoms

pro-Zionist sympathies of his colleagues and the former administration.[38] "Bevin repudiated all the pledges that had been made officially and unofficially by Labour speakers for the last ten years, some of which may have helped the Party win the election."[39]

Several changes made this reversal of policy the politically prudent course for the new foreign secretary. The Arab world was gaining prestige and becoming a factor to be reckoned with. It had just added several independent states to its number and its oil power was claiming international respect. In juggling interests in the Mideast, Bevin tended to favor the Arabs and downplay the rights of Jews. To this end, Bevin came to fiercely oppose the creation of a Jewish state in the troubled area.[40]

Another factor contributing to this reversal was the MacDonald "White Paper" of 1939, an anti-Jewish document that continued in effect throughout the war. Designed to mollify the Arabs, it in fact reduced Jewish immigration to Palestine to a trickle and intended to cut it off entirely. Had the White Paper been fully carried out, the hard-won advantages guaranteed the Jews in the Balfour Declaration would have been nullified. Arabs responded to this British reversal by increasing their opposition to Jewish immigration. Encouraged by Bevin, they boldly demanded that all Jewish immigration be stopped and a new Arab State be set up in Palestine.[41]

The irony is that none of these Arab nations (except for Transjordan) supported the Allies in World War II. They remained carefully neutral until the final months when Allied victory was assured. The Palestinian leader (ex-Mufti Haj Amin Husseini), in fact, defected to Iraq before the war and later joined Hitler and Eichmann in Germany in their butchery of Jews.[42] Yet, the Arab states were shown amazing respect by the Allied powers in the postwar era; seven seats were given them in the United Nations Assembly.[43]

The Jewish Resistance Movement

When many Zionists began to realize that a political solution to establish a national homeland for the Jewish people *(house of Judah)* could not be achieved, they saw the need for military action. The main Jewish resistance groups were the *Haganah*, the *Irgun* and *Lehi*.

Arab riots in the land of Palestine in 1920 and 1921 strengthened the view that it was impossible to depend upon the British authorities to defend and protect the Jewish people in the land of Palestine. Furthermore, the Arabs would disrupt the agricultural settlements set up by the *Yishuv*. In addition, after initially encouraging the immigration of Jews to Israel, the British now openly banned Jewish immigration. From these events, it became apparent that the British were not interested in providing security for the Jewish settlers in the land. Therefore, the *yishuv* needed to create an independent defense force completely free of foreign authority.

The Creation of the Haganah

With the help of the worldwide Jewish Agency, the *Hagonah* was created. In June 1920, the *Haganah* was founded by the *Histadrut* (General Federation of Jewish

Israel: The Fig Tree Blossoms

Labor). At the time, it was considered illegal by the British mandatory authorities. The *Haganah* became the underground defense organization of the *yishuv* from 1920 to the establishment of the state of Israel in 1948.

As Arab hostilities increased, the members of the *Haganah* split over the question of how to react to Arab terrorism. Following Arab disturbances in the summer of 1929, a group of commanders and members of the *Haganah*, led by Avraham Tehomi, decided to split from the main group and set up their own organization to be more active in pursuing the Arab terrorists.

The Creation of the Irgun

This new organization was named the *Irgun Zva'i Leumi* (National Military Organization) also known by the name of *Etzel*. It was founded in 1931 and became an underground organization that operated in Palestine in the 1930s and 1940s.

Irgun rejected the "restraint" policy of the *Haganah*. They carried out armed reprisals against Arabs and preferred to use political powers to forward the goal of reclaiming the land. While the armed reprisals against the Arabs provided relief for the Jewish settlers, it was condemned by the Jewish Agency and brought political embarrassment to them. While the Jewish Agency tried to provide an image of the Jew being a good moral person who was being terrorized by the Arabs in order to win support from the non-Jewish world, the *Irgun* gave it's full support to the settlers.

On December 5, 1936, Avraham Tehomi signed an accord with Ze'ev (Vladimir) Jabotinsky, the leader of the

Revisionist Movement, making Jabotinsky commander of *Irgun*. In April 1937, during the Arab riots, the *Irgun* split. About half its members returned to the *Haganah*. The rest formed a new Irgun Zeva'i Le'umi (National Military Organization), which was ideologically linked with the Revisionist Movement and accepted the authority of its leader, Vladimir Jabotinsky.

Vladimir Jabotinsky and the Revisionist Movement

Ze'ev (Vladimir) Jabotinsky was born on October 18, 1880, in the city of Odessa, Russia. The pogrom against the Jews of Kishinev in 1903 spurred Jabotinsky to undertake Zionist activity. Jabotinsky was deeply impressed by Theodor Herzl. Jabotinsky was elected as a delegate to the 6th Zionist Congress, the last in which Theodor Herzl participated.

After World War I, Jabotinsky became disenchanted when Great Britain severed almost 80% of the British Mandate originally designated for a Jewish Homeland to create Transjordan (1922). Disillusioned with Britain and angry at Zionist acquiescence to British reversals, Jabotinsky became unhappy with the direction of the Zionist Movement. He was unconvinced that the Turks or the Arabs would accommodate the aims of Zionism. So, he advocated bolder tactics.

Jabotinsky set about establishing a separate Zionist federation based on "revision" of the relationship between the Zionist movement and Great Britain. This

Israel: The Fig Tree Blossoms

federation would actively challenge British policy and openly demand self-determination or Jewish statehood. The goals of the Revisionist movement included restoration of a Jewish Brigade to protect the Jewish community and mass immigration to Palestine of up to 40,000 Jews a year.

In 1925, the establishment of the World Union of Zionist Revisionists *(Hatzohar)* was announced with Paris as its headquarters. In 1931, Jabotinsky demanded that the Seventeenth Zionist Congress make a clear announcement of its Zionist aims (a Jewish state) but the delegates refused to do so.

In 1923, the youth movement Betar (*Brith* Joseph Trumpeldor) was created. The new youth movement was aimed at educating its members so that they would have a military and nationalistic spirit. Jabotinsky was also the leader of this movement.

In 1935, after the Zionist Executive rejected his political program and refused to clearly define that "the aim of Zionism was the establishment of a Jewish state," Jabotinsky decided to resign from the Zionist Movement. He founded the New Zionist Organization (NZO) to conduct independent political activity for free immigration and the establishment of a Jewish State.

In 1937, the Irgun Tzvai Leumi (IZL) became the military arm of the Jabotinsky movement and he became its commander. The three bodies headed by Jabotinsky, The New Zionist Organization (NZO), the Betar youth movement and the *Irgun Tzvai Leumi* (IZL) were three extensions of the same movement.

Restoring the Two Houses of Israel

With the outbreak of World War II, *Irgun* declared a truce, which led to a second split. Some forces decided to fight with the British against the Nazi Axis powers. This group declared a truce and joined the British army and the Jewish Brigade. The second group led by Avraham Stern was known as the Stern Gang or **Lehi**. They operated as an underground organization from 1940 to 1948.

The Creation of Lehi

Lehi was an acronym for *Lohamei Herut Yisrael* (Fighters for the Freedom of Israel). The split with the Irgun was due to disagreement on three main issues:

1) The group's demand that the military struggle against the British government be continued irrespective of the war against Nazi Germany;

2) Opposition to enlistment in the British army, which Jabotinsky supported; and

3) Willingness to collaborate, as a tactical measure, with anyone who supported the struggle against the British in Palestine.

Lehi's goals were:

1) Conquest and liberation of *Eretz Israel;* war against the British Empire;

2) Complete withdrawal of Britain from Palestine;

3) Establishment of a "Hebrew kingdom from the Euphrates to the Nile."

Israel: The Fig Tree Blossoms

Menachem Begin Becomes Leader of the Irgun

In December of 1943, Menachem Begin became leader of the *Irgun*. Begin was a Polish Jew who had escaped a Siberian labor camp in 1943 and made his way to Palestine to join the *Irgun*.

Menachem Begin was born in Brest-Litovsk in 1913. As a child he was forced to flee with his family to escape the fighting between the German and Russian armies in World War I. A passionate Zionist from an early age, he joined Ze'ev Jabotinsky's Betar youth movement in his teens, rising quickly to important administrative and leadership positions.

In February 1944, *Irgun* declared war against the British administration. It attacked and blew up government offices, military installations and police stations. The Jewish Agency and their group, the *Haganah* responded against the *Irgun* in a campaign nicknamed the *Sezon*. The *Haganah* kidnapped several of the *Irgun's* members and handed them over to the British.

The Jewish Resistance Movements Become United in Purpose

After World War II, the *Haganah* realized that the British were not relenting their ban on immigration, nor were they helpful in combating Arab terrorism. In late 1945, the three groups (the *Irgun*, the *Haganah*, and *Lechi*) reached an understanding to coordinate the struggle to fight the British.

Restoring the Two Houses of Israel

The unity of the groups was short-lived. In May 1946 the *Irgun* blew up the wing of the King David hotel in Jerusalem, which housed the British Palestine Command. The organizations' cooperation broke up following *Irgun*'s bombing because *Haganah* claimed that the attack had not been coordinated with them.

The Jewish Resistance Movements Are Merged into the IDF

After the end of World War II, the *Haganah* was the largest and most important Jewish military force operating against the British. On May 26, 1948, the Provisional Government of Israel decided to transform the *Haganah* into the regular army of the State to be called "*Zeva Haganah Le-Yisrael*" or The Israel Defense Forces (IDF). When the IDF was established on May 31, 1948, *Irgun* and *Lehi* announced that its members would join also.

Haganah and Irgun became the Labor and Likud political parties in Israel. The *Haganah* and the *Irgun* have had their political differences since they were created to fight against the British in order that the Jewish people *(house of Judah)* could have a national homeland. There was an event that took place before they merged themselves into the IDF that highlights the division and tension between these two groups. This division continues to the present day through the modern day political parties in Israel named *Labor* and *Likud* whose political roots go back to the *Haganah* and the *Irgun.*

The *Irgun* had a boat, the *Altalena*, which had supplies and men coming into Jaffa port. The boat was laden with munitions needed by the Jewish defenders. The *Haganah* wanted to take all supplies. Negotiation between the *Irgun* and the *Haganah* ensued. No agreement was forged. The *Haganah* opened fire on the *Altalena*, sinking the boat, killing and wounding Jewish lives and destroying supplies. The commander of the *Haganah* was Yitzhak Rabin. When the nation of Israel was established, the Jewish Agency and its followers took up the leadership of Israel. Today, their political party is known as "*Labor*." The opposition party, led by the soldiers in the *Irgun*, became the opposition party to the *Haganah* and is known today as the "*Likud*." Still today, these two groups are politically fighting it out between themselves just as they did in the time of the birth of the state of Israel.

The British Mandate Is Turned Over to the UN

When the *Irgun* blew up the King David Hotel in Jerusalem *(Yerushalayim)* where the British government kept their office on July 22, 1946, twenty-eight British were killed. By the beginning of 1947, the British had decided they wanted nothing more than to wash their hands of the whole mandate affair. [44]

Thus it was becoming more and more evident that British anti-Zionist policy was bankrupt and that a new approach was needed. The fault lay primarily with "Bevin's agonized intransigence on the immigration issue, provoking maximal Zionist demands for Jewish statehood." This "ignited the terrorism, launched the illegal refugee traffic to Palestine, undermined Britain's economy, eroded its international reputation, and finally doomed the Palestine Mandate itself."[45] The Atlee-Bevin government came to see how impossible it was to carry out the British Mandate with conflicting policies toward the Jews and the Arabs.[46]

Acknowledging a deadlock on the issue, the British cabinet on April 2, 1947, announced it was referring the Palestine problem to the United Nations General Assembly. This body set up an eleven-nation investigative board (UNSCOP) to devise a plan of action. After several months of review, they recommended endorsing the principle of independence for both the Jews and the Arabs. However, they were divided regarding who should control what area. The majority voted for "partitioning" Palestine, advocating three divisions, an Arab state, a Jewish state, and an international zone in the Jerusalem area.[47]

The General Assembly of the United Nations voted on November 29, 1947, to support partitioning. The vote was thirty-three to thirteen, mainly the Western bloc against the Moslems and Asian blocs. Eleven nations abstained, including Britain. It was to be implemented at the termination of the British Mandate on May 14, 1948.[48]

The partition plan vote became UN Resolution 181. In Part III, Section A of UN Resolution 181, the city of Jerusalem was established as a *"corpus separatum"* under a special international regime and shall be administered by the United Nations. Thus, the plan of the UN was for Jerusalem *(Yerushalayim)* to become an international city.

Israel: The Fig Tree Blossoms

Copyright © 1998-1999 STIK-Media, Norway

The Arabs unequivocally rejected it, perceiving it as another step in Zionist expansionism. To maintain good relations with the Arab League, Britain also rejected it. Joining them, the United States State Department under Secretary of State George Marshall cautioned against the plan. In May 1947, the Soviet delegation surprised everyone by endorsing partitioning. In October, the Arab League began a troop buildup in Palestine.[49]

Restoring the Two Houses of Israel

President Truman chose to disagree with Secretary of State George Marshall on the issue. Truman accused the State Department of having an Arabic mentality. "Like most of the British diplomats," he quipped, "some of our diplomats also thought that the Arabs, on account of their numbers and because of the fact that they controlled such immense oil resources, should be appeased. I am sorry to say that there were some among them who were inclined to be anti-Semitic."[50] He then instructed the State Department to support the United Nations plan of partitioning Palestine.[51]

Many commentators believe that this courageous action by Truman received the smile of heaven. That fall, Truman ran for reelection against the highly favored Republican governor of New York, Tom Dewey, and won. Truman later referred to himself as "Cyrus," the biblical Gentile who in Persian times had assisted the post-exilic remnant in returning from dispersion.[52]

Israel's 1948 War of Independence

The Arabs responded to the Partition Resolution by carrying out their oft-repeated threats. Jewish homes and synagogues in the major cities were immediately attacked while the British stood by. Calls went out for all available forces from the Arabic States to mobilize for war. Arabs saw the British withdrawal as an opportunity to drive out the Jews and settle the immigration question once and for all. The Mufti moved from Cairo to Lebanon to take charge of the Palestinian operation.[53]

In the late afternoon of May 14, 1948, the British kept their word and hauled down the Union Jack. Israel proceeded to raise its newly designed flag featuring the

Israel: The Fig Tree Blossoms

Star of David the same day. David Ben-Gurion became Israel's first prime minister. Chaim Weizmann later became the first President of the new republic. Within minutes, President Truman issued a statement extending de facto recognition to Israel as a sovereign state.[54]

Before the day ended, Egyptian planes were already bombing Tel Aviv. Most of the Arab states sent men and material to the attack, including Syria, Transjordan, Lebanon, Egypt, Yemen, Iraq, and Saudi Arabia. Additional forces came from North African states.[55]

The Arab's initial attack was full-scale on all sides, confident that their sheer numbers and superior armament would quickly overwhelm the ill-equipped Jews.[56] Their plan was to take Palestine's key cities within a few weeks and then quickly "drive the Jews into the sea."

From a statistical standpoint, an easy triumph was practically a given: the Arab's overwhelming power came from seven nations with a combined population of over 140 million; the Jewish remnant they opposed totaled only 650,000 in all Palestine, with no promise of backing from other nations; the Arab Legion of Transjordan was "financed and officiated by the British."[57] However, with divine help from the G-d of Israel, the Jewish people *(house of Judah)* won the war and the nation of Israel was born.

The UN plan had assigned her 5,500 square miles and the new Arab state 4,500. The spoils of war added additional territory, which gave Israel a total of 8,050 of the total 10,400 square miles in Palestine.[58] King Abdullah of Transjordan acquired 2,350 square miles in the West Bank plus over 750,000 Palestinians.[59]

In May 1949, the new nation of Israel was accepted into the United Nations, recognized as an independent, sovereign nation.[60]

On four occasions in the next twenty-five years, Israel was forced to mobilize her troops to defend her borders. Each of these was a traumatic episode in itself, but each also resulted in further gain that fortified her position in the Middle East.[61]

Israel's 1956 War with Egypt

Egyptian General Gamal Abdel Nasser was elected president of Egypt in 1956. From 1948, Egypt had closed the Suez Canal to Israeli ships. Then in 1955, she began a blockade also of the Gulf of Aqaba, cutting off Israel's access to the Red Sea and Indian Ocean. Responding to this challenge, Israel again mobilized her citizen army in October 1956, striking at Egypt through the rugged Sinai wasteland. That desert campaign became known as *"Operation Kadesh."*[62] With divine help from the G-d of Israel, the Jewish people *(house of Judah)* defeated the plans of Nasser and Egypt and won the 1956 war.

Israel's 1967 War with Her Arab Neighbors

In the spring of 1967 following a vast military buildup of Russian equipment, Nasser again closed the Gulf of Aqaba to Israeli shipping and demanded that UN observers withdraw from the demilitarized zone. By May 17, seven Arabic nations had mobilized armor

Israel: The Fig Tree Blossoms

on three fronts, broadcasting their intentions to "cut the Jews throats." King Hussein of Jordan decided to join the fray, collaborating with Iraqi troops. He hoped to seize the Islamic shrines in Jerusalem for his Hashemite kingdom.[63]

When Nasser blockaded the Straits of Tiran and closed off the Israeli port of Eilat, he prevented Israel's only access from the Gulf of Aqaba to the Red Sea, and from there to the Gulf of Aden and the Arabian Sea, and it meant Israel's access to oil from the Persian Gulf was cut off. The blockade, considered an act of war by Israel, was provocation of the first order. Israel had already notified the UN Security Council that it would soon have to act in its own self-defense. But, the UN failed to enforce the conditions of the truce that had existed since 1956.[64]

The Arabs massed 547,000 troops, 2,504 tanks, and 957 combat aircraft. Israel mustered 264,000 troops, 800 tanks, and 300 combat airplanes. Israeli generals Yitzchak Rabin and Moshe Dayan foresaw that surprise was their only hope.[65] The preemptive strike was decisive. "In 170 minutes Israel's pilots had smashed Egypt's best-equipped air bases and had turned three hundred of Nasser's combat planes into flaming wrecks … The Egyptian air force, the largest in the Middle East, was in ruins."[66] The same scenario was replayed in Syria, Jordan, and Iraq. "By nightfall of June 6, Israel had destroyed 416 planes, 393 on the ground. It had lost twenty-six planes during that time, all to antiaircraft."[67]

In two days, the Egyptian army in the Sinai was virtually wiped out, leaving Israel to occupy the Gaza Strip. To the north, after a desperate and costly tank

Restoring the Two Houses of Israel

battle, the Syrians were routed and the strategic Golan Heights was taken. Thus ended the long nightmare of Syrian bombardment of Galilean villages. Israel was now secure on her northern border.[68]

In the battle with Jordan, Israel gained control of the West Bank and the old city of Jerusalem fell into Israeli hands. By gaining control of the West Bank, the cities of Bethlehem, Hebron, Jericho, and Shechem as well as Jerusalem came into Israel hands. For the first time in nineteen hundred years, the Jews had control of the old city of Jerusalem. A newly composed ballad, "Jerusalem the Golden," became Israel's popular anthem in the aftermath of the Six-Day War.[69]

In the war, "The Arabs suffered 15,000 casualties; Israel's losses were 777 killed, 2,186 wounded."[70] To its previous eighty-five hundred square miles, it added twenty-eight thousand square miles in the Sinai, Golan Heights, and West Bank.[71] The occupied territories proved to be an ideal bone of contention for the Arabs, leading to further conflicts that would dwarf even the monumental battles of Israel's first twenty years of nationhood.[72]

Israel's 1973 Yom Kippur War

On October 6, 1973 on Yom Kippur, the Arabs attacked Israel once again. They had 750,000 troops, 3,200 Soviet tanks, 860 planes, and the latest Soviet missiles.[73] In the first grim hours at the Canal Zone, Israeli reservists were obliterated. Their token defenses consisted of "precisely 436 Israeli soldiers in a series of bunkers seven to ten miles apart, together with three tanks and

Israel: The Fig Tree Blossoms

seven artillery batteries."[74] Coming at them, "were five Egyptian infantry divisions, three mixed infantry and tank divisions, and twenty-two independent infantry, commando, and paratroop brigades. With the air force, the enemy constituted not less than 600,000 men, 2,000 tanks, 2,300 artillery pieces, 160 SAM missile batteries, and 550 combat planes."[75]

In the third and fourth days of the war, Israel began to win the war. First, Israel was able to defeat Syria in the north. By October 18, Israeli troops headed toward Damascus. In the battle with Egypt in the Suez, Israel gained the upper edge over Egypt. By October 23, the Israeli army was at the Gulf of Suez. As a result, Egypt and Russia demanded that the United Nations Security Council require Israel to pull back to its pre-1967 borders.

As a result of the war, the United Nations demanded that Israel withdrawal from the West Bank and Gaza Strip based upon UN Resolution 242. When Israel refused to comply, the council nearly voted her out of the United Nations in the summer of 1975.[76]

The Politics of Oil in the Middle East

The 1973 Yom Kippur war highlighted how imported Arab oil has become an important political and economic issue in understanding the present Israel / Arab conflict. The world economy depends on imported Arab oil and the Arab oil producing countries decided to use oil as an economic and political weapon to influence world opinion against Israel. On October 17, 1973, Arab petroleum ministers met during the Yom Kippur

War and decided to cut oil production and exports. "It was under the façade of the war crisis … that the Arabs seized the opportunity to launch a drastic escalation of oil prices. Libya announced on October 18 that the cost of its oil would go up 28 percent — irrespective of the war and Israel's misdeeds. Iraq thereupon declared a 70 percent price rise. Kuwait matched this figure." [77]

Members of the European Common Market took immediate measures to placate Arab oil barons, making new demands on Israel to give up the occupied territories. Thus an oil-thirsty world forced Israel into a diplomatic ghetto. Though the Arabs suffered a devastating loss in the Yom Kippur war, they discovered a powerful new weapon and found themselves in the driver's seat of the world economy. By a simple turn of oil valves they could further the goals of Palestine. [78]

The Palestinian People and Arab Politics

As a result of Israel winning her war of independence and her succeeding wars against her Arab neighbors, the Arabs living in Israel did not have a country of their own. They called themselves Palestinians. Following the 1973 Yom Kippur war, the Palestinians became an increasingly important political issue in the Israel/Arab conflict. Since the creation of the Arab states, the Palestinian people have been mistreated by Arab states and have had bad relations with many of them. During this time, Arab leaders have fought among themselves for the title of being the leader of the Arab world. By not having a state of their own, the Palestinians have been used by the Arab world for their own political purpose

Israel: The Fig Tree Blossoms

and as a political weapon against Israel. While the Arab states all recognize the Palestinians as their cousins, only Jordan was willing to take their refugees.

The root of Arab politics toward the Palestinian people goes back to the early 1920's when the Arab states were being created following the defeat of the Turks in World War I. Following WWI, the British and French allowed the gradual formation of seven independent Arabic states in the region (Egypt, Syria, Lebanon, Transjordan, Iraq, Saudi Arabia, and Yemen, followed later by ten others).[79]

Winston Churchill gave the area of Transjordan to Abdullah of Arabia. This he did to mollify the Arab leader for the help his father, the sharif of Mecca, had given the British in diverting the Turks in Arabia in 1917.[80] This gift of East Jordan (Transjordan) to Abdullah constituted three-quarters of the area known as Palestine.

The Arabs west of the Jordan also wanted an independent state and had candidates chomping at the bit for rulership. For many years, two leading families, the al-Husseinis and Nashashibis, had alternated in filling the position of Grand Mufti of Jerusalem.[81] Though a religious position, it carried strong political clout throughout Palestine. Both families claimed descent from the Grand Sharif of Mecca, who in turn claimed descendancy from Muhammad himself. These two clans exerted much influence in mayoral offices in the region, but were constantly at loggerheads. From the Nashashibis came King Abdullah, who was given

Restoring the Two Houses of Israel

Transjordan, and his brother Feisal. Feisal was first given Syria (until the French took it over) and was later made King of Iraq. At the assassination of Abdullah in 1951, Hussein, his grandson (not of the al-Husseines), became King of Jordan. This family was known as the Hashemites. [82]

The al-Husseini family in Jerusalem was represented by Haj Amin al-Husseini who was appointed Grand Mufti by the British in 1921 when only twenty-one. Amin al-Husseini was a Muslim extremist who violently opposed Zionism. Insisting on Palestine becoming an Arab state, he used every influence to halt Jewish immigration. On August 23, 1929, he inspired a massacre of Jews praying at the Wailing Wall. Prior to that, "Haj Amin had instituted a plan to restore the mosques in order to reestablish the primacy of Islam over all of Palestine and to counter the increasingly vocal religious claims of the Zionists to a portion of Jerusalem." [83]

When World War II erupted, Haj Amin was forced to flee, first to Iraq and then to Germany where he was welcomed by Hitler and Himmler. [84]

These two families, the Hashemites and the al-Husseinis, came to represent the moderate and extreme factions of Palestinian Arabs. [85] Their special bitterness toward each other stemmed from Britain's bestowal of kingdoms on the Hashemites, which the al-Husseinis viewed as a sellout to the enemy. For this Haj Amin and his followers came to regard both the Jews and the Jordanian Hashemites as bitter enemies. [86]

Israel: The Fig Tree Blossoms

The Establishment of the PLO

The Palestinian Liberation Organization was actually the brainchild of Gamal Addel Nasser of Egypt. The PLO was first organized in Cairo in 1964. Its founding document is the Palestine National Covenant. This declaration rejects the Balfour Declaration of 1917, the UN Partition Agreement of 1948, the Jews' biblical claims to the land, and it denies the right of the Jewish people to have a nation. The Covenant has been revised several times over the years, but it still contains the vehement anti-Jewish sentiments of the original document. It insists that all the territory of the nation of Israel properly belongs to the Palestinian Arabs, and only those Jews living in Palestine prior to the "Zionist invasion" can be regarded as legitimate Palestinians and thus allowed to stay in the land. [87]

Nasser sought to promote an underground forum for the Palestinian people. This was first called the Palestine Liberation Army (later the PLO). Chosen as leader was Ahmad Shuqairi, a puppet of Nasser, who set up headquarters in Cairo. The expressed purpose of this organization was to allow the Palestinian people, "to play a role in the liberation of their country and their self-determination." [88] The Arab leaders who set it up, however, had other designs for the organization. They intended to make it an instrument of guerrilla warfare against Israel under their control. They had no intention of creating an independent Palestinian movement. [89]

Yasser Arafat and The Fatah

Six years before Nasser created the PLO, Yasser Arafat started his own group in Syria to "liberate Palestine." Then living in Kuwait, Arafat and a handful of revolutionaries created a military organization. They called it the Palestinian National Liberation Movement. In Arabic, the initials spelled out HATAF (*Harekat at-Tahrir al-Wataniyyeh al-Falastiniyyeh*).[90] They turned the letters around to spell FATAH, which is a reverse acronym of the name of the movement in Arabic. The word "Fatah" means "conquest by means of *jihad* [Islamic holy war]."

The major figures in FATAH were two young dyed-in-the-wool guerrilla operators, Yasser Arafat and Abu Jihad.[91] Both were from the militant Muslim community of Gaza. Arafat was born in Cairo in 1929 and grew up in the Gaza strip during the tumultuous Jewish-Arab conflicts of the 1930s and 1940s. His full name is Rahman Abdul Rauf Arafat al-Qudwa al-Husseini. He was later nicknamed as "Yasser" by his guerrilla tutor after a great Arab hero.[92] Through his mother, Arafat was related to Haj Amin, the Grand Mufti of Jerusalem, and a proud member of the al-Husseini family. That lineage supposedly traced back to Husayn ibn Ali, the son of Fatima, the daughter of Muhammad.[93]

From his earliest years, Arafat was engrossed in liberation tactics, devising terrorist activities against the Israelis whom he saw as invaders. As he and his cronies began the Fatah, they saw themselves as the "generation of revenge" — seeking vengeance for the loss of Palestine.[94] Originally, FATAH opposed the founding of the PLO. By 1969, FATAH had become the largest guerrilla group affiliated with the PLO. At that year's meeting of the PLO's executive body, the Palestinian

Israel: The Fig Tree Blossoms

National Council, Yasser Arafat won complete control of the PLO.[95]

Arafat Becomes the Leader of the PLO

The very establishment of the PLO by Nasser in 1964 was intended to rebuff Arafat and his FATAH. Incensed by Arafat's deriding him in his paper, *Our Palestine*, Nasser "ordered his intelligence service to see to Arafat's liquidation."[96]

Arafat became the leader of the PLO in 1969. Prior to 1968, Palestinians had looked to the pan-Arab nations to liberate their land. In the wake of the 1967 war, they gave up on the promises of the Arab League and determined that they would have to go it alone if they were to "restore their land."[97]

When Arafat took over the PLO, the organization reverted to cell groups developed by its FATAH members in Syria. First, it was basically a guerrilla organization that worked underground apart from national armies or agencies. Its single purpose was to evict the Israelis from the land and set up an independent Palestinian state, not one in tandem with Jordan or any other Arab state. Second, it intended to achieve its goals by armed conflict, using infiltration and terror to drive out the occupiers of the West Bank and Gaza Strip.[98]

The PLO and The Intifada

In December 1987, Palestinian patience ran out and long pent-up feelings were suddenly unleashed with stones and homemade bombs. This uprising was known as the *Intifada*. It quickly spread through the Gaza Strip and the West Bank. The cities of Nablus, Hebron, and Jerusalem in the West Bank soon became centers of agitation.[99]

Most irritating to the Palestinians was the Israeli settlement of Jewish communities in the West Bank. This has received almost continuous coverage by the press since 1977 when Begin began encouraging the program.[100] Various reasons were given for this colonization. Some Jews settled there for religious reasons, such as the hard-core Gush Emunists, searching for their biblical heritage. Others simply sought a place of residence from which to commute to the big cities of Tel Aviv and Jerusalem.[101]

Through the *intifada*, the Palestinians have looked to the world media to dramatize their fight against Israel.[102] By being successful at this, it has forced Israel to rethink its policies regarding the settlements in biblical Judea and Samaria (West Bank). While the settlements are a security issue for Israel, world public opinion is demanding a compromise on the issue and encouraging Israel to trade "land for peace." However, will trading land result in peace for Israel? It is highly unlikely because "PLO" after all, means the "Liberation of Palestine," which is not negotiable to the leaders of the movement.[103]

The PLO Phased Plan Destruction of Israel

Following the 1967 war, two different schools of thought developed among the Arabs concerning their di-

Israel: The Fig Tree Blossoms

lemma of what to do with Israel. With the increased territory Israel gained as a result of the war, it was believed impossible to defeat Israel by conventional means.

The first school of thought held that since it was no longer possible to defeat Israel by conventional means, then there was no choice but to make formal peace with the Jewish nation. This view was held by Anwar Sadat of Egypt, who accepted Menachem Begin's invitation to help negotiate a settlement with Israel. The peace treaty, called the Camp David Accords, was drafted in late 1978 and signed in early 1979.

The second school of thought held that since it was no longer possible to defeat Israel within her existing boundaries, then the course of action should be to first reduce Israel to the pre-1967 borders and then destroy her. This view was officially adopted by the PLO at their 1974 conference in Cairo. It was formalized in a document known as the Phased Plan. Dr. Aaron Lerner, a Middle East analyst, summarizes the goals of the PLO's Phased Plan as follows:

"First, to establish a combatant national authority over every part of Palestinian territory that is liberated (article 2); second, to use that territory to continue the fight against Israel (article 4); finally, to start a pan-Arab war to complete the liberation of all the Palestinian territory (article 8)." [104] The PLO phased plan destruction of Israel and articles 1-4 and 8 are highlighted below.

The PLO's Phased Plan

Political Programme: Adopted at the 12th Session of the Palestinian National Council, Cairo, June 9, 1974. The text of the Phased Plan resolution:

Restoring the Two Houses of Israel

The Palestinian National Council:

On the basis of the Palestinian National Charter and the Political Programme drawn up at the eleventh session, held from January 6-12, 1973; and from its belief that it is impossible for a permanent and just peace to be established in the area unless our Palestinian people recover all their national rights and, first and foremost, their rights to return and to self-determination on the whole of the soil of their homeland; and in the light of a study of the new political circumstances that have come into existence in the period between the Council's last and present sessions, resolves the following:

1. To reaffirm the Palestine Liberation Organization's previous attitude to Resolution 242, which obliterates the national right of our people and deals with the cause of our people as a problem of refugees. The Council therefore refuses to have anything to do with this resolution at any level, Arab or international, including the Geneva Conference.

2. The Liberation Organization will employ all means, and first and foremost armed struggle, to liberate Palestinian territory and to establish the independent combatant national authority for the people over every part of Palestinian territory that is liberated. This will require further changes being effected in the balance of power in favor of our people and their struggle.

3. Any step taken towards liberation is a step towards the realization of the Liberation

Israel: The Fig Tree Blossoms

Organization's strategy of establishing the democratic Palestinian State specified in the resolutions of previous Palestinian National Councils.

4. Struggle along with the Jordanian national forces to establish a Jordanian-Palestinian national front whose aim will be to set up in Jordan a democratic national authority in close contact with the Palestinian entity that is established through the struggle.

8. The Liberation Organization will strive to strengthen its solidarity with the socialist countries, and with forces of liberation and progress throughout the world, with the aim of frustration all the schemes of Zionism, reaction and imperialism.

The Executive Committee of the Palestine Liberation Organization will make every effort to implement this programme, and should a situation arise affecting the destiny and the future of the Palestinian people, the National Assembly will be convened in extraordinary session.

The Oslo Accords and the Phased Destruction of Israel

The PLO has decided that it would be acceptable to get rid of Israel in stages (by trading land for peace) if it couldn't be done all at once (by war). Arafat has publicly told his followers, on numerous occasions, that the Declaration of Principles signed with Israel in 1993

Restoring the Two Houses of Israel

(Oslo I) is actually a part of the PLO's Phased Plan. In November 1994, in a speech marking the celebration of Palestine National Day, Arafat said:

> "What has been a dream has become a reality. In 1974, the PNC decided on establishing a Palestinian Authority on the first piece of land from which the enemy has withdrawn or that we have liberated."

Another clue that the PLO has not totally renounced its idea of eliminating Israel, but has merely postponed it, is the fact that the official PLO letterhead still has for its logo a map of the nation of Israel labeled "Palestine." Textbooks in Egyptian and Jordanian schools, as well as those used in Palestinian schools, do not even show the nation of Israel on their maps. [105]

Furthermore, Arafat has not eliminated terrorism in his government. Instead, he has elevated it to official status. In May 1996, Arafat set aside four cabinet seats in the Palestinian Authority for representatives of the most active terrorist groups: Hamas, Islamic Jihad, and two PLO rejectionist groups, the Popular Front for the Liberation of Palestine (PFLP), and the Democratic Front for the Liberation of Palestine (DFLP). The US law that provides financial aid to the PA specifically says that aid will be cut off if the PLO allows terrorists to be included in the governing agencies. But to date, Congress has made no move to terminate the annual one hundred million in financial aid to the Palestinians.

The PLO has threatened that if Israel doesn't exchange "land for peace" that they will continue the

Israel: The Fig Tree Blossoms

struggle to liberate Palestine by any other means. Hamas and Islamic Jihad are part of the "war by other means" by the PLO against Israel. These two Islamic fundamentalist groups are funded, trained, and armed by Iran and Syria. The Hezbollah, or Party of Allah, which operates against Israel primarily out of Syrian-controlled southern Lebanon, is also sponsored by Iran. These groups are adamantly opposed to peace with Israel and, in fact, they are fanatically dedicated to waging continual "war by other means" against all non-Muslim countries.[106]

During his youth in Cairo, Arafat's family had close ties to a group called the Muslim Brotherhood, an Islamic fundamentalist group active in Egypt and the Middle East. As a teenager Arafat fought with the Muslim Brothers in Jerusalem in 1948 and, during his university days, he often went on secret missions with the Brothers when they were fighting the British at the Suez Canal. Many of the early Fatah members were tied to the Muslim Brotherhood, which once tried to assassinate Egyptian president Gamal Adbel Nasser.[107]

The Islamic Resistance Movement (Hamas) Charter, released to the public in 1988, states that "Hamas is one of the links in the Chain of Jihad in the confrontation with the Zionist invasion. It links up with ... the Muslim Brotherhood who fought the Holy War in 1936; it further relates to another link of the Palestinian Jihad and the efforts of the Muslim Brothers during the 1948 War, and to the Jihad operations of the Muslim Brothers in 1968 and thereafter ..." So the current masters of terrorism affirm their historic link to the Muslim Brotherhood. And it's a link that joins them directly to Yasser Arafat.[108]

Restoring the Two Houses of Israel

Israel Wants Peace with Her Arab Neighbors

Beginning in the late 1800s in Europe, political Zionism was birthed. With political Zionism, the Jewish people *(house of Judah)* dreamed of living in the ancient homeland of their forefathers Abraham *(Avraham)*, Isaac *(Yitzchak)* and Jacob *(Ya'acov)* where they would be free from anti-Semitism while living in security and being at peace with her neighbors.

Theodor Herzl is the father of modern Zionism. He established the World Zionist Organization in 1897 with the purpose of establishing a national homeland for the Jewish people *(house of Judah)*. His dream was carried by Chaim Weizmann who influenced the British to help establish a homeland for the Jewish people *(house of Judah)* by signing the Balfour Declaration.

The Arabs responded to the Jewish *(house of Judah)* desire for a national homeland with great protest. Because of British politics to appease the Arabs, the Jewish *(house of Judah)* Zionist dream was delayed until 1948. It was only achieved because of world outrage to the horrors of the holocaust and the Jewish Resistance Movement against the British. With political division, the United Nations approved the partitioning of Palestine into a Jewish state, an Arab state and Jerusalem being an international city through UN Resolution 181 in 1947.

The Arabs rejected this plan and went to war with Israel in 1948 following the passing of the UN partition

Israel: The Fig Tree Blossoms

plan. Israel defeated the Arabs and won her independence. The Arabs went to war with Israel again in 1956, 1967 and 1973 to liberate the land of Palestine. However, Israel won all these wars and increased the territory that she controlled and began to build settlements in these territories.

The Arab world and the PLO became infuriated with Israel for building settlements in these newly conquered land areas. These settlements and Israel's existence as a nation continued to be a thorny issue to Yasser Arafat and the PLO. Because the PLO and the Arab world could not conquer Israel by war, they decided to go forward with a phased plan destruction of Israel by trading *"land for peace."*

With the passing of UN Resolution 242 following the 1967 war and UN Resolution 338 following the 1973 war, the principle of Israel trading *"land for peace"* was established in the international world community. Because UN Resolutions 242 and 338 could be used as a means to accomplish the phased plan destruction of Israel, it was acceptable to the PLO and the Arab world. Because UN Resolution 242 and 338 is a part of the plan to establish the credibility of the UN as an organization to promote World Government and the *"New World Order,"* trading *"land for peace"* is a high priority to the framers who want to establish World Government. Therefore, the goals to establish World Government and the goal of the PLO to destroy Israel through its phased plan are being united through UN Resolutions 242 and 338. Because of this, Israel is being pressured to trade *"land for peace."*

Restoring the Two Houses of Israel

In the next chapter, we will learn that all of Israel's peace agreements with her Arab neighbors beginning with Egypt and the Camp David Accords in the late 1970s have been based upon UN Resolutions 242 and 338. Because the United States has been actively involved in promoting Israel having peace with her neighbors based upon UN Resolutions 242 and 338, it is easy to discern that the United States strongly advocates and promotes the idea of establishing World Government.

Because Israel desires so strongly to have peace with her Arab neighbors, she has agreed to "peace" with her Arab neighbors based upon UN Resolutions 242 and 338. While Israel desires peace with her neighbors, by agreeing to trade *"land for peace,"* she is rejecting the covenant that the G-d of Israel made with Abraham *(Avraham)* when He promised Abraham *(Avraham)* and his descendents an eternal Promised Land. This land would include the biblical areas of Judea and Samaria (West Bank).

By desiring to have World Government without the rulership of the G-d of Israel, the nations of the world have rejected the G-d of Israel as King of the Universe and have also rejected the covenant that the G-d of Israel made with Abraham *(Avraham)*. By rejecting the covenant that the G-d of Israel made with Abraham *(Avraham)*, the judgment of the G-d of Israel will fall upon Israel and the nations. Rather than having peace *(shalom)* with her Arab neighbors based upon UN Resolutions 242 and 338, the words of the prophet Jeremiah *(Yermiyahu)* ring loud and clear. In Jeremiah *(Yermiyahu)* 6:14 it is written:

Israel: The Fig Tree Blossoms

"They have healed also the hurt of the daughter of my people slightly, saying, **Peace, peace; when there is no peace.***"*

In the *Brit Hadashah* (New Testament), in I Thessalonians 5:3 it is written:

"For when they shall say, **Peace and safety** *[security]; then* **sudden destruction** *cometh upon them, as travail upon a woman with child* [Chevlai shel Mashiach/birthpangs of the Messiah] *and they shall not escape."*

However, it is during Jacob's trouble *(Chevlai shel Mashiach)*, that the prophet Jeremiah *(Yermiyahu)* declares that the two houses of Israel will be reunited in the land of Israel (Jeremiah [*Yermiyahu*] 30:1-7) when they return to the mountains of Israel (Judea and Samaria/West Bank) (Ezekiel [*Yechezekel*] 37:15-22).

May the G-d of Israel pour out His Holy Spirit *(Ruach HaKodesh)* and bring redemption, restoration, reconciliation and unity to both the *house of Judah* (Judaism) and the *house of Israel* (Christianity) speedily in our days. Amen !!

Chapter 9

The United Nations-Israel-Arab Peace Process

Since Israel became a nation in 1948, she has fought numerous wars with her Arab neighbors. While Israel has won all of these wars, she may be losing the *"peace."* In the June 1967 Six-Day War, Israel defeated her Arab neighbors and captured the Biblical land of Judea and Samaria (West Bank) and the city of Jerusalem *(Yerushalayim)* became a united city under Israeli control. The Biblical land of Judea and Samaria is known in the Western world as the "West Bank." In the 1973 Yom Kippur War, Israel gained control of the Golan Heights. Following these wars, the nation of Israel became increasingly interested in having peace and entering into peace agreements with her Arab neighbors. Therefore, in the years to come, Israel made peace agreements with Egypt (1979) and with Jordan (1994). The United States became the facilitator of these peace agreements.

In the early 1990s, Israel began to enter into peace negotiations with the Palestinian Liberation Organization (PLO). With the help of the United States, the result of these peace negotiations was the signing of the Declaration of Principles with the PLO (Oslo I) on September 13,

Restoring the Two Houses of Israel

1993 at the White House in Washington DC. With further help by the United States, Israel and the PLO signed Oslo II in 1995. The Oslo Accords are intended to become the framework for establishing a permanent peace between Israel and the PLO as well as the basis for Israel to establish peace with all of her Arab neighbors in the years to come.

Because the United States has played such a central and active role in bringing Israel and her Arab neighbors together to discuss peace with each other, it **could** be perceived that the United States is acting *independently* to achieve peace between Israel and her Arab neighbors so that they could sign *bilateral agreements* with each other. However, it may come as a surprise to most of our readers that nothing could be farther from the truth. In fact, it is the desire of the United States that all peace agreements between Israel and her Arab neighbors be **United Nations based peace agreements**. In reality, the United States is working as an agent in the peace agreements between Israel and her Arab neighbors to ensure that the goals, intent and purpose for the founding of the United Nations is realized. In other words, in desiring for Israel to make peace with her Arab neighbors, the foreign policy of the United States is to advance the cause of the United Nations.

The purpose of this chapter is to show our readers that the United States has been actively involved in promoting peace between Israel and her Arab neighbors making sure that any signed agreements are based upon United Nations resolutions. It was the goal of the founders of the United Nations that the United Nations would be an organization that would be used to promote, encourage and establish World Government at some point in the future.

The United Nations-Israel-Arab Peace Process

The Bible teaches that at some point in history, there will be World Government headed by the *False Messiah* known to the *house of Israel* (Christianity) as the Antichrist (Daniel 7, Revelation 13). When World Government is established, the *False Messiah* will enter into a peace agreement with the nation of Israel guaranteeing her peace and security. In I Thessalonians 5:1-3 it is written:

> *"But of the times and the seasons, brethren, ye have no need that I write unto you. For yourselves know perfectly that the day of the* Lord *so cometh as a thief in the night. For when they shall say, Peace and safety* [security] *then sudden destruction cometh upon them, as travail upon a woman with child* [Chevlai shel Mashiach/birth pangs of the Messiah]; *and they shall not escape."*

In this chapter, we will see how the peace agreements that the United States has helped to negotiate between Israel and her Arab neighbors have been based upon United Nations Resolutions 242 and 338. Furthermore, United Nations Resolutions 242 and 338 is based upon the principle of peace with security. Therefore, the United States is hastening the day when Israel will enter into an ominous peace agreement with the *False Messiah* in the end of days. Quite possibly, the *False Messiah* will try to enforce peace between Israel and her Arab neighbors by guaranteeing the terms and conditions of United Nations Resolutions 242 and 338 — peace with security.

In the rest of this chapter, the text of United Nations Resolutions 242 and 338 will be shown. Then, peace agreements and peace negotiations between Israel and her Arab neighbors will be reviewed highlighting those parts of the agreements which specify that these agreements are based upon United Nations Resolutions 242 and 338.

The source of the text of the peace agreements and negotiations between Israel and her Arab neighbors comes from the Israel Ministry of Foreign Affairs website located at http://www.mfa.gov.il and is used with permission. For further detailed study of these documents and other matters pertaining to the nation of Israel, please visit the Israel Ministry of Foreign Affairs website.

UN Security Council Resolution 242
(November 22, 1967)

The Security Council:

Expressing its continuing concern with the grave situation in the Middle East,

Emphasizing the inadmissibility of the acquisition of territory by war and the need to work for a just and lasting peace in which every State in the area can live in security,

Emphasizing further that all Member States in their acceptance of the Charter of the United Nations have undertaken a commitment to act in accordance with Article 2 of the Charter,

The United Nations-Israel-Arab Peace Process

1. Affirms that the fulfillment of Charter principles requires the establishment of a just and lasting peace in the Middle East which should include the application of both the following principles:

    (a) Withdrawal of Israeli armed forces from territories occupied in the recent conflict;
    (b) Termination of all claims or states of belligerency and respect for and acknowledgment of the sovereignty, territorial integrity and political independence of every State in the area and their right to live in peace within secure and recognized boundaries free from threats or acts of force;

2. Affirms further the necessity:

    (a) For guaranteeing freedom of navigation through international waterways in the area;
    (b) For achieving a just settlement of the refugee problem;
    (c) For guaranteeing the territorial inviolability and political independence of every State in the area, through measures including the establishment of demilitarized zones;

3. Requests the Secretary General to designate a Special Representative to proceed to the Middle East to establish and maintain contacts with the States concerned in order to promote agreement and assist efforts to achieve a peaceful and accepted settlement in accordance with the provisions and principles in this resolution;

4. Requests the Secretary-General to report to the Security Council on the progress of the efforts of the Special Representative as soon as possible.

UN Security Council Resolution 338
(October 22, 1973)

The Security Council:

1. Calls upon all parties to the present fighting to cease all firing and terminate all military activity immediately, no later than 12 hours after the moment of the adoption of this decision, in the positions after the moment of the adoption of this decision, in the positions they now occupy;

2. Calls upon all parties concerned to start immediately after the cease-fire the implementation of Security Council Resolution 242 (1967) in all of its parts;

3. Decides that, immediately and concurrently with the cease-fire, negotiations start between the parties concerned under appropriate auspices aimed at establishing a just and durable peace in the Middle East.

Israel Enters into Peace With Egypt

In the late 1970s, Israel entered into peace negotiations with the nation of Egypt. After twelve days of secret negotiations at Camp David, the Israeli-Egyptian negotiations were concluded with the signing at the

The United Nations-Israel-Arab Peace Process

White House of two agreements. First, the Camp David Accords were signed on September 17, 1978. Then, a full peace agreement between Israel and Egypt was signed on March 26, 1979. President Carter witnessed the accords that were signed by Egyptian President Sadat and Israeli Prime Minister Begin. The United States helped to negotiate these agreements. They are based upon United Nations Resolutions 242 and 338. Those parts of the agreement which highlight that they are based upon United Nations Resolution 242 and 338 will be presented.

The Camp David Accords
(September 17, 1978)

The Framework for Peace in the Middle East

Muhammad Anwar al-Sadat, President of the Arab Republic of Egypt, and Menachem Begin, Prime Minister of Israel, met with Jimmy Carter, President of the United States of America, at Camp David from September 5 to September 17, 1978, and have agreed on the following framework for peace in the Middle East. They invite other parties to the Arab-Israel conflict to adhere to it.

Preamble

The search for peace in the Middle East must be guided by the following:

The agreed basis for a peaceful settlement of the conflict between Israel and its neighbors is **United Nations**

Restoring the Two Houses of Israel

Security Council Resolution 242, in all its parts ... The provisions of the Charter of the United Nations and the other accepted norms of international law and legitimacy now provide accepted standards for the conduct of relations among all states.

To achieve a relationship of peace, in the spirit of Article 2 of the United Nations Charter, future negotiations between Israel and any neighbor prepared to negotiate **peace and security** with it are necessary for the purpose of carrying out all the provisions and principles of **Resolutions 242 and 338**.

Framework

Taking these factors into account, the parties are determined to reach a just, comprehensive, and durable settlement of the Middle East conflict through the conclusion of peace treaties based on **Security Council Resolutions 242 and 338** in all their parts. Their purpose is to achieve peace and good neighborly relations. They recognize that for peace to endure, it must involve all those who have been most deeply affected by the conflict. They therefore agree that this framework, as appropriate, is intended by them to constitute a basis for peace not only between Egypt and Israel, but also between Israel and each of its other neighbors which is prepared to negotiate peace with Israel on this basis. With that objective in mind, they have agreed to proceed as follows:

A. West Bank and Gaza

1. Egypt, Israel, Jordan and the representatives of the Palestinian people should participate in ne-

gotiations on the resolution of the Palestinian problem in all its aspects. To achieve that objective, negotiations relating to the West Bank and Gaza should proceed in three stages ... **The negotiations shall be based on all the provisions and principles of UN Security Council Resolution 242** ...

The United States shall be invited to participate in the talks on matters related to the modalities of the implementation of the agreements and working out the timetable for the carrying out of the obligations of the parties. The United Nations Security Council shall be requested to endorse the peace treaties and ensure that their provisions shall not be violated. The permanent members of the Security Council shall be requested to underwrite the peace treaties and ensure respect or the provisions...

For the Government of Israel:
Menachem Begin

For the Government of the Arab Republic of Egypt
Muhammed Anwar al-Sadat

Witnessed by
Jimmy Carter,
President of the United States of America

Framework For the Conclusion of a Peace Treaty Between Egypt and Israel

In order to achieve peace between them, Israel and Egypt agree to negotiate in good faith with a goal of concluding within three months of the signing of this framework a peace treaty between them:

It is agreed that:

The site of the negotiations will be under a **United Nations flag** at a location or locations to be mutually agreed. **All of the principles of UN Resolution 242** will apply in this resolution of the dispute between Israel and Egypt...

For the Government of
the Arab Republic of Egypt:
Muhammed Anwar al-Sadat

For the Government of Israel:
Menachem Begin

Witnessed by:
Jimmy Carter,
President of the United States of America

Israel's Peace Treaty with Egypt Is Based Upon UN Resolutions 242 and 338

Sixteen months after Sadat's visit to Israel, the Israel-Egypt peace treaty was signed in Washington. This peace treaty between Israel and Egypt was based upon United Nations Resolutions 242 and 338. Those parts of the agreement which highlight that this peace treaty was based upon United Nations Resolution 242 and 338 will be presented.

The United Nations-Israel-Arab Peace Process

Peace Treaty Between Israel and Egypt
(March 26, 1979)

The Government of the Arab Republic of Egypt and the Government of the State of Israel;

Preamble

Convinced of the urgent necessity of the establishment of a just, comprehensive and lasting peace in the Middle East in accordance **with Security Council Resolutions 242 and 338**;

Reaffirming their adherence to the "Framework for Peace in the Middle East Agreed at Camp David," dated September 17, 1978;

Noting that the aforementioned Framework as appropriate is intended to constitute a basis for peace not only between Egypt and Israel but also between Israel and each of its other Arab neighbors which is prepared to negotiate peace with it on this basis…

For the Government of Israel

For the Government of the
Arab Republic of Egypt

Witnessed by:
Jimmy Carter,
President of the United States of America

Restoring the Two Houses of Israel

Israel's Peace Initiative with the Arabs

The following peace initiative was formulated by Prime Minister Shamir (*Likud*) and Defense Minister Rabin (*Labour*) and represents the consensus of Israel policy in the National unity government in the late 1980s. The part of the peace initiative that highlights the commitment to United Nations Resolution 242 and 338 will be presented.

Israel's Peace Initiative
(May 14, 1989)

General

1. This document presents the principles of a political initiative of the Government of Israel which deals with the continuation of the peace process; the termination of the state of war with the Arab states; a solution for the Arabs of Judea, Samaria and the Gaza district; peace with Jordan; and a resolution of the problem of the residents of the refugee camps in Judea, Samaria and the Gaza district...

The Principles Constituting the Initiative

...The interlock between the stages is a timetable on which the Plan is built: the peace process delineated by the initiative is based on **Resolutions 242 and 338** upon which the Camp David Accords are founded...

The Madrid Peace Conference

Following the 1991 Gulf War, US Secretary of State James Baker made eight trips to the Middle East in eight

The United Nations-Israel-Arab Peace Process

months. As a result of the shuttle diplomacy by James Baker, the United States invited Israel, Syria, Lebanon, Jordan and the Palestinians to enter into peace negotiations that were to be held in Madrid, Spain. The following contains the invitation to the Madrid Peace Conference that was held on October 30, 1991. The invitation was jointly issued by the United States and the Soviet Union. Only the part of the invitation that highlights the commitment of the peace talks to United Nations Resolution 242 and 338 will be presented.

Letter of Invitation to Madrid Peace Conference
(October 30, 1991)

After extensive consultations with Arab states, Israel and the Palestinians, the United States and the Soviet Union believe that an historic opportunity exists to advance the prospects for genuine peace throughout the region. The United States and the Soviet Union are prepared to assist the parties to achieve a just, lasting and comprehensive peace settlement, through direct negotiations along two tracks, between Israel and the Arab states, and between Israel and the Palestinians, based on **United Nations Security Council Resolutions 242 and 338**. The objective of this process is real peace. Toward that end, the president of the US and the president of the USSR invite you to a peace conference, which their countries will cosponsor, followed immediately by direct negotiations. The conference will be convened in Madrid on October 30, 1991.

President Bush and President Gorbachev request your acceptance of this invitation no later than 6 PM

Restoring the Two Houses of Israel

Washington time, October 23, 1991, in order to ensure proper organization and preparation of the conference ... The European Community will be a participant in the conference, alongside the United States and the Soviet Union and will be represented by its presidency ... the negotiations between Israel and the Arab states, will take place on the basis of **Resolutions 242 and 338**...

Yasser Arafat Accepts United Nations Resolutions 242 and 338

Beginning with the Madrid peace conference, talks continued between Israel and the PLO. Eventually, these talks resulted in an agreement between Israel and the PLO termed the "Declaration of Principles" which was signed at the White House in Washington D.C. on September 13, 1993. In preparation for the signing of this agreement, Yasser Arafat sent a letter to Prime Minister Yitzchak Rabin acknowledging Israel's right to exist while reaffirming that peace negotiations would be based upon United Nations Resolutions 242 and 338. The letter from Yasser Arafat to Prime Minister Yitzchak Rabin is given below. Following Arafat's letter to Rabin is Prime Minister Rabin's reply to PLO leader Yasser Arafat.

Letter From Yasser Arafat to Prime Minister Rabin

September 9, 1993

Yitzhak Rabin
Prime Minister of Israel

Mr. Prime Minister,

The signing of the Declaration of Principles marks a new era in the history of the Middle East. In firm conviction thereof, I would like to confirm the following PLO commitments:

The PLO recognizes the right of the State of Israel to exist in peace and security.

The PLO accepts **United Nations Security Council Resolutions 242 and 338**.

The PLO commits itself to the Middle East peace process, and to a peaceful resolution of the conflict between the two sides and declares that all outstanding issues relating to permanent status will be resolved through negotiations...

In view of the promise of a new era and the signing of the Declaration of Principles and based on Palestinian acceptance of **Security Council Resolutions 242 and 338**, the PLO affirms that those articles of the Palestinian Covenant which deny Israel's right to exist, and the provisions of the Covenant which are inconsistent with the commitments of this letter are now inoperative and no longer valid. Consequently, the PLO undertakes to submit to the Palestinian National Council for formal approval the necessary changes in the Palestinian Covenant.

Sincerely,

Yasser Arafat
Chairman
The Palestine Liberation Organization

Restoring the Two Houses of Israel

Letter From Prime Minister Rabin to Yasser Arafat

September 9, 1993

Yasser Arafat
Chairman
The Palestinian Liberation Organization

Mr. Chairman,

In response to your letter of September 9, 1993, I wish to confirm to you that, in light of the PLO commitments included in your letter, the Government of Israel has decided to recognize the PLO as the representative of the Palestinian people and commence negotiations with the PLO within the Middle East peace process.

Yitzhak Rabin
Prime Minister of Israel

The Declaration of Principles Agreement Is Based Upon UN Resolutions 242 and 338

Declaration of Principles on Interim
Self-Government Arrangements
September 13, 1993

The Government of the State of Israel and the PLO team (in the Jordanian-Palestinian delegation to the Middle East Peace Conference) (the "Palestinian Delegation"), representing the Palestinian people, agree

The United Nations-Israel-Arab Peace Process

that it is time to put an end to decades of confrontation and conflict, recognize their mutual legitimate and political rights, and strive to live in peaceful coexistence and mutual dignity and security and achieve a just, lasting and comprehensive peace settlement and historic reconciliation through the agreed political process. Accordingly, the two sides agree to the following principles;

Article I
Aim of the Negotiations

The aim of the Israeli-Palestinian negotiations within the current Middle East peace process is, among other things, to establish a Palestinian Interim Self-Government Authority, the elected Council (the "Council"), for the Palestinian people in the West Bank and the Gaza Strip, for a transitional period not exceeding five years, leading to a **permanent settlement based on Security Council Resolutions 242 and 338**. It is understood that the interim arrangements are an integral part of the whole peace process and that the negotiations on the permanent status **will lead to the implementation of Security Council Resolutions 242 and 338** ...

Done at Washington, DC, this thirteenth day of September 1993.

For the Government of Israel
For the PLO

Witnessed By:

The United States of America
The Russian Federation

Restoring the Two Houses of Israel

Israel's Peace Treaty With Jordan Is Based Upon UN Resolutions 242 And 338

Following the signing of the Declaration of Principles between Israel and the PLO on September 13, 1993, Israel signed a declaration to enter into peace with Jordan on July 25, 1994. This declaration resulted in a peace treaty between Israel and Jordan on October 26, 1994. The United States helped to make this peace treaty possible. This peace treaty is also based upon United Nations Resolutions 242 and 338. The part of the peace treaty that highlights the commitment to United Nations Resolutions 242 and 338 will be presented.

The Washington Declaration Israel- Jordan- the United States
(July 25th, 1994)

After generations of hostility, blood and tears and in the wake of years of pain and wars, His Majesty King Hussein and Prime Minister Yitzhak Rabin are determined to bring an end to bloodshed and sorrow. It is in this spirit that His Majesty King Hussein of the Hashemite Kingdom of Jordan and Prime Minister and Minister of Defense, Mr. Yitzhak Rabin of Israel, met in Washington today at the invitation of President William J. Clinton of the United States of America. This initiative of President William J. Clinton constitutes an historic landmark in the United States' untiring efforts in promoting peace and stability in the Middle East ... In their meeting, His Majesty King Hussein and Prime Minister Yitzhak Rabin have jointly reaffirmed the five underlying principles of their understanding on an

The United Nations-Israel-Arab Peace Process

Agreed Common Agenda designed to reach the goal of a just, lasting and comprehensive peace between the Arab States and the Palestinians, with Israel.

1. Jordan and Israel aim at the achievement of a just, lasting and comprehensive peace between Israel and its neighbors and at the conclusion of a Treaty of Peace between both countries.

2. The two countries will vigorously continue their negotiations to arrive at a state of peace, based on **Security Council Resolutions 242 and 338** in all their aspects, and founded on freedom, equality and justice…

…In recognition of their appreciation to the President, His Majesty King Hussein and Prime Minister Yitzhak Rabin have asked President William J. Clinton to sign this document as a witness and as a host to their meeting.

His Majesty King Hussein
Prime Minister Yitzhak Rabin
President William J. Clinton

Treaty of Peace Between the State of Israel and the Hashemite Kingdom of Jordan
(October 26, 1994)

Preamble

The Government of the State of Israel and the Government of the Hashemite Kingdom of Jordan:

Restoring the Two Houses of Israel

Bearing in mind the Washington Declaration , signed by them on July 25, 1994, and which they are both committed to honor;

Aiming at the achievement of a just, lasting and comprehensive peace in the Middle East based an **Security Council Resolutions 242 and 338** in all their aspects...

Reaffirming their faith in the purposes and principles of the Charter of the United Nations and recognizing their right and obligation to live in peace with each other as well as with all states, within secure and recognized boundaries...

Bearing in mind that in their Washington Declaration of July 25, 1994, they declared the termination of the state of belligerency between them;

Deciding to establish peace between them in accordance with this Treaty of Peace;

Have agreed as follows...

For the State of Israel
Yitzhak Rabin, Prime Minister

For the Hashemite Kingdom of Jordan
Abdul Salam Majali, Prime Minister

Witnessed by:

William J. Clinton
President of the United States of America

The United Nations-Israel-Arab Peace Process

Agreement Between Israel and the PLO on the Gaza Strip and Jericho Is Based Upon UN Resolutions 242 and 338

As a part of the Declaration of Principles agreement signed between Israel and the PLO on September 13, 1993, Israel agreed to withdraw from the Gaza Strip and Jericho. This agreement was signed on May 4, 1994. It is also based upon United Nations Resolutions 242 and 338. The part of the agreement that highlights the commitment to UN Resolutions 242 and 338 will be presented.

Agreement on the Gaza Strip and the Jericho Area
(May 4, 1994)

The Government of the State of Israel and the Palestine Liberation Organization (hereinafter "the PLO"), the representative of the Palestinian people;

Preamble

WITHIN the framework of the Middle East peace process initiated at Madrid in October 1991;

REAFFIRMING their determination to live in peaceful coexistence, mutual dignity and security, while recognizing their mutual legitimate and political rights;

REAFFIRMING their desire to achieve a just, lasting and comprehensive peace settlement through the agreed political process;

Restoring the Two Houses of Israel

REAFFIRMING their adherence to the mutual recognition and commitments expressed in the letters dated September 9, 1993, signed by and exchanged between the Prime Minister of Israel and the Chairman of the PLO;

REAFFIRMING their understanding that the interim self-government arrangements, including the arrangements to apply in the Gaza Strip and the Jericho Area contained in this Agreement, are an integral part of the whole peace process and that the negotiations on the permanent status will lead to the implementation of **Security Council Resolutions 242 and 338**...

Done in Cairo this fourth day of May, 1994.

For the Government of the State of Israel for the PLO

Witnessed By:

The United States of America
The Russian Federation
The Arab Republic of Egypt

Interim Agreement Between Israel and the PLO (Oslo II) Is Based Upon UN Resolutions 242 and 338

The Israeli-Palestinian Interim Agreement on the West Bank and Gaza Strip (Oslo II) is based upon United Nations Resolutions 242 and 338. The part of the agreement that highlights the commitment to UN Resolutions 242 and 338 will be presented.

The United Nations-Israel-Arab Peace Process

Israeli-Palestinian Interim Agreement on the West Bank and the Gaza Strip

Washington, DC,
September 28, 1995

The Government of the State of Israel and the Palestine Liberation Organization (hereinafter "the PLO"), the representative of the Palestinian people;

Preamble

WITHIN the framework of the Middle East peace process initiated at Madrid in October 1991;

REAFFIRMING their determination to put an end to decades of confrontation and to live in peaceful coexistence, mutual dignity and security, while recognizing their mutual legitimate and political rights;

REAFFIRMING their desire to achieve a just, lasting and comprehensive peace settlement and historic reconciliation through the agreed political process;

RECOGNIZING that the peace process and the new era that it has created, as well as the new relationship established between the two Parties as described above, are irreversible, and the determination of the two Parties to maintain, sustain and continue the peace process;

RECOGNIZING that the aim of the Israeli-Palestinian negotiations within the current Middle East peace process is, among other things, to establish a Palestinian Interim Self-Government Authority, i.e. the elected Council (hereinafter "the Council" or "the Palestinian Council"), and the elected Ra'ees of the Executive Authority, for the Palestinian people in the West Bank and the Gaza Strip, for a transitional period not exceeding five years from the date of signing the Agreement on the Gaza Strip and the Jericho Area (hereinafter "the Gaza-Jericho Agreement") on May 4, 1994, leading to a **permanent settlement** based on **Security Council Resolutions 242 and 338**...

Madeline Albright Reaffirms the Commitment of the United States to UN Resolutions 242 and 338

At this point, there should be no doubt in the reader's mind that the Middle East peace process between Israel and her Arab neighbors is based upon United Nations Resolutions 242 and 338. Furthermore, there should be no doubt in the reader's mind that the United States fully supports United Nations Resolutions 242 and 338 and has played a central and active role in making sure that any peace agreements between Israel and her Arab neighbors is based upon United Nations Resolutions 242 and 338. Therefore, it can be reasonably concluded that the United States is in favor of future World Government and is actively working to help bring it into reality.

The following article appeared in the *Jerusalem Post Internet Edition* on November 17, 1997. At the time of the writing of this book, the article could be found on the *Jerusalem Post* website located at:

The United Nations-Israel-Arab Peace Process

http://www.jpost.com/com/Archive/17.Nov.1997/News/Article-0.html

In this article, the United States Secretary of State Madeline Albright reaffirms the United States commitment to the peace process between Israel and the PLO based upon United Nations Resolutions 242 and 338.

Albright to Israel: Time Is Running Out
By Steve Rodan

DOHA, Qatar (November 17) — Warning that time is running out for the peace process, US Secretary of State Madeline Albright yesterday called on Israel to implement the interim agreements with the Palestinians.

"Palestinian leaders must intensify cooperation on security issues and speak more consistently the language of peace," Albright told the opening of the Middle East and North Africa economic conference in the Qatari capital.

"Israeli leaders must meet their responsibilities by taking steps to restore Palestinian and Arab confidence in their commitment to implementing Oslo."

…**She reiterated US support for UN Security Council Resolutions 242 and 338**, "including the principle of land for peace."

Her words reflected what US officials said is Washington's frustration with the stalled peace process.

Restoring the Two Houses of Israel

President Bill Clinton Reaffirms the Commitment of the United States to UN Resolutions 242 and 338

In the May 14, 1999 edition of the *Jewish Press* newspaper (Brooklyn, New York) on page 80, there was an article that featured a letter from President Bill Clinton to Yasser Arafat that was sent to him on April 26, 1999. An excerpt of the letter reads as follows:

> "Dear Mr. Chairman, I appreciated the opportunity to see you at the White House last month and exchange views on the current situation ... I am asking that you continue to rely on the peace process as the way to fulfill the aspirations of your people ... the objective of the negotiating process is the implementation of UN Security Council Resolutions 242 and 338, including land for peace..."

The United Nations Israel/Arab Peace Process

At this point, it should be understood that the Middle East peace process between Israel and her Arab neighbors has been based upon United Nations Resolutions 242 and 338. The basis of UN Resolutions 242 and 338 is for Israel to exchange *"land for peace."* These resolutions are intended to grant Israel the assurance of having *"peace with security."*

The United States has played a central and active role in each and every peace negotiation and agreement between Israel and her Arab neighbors. The United States fully supports United Nations Resolutions 242 and 338

The United Nations-Israel-Arab Peace Process

and wants to ensure that each peace agreement between Israel and her Arab neighbors is based upon these UN resolutions. In doing so, the United States is taking an active role in promoting the intent, purpose and goals of the founders of the United Nations to use the United Nations as an instrument to help bring about World Government. By looking at the United States involvement in the Middle East peace process and how the United States seeks to promote United Nations Resolutions 242 and 338 as a central part of this process, it can be easily discerned that the foreign policy of the United States is to help promote the empowering of the United Nations and to advance the goal to eventually establish One World Government.

Knowledgeable students of Bible prophecy also know that the *False Messiah* will eventually be the leader of this coming World Government. Furthermore, the G-d of Israel declares in His Holy Word that the second coming of the Jewish Messiah (*Mashiach*) *Yeshua*/Jesus as the Kingly Messiah known as *Messiah ben David* will crush to pieces the world rule of this *False Messiah* through ushering in the Messianic Age *(Athid Lavo)* (Daniel 7, Revelation 13).

Because the United States is leading a world wide rebellion against the nation of Israel by basing Israel's peace negotiations and treaties with her Arab neighbors upon United Nations Resolutions 242 and 338 and subsequently, hastening the advent of World Government and the rise of the eventual *False Messiah* who will be the ruler of this World Government, the wrath and curse of the G-d of Israel will come upon the United States because she is turning her back on the nation of

Restoring the Two Houses of Israel

Israel and siding with Ishmael rather than Isaac in this conflict. The G-d of Israel made a promise to Abraham *(Avraham)* in Genesis *(Bereishit)* 12:3 as it is written:

> *"And I will bless them that bless thee, and curse him that curseth thee: and in thee shall all families of the earth be blessed."*

In Zechariah *(Zecharyah)* 2:8 it is written:

> *"...he that toucheth you toucheth the apple of his eye."*

Therefore, let us remember the inspired words of the G-d of Israel in Psalm *(Tehillim)* 121:4 as it is written:

> *"Behold, he that keepeth Israel shall neither slumber nor sleep."*

And let us also remember the inspired words of the G-d of Israel in Psalm *(Tehillim)* 122:6 as it is written:

> *"Pray for the peace of Jerusalem: they shall prosper that love thee."*

On behalf of the covenant that the G-d of Israel made with Abraham *(Avraham)* when the G-d of Israel promised ALL twelve tribes of Israel a Promised Land and for the sake of the city of Jerusalem *(Yerushalayim)* which He has chosen, may the G-d of Israel pour out His Holy Spirit *(Ruach HaKodesh)* upon the *house of Judah* (Judaism) and upon the *house of Israel* (Christianity) and unite our hearts by bringing redemption, restoration, reconciliation and unity to both houses of Israel speedily in our days because of our love for Zion. Amen!

Chapter 10

Jerusalem: The City of the Great King

There is no other city on the earth that is closer to the heart of the G-d of Israel than the city of Jerusalem *(Yerushalayim)*. Combining both the *TeNaKh* (Old Testament) and the *Brit Hadashah* (New Testament), it is mentioned over 800 times. The heavenly Jerusalem *(Yerushalayim)* is the city of the G-d of Israel (Hebrews 12:22). It is the city of the great King (Psalm *[Tehillim]* 48:2, Matthew *[Mattityahu]* 5:35). The throne of the G-d of Israel is located in Jerusalem *(Yerushalayim)* (Ezekiel *[Yechezekel]* 43:7). It is from the heavenly Jerusalem *(Yerushalayim)* that He sits upon His throne as King of the universe (Psalm *[Tehillim]* 47:2). The heavenly Jerusalem *(Yerushalayim)* is also the city of the Bride of the G-d of Israel (Revelation 21:2, 9-10).

Both in ancient and in modern times, Jerusalem *(Yerushalayim)* has always been the heartbeat of religious life for the nation of Israel. The special significance of Jerusalem *(Yerushalayim)* is emphasized throughout the Bible.

1) The G-d of Israel placed His name in Jerusalem *(Yerushalayim)* (II Kings *[Melachim]* 21:4) and His

name would be there forever (II Chronicles 6:6, 7:16, 33:4).

2) Abraham *(Avraham)* offered his son Isaac *(Yitzchak)* on mount Moriah in Jerusalem *(Yerushalayim)* in the event known by the *house of Judah* (Judaism) as the *Akeida* (Genesis *[Bereishit]* 22).

3) Three times a year, males from the nation of Israel went to Jerusalem *(Yerushalayim)* to celebrate the Biblical Festivals. (Deuteronomy *[Devarim]* 16:16).

4) The Temple *(Beit HaMikdash)* was built in Jerusalem *(Yerushalayim)*. (Psalm *[Tehillim]* 68:29).

5) The Priests *(Cohanim)* and Levites *(Levi'im)* taught the Torah and the *Sanhedrin* administered the G-d of Israel's court of justice from Jerusalem *(Yerushalayim)*. (Deuteronomy *[Devarim]* 16:18, 17:8-11).

6) The throne of David was in Jerusalem *(Yerushalayim)* (I Chronicles 11:3-7).

7) The Jewish Messiah *(Mashiach)* Yeshuu/Jesus died as the suffering Messiah *(Mashiach)* known as *Messiah ben Yosef* (Joseph) on a tree in Jerusalem *(Yerushalayim)*. (Matthew *(Mattityahu)* 16:21, 20:17-19).

8) The Holy Spirit *(Ruach HaKodesh)* indwelled and empowered the early Jewish believers in the Jewish Messiah *(Mashiach)* Yeshua/Jesus in Jerusalem *(Yerushalayim)* (Acts 2).

Jerusalem: The City of the Great King

9) Jerusalem *(Yerushalayim)* will become the center of controversy and a cup of trembling to the nations of the world and all nations will be gathered against her in the end of days (Isaiah *(Yeshayahu)* 34:8, Zechariah *(Zecharyah)* 12:2, 14:2).

10) Jerusalem *(Yerushalayim)* is the apple of the G-d of Israel's eye and He will fight against those nations who fight against Jerusalem *(Yerushalayim)* with the plague of nuclear war (Zechariah *[Zecharyah]* 2:1-2, 8, 14:3, 12).

11) The Jewish Messiah *(Mashiach)* Yeshua/Jesus will set His feet upon the mount of Olives in Jerusalem *(Yerushalayim)* as the Kingly Messiah *(Mashiach)* known as *Messiah ben David* at His second coming (Zechariah *[Zecharyah]* 14:4).

12) The Torah will be taught from Jerusalem *(Yerushalayim)* by the Jewish Messiah *(Mashiach)* Yeshua/Jesus during the Messianic age *(Athid Lavo)* (Isaiah *[Yeshayahu]* 2:2-3) and all nations will celebrate the Feast of Tabernacles *(Sukkot)* (Zechariah *[Zecharyah]* 14:16).

Jerusalem and the Jewish People

The city of Jerusalem *(Yerushalayim)* is constantly in the remembrance of the Jewish people *(house of Judah)* as they live their lives. She is regarded as the *"mother of Israel."* Prayers are said daily for Jerusalem *(Yerushalayim)*. She is remembered in the prayers of the Jewish people when they thank the G-d of Israel for their food and when they have their Sabbath *(Shabbat)* and holy-day observances. In fact, the Passover *(Pesach)* Seder and the Yom Kippur service ends by proclaiming, *"Next Year in Jerusalem."* When a Jew says, *"Next Year in Jerusalem,"* it is actually a prayer for the coming of the Messianic Age *(Athid Lavo)*.

At the conclusion of every Jewish wedding ceremony, it is a tradition for the groom to break a glass *(Orach Chaim* 560:2, *Evven HaEzer* 65:3 in *Hagah.* See *Tosafot, Berakhot* 31a, s.v. "Isi."). Among Ashkenazic Jews, the custom is to shout *Mazel Tov* at this point. However, Sefardic Jews recite the verse:

> *"If I forget thee O Jerusalem, let my right hand forget its cunning"* (Psalm *[Tehillim]* 137:5).

The glass is broken so that even at the happiest moment of their lives, the bride and groom should recall the destruction of Jerusalem *(Yerushalayim)*. This is in keeping with the next verse:

> *"Let my tongue stick to my palate if I remember you not, if I set not Jerusalem above my greatest joy"* (Psalm *[Tehillim]* 137:6).

The joy of marriage is associated with the city of Jerusalem *(Yerushalayim)*. In Jeremiah *(Yermiyahu)* 33:10-11 it is written:

> *"Thus saith the* Lord; *Again there shall be heard in this place ... even in the cities of Judah, and in the streets of* **Jerusalem ... the voice of joy**, *and the voice of gladness,* **the voice of the bridegroom,** *and* **the voice of the bride**..."

Jerusalem: The City of the Great King

The heavenly Jerusalem *(Yerushalayim)* is the city of the Bride of the G-d of Israel. In Revelation 21:2, 9-10 it is written:

> *"And I John saw the holy city,* **new Jerusalem***, coming down from God out of heaven,* **prepared as a bride adorned for her husband** *... and there came unto me one of the seven angels ... saying, Come hither, I will show thee the bride, the Lamb's wife. And he carried me away in the spirit to a great and high mountain, and showed me that great city, the holy Jerusalem, descending out of heaven from God."*

Every synagogue in the world is built with the ark on the side toward Jerusalem *(Yerushalayim)*. Therefore, whenever a Jew prays, he faces the Holy city of Jerusalem *(Yerushalayim)*. Whenever King Solomon *(Shlomo)* dedicated the Temple *(Beit HaMikdash)* to the G-d of Israel, it was established that all prayer to the G-d of Israel should be directed toward Jerusalem *(Yerushalayim)*. In I Kings *(Melachim)* 8:1, 3, 22-23, 28-30 it is written:

> *"Then Solomon assembled the elders of Israel, and all the heads of the tribes, the chief of the fathers of the children of Israel, unto king Solomon in* **Jerusalem***, that they might bring up the ark of the covenant of the* LORD *out of the city of David, which is Zion ... and all the elders of Israel came, and the priests took up the ark ... and Solomon stood before the altar of the* LORD *in the presence of all the congregation of Israel, and spread forth his hands toward heaven: And he said,* LORD *God of Israel ... yet have thou respect unto the prayer of thy servant, and to his supplication, O* LORD *my*

Restoring the Two Houses of Israel

> *God, to hearken unto the cry and to the* **prayer**, *which thy servant prayeth before thee today: that mine eyes may be open toward this house night and day, even toward* **the place** *of which thou hast said,* **My name shall be there**: *that thou mayest hearken unto the prayer which thy servant shall make toward this place. And hearken thou to the supplication of thy servant, and of thy people Israel,* **when they shall pray toward this place**..."

To the Jewish people, Jerusalem *(Yerushalayim)* is known as the *"gate of heaven."* So much is Jerusalem *(Yerushalayim)* a focal point of Jewish heart and life and the joy of the whole earth that it is written in the Talmud:

> "Ten measures of beauty descended to this world. Nine were given to Jerusalem and one to the rest of the world."

To the Jewish people, the remembrance of Jerusalem *(Yerushalayim)* radiates in every aspect of their lives. In truth, it is more than just a city. It is the heart and soul of the Jewish people and the entire nation of Israel.

Jerusalem: The City of Peace

Jerusalem *(Yerushalayim)* is first mentioned in the book of Genesis *(Bereishit)* 14:18 by the name of Salem. Salem was an early name for Jerusalem (Josephus, *Antiquity of the Jews*, Book 1, Chapter 10:2). In Genesis *(Bereishit)* 14:18-20 it is written:

> "*And* **Melchizedek king of Salem** *brought forth bread and wine: and he was the priest of the*

Jerusalem: The City of the Great King

most high God. And he blessed him, and said, Blessed be Abram of the most high God, possessor of heaven and earth: And blessed be the most high God, which hath delivered thine enemies into thy hand. And he gave him tithes of all."

The word *Salem* is the Strong's word (8004) in the Hebrew dictionary. *Shalom* is the Strong's word (7965) in the Hebrew dictionary. *Shalom* in Hebrew means *"peace, wholeness or to be complete."* Both *Salem* (8004) and *Shalom* (7965) come from the Hebrew word *Shalam*, which is the Strong's word (7999).

Jerusalem *(Yerushalayim)* is the Strong's word 3389. It is also related to the Hebrew word *shalam* which is the Strong's word (7999) and the Hebrew word *shalom* (7965). These are the Hebrew words for *"peace, wholeness or completeness."* Therefore, the Hebrew name for Jerusalem is associated with *shalom* or peace.

In Genesis *(Bereishit)* 14:18, *Melchizedek* is mentioned as being the king of Salem. *Melchizedek* is the Strong's word (4442) in the Hebrew dictionary. *Melchizedek* comes from two Hebrew words, *Melech*, and *tzedek*. *Melech* is the Strong's word (4428) which means, *"king."* *Tzedek* is the Strong's word (6664) which means, *"righteous."* Therefore, the king of Salem *(peace)* was Melchizedek *(the king of righteousness)*.

The Jewish Messiah Is the King of Peace and Righteousness

The Jewish Messiah *(Mashiach) Yeshua*/Jesus is the King of peace and the King of righteousness. He is the

High Priest of the G-d of Israel after the order of Melchizedek. In Hebrews 3:1, 6:20, 7:1-2 it is written:

> *"Wherefore, holy brethren, partakers of the heavenly calling, consider the Apostle* [Shaliach] *and High Priest* [Cohen HaGadol] *of our profession Christ Jesus ...* **made a high priest forever after the order of Melchisedec.** *For this Melchisedec, king of Salem, priest of the most high God, who met Abraham returning from the slaughter of the kings, and blessed him; To whom also Abraham gave a tenth part of all; first being by interpretation King of righteousness, and after that also King of Salem, which is, King of peace."*

The Jewish Messiah *(Mashiach) Yeshua*/Jesus is not only a High Priest *(Cohen HaGadol)* forever after the order of Melchizedek (Psalm *[Tehillim]* 110:4) and the King of righteousness but He is also the King of peace. In Isaiah *(Yeshayahu)* 9:6 it is written about the Jewish Messiah *(Mashiach) Yeshua*/Jesus:

> *"For unto us a child is born, unto us a son is given: and the government shall be upon his shoulder: and his name shall be called Wonderful, Counselor, The mighty God, The everlasting Father,* **The Prince of Peace** [Sar Shalom].*"*

The *Akeidah*: Abraham Binds Isaac on Mount Moriah

Genesis *(Bereishit)* 22 is one of the most important Torah readings to the *house of Judah* (Judaism). In some

Jerusalem: The City of the Great King

Jewish communities, it is read every day of the week except for the Sabbath *(Shabbat)*. It is the primary Torah reading for *Rosh HaShanah* (Feast of Trumpets). The major event of the chapter is Abraham's obedience to the G-d of Israel to offer his son Isaac *(Yitzchak)* as a burnt offering *(olah)* and bind him upon an altar. This event is known to the *house of Judah* (Judaism) as the *Akeidah*.

What is also important in this chapter is that the G-d of Israel provided for Abraham *(Avraham)* a lamb for a burnt offering *(olah)* as a substitute for Isaac *(Yitzchak)*. When He did, Abraham *(Avraham)* called the name of that place *"Jehovah-Jireh"* which means *"the LORD will see."* In Genesis *(Bereishit)* 22:1-2, 4, 6-8, 13-14 it is written:

> *"And it came to pass after these things, that God did tempt Abraham, and said unto him, Abraham: and he said, Behold, here I am. And he said, Take now thy son, thy only son Isaac, whom thou lovest, and get thee into the land of Moriah; and offer him there for a* **burnt offering** *upon one of the mountains which I will tell thee of ... Then on the third day Abraham lifted up his eyes, and saw the place afar off ... And Abraham took the wood of the burnt offering, and laid it upon Isaac his son; and he took the fire in his hand, and a knife; and they went both of them together. And Isaac spake unto Abraham his father, and said, My father: and he said, Here am I, my son. And he said, Behold the fire and the wood: but* **where is the lamb** *for a burnt offering? And Abraham said, My son, God will provide himself a lamb for a burnt offering: so they went both of them together ... And Abraham lifted up his eyes, and looked and behold behind*

him **a ram caught in a thicket** *by his horns: and Abraham went and took the ram, and offered him up for a burnt offering in the stead of his son. And Abraham called the name of that place Jehovah-jireh: as it is said to this day,* **In the mount of the LORD it shall be seen.**"

Mount Moriah is located in Jerusalem *(Yerushalayim)*. In II Chronicles 3:1, it is written:

> *"Then Solomon began to build the house of the LORD at Jerusalem in mount Moriah..."*

The Lamb of G-d Is the Jewish Messiah

The Jewish Messiah *(Mashiach) Yeshua*/Jesus referred to the binding of Isaac upon the altar as a prophetic foreshadowing of Himself. In John *(Yochanan)* 8:56-58, it is written:

> *"Your father Abraham rejoiced to see my day: and he saw it, and was glad. Then said the Jews unto him, Thou art not yet fifty years old, and hast thou seen Abraham? Jesus said unto them, Verily, verily, I say unto you, Before Abraham was, I AM."*

Spiritually, (*sod*/deeper meaning), Abraham *(Avraham)* is a type of the G-d of Israel. Isaac *(Yitzchak)* is a type of the Jewish Messiah *(Mashiach) Yeshua*/Jesus. In a Orthodox Rabbinical commentary of Genesis *(Bereishit)* 22, the *"thicket"* represents the sins of the children of Israel. When the Jewish Messiah *(Mashiach) Yeshua*/Jesus died upon the tree (Deuteronomy [*Devarim*] 21:22-23, Galatians 3:13, I Peter [*Kefa*] 2:24) as

Jerusalem: The City of the Great King

the suffering Messiah known as *Messiah ben Yosef* (Joseph), He did so as the spiritual Lamb of the G-d of Israel whom the G-d of Israel willingly gave as a burnt offering *(olah)* when He allowed Him to be bound to the tree to take away the sin of the entire world. In John *(Yochanan)* 1:29, it is written:

> *"The next day John seeth,* **Jesus** *coming unto him, and saith, Behold the* **Lamb of God,** *which* **taketh away** *the* **sin of the world.***"*

A burnt offering *(olah)* is an offering that is totally consumed. It is freely given and done freely, willingly, and joyfully by both parties involved. The Bible tells us that the G-d of Israel freely offered the Jewish Messiah *(Mashiach) Yeshua*/Jesus who is also the only Son of the G-d of Israel (Proverbs *[Mishlei]* 30:4) freely and the Jewish Messiah *(Mashiach) Yeshua*/Jesus was willing and obedient to His death upon the tree. In Philippians 2:8-11 it is written:

> *"And being found in fashion as a man,* **he humbled himself,** *and became* **obedient unto death,** *even* **the death of the cross [tree]**. *Wherefore God also hath highly exalted him, and given him a name which is above every name: That at the name of Jesus every knee should bow, of things in heaven, and things in earth, and things under the earth; And that every tongue should confess that Jesus Christ is* LORD, *to the glory of God the Father."*

Isaiah *(Yeshayahu)* 53 is written about the suffering Messiah *(Mashiach)* known as *Messiah ben Yosef* (Joseph). In Isaiah *(Yeshayahu)* 53:1, 4-5, 10, it tells us that

G-d the Father offered up the Jewish Messiah *(Mashiach) Yeshua*/Jesus willingly as a burnt offering *(olah)* for the sins of His people as it is written:

> *"Who hath believed our report? and to whom is the arm* [zeroa] *of the* LORD *revealed? ... Surely he hath borne our griefs, and carried our sorrows: yet we did esteem him stricken, smitten of God, and afflicted. But he was wounded for our transgressions, he was bruised for our iniquities: the chastisement of our peace was upon him; and with his stripes we are healed ... Yet it* **pleased the** LORD **to bruise him**; *he hath put him to grief: when thou shalt make* **his soul an offering for sin**..."

Therefore, the binding of Isaac *(Yitzchak)* to the altar by Abraham *(Avraham)* has great significance to both the *house of Judah* (Judaism) and the *house of Israel* (Christianity).

The G-d of Israel Chose Jerusalem To Put His Name There

The G-d of Israel chose Jerusalem *(Yerushalayim)* as His holy city and has chosen to put His name there. In II Chronicles 6:6 it is written:

> *"But I have* **chosen Jerusalem**, *that* **my name might be there**..."

The G-d of Israel's name will be in Jerusalem *(Yerushalayim)* forever. In II Chronicles 7:11-12, 16 it is written:

Jerusalem: The City of the Great King

"Thus Solomon finished the house of the LORD *... And the* LORD *appeared to Solomon by night, and said unto him ... For now have I chosen and sanctified this house, that* **my name may be there forever***: and mine eyes and mine heart shall be there perpetually."*

The Priests and Levites Ministered From Jerusalem

It was the duty of the Priests *(Cohanim)* and the Levites *(Levi'im)* to teach the Torah from Jerusalem *(Yerushalayim)* to the children of Israel. In Deuteronomy *(Devarim)* 17:8-11 it is written:

"If there arise a matter too hard for thee in judgment, between blood and blood, between plea and plea, and between stroke and stroke, being matters of controversy within thy gates: then shalt thou arise, and get thee up into the place which the LORD *thy God shall choose; And thou shalt come unto the* **priests the Levites***, and unto the judge that shall be in those days, and inquire; and they shall show thee the sentence of judgment: And thou shalt do according to the sentence, which they of that place which the* LORD *shall choose shall show thee: and thou shalt observe to do according to all that they inform thee; According to the sentence of the* **law [Torah]** *which they shall* **teach thee***, and according to the judgment which they shall tell thee, thou shalt do: thou shalt not decline from the sentence which they shall show thee, to the right hand, nor to the left."*

Restoring the Two Houses of Israel

The Court of Justice Is in Jerusalem

The G-d of Israel established that a court of justice be set up to judge the children of Israel with righteous judgments. In Deuteronomy *(Devarim)* 16:18 it is written:

> *"Judges and officers shalt thou make thee in all thy gates, which the* Lord *thy God giveth thee, throughout thy tribes: and they shall judge the people with just judgment."*

This commandment was carried out by the *Sanhedrin*. The *Sanhedrin* consisted of 71 members. Their commissioning is derived from Numbers *(Bamidbar)* 11:16 as it is written:

> *"And the* Lord *said unto* **Moses**, *Gather unto me* **seventy men** *of the elders of Israel ... and bring them unto the tabernacle of the congregation, that they may stand there with thee."*

It was believed that Moses *(Moshe)* was the head of the original seventy elders. Therefore, they consisted of 71 members. During the days of the Temple *(Beit HaMikdash)*, the *Sanhedrin* met in the outer north wall of the Temple in a room known as the Chamber of Cut Stone. As long as the *Sanhedrin* convened, it functioned as both the supreme court and the central legislative body for all Israel. The *Sanhedrin* ceased to exist after the destruction of the Temple *(Beit HaMikdash)* by the Romans.

Jerusalem: The City of the Great King

The Festivals are to Be Celebrated in Jerusalem

Three times a year, the G-d of Israel instructed the males from the nation of Israel to keep the **Feasts of the** L*ORD* (Leviticus *[Vayikra]* 23) in Jerusalem *(Yerushalayim)*. In Deuteronomy *(Devarim)* 16:16 it is written:

> *"Three times in a year shall all thy males appear before the* L*ORD* *thy God in the place which he shall choose; in the* **feast of unleavened bread***, and in the feast of weeks, and in the* **feast of tabernacles***..."*

The Jewish Messiah Celebrated the Festivals

The Jewish Messiah *(Mashiach) Yeshua*/Jesus celebrated the Festivals of the G-d of Israel. In Luke 2:41-42, He celebrated Passover *(Pesach)* as it is written:

> *"Now his parents went to* **Jerusalem every year** *at the* **feast of the passover***. And when he was twelve years old, they went up to Jerusalem after the custom of the feast."*

The Jewish Messiah *(Mashiach) Yeshua*/Jesus celebrated the Feast of Tabernacles *(Sukkot)*. In John *(Yochanan)* 7:2, 37-38 it is written:

> *"Now the Jews* **feast of tabernacles** *was at hand ...In the last day, that great day of the feast, Jesus stood and cried, saying, If any man thirst, let him come unto me, and drink. He that believeth on me,*

as the Scripture hath said, out of his belly shall flow rivers of living water."

Sacrifices and Offerings Are Given in Jerusalem

The G-d of Israel commanded that various kinds of sacrifices and offerings be given in Jerusalem *(Yerushalayim)*. In Deuteronomy *(Devarim)* 12:11, 14:22-23, it is written:

> *"Then there shall be a place which the* LORD *your God shall choose to cause his name to dwell there; thither shall ye bring all that I command you; your* **burnt offerings**, *and your* **sacrifices**, *your* **tithes**, *and the* **heave offering** *of your hand, and all your choice vows which ye vow unto the* LORD ... *Thou shalt truly tithe all the increase of thy seed, that the field bringeth forth year by year. And thou shalt eat before the* LORD *thy God, in the place which he shall choose to place his name there, the tithe of thy corn, of thy wine and of thine oil, and the* **firstlings** *of thy* **herds** *and of thy* **flocks**; *that thou mayest learn to fear the* LORD *thy God always...*

The Temple Was Built in Jerusalem

The Temple *(Beit HaMikdash)* was built in Jerusalem *(Yerushalayim)*. In Psalm *(Tehillim)* 68:29 it is written:

> *"Because of* **thy temple at Jerusalem** *shall kings bring presents unto thee."*

Jerusalem: The City of the Great King

The Throne of David Was In Jerusalem

The throne of David was in Jerusalem *(Yerushalayim)*. In I Chronicles 11:3-5 it is written:

> *"Therefore came all the elders of Israel ... and they anointed* **David king over Israel** *... and David and all Israel went to* **Jerusalem** *... David took the castle of Zion, which is the city of David..."*

The Jewish Messiah Will Sit on the Throne of David

The Jewish Messiah *(Mashiach) Yeshua*/Jesus was born to sit on the throne of David and rule over the *house of Jacob* which consists of the *house of Judah* (Judaism) and the *house of Israel* (Christianity) forever. In Luke 1:30-33 it is written:

> *"And the angel said unto her, Fear not, Mary* [Miryam]: *for thou hast found favor with God. And, behold, thou shalt conceive in thy womb, and bring forth a son, and shalt call his name* **Jesus** [Yeshua]. *He shall be great, and shall be called the Son of the Highest: and the* LORD *God shall give unto him the* **throne of his father David**: *And he shall reign over the house of Jacob forever; and of his kingdom there shall be no end."*

The Jewish Messiah Died and Was Resurrected in Jerusalem

The Jewish Messiah *(Mashiach) Yeshua*/Jesus died as the suffering Messiah *(Mashiach)* known as *Messiah ben*

Yosef (Joseph) on a tree in Jerusalem *(Yerushalayim)*. In Matthew *(Mattityahu)* 16:21, it is written:

> *"From that time forth began* **Jesus** [Yeshua] *to show unto his disciples* [talmidim], *how that he must* **go unto Jerusalem**, *and suffer many things of the elders and chief priests and scribes, and* **be killed,** *and* **be raised again the third day."**

The Holy Spirit Empowered Jewish Believers of Yeshua in Jerusalem

The Holy Spirit *(Ruach HaKodesh)* empowered the Jewish *(house of Judah)* believers in *Yeshua*/Jesus as the Jewish Messiah *(Mashiach)* to be His witnesses on the day of *Shavuot* (Pentecost). In Luke 24:44-49 it is written:

> *"And he said unto them, These are the words which I spake unto you, while I was yet with you, that all things must be fulfilled which were written in the law* [Torah] *of Moses, and in the prophets* [Nevi'im] *and in the Psalms* [Ketuvim], *concerning me. Then opened he their understanding that they might understand the Scriptures, And said unto them, Thus it is written, and thus it behooved Christ* [Mashiach] *to suffer, and to rise from the dead the third day: And that repentance* [Teshuvah] *and remission of sins should be preached in his name among all nations,* **beginning at Jerusalem.** *And* **ye are witnesses** *of these things. And, behold, I send the promise of my Father upon you: but tarry ye in the city of Jerusalem, until ye* **be endued with power** *from on high."*

Jerusalem: The City of the Great King

This was fulfilled in Jerusalem *(Yerushalayim)* on the day of Pentecost *(Shavuot)*. In Acts 2:1-5 it is written:

> *"And when* **the day of Pentecost** *was fully come, they were all with one accord in one place. And suddenly there came a sound from heaven as of a rushing mighty wind, and it filled all the house where they were sitting. And there appeared unto them cloven tongues like as of fire, and it sat upon each of them.* **And they were all filled with the Holy Ghost [Ruach HaKodesh]**, *and began to speak with other tongues, as the Spirit gave them utterance. And* **there were dwelling at Jerusalem Jews**, *devout men, out of every nation under heaven."*

The Ancient Battle for Jerusalem

The prophets of Israel wrote that the final battle of the age before the coming of the Jewish Messiah *(Mashiach)* will be a battle of the nations over Jerusalem *(Yerushalayim)*. In truth, this battle over Jerusalem *(Yerushalayim)* is an ancient battle between the kingdom of darkness *(HaSatan)* and the kingdom of light (the kingdom of G-d of Israel).

The modern battle over Jerusalem *(Yerushalayim)* is being played out among the actors on the world's stage who are participating in this ancient battle. For those who have rejected the G-d of Israel as King of the Universe, their plans, ideas, beliefs and ideology are being influenced by the kingdom of darkness *(HaSatan)*. They desire to divide the Promised Land of the G-d of Israel and desire to make Jerusalem *(Yerushalayim)* an international city. For those who put their faith, trust and confidence *(emunah)* in the G-d of Israel and His promises to His people and follow after the kingdom of light, they oppose dividing the land which the G-d of Israel promised to Abraham *(Avraham)* and his descendents forever through Isaac *(Yitzchak)* and Jacob *(Ya'acov)* and want Jerusalem *(Yerushalayim)* to be the eternal undivided capital of the nation of Israel.

Lucifer Desires G-d's Throne

The origin of this battle over Jerusalem took place before the creation of Adam in the Garden of Eden *(Gan Eden)* when *HaSatan* tried to overthrow the throne of the G-d of Israel in the heavenly Jerusalem *(Yerushalayim)*. In Isaiah *(Yeshayahu)* 14:12-14 it is written:

> *"How art thou fallen from heaven, O* **Lucifer***, son of the morning! How art thou cut down to the ground, which didst weaken the nations!* **For thou hast said in thine heart***, I will ascend into heaven, I will exalt my throne above the stars of God:* **I will sit also upon the mount of the congregation in the sides of the north***: I will ascend above the heights of the clouds; I will be like the most High."*

The throne of the G-d of Israel is in the heavenly Jerusalem *(Yerushalayim)* (Hebrews 12:22) in mount Zion, on the sides of the north, which is the city of the great King. In Psalm *(Tehillim)* 48:1-2 it is written:

Jerusalem: The City of the Great King

*"Great is the L*ORD*, and greatly to be praised in the city of our God, in the mountain of his holiness. Beautiful for situation the joy of the whole earth, is* **mount Zion, on the sides of the north**, *the city of the great King."*

Therefore, *HaSatan* stirred a rebellion against the G-d of Israel in the heavenlies with the desire and purpose to exalt his throne above the G-d of Israel and to sit upon the throne of the G-d of Israel in the heavenly Jerusalem *(Yerushalayim)*. In doing so, *HaSatan* wanted to establish a government in the heavenlies without the G-d of Israel.

Satan Is Cast Out of Heaven

When *HaSatan* rebelled against the G-d of Israel, he was cast down. The Jewish Messiah *(Mashiach) Yeshua*/Jesus witnessed this event. In Luke 10:18 it is written:

"And he said unto them, I beheld Satan as lightning fall from heaven."

When *HaSatan* was cast out of heaven, one-third of the angelic hosts rebelled with *HaSatan* against the G-d of Israel and were cast out of heaven also. In Revelation 12:3-4 it is written:

"And there appeared another wonder in heaven; and behold a great **red dragon***, having seven heads and ten horns, and seven crowns upon his heads. And* **his tail drew** *the* **third part** *of the stars of heaven, and did cast them to the earth…"*

Restoring the Two Houses of Israel

The Tower of Babel: World Government on the Earth

When the G-d of Israel created Adam in the Garden of Eden *(Gan Eden)*, this ancient battle between the G-d of Israel and *HaSatan* began to be played out on the earth through mankind. When *HaSatan* tempted Eve, he told her the ancient lie that he believed when he tried to overthrow the throne of the G-d of Israel in the heavenly Jerusalem *(Yerushalayim)* by telling her that she could be like gods. In Genesis *(Bereishit)* 3:4-5 it is written:

> *"And the serpent said unto the woman, Ye shall not surely die: For God doth know that in the day ye eat thereof, then your eyes shall be opened,* **and ye shall be as gods***, knowing good and evil."*

In the process of time, *HaSatan* inspired the people on the earth to try to establish the first world government without the G-d of Israel and exalt themselves and their name above the G-d of Israel and reject Him as being King over all the earth. In Genesis *(Bereishit)* 11:1, 4 it is written:

> *"And the whole earth was of one language, and of one speech ... And they said, Go to, let us build* **us a city** *and a tower, whose top may reach unto heaven; and let us make* **us a name***, lest we be scattered abroad upon the face of the whole earth."*

When the people of the earth through the inspiration of the kingdom of darkness (*HaSatan*) rebelled against the G-d of Israel and tried to build a city and a tower

Jerusalem: The City of the Great King

that would reach unto heaven and exalt their name above the G-d of Israel, the G-d of Israel judged their evil plan and it was called the tower of Babel. In Genesis *(Bereishit)* 11:8-9 it is written:

> *"So the* Lord *scattered them abroad from thence upon the face of all the earth: and they left off to build the city.* **Therefore is the name of it called Babel;** *because the* Lord *did there confound the language of all the earth: and from thence did the* Lord *scatter them abroad upon the face of all the earth."*

The Resurrection of the Tower of Babel

The tower of Babel became a blueprint of *HaSatan's* rebellion against the G-d of Israel through the people living on the earth. This has continued throughout the ages and will be brought to its final conclusion in the ends of days when the nations of the world try to resurrect the tower of Babel and establish a world government without the G-d of Israel. The goal of the framers of world government is to make the city of Jerusalem *(Yerushalayim)* the capital of this godless *"New World Order."*

This end-time plan of the nations to resurrect the tower of Babel and to create a world government without the rule of the G-d of Israel was given for us to understand as a type and shadow by the G-d of Israel through the world empires of Egypt *(Mitzrayim)*, Babylon, Greece and Rome. The preview of these world kingdoms as a type and shadow of world government at the end of the age *(Olam Hazeh)* was given to Daniel the prophet. With the conclusion of the last world kingdom seen by Daniel the prophet (which is world government or the *"New World Order"* and a resurrection of the tower of Babel of old), the G-d of Israel will crush this end-time world government at the same time when they try to make Jerusalem *(Yerushalayim)* an international city. After this, the G-d of Israel through the Jewish Messiah *(Mashiach) Yeshua*/Jesus will set up His world government which will be a Torah based government during the Messiah age *(Athid Lavo)*. In Daniel 7:1-3, 7, 9-10, 13-14 it is written:

> *"In the first year of Belshazzar king of Babylon Daniel had a dream and visions of his head upon his bed: then he wrote the dream, and told the sum of the matters. Daniel spake and said, I saw in my vision by night, and, behold, the four winds of the heaven strove upon the great sea. And* **four great beasts** [future world kingdoms] *came up from the sea,* **diverse one from another** ... *After this I saw in the night visions, and behold a fourth beast* [the last world kingdom which is world government or the "New World Order"] **dreadful and terrible**, *and strong exceedingly ... and it had* **ten horns** ... *I beheld till the thrones were cast down, and the Ancient of days did sit, whose garment was white as snow, and the hair of his head like the pure wool: his throne was like the fiery flame, and his wheels as burning fire. A fiery stream issued and came forth from before him: thousand thousands ministered unto him, and ten thousand times ten thousand stood before him: the judgment was set, and the books were opened ... I saw in the night visions, and, behold, one like the*

Jerusalem: The City of the Great King

Son of man *came with the clouds of heaven, and came to the Ancient of days, and they brought him near before him. And there was* **given him dominion***, and* **glory***, and* **a kingdom***, that all people, nations, and languages, should serve him: his dominion is an* **everlasting dominion***, which shall not pass away, and his kingdom that which shall not be destroyed."*

Daniel's vision will be fulfilled in the end of days when the Jewish Messiah *(Mashiach) Yeshua*/Jesus will return to the earth as the Kingly Messiah known as *Messiah ben David*, defend Jerusalem *(Yerushalayim)* and crush the resurrected tower of Babel known as world government or the *"New World Order."* This will happen during the days when the nations of the world seek to divide the land of Israel and make Jerusalem *(Yerushalayim)* an international city and the capital of their world government.

The ancient battle between the kingdom of darkness *(HaSatan)* and the kingdom of light (the kingdom of the G-d of Israel) which originated before the creation of Adam in the Garden of Eden *(Gan Eden)* when *HaSatan* tried to overtake the throne of the G-d of Israel in the heavenly Jerusalem *(Yerushalayim)* will be played out on the earth in the end of days over the land that the G-d of Israel promised Abraham *(Avraham)* and His descendents forever through Isaac *(Yitzchak)* and Jacob *(Ya'acov)* and over the sovereignty of the city of Jerusalem *(Yerushalayim)*. The G-d of Israel described this battle through the prophet Isaiah *(Yeshayahu)* as the *"controversy of Zion."*

Restoring the Two Houses of Israel

The *"controversy of Zion"* (Isaiah *[Yeshayahu]* 34:8) will conclude with the Jewish Messiah *(Mashiach) Yeshua/*Jesus fighting against the nations (Zechariah *[Zecharyah]* 14:2-3), defending the city of Jerusalem *(Yerushalayim)*, delivering/saving the nation of Israel from her enemies, ending the exile and bringing about the reunification of the two houses of Israel (Ezekiel *[Yechezekel]* 37:15-28) and establishing the Messianic Age *(Athid Lavo)*.

The Controversy of Zion

In the end of days, the city of Jerusalem *(Yerushalayim)* will become a stumbling block and a cup of trembling for all the nations who will be gathered against her because of the controversy of Zion. In Zechariah *(Zecharyah)* 12:1-3 it is written:

> *"The burden of the word of the* Lord *for Israel saith the* Lord, *which stretcheth forth the heavens, and layeth the foundation of the earth, and formeth the spirit of man within him. Behold, I will make* **Jerusalem a cup of trembling** *unto all the people round about, when they shall be in the siege both against Judah and against Jerusalem. And in that day will I make* **Jerusalem a burdensome stone** *for all people: all that burden themselves with it shall be cut in pieces, though all the people of the earth be gathered together against it."*

In Isaiah *(Yeshayahu)* 34:1-3, 8 it is written:

> *"Come near, ye nations, to hear; and hearken, ye people: let the earth hear, and all that is therein; the world, and all things that come forth of it. For*

the **indignation of the** L*ORD* **is upon all nations**, *and his fury upon all their armies: he hath utterly destroyed them, he hath delivered them to the slaughter. Their slain also shall be cast out, and their stink shall come up out of their carcasses, and the mountains shall be melted with their blood … for it is* **the day of the Lord's vengeance**, *and the year of recompences for* **the controversy of Zion.**"

What Is the Controversy of Zion?

How will the nations be gathered against Jerusalem *(Yerushalayim)* and what is the controversy of Zion? The controversy of Zion is over two primary issues. The first is the controversy of the covenant that the G-d of Israel made with Abraham *(Avraham)* and His descendents forever when He promised them a land. The descendents of Abraham *(Avraham)* became the *house of Jacob*. The *house of Jacob* consists of the *house of Judah* (Southern Kingdom) and the *house of Israel* (Northern Kingdom). Secondly, the controversy of Zion is over the future, destiny and sovereignty of the city of Jerusalem *(Yerushalayim)*.

G-d Will Judge the Nations For Dividing His Land

The G-d of Israel promised that He will judge all the nations for dividing His land. In Joel *(Yoel)* 3:1-2 it is written:

> *"For, behold, in those days, and in that time, when I shall bring again the captivity of Judah and*

Restoring the Two Houses of Israel

Jerusalem, I will also gather all nations, and will bring them down into the valley of Jehoshaphat, and will plead with them there for my people and for my heritage Israel, whom they have scattered among the nations, and **parted my land.**"

UN Resolutions: Land For Peace

The plan of the nations of the world to divide the land that the G-d of Israel promised to Abraham *(Avraham)* and His descendents forever through Isaac *(Yitzchak)* and Jacob *(Ya'acov)* is being expressed by the nations of the world through the United Nations based upon UN Resolutions 181, 242 and 338. UN Resolution 181 was passed by the United Nations in 1947. The idea of this plan was to establish a Jewish state, a Palestinian state and make Jerusalem *(Yerushalayim)* an international city. This plan by the nations is the foundation for the controversy of Zion. This plan does not recognize the covenant that the G-d of Israel made with Abraham *(Avraham)* and does not recognize the sovereignty of the G-d of Israel over the city of Jerusalem *(Yerushalayim)*.

UN Resolution 242 was passed following Israel's 1967 war with her Arab neighbors when the entire city of Jerusalem *(Yerushalayim)* came into the hands of the Jewish people *(house of Judah)*. UN Resolution 338 was passed following Israel's 1973 Yom Kippur war with her Arab neighbors. UN Resolutions 242 and 338 is based upon the principle of Israel trading *"land for peace."*

In trading *"land for peace"*, the nations of the world are rejecting the covenant that the G-d of Israel made

Jerusalem: The City of the Great King

with Abraham *(Avraham)* and His descendents forever through Isaac *(Yitzchak)* and Jacob *(Ya'acov)*. In Leviticus *(Vayikra)* 25:23 it is written:

> "**The land shall not be sold forever**: *for the land is mine; for ye are strangers and sojourners with me.*"

The PLO and the Arab Nations Seek to Destroy the Nation of Israel

Furthermore, the nations of the world are putting their trust in having a *"just, lasting and comprehensive peace in the Middle East"* into the hands of Yasser Arafat and the PLO. Yasser Arafat is a murderer and a terrorist and the PLO was founded to destroy the nation of Israel and drive them into the sea. It is completely illogical for the nations of the world to believe that there can be a *"just, comprehensive and lasting peace in the Middle East"* by putting their trust for peace into the hands of a murderer and a terrorist (Yasser Arafat) and an organization (PLO) which was founded with the initial goal of destroying the nation of Israel and driving them into the sea. The plans of the PLO in confederacy with her Arab nations to destroy the nation of Israel and drive them into the sea is prophesied in Psalm *(Tehillim)* 83:1-8 as it is written:

> *"Keep not thou silence, O God: hold not thy peace, and be not still, O God. For, lo, thine enemies make a tumult: and they that hate thee have lifted up the head. They have taken crafty counsel against thy people, and consulted against thy hidden ones. They have said, Come, and* **let us cut**

them off from being a nation; that the **name of Israel** may be **no more in remembrance**. *For they have consulted together with one consent: they are confederate against thee: The tabernacles of Edom, and the Ishmaelites; of Moab, and the Hagarenes; Gebal, and Ammon, and Amalek; the Philistines with the inhabitants of Tyre; Assur also is joined with them: they have helped the children of Lot. Selah."*

G-d Will Judge the Nations

This injustice by the nations of the world against the Jewish people and the nation of Israel by rejecting the covenant that the G-d of Israel made with Abraham and His descendents forever and by rejecting the sovereignty of the city of Jerusalem *(Yerushalayim)* will bring the wrath of the G-d of Israel upon the nations of the world. The wrath of the G-d of Israel will be fully expressed during the period of time known as the tribulation or Jacob's *(Ya'acov's)* trouble to the *house of Israel* (Christianity) and as the *Chevlai shel Mashiach* or the *birth pangs of the Messiah* to the *house of Judah* (Judaism). The wicked plan of the nations and the judgment of the G-d of Israel against the nations because of the controversy of Zion is spoken about in Psalm *(Tehillim)* 2:1-4 as it is written:

> *"Why do the heathen rage, and the people imagine a vain thing?* **The kings of the earth** *set themselves and the rulers* **take counsel** *together,* **against the** L ORD, *and* **against his anointed***, saying, Let us break their bands asunder, and cast away their cords from us. He that sitteth in the*

Jerusalem: The City of the Great King

heavens shall laugh: **the** L*ORD* **shall have them in derision.**"

Because of the wicked plans of the kings of the earth against the L-RD, against His land, against His people and against His holy city of Jerusalem *(Yerushalayim)*, the nations of the world will drink the cup of the wrath of the G-d of Israel. In Jeremiah *(Yermiyahu)* 25:15-17, 27-28 it is written:

> *"For thus saith the* LORD *God of Israel unto me; Take the* **wine cup** *of this* **fury** *at my hand, and* **cause all the nations**, *to whom I send thee,* **to drink it**. *And they shall drink, and be moved, and be mad, because of the sword that I will send among them. Then took I the cup at the Lord's hand, and made all the nations to drink, unto whom the* LORD *had sent me ...Therefore thou shalt say unto them, thus saith the* LORD *of hosts, the God of Israel; Drink ye, and be drunken, and* **spew**, *and* **fall**, *and rise no more, because of the sword which I will send among you. And it shall be, if they refuse to take the cup at thine hand to drink, then shalt thou say unto them, Thus saith the* LORD *of hosts; Ye shall certainly drink."*

The G-d of Israel will judge the nations who come against the city of Jerusalem *(Yerushalayim)* with the plague of nuclear warfare. In Zechariah *(Zecharyah)* 14:12 it is written:

> *"And this shall be the* **plague** *wherewith the* LORD *will smite all the people that have* **fought against Jerusalem**; *Their* **flesh** *shall* **consume away**

while they stand upon their feet, *and their eyes shall consume away in their holes, and their tongue shall consume away in their mouth."*

The Scornful Men Who Rule Jerusalem

Not only will the nations of the world be severely chastised because of the controversy of Zion but the nation of Israel will also be severely chastised by the G-d of Israel for agreeing to the plan of the nations of the world to divide the land of Israel and make Jerusalem *(Yerushalayim)* an international city. By agreeing to these plans, the nation of Israel will experience the most difficult time in her existence as a nation. This period of time is known by the *house of Israel* (Christianity) as the tribulation or Jacob's *(Ya'acov's)* trouble and to the *house of Judah* (Judaism) as the *Chevlai shel Mashiach* or the *birth pangs of the Messiah.*

The G-d of Israel through the prophet Isaiah *(Yeshayahu)* warns of the scornful attitude of the modern day leaders of the nation of Israel who have no regard for the land that the G-d of Israel promised to Abraham *(Avraham)* and his descendents forever through Isaac *(Yitzchak)* and Jacob *(Ya'acov)* and the judgment which will come upon them and the nation of Israel as a result of their scornful attitude. In Isaiah *(Yeshayahu)* 28:14-18 it is written:

> *"Wherefore hear the word of the* LORD, *ye* **scornful men,** *that* **rule this people** *which is in* **Jerusalem.** *Because ye have said, We have made* **a covenant with death,** *and with hell are we at agreement; when the overflowing scourge shall*

Jerusalem: The City of the Great King

pass through, it shall not come unto us: for **we have made lies our refuge**, *and under falsehood have we hid ourselves: Therefore, thus saith the LORD God, Behold, I lay in Zion for a foundation a stone, a tried stone, a precious corner stone, a sure foundation; he that believeth shall not make haste.* **Judgment also will I lay to the line**, *and righteousness to the plummet: and the hail shall sweep away the refuge of lies, and the waters shall overflow the hiding place. And your covenant with death shall be disannulled, and your agreement with hell shall not stand; when the overflowing scourge shall pass through, then ye shall be trodden down by it."*

The Nation of Israel Will Suffer Great Tribulation

Because of the rejection of the covenant that the G-d of Israel made with Abraham *(Avraham)* and the embracing of the *"covenant with death"* as advocated by the nations of the world, the scornful leaders and the entire nation of Israel will experience their most difficult time that they have ever experienced as a nation. However, the wise will understand these things and give instruction and counsel to many. In Daniel 12:1-3 it is written:

"And at that time shall Michael stand up, the great prince which standeth for the children of thy people: and there shall be a **time of trouble such as never was since there was a nation** *even to that same time: and at that time thy people shall be delivered, every one that shall be found written in the book. And many of them that sleep in the dust*

of the earth shall awake, some to everlasting life, and some to shame and everlasting contempt. And they that be **wise shall shine** *as the brightness of the firmament; and they that* **turn many to righteousness** *as the stars forever and ever."*

The G-d of Israel Will Purify His People

During this time, the G-d of Israel will bring His people through the fire and refine them as silver is refined and try them as gold is tried. They will call upon the name of the L-RD and the L-RD will deliver His people through the Jewish Messiah (*Mashiach*) *Yeshua*/Jesus. In Zechariah (*Zecharyah*) 13:9 it is written:

> *"And I will bring the* **third part** *through the* **fire**, *and will* **refine them** *as silver is refined, and will try them as gold is tried: they shall call on my name, and I will hear them: I will say, It is my people: and they shall say, The* LORD *is my God."*

The Jewish Messiah Will Save the Nation of Israel

The Jewish Messiah (*Mashiach*) *Yeshua*/Jesus will arise as a mighty warrior and save the nation of Israel and deliver them from their enemies when they call upon His name. In Luke 13:35 it is written:

> *"...verily I say unto you, Ye shall not see me, until the time come when ye shall say,* **Blessed is he that cometh in the name of the** LORD.*"*

In that day when the nations of the world seek to destroy the city of Jerusalem (*Yerushalayim*), the G-d of

Jerusalem: The City of the Great King

Israel will pour out the spirit of grace and supplication upon the house of David and the city of Jerusalem *(Yerushalayim)*. When the nation of Israel calls upon the Jewish Messiah *(Mashiach) Yeshua*/Jesus, He will save them and deliver them from their enemies. In Zechariah *(Zecharyah)* 12:8-10 it is written:

> *"In that day shall the L*ORD *defend the inhabitants of Jerusalem; and he that is feeble among them at that day shall be as David; and the house of David shall be as God, as the angel of the L*ORD *before them. And it shall come to pass in that day, that* **I will seek to destroy all the nations that come against Jerusalem**. *And I will pour upon the house of David, and upon the inhabitants of Jerusalem, the spirit of grace and supplications: and* **they shall look upon me whom they have pierced**, *and they shall mourn for him, as one mourneth for his only son, and shall be in bitterness for him, as one that is in bitterness for his firstborn."*

The Jewish Messiah Will Fight For Jerusalem

When the nations of the world seek to destroy Jerusalem *(Yerushalayim)* and when the nation of Israel calls upon the Jewish Messiah *(Mashiach) Yeshua*/Jesus for their deliverance, the Jewish Messiah *(Mashiach) Yeshua*/Jesus will fight against those nations and defend the covenant that the G-d of Israel made with Abraham *(Avraham)* and His descendents forever, the land, the people and the city of Jerusalem *(Yerushalayim)*. Then, He will set His feet down upon the mount of Olives and be King over all the earth. In Zechariah *(Zecharyah)* 14:2-4, 9 it is written:

*"For I will **gather all nations against Jerusalem** to battle ... then shall the L<small>ORD</small> go forth, and **fight against those nations**, as when he fought in the day of battle. And **his feet shall stand** in that day upon the **mount of Olives**, which is before Jerusalem on the east ... And the L<small>ORD</small> shall be **king over all the earth**: in that day shall there be one L<small>ORD</small>, and his name one."*

The G-d of Israel Is King of the Universe and His Throne Is in Jerusalem

The G-d of Israel is King over all the earth and the city of Jerusalem (*Yerushalayim*) is the place of His throne. Psalm 47 is a coronation psalm proclaiming that the G-d of Israel is King over all the earth. In Psalm *(Tehillim)* 47:1-9, it is written:

> *"O clap your hands, all ye people; shout unto God with the voice of triumph. For the L<small>ORD</small> most high is terrible; he is a great King over all the earth. He shall subdue the people under us, and the nations under our feet. He shall choose our inheritance for us, the excellency of Jacob* [both the house of Israel (Christianity) and the house of Judah (Judaism)] *whom he loved. Selah. God is gone up with a shout, the L<small>ORD</small> with the sound of a trumpet. Sing praises to God, sing praises: sing praises unto our King, sing praises. For **God is the King of all the earth**: sing ye praises with understanding. God reigneth over the heathen: **God sitteth upon the throne** of his holiness. The princes of the people are gathered together, even the people of the God of Abraham: for the shields of the earth belong unto God: he is greatly exalted."*

Jerusalem: The City of the Great King

The G-d of Israel is our King of glory. In Psalm *(Tehillim)* 24:1, 8, 10 it is written:

> *"The earth is the Lord's and the fulness thereof; the world, and they that dwell therein …* **Who is this King of glory?** *The* L<small>ORD</small> *strong and mighty, the* L<small>ORD</small> **mighty in battle** *… Who is this King of glory? The* L<small>ORD</small> *of hosts, he is the King of glory. Selah."*

In Psalm *(Tehillim)* 48:2, it is written:

> *"Beautiful for situation, the joy of the whole earth, is* **mount Zion***, on the sides of the north, the* **city of the great King***."*

The throne of the G-d of Israel is in Jerusalem *(Yerushalayim)*. In Jeremiah *(Yermiyahu)* 3:17 it is written:

> *"At that time they shall call* **Jerusalem the throne of the** L<small>ORD</small>*…"*

The G-d of Israel Will Always Remember the City of Jerusalem

Jerusalem *(Yerushalayim)* is always in the remembrance of the G-d of Israel. In Psalm *(Tehillim)* 137:5-6 it is written:

> *"If I forget thee, O Jerusalem, let my right hand forget her cunning. If I do not remember thee, let my tongue cleave to the roof of my mouth; if I prefer not Jerusalem above my chief joy."*

Restoring the Two Houses of Israel

The Messiah Remembers the City of Jerusalem

Traditional Judaism *(house of Judah)* expects that the Jewish Messiah *(Mashiach)* will fulfill two primary roles. He will be a suffering Messiah *(Mashiach)* known as *Messiah ben Yosef* (Joseph) as well as being a Kingly Messiah *(Mashiach)* known as *Messiah ben David*. However, traditional Judaism *(house of Judah)* believes that these two roles will be fulfilled by two different people. The suffering Messiah *(Mashiach)* was seen as being a humble Messiah *(Mashiach)* who would ride into Jerusalem *(Yerushalayim)* on a donkey. On the other hand, the Kingly Messiah *(Mashiach)* was seen as riding on a white horse.

In the weekly Internet Orthodox Jewish *Parasha Ki-Tetze* 5757 written by Orthodox Jewish Rabbi Mordecai Kornfeld who is associated with *Ohr Somayach*, he writes about the Messiah *(Mashiach)* and his role of riding on a donkey and on a (white) horse. In the article, he explains that horses represent war and conquest. Furthermore, he states in this *parasha* that the prophet *(Zecharyah 9:9)* describes the Messiah as "a poor man, riding upon a **donkey**." He then explains that the *Gemara (Sanhedrin 98a)* describes how King Shevor of Persia scoffed:

> "Why doesn't your Messiah come riding on a horse? If he lacks one, I'll be glad to provide him with one of my best!"

The article continues and the question is asked:

Jerusalem: The City of the Great King

"Why, indeed, should the Messiah come on a donkey? Isn't a horse a more appropriate sign of military victory?"

Rabbi Kornfeld's article concludes with the response that the answer may be learned from the words of the *Gemara* earlier on that same page (ibid.). A poor man on a donkey is a description of how the Messiah will appear if the Jews are **not** found deserving of a spectacular salvation. Whether we deserve it or not, we will eventually be redeemed; however, if we are not deserving the Messiah will only arrive riding on a donkey. A horse is a sign of proud conquest; this Messiah will provide but a humble Exodus. As the *Gemara* says in *Shabbat 152a*:

"One who rides a horse is a king; one who rides a donkey is but a freeman."

The Jewish Messiah Rode on a Donkey

The *house of Israel* (Christianity) understands that the Jewish Messiah *(Mashiach) Yeshua*/Jesus will fulfill both the role of the suffering Messiah *(Mashiach)* known by the *house of Judah* (Judaism) as *Messiah ben Yosef* (Joseph) as well as the role of the Kingly Messiah *(Mashiach)* known as *Messiah ben David*. The suffering Messiah rode humbly into Jerusalem *(Yerushalayim)* at His first coming on a **donkey** and proceeded to weep over the city of Jerusalem *(Yerushalayim)* because of her future destruction which happened in 70 CE. At His second coming, He will ride in conquest and victory on a **white horse**. In Matthew *(Mattityahu)* 21:1-9 it is written:

"And when they drew nigh unto Jerusalem, and were come to Bethphage, unto the mount of Olives,

> *then sent Jesus two disciples, Saying unto them, Go into the village over against you, and straightway ye shall find an ass tied, and a colt with her: loose them, and bring them unto me. And if any man say aught unto you, ye shall say, The LORD hath need of them; and straightway he will send them. All this was done, that it might be fulfilled which was spoken by the prophet, saying, Tell ye the daughter of Zion, Behold, thy king cometh unto thee, meek, and sitting upon an ass, and a colt the foal of an ass. And the disciples went, and did as Jesus commanded them, And brought the ass, and the colt, and put on them their clothes, and they set him thereon. And a very great multitude spread their garments in the way; others cut down branches from the trees, and strewed them in the way. And the multitudes that went before, and that followed, cried, saying, Hosanna to the son of David: Blessed is he that cometh in the name of the LORD; Hosanna in the highest."*

After the Jewish Messiah *(Mashiach) Yeshua*/Jesus rode into the city of Jerusalem *(Yerushalayim)* humbly on a donkey as the suffering Messiah *(Mashiach)* known as *Messiah ben Yosef* (Joseph), He wept over the city of Jerusalem (*Yerushalayim*) realizing her future destruction to come by the Romans in 70 CE. In Luke 19:41-44 it is written:

> "And when he was come near, he beheld the city, and wept over it, Saying, If thou hadst known, even thou, at least in this thy day, the things which belong unto thy peace! But now they are hid from thine eyes. For the days shall come upon thee,

Jerusalem: The City of the Great King

that thine enemies shall cast a trench about thee, and compass thee round, and keep thee in on every side, and shall lay thee even with the ground, and thy children within thee; and they shall not leave in thee one stone upon another; because thou knewest not the time of thy visitation."

The Jewish Messiah Will Ride on a White Horse

When the Jewish Messiah *(Mashiach) Yeshua*/Jesus returns to the earth at His second coming as the Kingly Messiah *(Mashiach)* known as *Messiah ben David*, He will ride on a white horse as a mighty warrior in victory over His enemies. In Revelation 19:11-16 it is written:

"And I saw heaven opened, and behold a **white horse***; and* **he that sat upon him** *was called Faithful and True, and in righteousness he doth judge and make war. His eyes were as a flame of fire, and on his head were many crowns; and he had a name written that no man knew, but he himself. And he was clothed with a vesture dipped in blood: and his name is called* **The Word of God***. And the armies which were in heaven followed him upon white horses, clothed in fine linen, white and clean. And out of his mouth goeth a sharp sword, that with it he should smite the nations: and he shall rule them with a rod of iron: and he treadeth the winepress of the fierceness and wrath of Almighty God. And he hath on his vesture and on his thigh a name written,* **KING OF KINGS, AND LORD OF LORDS***."*

Restoring the Two Houses of Israel

When the nations of the world gather against Jerusalem *(Yerushalayim)*, the Jewish Messiah *(Mashiach)* Yeshua/Jesus will fight against those nations as a mighty man of war. Following His victory over the nations in battle, He will set His feet down on the mount of Olives and be King over all the earth. In Zechariah *(Zecharyah)* 14:2-4, 9 it is written:

> *"For I will gather all nations against Jerusalem to battle ... Then shall the* Lord *go forth, and fight against those nations, as when he fought in the day of battle. And his feet shall stand in that day upon the mount of Olives ... And the* Lord **shall be king over all the earth**: *in that day shall there be one* Lord*, and his name one."*

Following this event, the Jewish Messiah *(Mashiach)* Yeshua/Jesus will set up His Messianic Kingdom and rule and reign on the earth from Jerusalem *(Yerushalayim)* teaching the Torah to all nations. In Isaiah *(Yeshayahu)* 2:2-3 it is written:

> *"And it shall come to pass in the last days, that the mountain of the Lord's house shall be established in the top of the mountains, and shall be exalted above the hills; and all nations shall flow unto it. And many people shall go and say, Come ye, and let us go up to the mountain of the* Lord*, to the house of the G-d of Jacob; and he will teach us of his ways, and we will walk in his paths: for* **out of Zion shall go forth the law [TORAH]**, *and the word of the* Lord *from Jerusalem."*

Jerusalem: The City of the Great King

The G-d of Israel desires to someday have a **Torah based world government** with the Jewish Messiah *(Mashiach) Yeshua*/Jesus ruling, reigning and teaching the nations of the world the Torah of the G-d of Israel from Jerusalem *(Yerushalayim)*. When this happens, peace *(shalom)* will come upon the entire earth. May the Jewish Messiah *(Mashiach) Yeshua*/Jesus come to the earth as the Kingly Messiah known as *Messiah ben David* and bring redemption, restoration, reconciliation and unity to both houses of Israel and usher in the Messianic Age speedily in our days. Amen!

NEXT YEAR IN JERUSALEM !!!

Chapter 11

The Judgment of the Nations

By Israel embracing the plan of the nations of the world (UN Resolutions 242 and 338) for her to have *"peace"* with her Arab neighbors rather than believing the ETERNAL covenant that the G-d of Israel made with Abraham *(Avraham)* whereby his descendents would inherit the land of Canaan (Genesis *[Bereishit]* 17:7-8), the nation of Israel will experience a time of trouble such that she has never experienced in her entire history as a nation and as a people (Jeremiah *[Yermiyahu]* 30:7, Daniel 12:1). However, she will be redeemed/saved/delivered through it. This time of trouble is known as the tribulation to the *house of Israel* (Christianity). It is known as the birth pangs of the Messiah *[Chevlai shel Mashiach]* to the *house of Judah* (Judaism).

During this time, the G-d of Israel will judge ALL the nations on the earth. Some nations will NOT make it through the entire tribulation or birth pangs of the Messiah *(Chevlai shel Mashiach)*. In Jeremiah *(Yermiyahu)* 30:10-11 it is written:

> *"Therefore fear thou not, O my servant Jacob, saith the* LORD*; neither be dismayed, O Israel: for, lo, I will save thee from afar, and thy seed from the*

> land of their captivity; and Jacob shall return, and shall be in rest, and be quiet, and none shall make him afraid. For I am with thee, saith the LORD, to save thee: though I make a full end of all nations whither I have scattered thee, yet will I not make a full end of thee: but I will correct thee in measure, and will not leave thee altogether unpunished."

The G-d of Israel will judge the nations based on three primary things:

1) The dividing of Israel's Promised Land.
2) The dividing of the city of Jerusalem.
3) The historical treatment of the nations of the world toward the *house of Judah* (Jewish people) when they were in exile in the nations.

The Judgment of the Nations Over the Controversy of Zion

The G-d of Israel will judge the nations over the controversy of Zion. What is the controversy of Zion? The controversy of Zion is the dispute and rejection among the nations of the covenant that the G-d of Israel made with Abraham *(Avraham)* giving him and his seed the land of Canaan as an everlasting possession (Genesis *[Bereishit]* 17:7-8) and the plan of the nations to make Jerusalem *(Yerushalayim)* an international city. By rejecting the covenant that the G-d of Israel made with Abraham *(Avraham)*, the nations of the world will be OPPOSED to the restoration and reunification of BOTH houses of Israel (*house of Judah* [Judaism] and *house of Israel*/Christianity) to the land of Israel (Ezekiel

The Judgment of the Nations

(Yechezekel) 37:15-28). Regarding the controversy of Zion and the judgment of the nations, in Isaiah *(Yeshayahu)* 34:1-2, 4, 8 it is written:

> *"Come near, ye nations, to hear; and hearken, ye people: let the earth hear, and all that is therein; the world, and all things that come forth of it. For the indignation of the LORD is upon all nations, and his fury upon all their armies: he hath utterly destroyed them, he hath delivered them to the slaughter ... And all the host of heaven shall be dissolved, and the heavens shall be rolled together as a scroll:* [nuclear war] *and all their host shall fall down, as the leaf falleth off from the vine, and as a falling fig from the fig tree ... for it is the day of the Lord's vengeance, and the year of recompences for the controversy of Zion."*

Judgment for Dividing the Promised Land

The G-d of Israel will judge the nations of the world for their plan to divide/part the land that the G-d of Israel promised the seed of Abraham *(Avraham)*. In Joel *(Yoel)* 3:1-2 it is written:

> *"For, behold, in those days, and in that time* [a Jewish idiom for the advent of the Messianic Age], *when I shall bring again the captivity of Judah and Jerusalem, I will also gather all nations, and will bring them down into the valley of Jehoshaphat, and will plead with them there for my people and for my heritage Israel, whom they have scattered among the nations, and parted my land."*

Judgment for Dividing the City of Jerusalem

The G-d of Israel will judge the nations of the world for dividing the city of Jerusalem (making it an international city). In Zechariah *(Zecharyah)* 14:2-3 it is written:

> *"For I will **gather all nations** against Jerusalem to battle; and the city shall be taken, and the houses rifled, and the women ravished; and **half** of the city shall go forth into captivity, and the residue of the people shall not be cut off from the city. Then shall the* LORD *go forth, and **fight against those nations**, as when he fought in the day of battle."*

The Judgment of Nuclear War

The judgment of the nations that have fought against Jerusalem *(Yerushalayim)* will be nuclear war. ONLY the nations who fight against Jerusalem *(Yerushalayim)* and SURVIVE will celebrate *Sukkot* (the Feast of Tabernacles) during the Messianic Age *(Athid Lavo)*. In Zechariah *(Zecharyah)* 14:12, 16 it is written:

> *"And this shall be the **plague** wherewith the* LORD *will smite all the people that have **fought against Jerusalem**; Their flesh shall consume away while they stand upon their feet, and their eyes shall consume away in their holes, and their tongue shall consume away in their mouth* [nuclear war] *... And it shall come to pass, that every one that is **left** of all the **nations** which came **against***

The Judgment of the Nations

Jerusalem *shall even go up from year to year to worship the King, the* LORD *of hosts, and to* **keep** *the* **feast of tabernacles**.*"*

The Judgment for the Treatment of the Jewish People

In Genesis *(Bereishit)* 12:1-3, the G-d of Israel made a promise to Abraham *(Avraham)* and to his seed as it is written:

> *"Now the* LORD *had said unto Abram, Get thee out of thy country ... And I will make of thee a great nation ... And I will bless them that bless thee, and curse him that curseth thee, and in thee shall all families of the earth be blessed."*

The Jewish Messiah *(Mashiach) Yeshua*/Jesus calls those nations of the world who bless the Jewish people *"sheep nations"* and those nations of the world who curse the Jewish people *"goat nations."* The *"sheep nations"* will enter into the Messianic Age *(Athid Lavo)*. The *"goat nations"* will not enter into the Messianic Age *(Athid Lavo)*. In Matthew *(Mattityahu)* 25:31-46 it is written:

> *"When the Son of man shall come in his glory, and all the holy angels with him, then shall he sit upon the throne of his glory: And before him shall be gathered all nations: and he shall separate them one from another, as a shepherd divideth his sheep from the goats: And he shall set the sheep on his*

right hand, but the goats on the left. Then shall the King say unto them on his right hand, Come, ye blessed [Genesis 12:3] *of my Father, inherit the kingdom* [Messianic Age/Athid Lavo] *prepared for you from the foundation of the world: For I was hungry, and ye gave me meat: I was thirsty, and ye gave me drink: I was a stranger, and ye took me in: Naked, and ye clothed me: I was sick, and ye visited me: I was in prison, and ye came unto me. Then shall the righteous* [sheep nations] *answer him, saying,* Lord, *when saw we thee hungry, and fed thee? Or thirsty, and gave thee drink? When saw we thee a stranger, and took thee in? or naked, and clothed thee? Or when saw we thee sick, or in prison, and came unto thee? And the King shall answer and say unto them, Verily I say unto you, Inasmuch as ye have done it unto one of the least of these my brethren* [the JEWISH BRETHREN of the JEWISH MESSIAH], *ye have done it unto me. Then shall he say also unto them on the left hand* [goat nations], *Depart from me* [cannot enter the Messianic Age/Athid Lavo] *ye cursed* [Genesis 12:3], *into everlasting fire, prepared for the devil and his angels: For I was hungry, and ye gave me no meat: I was thirsty, and you gave me no drink: I was a stranger, and ye took me not in: naked, and ye clothed me not: sick, and in prison, and ye visited me not. Then shall they also answer him, saying,* Lord, *when saw we thee hungry, or athirst, or a stranger, or naked, or sick, or in prison, and did not minister unto thee? Then shall he answer them, saying, Verily I say unto you, Inasmuch as ye did it not to one of the least of these* [the JEWISH BRETHREN of the JEWISH MESSIAH], *ye did it not to me. And these* [goat

The Judgment of the Nations

nations] *shall go away into everlasting punishment: but the righteous* [sheep nations] *into life eternal."* [Zoe/the highest form of life which in the case of the nations is the Messianic Age/Athid Lavo.]

The Judgment of the United States

While the G-d of Israel will judge ALL NATIONS during the tribulation or the birth pangs of the Messiah *(Chevlai shel Mashiach)*, I would like to focus the rest of this chapter upon the judgment of one particular country in the world. This country is the United States of America.

I was born in the United States. I love my country. I praise the G-d of Israel that He allowed me to be born in a country that has probably been blessed greater by Him than any other country since the creation of the world up until the beginning of the tribulation period. Furthermore, I have been blessed to live not only in probably the most blessed country but also in the most blessed generation of any generation since the birth of the United States. Therefore, I praise the G-d of Israel for His historical blessings upon the United States and I praise and thank the G-d of Israel that I have been blessed to live in the United States in the most blessed generation of its history.

However, in spite of being blessed so greatly by the G-d of Israel, no generation since the founding of the USA has sinned greater than the current generation. The USA has forgotten her Judeo/Christian heritage

Restoring the Two Houses of Israel

and has forgotten the L-RD G-d of Israel in the days of her richest blessings. The USA has fornicated with the god of materialism. Rather than using the blessings of the G-d of Israel to establish the covenant that the G-d of Israel made with Abraham *(Avraham)*, she has used the blessings of the G-d of Israel to satisfy her own lusts. Both the members from the *house of Israel* (Christianity) and the members from the *house of Judah* (Judaism) have been guilty of these sins. In the Torah, the G-d of Israel warned His people against behaving in such a manner in the time of great blessing. In Deuteronomy *(Devarim)* 8:11-14, 17-18 it is written:

> *"Beware that thou forget not the* LORD *thy God, in not keeping his commandments, and his judgments, and his statutes, which I command thee this day: Lest when thou hast eaten and art full, and hast built goodly houses, and dwelt therein; And when thy herds and thy flocks multiply, and thy silver and thy gold is multiplied, and all that thou hast is multiplied; Then thine heart be lifted up, and thou forget the* LORD *thy God, which brought thee forth out of the land of Egypt, from the house of bondage* [European religious persecution for the house of Israel/Christianity and pogroms and the holocaust in Europe and Russia for the house of Judah/Judaism] *... And thou say in thine heart, My power and the might of mine hand hath gotten me this wealth. But thou shalt remember the* LORD *thy God: for it is he that giveth thee power to get wealth, that he may establish his covenant which he sware unto thy fathers, as it is this day."*

The Judgment of the Nations

The USA Will Be Judged for Dividing the Land of Israel

The USA will be judged by the G-d of Israel for being the LEADER among the nations of the world in dividing the land of Israel. All of the peace agreements that Israel has made with her Arab neighbors have been based upon UN Resolutions 242 and 338. The USA has been the main negotiator with Israel and her Arab neighbors and has played a central role in ensuring that all peace agreements between Israel and her Arab neighbors would be based upon UN Resolutions 242 and 338. Because the USA had led the rebellion of the nations against Israel to part the land of Israel, she will be judged by the G-d of Israel for dividing/parting the land of Israel (Joel *[Yoel]* 3:2).

The USA Will Be Judged for Dividing the City of Jerusalem

The United States has not recognized Jerusalem *(Yerushalayim)* as being the capital of Israel since it came into the possession of the nation of Israel in 1967 following the June war between Israel and her Arab neighbors. The reason is because the USA desires for Jerusalem *(Yerushalayim)* to be an international city after the full implementation of UN Resolutions 242 and 338.

The United States maintains diplomatic relations with more than 160 countries, and in each of those countries our state department maintains a US embassy in the capital city. Each of those countries, that is, except Israel. Under pressure from the Arab world, the US has maintained its embassy in Tel Aviv since 1948.[1]

Restoring the Two Houses of Israel

To rectify this injustice, the US Congress finally enacted The Jerusalem Embassy Act of 1995, which calls for the embassy to be moved to Jerusalem by May 31, 1999. There was broad bipartisan support in both the House and the Senate, and the measure was passed by over 90 percent majorities. Campaigning for president in 1992, Bill Clinton said:

> "I do recognize Jerusalem as Israel's capital, and Jerusalem ought to remain an undivided city."

He even put it in writing. In a June 1992 letter to the Rabbinical Council of America he wrote:

> "I recognize Jerusalem as an undivided city and the eternal capital of Israel."

But by 1995, the president had changed his tune. His administration opposed the Jerusalem Embassy Act, and he refused to sign it when it was passed. Clinton could not veto the bill, with a 90 percent majority supporting its passage. However, nothing has been done about moving the US Embassy to Jerusalem. A waiver was written into the bill allowing the president to put the new embassy construction on hold for six-month intervals if he deems vital national security interests to be at risk and so reports to Congress. Since then, the Clinton administration immediately moved to take advantage of the waiver, claiming national security interests would be jeopardized by moving the embassy, because it might disrupt the Middle East peace process.[2]

Just two months after the Congressional vote to finally recognize Jerusalem as Israel's capital, the Fiftieth

The Judgment of the Nations

General Assembly of the United Nations passed a resolution chastising Israel for her claims on all of Jerusalem. The resolution passed by a vote of 133 to one — Israel was the only nation to vote against it. The United States, once Israel's staunch ally, abstained from voting.[3]

Because the USA does not recognize Jerusalem *(Yerushalayim)* and seeks to divide Jerusalem *(Yerushalayim)* and make it an international city, the USA will suffer the judgment of nuclear war and will NOT make it as a nation through the tribulation period (Zechariah *[Zecharyah]* 14:12, 16).

The USA Embraces Arafat the Murderer and Terrorist as a Man of Peace

Rather than the USA embracing the covenant that the G-d of Israel made with Abraham *(Avraham)* whereby He gave the seed of Abraham *(Avraham)* the land of Canaan as an EVERLASTING possession (Genesis *[Bereishit]* 17:7-8), the USA is embracing Yasser Arafat as a man of peace and a peace partner to the nation of Israel even though the USA once did not allow Yasser Arafat into the USA because he is a terrorist. The history of this event is as follows.

The Forty-third General Assembly of the United Nations was scheduled to take up the Palestinian issue at a session in early December 1988. Yasser Arafat requested a visa so he could come to New York and address a special session of the UN. Under the direction of President Reagan, Secretary of State George Shultz denied the visa because antiterrorist legislation in the

USA specified that no waiver on visa requirements could be issued to anyone known to be actively engaged in terrorist activity.[4]

The UN conference was rescheduled to be in Geneva, Switzerland. On December 14, 1988, Arafat called a press conference to announce that he recognized Israel's "right to exist," and he accepted the terms of UN Resolutions 242 and 338 and renounced the use of terrorism. From that point forward, the United States openly supported the PLO.[5]

The USA Is Modern Day Babylon

Spiritually (*sod*/deeper meaning), the USA is the land of Babylon. The word Babylon means *"confusion"* (Genesis [*Bereishit*] 11:9). Babylon is a generic term in the Bible that refers to the ways of the adversary *(HaSatan)* and his kingdom of darkness. The Bible talks about a financial Babylon, a political Babylon, a religious Babylon and a land of Babylon. Literally *(Peshat)*, the modern land of Babylon is the area of Iran and Iraq. However, today, very few members of the *house of Judah* (Judaism) and the *house of Israel* (Christianity) live in Iran and Iraq. Therefore, there must also be a spiritual (*sod*/deeper meaning) land of Babylon.

Today, the USA is the spiritual land of Babylon. The prophets of Israel had much to say about the judgment of the land of Babylon in the end of days. The judgment of the land of Babylon in the end of days is prophesied in Isaiah *(Yeshayahu)* chapter 13, 21:1-10 and chapter 47, Jeremiah *(Yermiyahu)* chapters 50 and 51. In the *Brit*

The Judgment of the Nations

Hadashah (New Testament), the judgment of the land of Babylon in the end of days is spoken about in Revelation 18.

The Characteristics of Babylon

1) Babylon is an end-time nation who is judged by the G-d of Israel *"in those days and in that time"* and in the *"day of trouble."* This is a reference to the time of Jacob's trouble or the birth pangs of the Messiah *(Chevlai shel Mashaich)* (Isaiah 13:8, 13, 21:3, Jeremiah 50:4, 20, 51:2, 43).

2) Babylon is a rich and economically prosperous country (Jeremiah 50:37, 51:13, Revelation 18:3, 19).

3) Babylon is a land of *"mixed/mingled people"* (Jeremiah 50:37).

4) Babylon is a world military power (Jeremiah 51:53).

5) Babylon is a country that has defeated mighty kingdoms through war (Jeremiah 50:23, 51:20-21).

6) Babylon is a land that sits among many waters (Jeremiah 51:13).

7) Babylon is a country that has a heritage in the G-d of Israel but has sinned and has turned from the G-d of Israel (Jeremiah 50:11, 14, 24, 29, 38, 51:7).

Restoring the Two Houses of Israel

8) The G-d of Israel would have healed the land of Babylon if she would have repented but she will not repent (II Chronicles 7:14, Jeremiah 51:8-9).

9) The good news of Messiah is going forth from the land of Babylon but it will be *"cut off"* in *"the time of harvest"* which is the end of the age (Jeremiah 50:16, Matthew 13:39).

10) Babylon is a country that does not believe that it will experience the wrath and judgment of the G-d of Israel (be a widow) (Isaiah 47:5, 7-10, Revelation 18:7-8).

11) The attacking power against Babylon is from the north (Jeremiah 50:3, 9, 26, 41, 51:48).

12) Babylon is destroyed by extremely accurate arrows (missiles) and the attack is devastating (Jeremiah 50:9, 14, 29, 42, 51:3, 11).

13) A fire is kindled in the cities of Babylon from the accurate arrows (missiles) (Jeremiah 50:32, Revelation 18:8).

14) Babylon will be destroyed in the way that Sodom and Gomorrah was destroyed (Isaiah 13:19, Jeremiah 50:40).

15) When Babylon is destroyed, it will never be inhabited again (Isaiah 13:19-20, Jeremiah 50:3, 13, 26, 39-40, 51:2-3, 26, 29, 37, 43, 63-64).

16) The nations of the world tremble and shake in fear at the defeat of Babylon (Jeremiah 50:46, Revelation 18:9-10).

The Judgment of the Nations

17) The *house of Judah* (Judaism) and the *house of Israel* (Christianity) who live in Babylon are called to flee from Babylon and go to the land of Israel (Isaiah 13:14, Jeremiah 50:4-5, 16-19, 28, 33, 51:9, 45, Revelation 18:4).

18) The *house of Judah* (Judaism) and the *house of Israel* (Christianity) who live in Babylon and who have escaped the sword (judgment upon the land of Babylon) are called by the G-d of Israel to let Jerusalem come to their mind (Jeremiah 50:4, 51:50).

19) When Babylon is destroyed, the sins of the *house of Judah* (Judaism) and the *house of Israel* (Christianity) will be pardoned (the exile will be over and the house of Judah and the house of Israel will be restored) (Jeremiah 50:20).

20) When the *house of Judah* (Judaism) and the *house of Israel* (Christianity) flees the land of Babylon and returns to the land of Israel, they will enter into an ETERNAL covenant that will not be forgotten (the Messianic Age/*Athid Lavo*) (Jeremiah 50:4-5 = Ezekiel 37:26-27).

From the 20 characteristics of the land of Babylon given above, I believe that the evidence is overwhelmingly conclusive that the nation being portrayed by these characteristics is the United States of America. Because of the just described characteristics of the USA and because the USA has been the most influential nation of the world in encouraging Israel to divide/part her land by trading *"land for peace"* and because the

USA desires to make Jerusalem *(Yerushalayim)* an international city, the USA will be totally destroyed during the tribulation period or the birth pangs of the Messiah *(Chevlai shel Mashiach)*.

Judah and Ephraim Flee Babylon and Return to the Land of Israel

During the tribulation period/Jacob's trouble, the *house of Judah* (Judaism) and the *house of Israel* (Christianity) will be fleeing from the land of Babylon and returning to the land of Israel. When both houses of Israel return to the land of their forefathers, the centuries of exile will be over. The *house of Judah* (Judaism) and the *house of Israel* (Christianity) will be one nation when they return to the land of Israel. They will be redeemed, restored, reconciled and unified in the land of Israel (Ezekiel *[Yechezekel]* 37:15-28). After this event happens, the Jewish Messiah *(Mashiach) Yeshua*/Jesus will set His feet on the mount of Olives and be King over all the earth (Zechariah *[Zecharyah]* 14:4, 9) and usher in the Messianic Age *(Athid Lavo)* teaching the Torah to the nations from the city of Jerusalem *(Yerushalayim)* (Isaiah *[Yeshayahu]* 2:2-3).

May the G-d of Israel bring redemption, restoration, reconciliation and unity to both houses of Israel speedily in our days. Amen!

Chapter 12

Ephraim and Judah Become One House

How will the two houses of Israel *(house of Israel/* Christianity and *house of Judah*/Judaism) become one house? When will the prophecy of Ezekiel *(Yechezekel)* 37:15-28 be fulfilled and Ephraim *(house of Israel)* and Judah *(house of Judah)* become one in the hand of the G-d of Israel? In this chapter, we will discuss how and when the two houses of Israel will be redeemed and restored to the G-d of Israel and reconciled to each other.

In order to understand how and when the two houses of Israel will be reunited, you need to understand how the restoration and unification of the two houses of Israel is related and associated with the covenant that the G-d of Israel made with Abraham *(Avraham)*. This covenant is also paramount in understanding the prophetic significance of the nation of Israel making peace with her Arab neighbors in the end of days. By being willing to trade "land for peace" based upon UN Resolutions 242 and 338, the leadership of the nation of Israel and all Jews *(house of Judah)* who approve of trading "land for peace" are rejecting the covenant that the G-d of Israel made with Abraham *(Avraham)*.

The covenant that the G-d of Israel made with Abra-

Restoring the Two Houses of Israel

ham *(Avraham)* is an **everlasting** covenant (Genesis [*Bereishit*] 17:7. In Genesis *(Bereishit)* 15:18-21, the G-d of Israel promised the descendents of Abraham *(Avraham)* a land forever. In Leviticus *(Vayikra)* 25:23, the G-d of Israel commanded that the land is not to be sold forever.

By rejecting the covenant that the G-d of Israel made with Abraham *(Avraham)* and by being willing to trade part of the eternal Promised Land for "peace," the nation of Israel will experience the greatest time of trouble that she has ever experienced since she has been a nation (Daniel 12:1-2). This period of time is also known as Jacob's trouble (Jeremiah *[Yermiyahu]* 30:7 or the birth pangs of the Messiah *(Chevlai shel Mashiach)*. However, during the time of Jacob's trouble, the two houses of Israel (Ephraim and Judah) will be reunited in the land of Israel (Jeremiah *[Yermiyahu]* 30:1-7) through a great outpouring of the Holy Spirit *(Ruach HaKodesh)* upon the remnant in the *house of Israel* (Christianity) and the *house of Judah* (Judaism) who believe the covenant that the G-d of Israel made with Abraham *(Avraham)*.

The restoration of both houses of Israel and a return to the land of Israel will be done by the G-d of Israel with a mighty hand and an outstretched arm in the sight of all the nations. The G-d of Israel will gather His people as a shepherd who gathers His lost sheep and bring them to the land of Israel (Ezekiel *[Yechezekel]* 34:11-13) from all the nations of the earth where they have been scattered (Deuteronomy *[Devarim]* 30:1-5). The restoration of both houses of Israel and their return upon the "mountains of Israel" (West Bank) (Ezekiel *[Yechezekel]* 37:18-22) will be the end of the exile of both

Ephraim and Judah Become One House

houses of Israel into all the nations of the earth. After returning to the land of Israel following this "Messianic redemption" and the ending of the exile of both houses of Israel from all the nations of the earth, the Jewish Messiah *(Mashiach) Yeshua*/Jesus will set His feet down upon the mount of Olives (Zechariah *[Zecharyah]* 14:4) and be King over all the earth (Zechariah *[Zecharyah]* 14:9) and rule and reign from Jerusalem *(Yerushalayim)* teaching the Torah to the nations during the Messianic Age *(Athid Lavo)* (Isaiah *[Yeshayahu]* 2:2-3) for 1,000 years (Revelation 20:4,6).

The Gospel According to Torah

In this chapter, we will learn how the covenant that the G-d of Israel made with Abraham *(Avraham)* is related and associated to the nation of Israel making peace with her Arab neighbors in the end of days and how this is related and associated with the restoration and unification of the two houses of Israel. We will do this by seeing how the G-d of Israel has historically judged His people based upon whether or not they believed the covenant that He made with Abraham *(Avraham)*. In doing so, we will see how the *TeNaKh* (Old Testament) is related and connected to the *Brit Hadashah* (New Testament) and reveals the role of the Jewish Messiah *Yeshua*/Jesus as the suffering Messiah *(Messiah ben Yosef)* and the Kingly Messiah *(Messiah ben David)* who will redeem and restore the two houses of Israel through the outpouring of the Holy Spirit *(Ruach HaKodesh)* upon both houses of Israel in the end of days prior to the Messianic Age *(Athid Lavo)*.

This is the covenant that the G-d of Israel made with Abraham *(Avraham)* and this is the Gospel according to Torah! (Galatians 3:8)

Restoring the Two Houses of Israel

The Grafting of The Seed of Abraham

In Genesis *(Bereishit)* 12:1-9, the G-d of Israel called Abraham *(Avraham)* out of Ur of the Chaldeeans and promised him that if he would obey the G-d of Israel that He would promise the seed of Abraham *(Avraham)* a land. Furthermore, the G-d of Israel declared to Abraham *(Avraham)* that He would bless those who would bless the seed of Abraham *(Avraham)* and curse those that would curse the seed of Abraham *(Avraham)*. In Genesis *(Bereishit)* 12:3 it is written:

> *"And I will bless them that bless thee, and curse him that curseth thee: and in thee shall* **all families** *of the earth* **be blessed.***"*

However, in Hebrew, this verse is more profound in understanding *how* ALL FAMILIES of the earth would be "blessed" through the seed of Abraham *(Avraham)*. In Hebrew, the phrase in Genesis *(Bereishit)* 12:3 that reads in English as *"And in thee shall all families of the earth be blessed"* is written:

> *"Ve nivrecu bekah kol mishpachot ha-adamah."*

The Hebrew word *"nivrecu"* is translated in most English texts as *"be blessed."* However, the usual Hebrew word for *"be blessed"* is not *nivrecu*. It is *yivrecu*. The word *"nivrecu"* is the "niphal" conjugation of the Hebrew word, *barak*. The Hebrew word *barak* has a deeper meaning than just "blessed." The simplest Hebrew meaning of the word *barak* is blessing which invokes the G-d of Israel's presence, favor or choice in a given situation. Jewish prayers *(house of Judah)* begin with the

Ephraim and Judah Become One House

phrase, *"Baruk atah Adonai..."* which in English is *"Blessed are you,* Lord*..."* and reflects the idea that "blessed" is related to being "chosen" or "favored" by the G-d of Israel.

In five places in the Talmud and other Rabbinic literature, *nivrecu* is translated as "**grafted** or intermingled." In the Orthodox Jewish *ArtScroll Tenakh Series*, Volume 1, page 432, it is written:

> There is ... an opinion shared by *Rashbam* [to Genesis 28:14], *Chizkuni, Da'as Zekeinum*, and quoted by *Tur* that the verb *(ve nivrecu)* in Genesis 12:3 is related to the root *barak* as in the Mishnaic term *mavreek* meaning to "intermingle or **graft**." [cf Kelaim 7:1, Sotah 43a.] As Heidenheim explains it, this interpretation is inspired by the fact that nowhere else besides here do we find *barak* in the sense of blessing in the niphal conjugation, while in the sense of **"grafting"** it is common in that form.

Therefore, based upon this insight of the Hebrew language by respected Hebrew scholars within the *house of Judah* (Judaism), Genesis *(Bereishit)* 12:3 is better understood to be translated as:

"And in thee shall all families of the earth **nivrecu** [will be **grafted** or intermingled]*."*

The only PHYSICAL way ALL FAMILIES of the earth would be *nivrecu* (**grafted** or intermingled) is by the seed of Abraham *(Avraham)* being assimilated into EVERY FAMILY of the earth.

Restoring the Two Houses of Israel

How does the Bible explain that this happened? Abraham *(Avraham)* had a son named Isaac *(Yitzchak)* who had a son named Jacob *(Ya'acov)* whose named was changed to Israel. Jacob *(Ya'acov)* had twelve sons who became head of the twelve tribes of Israel. Following the reign of king Solomon *(Shlomo)*, the kingdom of Israel was divided into Northern Kingdom *(house of Israel)* and Southern *Kingdom (house of Judah)*. The judgment of the Northern Kingdom *(house of Israel)* as recorded by the prophet Hosea in Hosea chapter 1 was that the Northern Kingdom *(house of Israel)* would be assimilated into **all families** of the earth in fulfillment of the G-d of Israel's promise to Abraham *(Avraham)* that his seed would be in **all families** of the earth.

While the seed of Abraham *(Avraham)* was prophesied by the G-d of Israel to be in **all families** of the earth, not every person and not every family of the earth will believe the "Gospel according to Torah" that the G-d of Israel preached to Abraham *(Avraham)* that through His seed **all families** of the earth would "be blessed" (**grafted** or intermingled). Spiritually *(sod/* deeper meaning), those who would believe the promise that the G-d of Israel made to Abraham *(Avraham)* would become a spiritual member of the family of the G-d of Israel by the salvation offered from the G-d of Israel through the Jewish Messiah *(Mashiach) Yeshua/* Jesus. In Galatians 3:8, 16, 29 it is written:

> *"And the Scripture,* [TeNaKh/Old Testament] *foreseeing that God would justify* [make righteous] *the heathen through faith* [emunah], *preached before the gospel unto Abraham, saying, In thee shall all nations be blessed* **[nivrecu/**

Ephraim and Judah Become One House

grafted or intermingled] ... *Now to Abraham and his seed were the promises made. He saith not, And to seeds, as of many; but as of one, And to thy seed, which is Christ* [Mashiach] *... And if ye be Christ's, then are ye Abraham's seed, and heirs according to the promise."*

Spiritually (*sod*/deeper meaning), any person on the earth who accepts that *Yeshua*/Jesus is the Jewish Messiah and repents *(teshuvah)* of their sins becomes a member of the **commonwealth of Israel** and **grafted** into the family of the G-d of Israel. In Ephesians 2:11-13 it is written:

"Wherefore remember, that ye being in time past Gentiles in the flesh ... That at that time ye were without Christ [Mashiach], *being aliens from the* **commonwealth of Israel** *... but now in Christ Jesus* [Yeshua HaMashiach] *ye who sometimes were far off are made nigh by the blood of Christ* [Mashiach]."

In Romans 11:13, 17 it is written:

"For I speak to you Gentiles ... and thou, being a wild olive tree, wast **GRAFTED** *in among them, and with them partakest of the root and fatness of the olive tree."*

When the **physical** seed of Abraham *(Avraham)* becomes grafted or intermingled in **every family** of the earth, the Bible calls this event the *"fullness of the Gentiles."* In Hebrew, this would be the *"melo ha goyim."* The Apostle Paul *(Rav Sha'ul)* talks about the "fullness of the

Restoring the Two Houses of Israel

Gentiles/*melo ha goyim"* being a mystery (*sod*/deeper meaning) that the family of the G-d of Israel should understand. In Romans 11:25 it is written:

> *"For I would not, brethren, that ye should be ignorant of this mystery* [sod/deeper meaning], *lest ye should be wise in your own conceits; that blindness in part is happened to Israel* [both the house of Israel/Christianity and the house of Judah/Judaism], *until the fullness of the Gentiles* [melo ha goyim] *be come in."*

Therefore, we can see how the **grafted** Northern Kingdom *(house of Israel)* would be recognized today as being *"Gentiles"* and Christians (followers of the Jewish Messiah *[Mashiach]* Yeshua/Jesus) by the *house of Judah* (Judaism). Upon the fullness of the Gentiles *(melo ha goyim)* (Romans 11:25), the G-d of Israel will gather the **grafted** and assimilated *house of Israel* (Christianity) along with the *house of Judah* (Judaism) in fulfillment of the two houses being reunited in Ezekiel *(Yechezekel)* 37:15-28 and allow them to return to the land of Israel (Ezekiel *[Yechezekel]* 37:21-22) in the end of days during Jacob's trouble (Jeremiah *[Yermiyahu]* 30:1-7) or the birth pangs of the Messiah *(Chevlai shel Mashiach).*

In the rest of this chapter, we will learn how the Bible details how the seed of Abraham *(Avraham)* would be **grafted** into **all families** of the earth (Genesis *[Bereishit]* 12:3) and how after being assimilated into all the nations of the earth for not believing the covenant that the G-d of Israel made with Abraham *(Avraham)* that the two houses of Israel would be reunited in the end of days and return to the land of Israel.

Ephraim and Judah Become One House
Abraham Is the Father of Our Faith

The complete redemptive plan of the G-d of Israel is fulfilled according to the covenant that the G-d of Israel made with Abraham *(Avraham)*. For this reason, Abraham *(Avraham)* is called the father of our faith *(emunah)* (Romans 4:16). Furthermore, the G-d of Israel tells His people that they are to look unto (understand the covenant that the G-d of Israel made with) Abraham *(Avraham)* our father and Sarah who bore us. In Isaiah *(Yeshayahu)* 51:1-4 it is written:

> *"Hearken to me, ye that follow after righteousness, ye that seek the LORD: look unto the rock whence ye are hewn, and to the hole of the pit where ye are digged. Look unto Abraham your father, and unto Sarah that bare you: for I called him alone, and blessed him, and increased him. For the LORD shall comfort Zion ... Hearken unto me, my people; and give ear unto me, O my nation: for a law [TORAH] shall proceed from me, and I will make my judgment to rest for a light of the people."*

In Genesis *(Bereishit)* 17:1-8, the G-d of Israel reaffirmed His covenant that He made with Abraham *(Avraham)* as it is written:

> *"And when Abram was ninety years old and nine, the LORD appeared to Abram, and said unto him ... I will make my covenant between me and thee, and will multiply thee exceedingly ... As for me, behold, my covenant is with thee, and thou shalt be a father of many nations ... And I will establish my covenant between me and thee and thy seed after*

thee in their generations for an **everlasting covenant**, *to be a God unto thee, and to thy seed after thee. And I will give unto thee, and to* **thy seed after thee***, the land wherein thou art a stranger, all* **the land of Canaan***, for an* **everlasting possession;** *and I will be their God."*

Seven Promises of the Covenant That G-d Made with Abraham

1. Exceedingly fruitful *(Genesis 17:6)*.
2. Nations shall come out of Abraham *(Genesis 17:6)*.
3. Kings shall come out of Abraham *(Genesis 17:6)*.
4. The covenant is with the seed of Abraham *(Genesis 17:7)*.
5. G-d's covenant with Abraham is everlasting *(Genesis 17:7)*.
6. The seed of Abraham will possess the land of Canaan *(Genesis 17:8)*.
7. The possession of the land of Canaan is an everlasting possession *(Genesis 17:8)*.

These seven promises that the G-d of Israel made with Abraham *(Avraham)* and his seed after him have never been fulfilled in their fullness. Even so, the covenant that the G-d of Israel made with Abraham *(Avraham)* will be fulfilled both physically and spiritually. Since the covenant that the G-d of Israel made with Abraham *(Avraham)* is everlasting and eternal, these promises are still valid today. The fullness of the fulfillment of these promises will be during the Messianic Age *(Athid Lavo)* when the Jewish Messiah *(Mashiach)* Yeshua/Jesus will teach the Torah to all nations from Jerusalem *(Yerushalayim)* (Isaiah [Yeshayahu] 2:2-3).

Ephraim and Judah Become One House

From Abraham to Isaac to Jacob

From Abraham *(Avraham)*, the covenant was passed to Isaac *(Yitzchak)*. In Genesis *(Bereishit)* 26:1-4 it is written:

> *"And there was a famine in the land, beside the first famine that was in the days of Abraham. And Isaac went unto Abimelech king of the Philistines unto Gerar. And the LORD appeared unto him, and said, Go not down into Egypt; dwell in the land which I shall tell thee of: Sojourn in this land, and I will be with thee, and will bless thee; for unto thee, and unto thy seed, I will give all these countries, and I will perform the oath which I sware unto Abraham thy father; And I will make thy seed to multiply as the stars of heaven, and will give unto thy seed all these countries; and in thy seed shall all the nations of the earth* **[nivrecu]** *be blessed* **[grafted** *or intermingled]."*

From Abraham *(Avraham)*, the covenant that the G-d of Israel made with him was passed to Isaac *(Yitzchak)* and then to Jacob *(Ya'acov)*. In Genesis *(Bereishit)* 28:10, 13-14 it is written:

> *"And Jacob went out from Beersheba, and went toward Haran … And, behold, the LORD stood above it, and said, I am the LORD God of Abraham thy father, and the God of Isaac: the land whereon thou liest, to thee will I give it, and to thy seed; And thy seed shall be as the dust of the earth, and thou shalt spread abroad to the west, and to the east, and to the north, and to the south: and in thee and in thy seed shall all the families of the earth be blessed* **[nivrecu/grafted** *or intermingled]."*

Later, the G-d of Israel reiterated His promise to Jacob *(Ya'acov)* and changed his name to Israel. In Genesis *(Bereishit)* 35:9-12 it is written:

> *"And God appeared unto Jacob again, when he came out of Padan-aram, and blessed him. And God said unto him, thy name is Jacob: thy name shall not be called any more Jacob, but Israel shall be thy name: and he called his name Israel. And God said unto him, I am God Almighty: be fruitful and multiply; a nation and a company of nations shall be of thee, and kings shall come out of thy loins."*

From Abraham to Isaac to Jacob to the Children of Jacob

Jacob *(Ya'acov)* had twelve sons. Each son became the head of one of the twelve tribes of Israel. In Genesis *(Bereishit)* 49:1-28, Jacob blesses his twelve sons. In Genesis *(Bereishit)* 49:28 it is written:

> *"All these are the* **twelve tribes of Israel**: *and this is it that their father spake unto them, and blessed them; every one according to his blessing he blessed them."*

The Full Blessing of Abraham Was Given to Ephraim and Manasseh

One of the twelve sons of Jacob *(Ya'acov)* was Joseph *(Yosef)*. The blessing of Abraham *(Avraham)*, Isaac *(Yitzchak)* and Jacob *(Ya'acov)* was bestowed upon the

Ephraim and Judah Become One House

grandsons of Jacob, Ephraim and Manasseh. Jacob *(Ya'acov)* adopts Ephraim and Manasseh and gives them the blessing of the covenant that the G-d of Israel made with Abraham *(Avraham)*, Isaac *(Yitzchak)*, and Jacob *(Ya'acov)* and they are given the rights of the first born son and the fruitful fulfillment of the G-d of Israel's covenant with Abraham *(Avraham)*. In Genesis *(Bereishit)* 48:3-6 it is written:

> *"And Jacob said unto Joseph, God Almighty appeared unto me at Luz in the land of Canaan, and blessed me, And said unto me, Behold, I will make thee fruitful, and multiply thee, and I will make of thee a multitude of people; and will give this land to thy seed after thee for an everlasting possession. And now thy two sons, Ephraim and Manasseh, which were born unto thee in the land of Egypt before I came unto thee into Egypt, are mine; as Reuben and Simeon, they shall be mine. And thy issue, which thou begettest after them, shall be thine, and shall be called after the name of their brethren in their inheritance."*

Reuben and Simeon are the natural first born sons of Jacob. The double portion blessing of the inheritance belongs to the first born son. Not only is Jacob *(Ya'acov)* adopting Ephraim and Manasseh into his family by giving them his blessing, but they are being given the double portion blessing of the firstborn. Jacob's blessing upon Ephraim and Manasseh is recorded in Genesis *(Bereishit)* 48:12-16, 19 as it is written:

Restoring the Two Houses of Israel

"And Joseph brought them out from between his knees, and he bowed himself with his face to the earth. And Joseph took them both, Ephraim in his right hand toward Israel's left hand, and Manasseh in his left hand toward Israel's right hand, and brought them near unto him. And Israel stretched out his right hand, and laid it upon Ephraim's head, who was the younger, and his left hand upon Manasseh's head, guiding his hands wittingly; for Manasseh was the firstborn. And he blessed Joseph, and said, God, before whom my fathers Abraham and Isaac did walk, the God which fed me all my life long unto this day, The Angel which redeemed me from all evil, bless the lads; and let my name be named on them, and the name of my fathers Abraham and Isaac; and let them grow into a multitude in the midst of the earth ... truly his younger brother [Ephraim] *shall be greater than he* [Manasseh]*, and his seed* [Ephraim] *shall become a multitude of nations* [melo ha goyim]*."*

Ephraim Is Fruitful

The word Ephraim is the Strong's word 669. The Hebrew word, Ephraim, means *"double fruit."* Being exceedingly fruitful was a promise that the G-d of Israel made to Abraham (*Avraham*) concerning his seed (Genesis *[Bereishit]* 17:6).

In Genesis *(Bereishit)* 48:19, Jacob *(Ya'acov)* prophesied that Ephraim would be a "multitude of nations." In Hebrew, a multitude of nations is *"melo ha goyim."* This phrase can also be translated as "fullness of the Gentiles." The Apostle Paul *(Rav Sha'ul)* referred to the "fullness of the Gentiles/*melo ha goyim*" in Romans

Ephraim and Judah Become One House

11:25. By being a "fullness of the Gentiles/*melo ha goyim*", Ephraim would be fruitful.

In order for this prophecy to be fulfilled, Ephraim would have to be recognized as being "Gentiles" to the *house of Judah* (Judaism) in the end of days when the two houses would be reunited (Ezekiel *[Yechezekel]* 37:15-28).

As mentioned in the first chapter of this book, there are various "Christian" groups who teach that there are two houses of Israel in the context of elitism (they are a special race of people) and replacement theology (Ephraim is the "New Israel") and have replaced the *house of Judah* (Judaism) in the redemptive plan of the G-d of Israel. Because there are many misplaced teachings which exist concerning Ephraim, let me take this opportunity to identify the unbiblical doctrines regarding Ephraim and the house of Israel. Ephraim is NOT the following:

1. Ephraim is NOT associated with British Israelism.
2. Ephraim is NOT associated with white supremacy.
3. Ephraim is NOT associated with replacement theology.

As has been expressed in explicit detail in this book, Ephraim (*the house of Israel*/Christianity) has been **grafted** into the olive tree of the G-d of Israel. The *house of Judah* (Judaism) is the **natural root** of this olive tree. Therefore, Ephraim, the (*house of Israel*/Christianity) has NOT replaced or superceded the *house of Judah* (Judaism) but has been grafted into the natural root of the *house of Judah* (Judaism).

Restoring the Two Houses of Israel

Ephraim (Northern Kingdom) Is a Spiritual Picture of Christianity

Ephraim (Northern Kingdom) is a spiritual picture of future Christianity. How is this so?

1. Ephraim was **adopted** into Jacob's family. Believer's in the Jewish Messiah *(Mashiach) Yeshua*/Jesus are adopted into the family of the G-d of Israel (Romans 8:14-17, 22-23, Galatians 4:4-6).

2. Ephraim is the Strong's word 669 and means "double fruit." The G-d of Israel promised Abraham that his descendants would be **exceedingly fruitful** (Genesis *[Bereishit]* 17:6). This alludes to the fact that Ephraim (the *house of Israel*/Christianity) would be numerically greater than the *house of Judah* (Judaism).

3. Ephraim is the masculine word in Hebrew for the female equivalent Ephratah. Ephratah is another name for Bethlehem and is the place where the Jewish Messiah *(Mashiach) Yeshua*/Jesus was born (Micah 5:2, Matthew *(Mattityahu)* 2:1-6).

4. Ephraim is a term for the Northern Kingdom of Israel who forsook the Torah of the G-d of Israel by calling the Torah "a strange thing." So has historical Christianity (Hosea *[Hoshea]* 8:12).

5. Ephraim, the Northern Kingdom, instituted a substitute place of worship (Dan and Bethel) rather than Jerusalem *(Yerushalayim)* (I Kings *[Melachim]* 12:29, Deuteronomy *[Devarim]* 16:16). When Christianity departed from her Jewish roots, she began to worship in a church rather than a synagogue where the Jewish Messiah *(Mashiach) Yeshua*/Jesus worshiped (Luke 4:16).

6. Ephraim, the Northern Kingdom, instituted substitute holidays (I Kings *[Melachim]* 12:32-33) rather than observing the dates and times of the Biblical holidays that the G-d of Israel gave to His people in Leviticus *(Vayikra)* 23. Christianity has adopted the original pagan holidays of Christmas and Easter from Roman Mythraism rather than keeping the Biblical holidays in Leviticus *(Vayikra)* 23.

7. Ephraim, the Northern Kingdom, instituted a substitute priesthood rather than have priests from the tribe of Levi (I Kings *[Melachim]* 12:31). Christianity allows pastors and priests to be ministers of the sheep of the G-d of Israel who are not anointed and called by the G-d of Israel into their office or ministry.

8. Ephraim, the Northern Kingdom, mixed paganism with the true worship of the G-d of Israel and called it the true worship of the G-d of Israel. The G-d of Israel called this the golden calf system of worship (I Kings *[Melachim]* 12:28). Historical Christianity has mixed Roman and Babylonian practices and beliefs with the true worship of the G-d of Israel and calls this mixture true worship of the G-d of Israel.

Deliverance from Egypt on Behalf of G-d's Covenant with Abraham

At mount Sinai, the covenant that the G-d of Israel made with Abraham *(Avraham)* was made with the twelve tribes of Jacob *(Ya'acov)*, the children of Israel. In Exodus *(Shemot)* 19:1, 3 it is written:

> *"In the third month, when the children of Israel were gone forth out of the land of Egypt, the same day, came they into the wilderness of Sinai ... And Moses went up unto God, and the* LORD *called unto him out of the mountain, saying, Thus shalt thou say to the* **house of Jacob**, *and tell the children of Israel."*

The G-d of Israel brought the children of Israel out of Egypt *(Mitzrayim)* because of the covenant that He made with Abraham *(Avraham)*. In Genesis *(Bereishit)* 15:13-14 it is written:

> *"And he said unto Abram, Know of a surety that thy seed shall be a stranger in a land that is not theirs, and shall serve them; and they shall afflict them four hundred years; And also that nation, whom they shall serve, will I judge: and afterward shall they come out with great substance."*

The G-d of Israel called Moses *(Moshe)* because of the covenant that He made with Abraham *(Avraham)*. In Exodus *(Shemot)* 2:23-25 it is written:

> *"And it came to pass in process of time, that the king of Egypt died: and the children of Israel sighed by reason of the bondage, and they cried, and their cry came up unto God by reason of the bondage. And God heard their groaning, and* **God remembered his covenant with Abraham, with Isaac, and with Jacob**. *And God looked*

Ephraim and Judah Become One House

upon the children of Israel, and God had respect unto them."

Moses *(Moshe)* delivered the children of Israel from Egypt *(Mitzrayim)* by the mighty hand of the G-d of Israel. After the G-d of Israel delivered the children of Israel from Egypt *(Mitzrayim)* and the rule of Pharaoh, the G-d of Israel instructed Moses *(Moshe)* to take the children of Israel to mount Sinai. In Exodus *(Shemot)* 3:1, 11-12 it is written:

> *"Now Moses kept the flock of Jethro his father in law, the priest of Midian: and he led the flock to the backside of the desert, and came to the mountain of God, even to Horeb ...And Moses said unto God, Who am I, that I should go unto Pharaoh, and that I should bring forth the children of Israel out of Egypt? And he said, Certainly I will be with thee; and this shall be a token unto thee, that I have sent thee: When thou hast brought forth the people out of Egypt, ye shall serve God upon this mountain."*

In Exodus *(Shemot)* 19:1-3, Moses *(Moshe)* brought the house of Jacob *(Ya'acov)*, the children of Israel, to mount Sinai where the G-d of Israel confirmed the covenant that He made with Abraham *(Avraham)* and entered into a marriage contract with the seed of Abraham *(Avraham)*.

G-d's Covenant with Abraham Was Made with Abraham's Descendants at Mount Sinai

Many members within the *house of Israel* (Christianity) view the covenant that the G-d of Israel made with

Restoring the Two Houses of Israel

Abraham *(Avraham)* and the marriage contract that the G-d of Israel made with the seed of Abraham *(Avraham)* as two independent events and two separate covenants. In reality, what happened at mount Sinai was an extension of the covenant that the G-d of Israel made with Abraham *(Avraham)*. At mount Sinai, the covenant that the G-d of Israel made with Abraham *(Avraham)* was formally made to the seed of Abraham *(Avraham)* and to his descendents forever just as the G-d of Israel promised Abraham *(Avraham)* in Genesis *(Bereishit)* 17:7. In Deuteronomy *(Devarim)* 29:14-15 it is written:

> *"Neither with you only do I make this covenant and this oath; But with him that standeth here with us this day before the* L<small>ORD</small> *our God, and also with him that is not here with us this day."*

Every generation who lives after the generation who was at mount Sinai are to see themselves as if they were actually redeemed from Egyptian bondage and passed through the Red Sea to mount Sinai on their way to the Promised Land. In I Corinthians 10:1-4 it is written:

> *"Moreover, brethren, I would not that ye should be ignorant, how that* **all our fathers** *were under the cloud, and* **all** *passed through the sea; And were all baptized unto Moses in the cloud and in the sea; And did all eat the same spiritual meat; And did all drink the same spiritual drink: for they drank of that spiritual Rock that followed them: and that Rock was Christ* [Mashiach].*"*

Spiritually (*sod*/deeper meaning), all those who have accepted the Jewish Messiah *(Mashiach) Yeshua*/Jesus

Ephraim and Judah Become One House

from among the nations and who are **grafted** into the olive tree of the G-d of Israel are heirs of the promise that the G-d of Israel made with Abraham *(Avraham)*. In Galatians 3:8, 16, 29 it is written:

> *"And the Scripture,* [TeNaKh/Old Testament] *foreseeing that God would justify* [make righteous] *the heathen through faith* [emunah], *preached before the gospel unto Abraham, saying, in thee shall all nations be blessed* **[nivrecu/ grafted or intermingled]** *... Now to Abraham and his seed were the promises made. He saith not, And to seeds, as of many; but as of one, And to thy seed, which is Christ* [Mashiach] *... And if ye be Christ's, then are ye Abraham's seed, and heirs according to the promise."*

The Children of Israel Become a Nation at Mount Sinai

As we just studied, the G-d of Israel called Moses *(Moshe)* because of the covenant that He made with Abraham *(Avraham)* (Genesis *[Bereishit]* 15:1-5, 13-14, 18-21, Exodus *[Shemot]* 2:23-25, 3:15-17) to deliver the children of Israel from the bondage of the Egyptians. The Torah of the G-d of Israel is a tree of life to the family of the G-d of Israel (Proverbs *[Mishlei]* 3:17-18). The leaves of the tree of life (the pages of the Torah scroll) is for the healing of the nations (Revelation 22:2). Abraham *(Avraham)* kept the Torah of the G-d of Israel (Genesis *[Bereishit]* 26:5). Because the tree of life was in the Garden of Eden *(Gan Eden)* and because Abraham *(Avraham)* kept the Torah of the G-d of Israel, the Torah of the G-d of Israel did not first come into existence at mount Sinai. The Torah of the G-d of Israel has always existed and will always exist.

The unique event at mount Sinai was that the G-d of Israel entered into a marriage contract with the seed of Abraham *(Avraham)*. When this was done, the seed of Abraham *(Avraham)* became a covenant nation of people unto the G-d of Israel. The Torah became the *ketubah* (marriage contract) or covenant agreement that made the seed of Abraham *(Avraham)* a nation of people unto the G-d of Israel. Therefore, the covenant that the G-d of Israel made with Abraham *(Avraham)* was extended to the seed of Abraham *(Avraham)* at mount Sinai and they became a covenant people and a holy nation unto the G-d of Israel. Never before in the history of the world did the G-d of Israel enter into a covenant with a specific nation of people. In Exodus *(Shemot)* 19:5-6 it is written:

> *"Now therefore, if ye will obey my voice indeed, and keep my covenant, then ye shall be a peculiar treasure unto me above all people: for all the earth is mine: And ye shall be unto me a kingdom of priests and a* **HOLY NATION...**"

G-d Betrothed Himself to Israel at Mount Sinai

At mount Sinai, the G-d of Israel betrothed Himself to the children of Israel and entered into a marriage contract with them. In Jeremiah *(Yermiyahu)* 2:1-3 it is written:

> *"Moreover the word of the* LORD *came to me, saying, go and cry in the ears of Jerusalem, saying,*

Ephraim and Judah Become One House

Thus saith the L‌ord; I remember thee, the kindness of thy youth, the love of thine espousals, when thou wentest after me in the wilderness, in a land that was not sown. Israel was holiness unto the L‌ord, and the firstfruits of his increase: all that devour him shall offend, evil shall come upon them, says the L‌ord."

There are two stages to the Biblical wedding. The first stage is betrothal and the second stage is the consummation of the marriage. During betrothal, you are legally married to your bride but you do not physically dwell with her.

At mount Sinai, the G-d of Israel betrothed Himself to the seed of Abraham *(Avraham)* and entered into a marriage contract with them. This marriage contract included a *"mixed multitude"* (Exodus *[Shemot]* 12:38) who came out of Egypt *(Mitzrayim)* with the seed of Abraham *(Avraham)*. These *"mixed multitude"* of people were **GRAFTED** into the natural seed of Abraham *(Avraham)*.

In order for a Biblical marriage to be legal, both the bride and the groom must agree to the terms of the marriage. The terms of the marriage are stated in a marriage document known in Hebrew as a *Ketubah*. When the G-d of Israel betrothed Himself to Israel at mount Sinai, the *Ketubah* (marriage contract) was seen as being the Torah. The children of Israel accepted the terms of the condition of the marriage by saying the words, *"I do."* In Exodus *(Shemot)* 19:8 it is written:

> *"And all the people answered together, and said, All that the L‌ord has spoken* **we will do***..."*

Restoring the Two Houses of Israel

The terms and the conditions of the marriage including the blessing for obedience and the curses for disobedience is stated in Leviticus *(Vayikra)* 26 and Deuteronomy *(Devarim)* 28. In order to understand the covenant that the G-d of Israel made with Abraham *(Avraham)*, we need to understand the blessings and the curses and the consequences for obedience and disobedience in the marriage contract.

The Biblical wedding that the G-d of Israel gave to His people will traditionally have two witnesses. They are called the friends of the bridegroom. One is assigned to the groom and one is assigned to the bride. Spiritually (*sod*/deeper meaning), there are two witnesses that *Yeshua*/Jesus is the Jewish Messiah *(Mashiach)*. These two witnesses are the Torah and the Prophets. In Luke 24:44, the Jewish Messiah *(Mashiach) Yeshua*/Jesus spoke to His disciples *(talmidim)* and stated that the Torah, Prophets and Writings *(TeNaKh)* speak of Him as it is written:

> *"And he said unto them, These are the words which I spake unto you, while I was yet with you, that all things must be fulfilled, which were written in the* **law [Torah]** *of Moses, and in the* **prophets** [Nevi'im], *and in the* **Psalms,** [Ketuvim] *concerning me."*

When the G-d of Israel betrothed Himself to Israel at mount Sinai, Moses *(Moshe)* was seen as being one of the two witnesses whose primary job was to escort the bride (Israel) to meet the groom under the *chuppah* (wedding canopy) which was seen as being mount Sinai. In Exodus *(Shemot)* 19:17, Moses *(Moshe)*

Ephraim and Judah Become One House

escorted the children of Israel to mount Sinai to be married to the G-d of Israel under the *chuppah* (mount Sinai) as it is written:

> *"And Moses brought forth* [escorted] *the people out of the camp to meet with God; and they stood at the nether part of the mount."*

What Is the Spiritual Meaning of Betrothal?

Spiritually (*sod*/deeper meaning), everybody who accepts *Yeshua*/Jesus as the Jewish Messiah *(Mashiach)* and asks Him into their heart and life by repenting *(teshuvah)* of their sins and by trusting *(emunah)* in His shed blood on the tree for the forgiveness of their sins is betrothed to Him.

The *ketubah* (marriage contract) for all believers in *Yeshua*/Jesus as the Jewish Messiah *(Mashiach)* is the **Torah** written upon our heart. This is the New Covenant (Jeremiah *[Yermiyahu]* 31:33, Hebrews 10:15-16). The fullness of the marriage will be when we live and dwell with the Jewish Messiah *(Mashiach) Yeshua*/Jesus during the Messianic Age *(Athid Lavo)*.

The Fulfillment of G-d's Promise to Abraham Is Conditional Upon Obedience to G-d and His Torah

The G-d of Israel promised Abraham *(Avraham)* that his seed would be given a land for all eternity (Genesis *[Bereishit]* 15:18-21, 17:7-8). In order to fulfill this promise that the G-d of Israel made to Abraham *(Avraham)*, it was conditional upon the seed of Abraham *(Avraham)* being an obedient people to the Torah of the G-d of Israel, keeping His commandments and loving the G-d of Israel with all your heart, soul, mind, and strength. In Deuteronomy *(Devarim)* 10:12-14 it is written:

> *"And now Israel, what does the* Lord *thy God require of thee, but to fear the* Lord *thy God, to walk in all his ways, and to love him, and to serve the* Lord *thy God with all thy heart and with all thy soul. To keep the commandments of the* Lord*, and his statutes, which I command thee this day for thy good?"*

In Deuteronomy (*Devarim*) 4:5-9 it is written:

> *"Behold, I have taught you statutes and judgments, even as the* Lord *my God commanded me, that you should do so in the land whither you go to possess it. Keep therefore and do them; for this is your wisdom and your understanding in the sight of the nations, which shall hear all these statutes, and say, Surely this great nation is a wise and understanding people. For what nation is there so great, who has God so nigh unto them, as the* Lord *our God is in all things that we call upon him for? And what nation is there so great, that has statutes and judgments* **SO RIGHTEOUS AS ALL THIS LAW [TORAH]***, which I set before you this day? Only take heed to thyself, and keep thy soul diligently, lest thou forget the things which thine eyes have seen, and lest they depart from thy*

Ephraim and Judah Become One House

heart all the days of thy life: but teach them thy sons, and thy sons' sons."

The terms and the conditions of the marriage contract *(ketubah)* that the G-d of Israel made with the seed of Abraham *(Avraham)* can be seen in Leviticus *(Vayikra)* 26 and Deuteronomy *(Devarim)* 28. The conditional aspect of obedience to the Torah in order to receive these blessings can be seen in Deuteronomy *(Devarim)* 28:1-2 as it is written:

> *"And it shall come to pass,* **IF** *thou shalt hearken diligently unto the voice of the* LORD *thy God, to observe and to do all his commandments which I command thee this day, that the* LORD *thy God will set thee on high above all nations of the earth: And all these blessings shall come on thee, and overtake thee,* **IF** *thou shalt hearken unto the voice of the* LORD *thy God."*

The relationship between the G-d of Israel fulfilling the covenant that He made with Abraham *(Avraham)* and his seed to give them an eternal Promised Land based upon obedience to the Torah of the G-d of Israel can also be seen in Leviticus *(Vayikra)* 26:1-12. In these scripture verses, we see the following:

IF you walk in my statutes and keep my commandments and do them (Leviticus *[Vayikra]* 26:3) ... then the G-d of Israel will give:

a) Rain in due season (Leviticus *[Vayikra]* 26:4)
b) Peace in the land (Leviticus *[Vayikra]* 26:6)
c) Victory over enemies (Leviticus *[Vayikra]* 26:7)

d) Be fruitful and multiply (Leviticus *[Vayikra]* 26:9)
e) G-d's covenant with Abraham *(Avraham)* would be established (Leviticus *[Vayikra]* 26:9)
f) G-d would set His tabernacle among His people (Leviticus *[Vayikra]* 26:11, Revelation 21:2-3)
g) G-d's family would be called my people (Leviticus *[Vayikra]* 26:12, Revelation 21:2-3)

The G-d of Israel setting His tabernacle *(Mishkan)* in the midst of His people is an allusion to the establishment of the Messianic Era *(Athid Lavo)* when the Jewish Messiah *(Mashiach)* would live and dwell with the family of the G-d of Israel teaching the Torah from Jerusalem *(Yerushalayim)* to all the nations of the earth (Isaiah *[Yeshayahu]* 2:2-3).

The Punishment for Disobedience Was Dispersion into the Nations

The G-d of Israel declared that the punishment of Abraham's seed for not believing and walking in His promise to them specifying that they would be given a Promised Land and by not being faithful to the marriage contract *(Ketubah)* made at mount Sinai (being obedient to the Torah) that they would be scattered unto all the nations in the earth. In Deuteronomy *(Devarim)* 28:15, 36-37, 45 it is written:

> *"But it shall come to pass, if thou wilt not hearken unto the voice of the* Lord *thy God, to observe to do all his commandments and his statutes which I command thee this day; that all these curses shall come upon thee, and overtake thee ... The* Lord *shall bring thee, and thy king which thou shall set*

Ephraim and Judah Become One House

over thee, unto a nation which neither thou nor thy fathers have known; and there shalt thou serve other gods, wood and stone. And thou shall become an astonishment, a proverb, and a byword, among all nations whither the LORD shall lead thee ... Moreover all these curses shall come upon thee, and shall pursue thee, and overtake thee, till thou be destroyed; because thou hearkenedst not unto the voice of the LORD thy God, to keep his commandments and his statutes which he commanded thee."

G-d Warns Against Adopting the Ways of the Other Nations

The G-d of Israel instructed the children of Israel that when they entered the land of Canaan that they were to totally destroy the culture of the Canaanite people. In Deuteronomy *(Devarim)* 7:1-5 it is written:

"When the LORD thy God shall bring thee into the land whither thou goest to possess it, and has cast out many nations before thee, the Hittites, and the Girgashites, and the Amorites, and the Canaanites, and the Perizzites, and the Hivites, and the Jebusites, seven nations greater and mightier than thou; And when the LORD thy God shall deliver them before thee; thou shalt smite them, and utterly destroy them; thou shalt make no covenant with them, nor show mercy unto them: Neither shalt thou make marriages with them; thy daughter thou shalt not give unto his son, nor his daughter shalt thou take unto thy son. For they will turn away thy son from following me, that they may serve other gods: so will the anger of the

Restoring the Two Houses of Israel

> L̲o̲r̲d̲ *be kindled against you, and destroy thee suddenly. But thus shall ye deal with them; ye shall destroy their altars, and break down their images, and cut down their groves, and burn their graven images with fire."*

In this scripture passage, the G-d of Israel warned the seed of Abraham *(Avraham)* not to mix paganism with their worship of Him. In the previous section of this chapter, we saw that the G-d of Israel declared that the punishment for disobeying His Torah and not believing His covenant with Abraham *(Avraham)* was dispersion into the nations of the world. However, the G-d of Israel made a promise to Abraham's seed in His marriage contract *(ketubah)* to them that if they would repent *(teshuvah)* after they had been scattered into the nations of the earth that He would redeem His people and bring them back to the Promised Land and fulfill the promise that He made with Abraham *(Avraham)*. In Deuteronomy *(Devarim)* 30:1-5 it is written:

> *"And it shall come to pass, when all these things are come upon thee, the blessing and the curse, which I have set before thee, and thou shalt call them to mind among all the nations whither the* L̲o̲r̲d̲ *thy God has driven thee, And shalt return unto the* L̲o̲r̲d̲ *thy God, and shalt obey his voice according to all that I command thee this day, thou and thy children with all thine heart, and with all thy soul; That then the* L̲o̲r̲d̲ *thy God will turn thy captivity, and have compassion upon thee, and will return and gather thee from all the nations, whither the* L̲o̲r̲d̲ *thy God has scattered thee. If any*

Ephraim and Judah Become One House

> *of thine be driven out unto the outmost parts of heaven, from thence will the LORD thy God gather thee, and from thence will he fetch thee: And the LORD thy God will bring thee into the land which your fathers possessed, and thou shalt possess it; and he will do thee good, and multiply thee above your fathers."*

The fulfillment of this promise is the restoration of the two houses of Israel (*house of Israel*/Christianity and the *house of Judah*/Judaism) as prophesied in Ezekiel *(Yechezekel)* 37:15-28.

The Children of Israel Are Commanded to Possess the Promised Land

The G-d of Israel commanded the seed of Abraham *(Avraham)* through the word of Moses *(Moshe)* to possess the land that the G-d of Israel had promised Abraham *(Avraham)*. In Deuteronomy *(Devarim)* 1:3, 5, 8 it is written:

> *"And it came to pass in the fortieth year, in the eleventh month, on the first day of the month, that Moses spake unto the children of Israel, according unto all that the LORD had given him in commandment unto them ... On this side Jordan, in the land of Moab, began Moses to declare this law [Torah] saying ... Behold I have set the land before you: go in and possess the land which the LORD sware unto your fathers, Abraham, Isaac, and Jacob, to give unto them and to their seed after them."*

Restoring the Two Houses of Israel

Twelve Spies Search Out the Land of Promise

In Numbers *(Bamidbar)* 13:1-17, the G-d of Israel commanded Moses *(Moshe)* to have the children of Israel select one individual from each of the twelve tribes and search the land of Canaan that the G-d of Israel had promised the seed of Abraham *(Avraham)*. A summary of this event is as follows:

1. One member from each of the 12 tribes was selected to spy out the land (Numbers *[Bamidbar]* 13:1-17).

2. Only Joshua and Caleb came back with news that the children of Israel could possess the land that the G-d of Israel promised Abraham *(Avraham)*.
    a) Joshua was from the tribe of Ephraim (Northern Kingdom).
    b) Caleb was from the tribe of Judah (Southern Kingdom).

3. Ten spies came back with an evil report that the children of Israel could not possess the land that the G-d of Israel promised Abraham *(Avraham)* (Numbers *[Bamidbar]* 13:17-20, 25-33)

4. The G-d of Israel's punishment for those that believed the evil report was traveling 40 years in the wilderness. One year for each day of searching (Numbers *[Bamidbar]* 14:26-34)

G-d Commands Joshua to Conquer the Promised Land

When the G-d of Israel commanded Joshua and the

Ephraim and Judah Become One House

seed of Abraham *(Avraham)* to enter the Promised Land, the G-d of Israel reiterated to Joshua the promise that He made with Abraham *(Avraham)*. In Joshua 1:1-4 it is written:

> *"Now after the death of Moses the servant of the* Lord *it came to pass, that the* Lord *spake unto Joshua the son of Nun, Moses' minister, saying, Moses my servant is dead; now therefore arise, go over this Jordan, thou, and all this people, unto the land which I do give to them, even to the children of Israel. Every place that the sole of your foot shall tread upon, that have I given unto you, as I said unto Moses. From the wilderness and this Lebanon even unto the great river, the river Euphrates, all the land of the Hittites, and unto the great sea toward the going down of the sun, shall be your coast."*

The Children of Israel Only Possess Part of the Promised Land

Following the death of Joshua, the children of Israel possessed (in part) the land of Canaan. (Joshua 21:43-45). The children of Israel did not possess the **fullness** of the land that the G-d of Israel promised Abraham *(Avraham)*. The G-d of Israel promised Abraham *(Avraham)* that His descendants would possess the land from the Nile to the Euphrates (Genesis *[Bereishit]* 15:18-21) including the land of Canaan (Genesis *[Bereishit]* 17:8).

G-d Appoints Judges to Finish Conquering the Promised Land

Following the death of Joshua, we enter into the period of the Judges. During this time, the entire land of Canaan was still not yet conquered (Judges *[Shoftim]* 1:27-34). The G-d of Israel allowed for some of the land of Canaan that He had promised Abraham (Genesis *[Bereishit]* 17:7-8) to be left unconquered to test the hearts of the seed of Abraham *[Avraham]* to determine if they would be obedient to His Torah and believe the covenant that He made with Abraham *[Avraham]*. In Judges *[Shoftim]* 3:1-4 it is written:

> *"Now these are the nations which the* Lord *left, to prove Israel by them, even as many of Israel as had not known all the wars of Canaan; Only that the generations of the children of Israel might know, to teach them war, at the least such as before knew nothing thereof; Namely, five lords of the Philistines, and all the Canaanites, and the Sidonians, and the Hivites that dwelt in mount Lebanon, from mount Baalhermon unto the entering in of Hamath; And they were to prove Israel by them, to know whether they would hearken unto the commandments of the* Lord*, which he commanded their fathers by the hand of Moses."*

The Sins of the Children of Israel in the Promised Land

When the G-d of Israel entered into a marriage contract *(ketubah)* with the seed of Abraham *(Avraham)* at mount Sinai to keep His Torah, He gave specific instructions to His people regarding how they were to conduct themselves in the presence of the other nations who dwelt in the land of Canaan (Deuteronomy *[Devarim]* 7:1-5). In these verses we see the G-d of Israel commanding His people to do the following things:

Ephraim and Judah Become One House

1. Do not make marriages with the daughters of the nations who dwell in the land of Canaan.

2. Do not serve the gods of the nations that dwell in the land of Canaan.

3. Destroy the places of worship of those nations who dwell in the land of Canaan including their altars, graven images and groves.

Spiritually (*sod*/deeper meaning), the G-d of Israel was asking the seed of Abraham *(Avraham)* to live among the people in the land of Canaan but don't practice the ways of their culture. The same cultural values that existed in the land of Canaan during the days when the G-d of Israel instructed the seed of Abraham *(Avraham)* to conquer the Promised Land is still present today in our society in the Western world through our Greco/Roman/Babylonian based value system. The G-d of Israel still commands the people who are called by His name within the *house of Israel* (Christianity) and the *house of Judah* (Judaism) to depart from practicing the ways and values of our Greco/Roman/Babylonian based culture. In Revelation 18:4 it is written:

> *"And I heard another voice from heaven, saying, Come out of her, my people, that ye be not partakers of her sins, and that ye receive not of her plaques."*

The Children of Israel Are Unfaithful to Their Marriage Contract

While in the land of Canaan, the seed of Abraham *(Avraham)* forsook their marriage contract (obedience to the Torah) and the covenant that the G-d of Israel made with Abraham *(Avraham)*. They served the gods of the Canaanite nations (Judges *[Shoftim]* 2:12) and intermarried with their people (Judges *[Shoftim]* 3:5-6). Because of these sins, the seed of Abraham *(Avraham)* did not conquer all of the land of Canaan that the G-d of Israel promised Abraham *(Avraham)* (Genesis *[Bereishit]* 17:7-8. Therefore, the **fullness** of the promise that the G-d of Israel made Abraham *[Avraham]* remained unfulfilled.

Nevertheless, when the seed of Abraham *(Avraham)* repented *(teshuvah)* to the G-d of Israel for their sins, the G-d of Israel raised up Judges who would deliver the seed of Abraham *(Avraham)* from their enemies. However, when the Judge died, the seed of Abraham *(Avraham)* returned to their ways of sin and disobedience to the Torah of the G-d of Israel (Judges *[Shoftim]* 2:11-21).

One of the gods that the seed of Abraham *(Avraham)* served in Canaan was Ashtaroth (Judges *[Shoftim]* 2:13). Ashtaroth was the goddess of sex and fertility. The *house of Israel* (Christianity) "Christianized" the original pagan worship of Ashtaroth during the days of the Roman Empire and has named this holiday Easter. The custom of Easter eggs and rabbits is associated with the worship of Ashtaroth and the fertility of the earth.

An overview of the seed of Abraham's sin during the time of the Judges and the G-d of Israel's judgment upon His people for not being faithful to their marriage contract (obedience to the Torah) is recorded in Judges *(Shoftim)* 2:11-21 as it is written:

Ephraim and Judah Become One House

"And the children of Israel did evil in the sight of the LORD*, and served Baalim: And they forsook the* LORD *God of their fathers, which brought them out of the land of Egypt, and followed other gods, of the gods of the people that were round about them, and bowed themselves unto them, and provoked the* LORD *to anger. And they forsook the* LORD*, and served Baal and Ashtaroth. And the anger of the* LORD *was hot against Israel, and he delivered them into the hands of the spoilers that spoiled them, and he sold them into the hands of their enemies round about, so that they could not any longer stand before their enemies. Whithersoever they went out, the hand of the* LORD *was against them for evil, as the* LORD *had said, and as the* LORD *had sworn unto them: and they were greatly distressed. Nevertheless the* LORD *raised up judges, which delivered them out of the hand of those that spoiled them. And yet they would not hearken unto their judges, but they went a whoring after other gods, and bowed themselves unto them: they turned quickly out of the way which their fathers walked in, obeying the commandments of the* LORD*; but they did not so. And when the* LORD *raised them up judges, then the* LORD *was with the judge, and delivered them out of the hand of their enemies all the days of the judge: for it repented the* LORD *because of their groanings by reason of them that oppressed them and vexed them. And it came to pass, when the judge was dead, that they returned, and corrupted themselves more than their fathers, in following other gods to serve them, and to bow down unto them; they ceased not from their own doings, nor from their stubborn way. And the*

anger of the L*ORD* *was hot against Israel; and he said, Because that this people hath transgressed my covenant which I commanded their fathers, and have not hearkened unto my voice; I also will not henceforth drive out any from before them of the nations which Joshua left when he died."*

Israel Desires a King

Following the period of the Judges, the seed of Abraham *(Avraham)* began to cry out for a king. Rather than allowing the G-d of Israel to be their King and to be a separate people from the nations who lived around them, the seed of Abraham *(Avraham)* wanted to have their own king. In I Samuel *(Sh'muel)* 8:1, 3-10 it is written:

"And it came to pass, when Samuel was old, that he made his sons judges over Israel ... And his sons walked not in his ways, but turned aside after lucre, and took bribes and perverted judgment. Then all the elders of Israel gathered themselves together, and came to Samuel unto Ramah, And said unto him, Behold, thou art old, and thy sons walk not in thy ways: now make us a king to judge us like all the other nations. But the thing displeased Samuel, when they said, Give us a king to judge us. And Samuel prayed unto the L*ORD**. And the* L*ORD* *said unto Samuel, Hearken unto the voice of the people in all that they say unto thee: for they have not rejected thee, but* **they have rejected me**, *that I should not reign over them. According to all the works which they have done since the day that I brought them up out of Egypt even unto this*

Ephraim and Judah Become One House

day, wherewith they have forsaken me, and served other gods, so do they also unto thee. Now therefore hearken unto their voice: howbeit yet protest solemnly unto them, and show them the manner of the king that shall reign over them. And Samuel told all the words of the LORD unto the people that asked of him a king."

The G-d of Israel warned the seed of Abraham *(Avraham)* that if they chose a king to rule over them that the king would treat them with hardship. Furthermore, the G-d of Israel warned the seed of Abraham *(Avraham)* that when they would cry out to Him because of the burden placed upon them by their king that He would not listen and answer their prayers. Nevertheless, the seed of Abraham *(Avraham)* desired and asked for a king so that they could be like all the other nations. Therefore, the G-d of Israel was upset with His people because they wanted a king and rejected Him as their King. In I Samuel *(Sh'muel)* 8:18-20 it is written:

"And ye shall cry out in that day because of your king which ye shall have chosen you; and the LORD will not hear you in that day. Nevertheless the people refused to obey the voice of Samuel; and they said, Nay, but we will have a king over us; That we also may be like all the nations; and that our king may judge us, and go out before us, and fight our battles."

Saul becomes the first king of Israel (I Samuel *[Sh'muel]* 10. After the reign of Saul, David became the next king of Israel (I Samuel *[Sh'muel]* 16:1-13).

Restoring the Two Houses of Israel

G-d's Promise of Mercy to David

David was a man after the G-d of Israel's own heart (Acts 13:22) because David **loved** the Torah of the G-d of Israel (Psalm *[Tehillim]* 119). Therefore, the G-d of Israel promised to extend mercy to David and to the seed of David. The G-d of Israel's promise of mercy to David and his seed is found in II Samuel *(Sh'muel)* 7:11-17 as it is written:

> *"And as since the time that I commanded judges to be over my people Israel, and have caused thee to rest from all thine enemies. Also the* LORD *telleth thee that he will make thee a house. And when thy days be fulfilled, and thou shalt sleep with thy fathers, I will set up thy seed after thee, which shall proceed out of thy bowels, and I will establish his kingdom. He shall build a house for my name, and I will establish the throne of his kingdom forever. I will be his father, and he shall be my son. If he commit iniquity, I will chasten him with the rod of men, and with the stripes of the children of men: But my mercy shall not depart away from him, as I took it from Saul, whom I put away before thee. And thine house and thy kingdom shall be established forever before thee: your throne shall be established forever. According to all these words, and according to all this vision, so did Nathan speak unto David."*

In Psalm *(Tehillim)* 89:1-4 it is written:

> *"I will sing of the mercies of the* LORD *forever: with my mouth will I make known thy faithfulness to*

Ephraim and Judah Become One House

all generations. For I have said, **Mercy** *shall be built up forever: thy faithfulness shalt thou establish in the very heavens. I have made a covenant with my chosen, I have sworn unto David my servant,* **Thy seed will I establish forever**, *and build up thy throne to all generations. Selah."*

Why Did G-d Extend Mercy to the Seed of David?

The G-d of Israel extended His mercy to the seed of David on behalf of the covenant that He made with Abraham *(Avraham)* and on behalf of the Torah that was given to the seed of Abraham *(Avraham)* at mount Sinai. Even though the seed of Abraham *(Avraham)* was unfaithful to their marriage contract (obedience to the Torah) and broke it, the G-d of Israel promised that His mercy would be extended to the seed of David. This was done so that the covenant that the G-d of Israel made with Abraham *(Avraham)* would be fulfilled through the redemptive work of the Jewish Messiah *(Mashiach) Yeshua*/Jesus who would be born of the seed of David. In Psalm *(Tehillim)* 89:20, 24, 28-36 it is written:

> *"I have found David my servant; with my holy oil have I anointed him ... But my faithfulness and* **my mercy shall be with him:** *and in my name shall his horn be exalted ... My mercy will I keep for him forevermore, and my covenant shall stand fast with him. His seed also will I make to endure forever, and his throne as the days of heaven. If his children forsake my law* [TORAH], *and walk not in my judgments; If they break my statutes, and keep not my commandments; Then will I visit*

> *their transgression with the rod, and their iniquity with stripes. Nevertheless my lovingkindness will I not utterly take from him, nor suffer my faithfulness to fail. My covenant will I not break, nor alter the thing that is gone out of my lips. Once have I sworn by my holiness that I will not lie unto David. His seed shall endure forever, and his throne as the sun before me."*

David reminded the seed of Abraham (*Avraham*) to **ALWAYS** remember the covenant that the G-d of Israel made with Abraham (*Avraham*). In I Chronicles 16:13-18 it is written:

> *"O ye seed of Israel his servant, ye children of Jacob, his chosen ones. He is the L*ORD *our God; his judgments are in all the earth. Be ye* **mindful always of his covenant;** *the word which he commanded to a thousand generations; Even of* **the covenant** *which he* **made with Abraham,** *and of his oath unto Isaac; And has confirmed the same to Jacob for a law, and to Israel for an* **EVERLASTING covenant***, Saying, Unto thee will I give the land of Canaan, the lot of your inheritance."*

Therefore, the G-d of Israel extended His mercy to the seed of David so that He could fulfill the covenant that He made with Abraham *(Avraham)* through the redemptive work of the Jewish Messiah *(Mashiach) Yeshua*/Jesus who was born of the seed of David. (Hebrews 7:14, Revelation 5:5)

The Reign of Solomon

Following the reign of David, Solomon *(Shlomo)* was

Ephraim and Judah Become One House

made king over Israel. Solomon *(Shlomo)* is widely believed to be one of the wisest persons who ever lived. Solomon *(Shlomo)* wrote the wisdom of the Proverbs *(Mishlei)*. Why was Solomon so wise? The wisdom and understanding that the G-d of Israel gave to rule the seed of Abraham *(Avraham)* through Solomon *(Shlomo)* was knowledge of how to rule them according to the Torah and keeping the commandments of the G-d of Israel.

The G-d of Israel appeared to Solomon *(Shlomo)* in a dream and asked Solomon *(Shlomo)* what He should give him. Solomon *(Shlomo)* responded by asking the G-d of Israel for wisdom to discern between good and bad (how to keep the Torah). In I Kings *(Melachim)* 3:9-12, 14 it is written:

> *"Give therefore thy servant an understanding heart to judge thy people, that I may discern between good and bad: for who is able to judge this thy so great a people? And the speech pleased the* Lord, *that Solomon had asked this thing. And God said unto him, Because thou hast asked this thing, and hast not asked for thyself long life; neither have not asked riches for thyself, nor hast asked the life of your enemies; but hast asked for yourself understanding to discern judgment; Behold, I have done according to thy words: lo, I have given you a wise and an understanding heart; so that there was none like thee before thee, neither after thee shall any arise like unto thee ... And if thou will walk in my ways, to keep my statutes and my commandments, as thy father David did walk, then I will lengthen thy days."*

Restoring the Two Houses of Israel

During the reign of Solomon *(Shlomo)*, the seed of Abraham *(Avraham)* enjoyed the greatest land area of its borders. The reign of Solomon *(Shlomo)* is a prophetic picture of the peace *(shalom)* that the nation of Israel will enjoy during the Messianic Age *(Athid Lavo)* when the Jewish Messiah *(Mashiach) Yeshua*/Jesus will be teaching the Torah to the nations from Jerusalem *(Yerushalayim)* (Isaiah *[Yeshayahu]* 2:2-3).

Solomon's Kingdom Is Divided

The G-d of Israel told Solomon *(Shlomo)* to keep His Torah, commandments and statutes. Failing to do so and following after other gods would result in the G-d of Israel dispersing the seed of Abraham *(Avraham)* into all the nations of the earth. In I Kings *(Melachim)* 9:1-9 it is written:

> *"And it came to pass, when Solomon had finished the building of the house of the* LORD*, and the king's house, and all Solomon's desire which he was pleased to do, That the* LORD *appeared to Solomon the second time, as he had appeared unto him at Gibeon. And the* LORD *said unto him ... if you will walk before me, as David thy father walked, in integrity of heart, and in uprightness, to do according to all that I have commanded thee, and will keep my statutes and my judgments: Then I will establish the throne of thy kingdom upon Israel forever, as I promised to David thy father, saying, There shall not fail thee a man upon the throne of Israel. But if ye shall at all turn from following me, ye or your children, and will not keep my commandments and my statutes which I*

Ephraim and Judah Become One House

> *have set before you, but go and serve other gods, and worship them: Then will I cut off Israel out of the land which I have given them; and this house, which I have hallowed for my name, will I cast out of my sight; and Israel shall be a proverb and a byword among all people:* [being scattered among the nations — Deuteronomy 28:37] *And at this house, which is high, every one that passes by it shall be astonished, and shall hiss; and they shall say, Why hath the LORD done thus unto this land, and to this house? And they shall answer, Because they forsook the LORD their God, who brought forth their fathers out of the land of Egypt, and have taken hold upon other gods, and have worshiped them, and served them: therefore has the LORD brought upon them all this evil."*

Solomon *(Shlomo)* disobeyed the G-d of Israel and His Torah by marrying the women of the nations who dwelt in the land of Canaan. The G-d of Israel warned His people in the Torah not to marry the women of the nations who dwelt in Canaan (Deuteronomy *[Devarim]* 7:1-4).

Because the G-d of Israel appeared to Solomon *(Shlomo)* twice and instructed him not to marry foreign women, the G-d of Israel became angry at Solomon *(Shlomo)* for his disobedience and told him that his kingdom would be divided. In I Kings *(Melachim)* 11:9-13 it is written:

> *"And the LORD was angry with Solomon, because his heart was turned from the LORD God of Israel, which had appeared unto him twice, And had commanded him concerning this thing, that he should*

> not go after other gods: but he kept not that which the LORD commanded. Wherefore the LORD said unto Solomon, Forasmuch as this is done of thee, and thou hast not kept my covenant and my statutes, which I have commanded thee, I will surely rend the kingdom from thee, and will give it to your servant. Notwithstanding in thy days I will not do it for David thy father's sake: but I will rend it out of the hand of thy son. Howbeit I will not rend away all the kingdom; but will give one tribe to thy son for David my servant's sake, and for Jerusalem's sake which I have chosen."

Solomon's kingdom was divided into Northern Kingdom and Southern Kingdom. The Northern Kingdom was called the *house of Israel*. The Northern Kingdom is a prophetic type of future Christianity. The Southern Kingdom was called the *house of Judah*. The Southern Kingdom is a prophetic type of future Judaism.

The Northern Kingdom of Israel

Following the death of Solomon *(Shlomo)*, his kingdom was divided. Jeroboam, an Ephrathite became the ruler of the Northern Kingdom of Israel. Rehoboam became the ruler of the Southern Kingdom of Israel. Concerning the selection of Jeroboam as king of the Northern Kingdom, in I Kings *(Melachim)* 11:30-38 it is written:

> "And Ahijah caught the new garment that was on him, and rent it in twelve pieces: And he said to Jeroboam, Take thee ten pieces: for thus says the LORD, the God of Israel, Behold, I will rend the kingdom out of the hand of Solomon, and will give

Ephraim and Judah Become One House

ten tribes to thee: (But he shall have one tribe for my servant David's sake, and for Jerusalem sake, the city which I have chosen out of all the tribes of Israel:) Because that they have forsaken me, and have worshiped Ashtoreth the goddess of the Zidonians, Chemosh the god of the Moabites, and Milcom the god of the children of Ammon, and have not walked in my ways, to do that which is right in mine eyes, and to keep my statutes and my judgments, as did David his father. Howbeit I will not take the whole kingdom out of his hand: but I will make him prince all the days of his life for David my servant's sake, whom I chose, because he kept my commandments and my statutes: But I will take the kingdom out of his son's hand, and will give it unto thee, even ten tribes. And unto his son will I give one tribe, that David my servant may have a light always before me in Jerusalem, the city which I have chosen me to put my name there. And I will take thee, and thou shalt reign according to all that thy soul desires, and shall be king over Israel. And it shall be, if thou wilt hearken unto all that I command thee, and wilt walk in my ways, and do that is right in my sight, to keep my statutes and my commandments, as David my servant did, that I will be with thee, and build thee a sure house, as I built for David, and will give Israel unto thee."

Jeroboam Was an Ephrathite Over the House of Joseph

Jeroboam was an Ephrathite over the house of Joseph. In I Kings *(Melachim)* 11:26, 28 it is written:

Restoring the Two Houses of Israel

"And Jeroboam the son of Nebat an **Ephrathite** *... and the man Jeroboam was a mighty man of valor ... ruler over all the charge of the* **house of Joseph.***"*

The Northern Kingdom was known by the following names:

  1. The house of Israel (I Kings 12:21, Jeremiah 31:31)
  2. The house of Joseph (I Kings 11:28)
  3. Samaria (Hosea 7:1, 8:5-6, 13:16)
  4. Ephraim (Hosea 4:17, 5:3, 7:1)

The Golden Calf System of Worship

The Northern Kingdom of Israel practiced the "golden calf" system of worship of the G-d of Israel. This is mixing paganism with the true worship of the G-d of Israel and calling this mixed worship the true worship of the G-d of Israel. The "golden calf" system of worship of the G-d of Israel is first mentioned in Exodus *(Shemot)* 32. In Exodus *(Shemot)* 32:3-6 it is written:

> *"And all the people broke off the golden earrings which were in their ears, and brought them unto Aaron. And he received them at their hand, and fashioned it with a graving tool, after he had made it a molten calf: and they said,* **these be thy gods, O Israel***, which brought thee up out of the land of Egypt. And when Aaron saw it, he built an altar before it; and Aaron made proclamation, and said,* **tomorrow is a feast to the** Lord*. And they rose up early on the morrow, and offered burnt offerings, and brought peace offerings; and the people sat down to eat and to drink, and rose up to play."*

Ephraim and Judah Become One House

The Northern Kingdom, Ephraim, the house of Joseph, under the leadership of Jeroboam instituted a "golden calf" system of worship of the G-d of Israel. In I Kings *(Melachim)* 12:28-30 it is written:

> *"Whereupon the king took counsel, and* **made two calves of gold***, and said unto them, It is too much for you to go up to Jerusalem:* **behold thy gods, O Israel***, which brought thee up out of the land of Egypt. And he set the one in Bethel, and the other put he in Dan. And this thing became a sin: for the people went to worship before the one, even unto Dan."*

Bethel in Hebrew means, *"House of God."* Dan comes from the Hebrew word, *Din*, which means, *"Judgment."* Spiritually (*sod*/deeper meaning), this is prophetic that the people called the system of worship, *"The House of God"* but the G-d of Israel viewed the system of worship as *"Judgment."*

Jeroboam's False System of Worship

Jeroboam instituted a "golden calf" system of worship that mixed paganism with the worship of the G-d of Israel and called that system of worship, the true worship of the G-d of Israel. In doing this, the Northern Kingdom is prophetic of historical Christianity.

The Jewish Messiah *(Mashiach) Yeshua*/Jesus and his disciples *(talmidim)* were Torah observant Jews. The original followers of the Jewish Messiah *(Mashiach) Yeshua*/Jesus was considered a sect of Judaism (Acts 28:22-23) and kept the Sabbath *(Shabbat)* and Biblical

Restoring the Two Houses of Israel

Festivals found in Leviticus *(Vayikra)* 23 and worshiped in the Jewish synagogue. Later, the followers in *Yeshua/*Jesus as the Jewish Messiah *(Mashiach)* were called Christians at Antioch (Acts 11:26).

When Christianity spread into the Western world and more and more non-Jews and less and less Jews became believers in *Yeshua/*Jesus as the Jewish Messiah *(Mashiach)*, Christianity through the influence of the Roman Catholic church began to mix paganism (mostly the Mythraic religion of the Roman Empire which has its roots in ancient Babylon) with Biblical faith in the G-d of Israel. The modern day *house of Israel* (Christianity) is still influenced and still practices this mixture of paganism and the true worship of the G-d of Israel through the celebration of Christmas and Easter (rather than the Biblical holidays of Leviticus 23) and Sunday worship (rather than on the Biblical Sabbath from Friday sundown to Saturday sundown).

The predominant religion in the Roman Empire prior to the adoption of Christianity was Mythraism. Mythraism was focused on the worship of the sun god. The worship day of the sun god was Sun Day. The birthday of the sun god was December 25. Through the influence of the Roman Catholic church, the Biblical Sabbath was replaced with Sun Day. Rather than worshipping the birthday of the sun god on December 25, the birthday of the Jewish Messiah *(Mashiach)* *Yeshua/*Jesus began to be celebrated on December 25.

The origin of Easter was a pagan practice of celebrating the rebirth of the fertility of the earth in the spring of the year. Historically, Easter was the worship of the sex goddess Ishtar. In the Bible, Ishtar is called, Ashtaroth. The G-d of Israel condemned the seed of Abraham *(Avraham)* for worshiping the sex goddess Ashtaroth (I Kings 11:5, 33, II Kings 23:13). While the modern day *house of Israel* (Christianity) does not **literally** worship the sun god or the goddess of sex and fertility, it still practices the **customs** of this system of worship. However, all of these customs have been "Christianized" in their meaning and understanding by the adversary *(HaSatan)* to disguise the original practices and customs behind this system of worship.

The Characteristics of the Golden Calf System of Worship

The main characteristics of the Northern Kingdom's golden calf system of worship was the following:

1. Forsaking the Torah of the G-d of Israel
2. A substitute day of worship
3. A substitute place of worship
4. A substitute priesthood

Let us examine these characteristics in greater detail seeing how these sins of the Northern Kingdom are prophetic of the sins of historical Christianity.

1. Ephraim, a term for the Northern Kingdom of Israel, forsook the G-d of Israel's Torah and called it a strange thing (Hosea 8:12). Today, corporate Christianity calls the Torah *"a strange thing."*

2. Ephraim, the Northern Kingdom, instituted a substitute place of worship (Dan and Bethel)

rather than Jerusalem (I Kings *[Melachim]* 12:29, Deuteronomy *[Devarim]* 16:16). Corporate Christianity worships in a church rather than a synagogue where the Jewish Messiah *[Mashiach]* *Yeshua*/Jesus worshiped (Luke 4:14-16).

3. Ephraim, the Northern Kingdom, instituted substitute holidays rather than observing the dates and times of the Biblical holidays that the G-d of Israel gave in Leviticus *(Vayikra)* 23. Jeroboam changed the observance of the feast of tabernacles *(Sukkot)* to the eighth month in the year (I Kings *[Melechim]* 12:32-33) rather than the seventh month which the G-d of Israel had declared in Leviticus *[Vayikra]* 23:34. Historical Christianity has adopted Christmas and Easter from Roman Mythraism rather than keeping the Biblical holidays that the G-d of Israel gave in Leviticus *[Vayikra]* 23. The Jewish Messiah *(Mashiach) Yeshua*/Jesus kept the Biblical holidays (Luke 2:41-42).

4. Ephraim, the Northern Kingdom, instituted a substitute priesthood rather than have priests from the tribe of Levi (I Kings *[Melachim]* 12:31). Christianity allows pastors and priests to be ministers of the sheep of the G-d of Israel who are not anointed and called by the G-d of Israel into their office and ministry.

5. Ephraim, the Northern Kingdom, mixed paganism with the true worship of the G-d of Israel and called this mixture the true worship of the G-d of Israel. The G-d of Israel called this a golden

Ephraim and Judah Become One House

calf system of worship (I Kings *[Melachim]* 12:28). Historical Christianity has mixed Roman and Babylonian practices and beliefs with the worship of the G-d of Israel and calls this the true worship of the G-d of Israel.

G-d's Judgment Upon His People For Forsaking His Torah

When the G-d of Israel betrothed Himself to the seed of Abraham *(Avraham)* at mount Sinai (Jeremiah *[Yermiyahu]* 2:1-3), He entered into a marriage contract with them. The terms and conditions of a Biblical marriage contract are specified in a written document called a *Ketubah*. Spiritually (*sod*/deeper meaning), the Torah is the marriage contract between the G-d of Israel and the seed of Abraham *(Avraham)*. The terms and conditions for breaking the marriage contract are given in Leviticus *(Vayikra)* 26 and Deuteronomy *(Devarim)* 28. One of the harshest judgments for breaking the marriage contract (obedience to the Torah) is dispersion into the nations of the world. In Deuteronomy *(Devarim)* 28:15, 36-37 it is written:

> *"But it shall come to pass, if thou wilt not hearken unto the voice of the* Lord *thy God, to observe to do all his commandments and his statutes which I command thee this day; that all these curses shall come upon thee, and overtake thee ... The* Lord *shall bring thee, and thy king thou shalt set over thee, unto a nation which neither thou nor thy fathers have known; and there shalt thou serve other gods, wood and stone. And thou shalt become an aston-*

ishment, a proverb, and a byword, among all the nations whither the LORD shall lead thee."

Because of disobedience to the marriage contract (obedience to Torah) at mount Sinai, the G-d of Israel's judgment came upon both the Northern and Southern Kingdoms of Israel. Initially, the Northern Kingdom of Israel was taken captive into Assyria and the Southern Kingdom of Israel was taken captive into Babylon. Eventually, the Northern Kingdom and the Southern Kingdom were taken into worldwide captivity. The Northern Kingdom of Israel went into worldwide captivity through assimilation into Gentile culture and eventually settled in all the nations of the world. The Southern Kingdom of Israel was taken into worldwide captivity following the destruction of the Temple *(Beit HaMikdash)* in 70 C.E. (Common Era) but have kept their Jewish identity and allegiance to the Torah of the G-d of Israel during this time.

The Northern Kingdom Was Taken Captive into Assyria

Because they broke their marriage contract (obedience to the Torah) through their "golden calf" system of worship, the G-d of Israel's judgment came upon the Northern Kingdom of Israel, Ephraim, the house of Joseph. In II Kings *(Melachim)* 17:7-23 it is written:

> *"For so it was, that the children of Israel had sinned against the* LORD *their God, which had brought them up out of the land of Egypt, from under the hand of Pharaoh king of Egypt, and had feared other gods, And walked in the statutes of the*

Ephraim and Judah Become One House

*heathen, whom the L*ORD *cast out from before the children of Israel, and of the kings of Israel, which they had made. And the children of Israel did secretly those things that were not right against the L*ORD *their God, and they built them high places in all their cities, from the tower of the watchmen to the fenced city. And they set them up images and groves in every high hill, and under every green tree: And there they burnt incense in all the high places, as did the heathen whom the L*ORD *carried away before them; and wrought wicked things to provoke the L*ORD *to anger: For they served idols, whereof the L*ORD *had said unto them, You shall not do this thing. Yet the L*ORD *testified against Israel, and against Judah, by all the prophets and by all the seers, saying, Turn you from your evil ways, and keep my commandments and my statutes, according to all the law* [Torah] *which I commanded your fathers, and which I sent to you by my servants the prophets. Notwithstanding they would not hear, but hardened their necks, like to the neck of their fathers, that did not believe in the L*ORD *their God. And they rejected his statutes, and his covenant that he made with their fathers, and his testimonies which he testified against them; and they followed vanity, and became vain and went after the heathen that were round about them, concerning whom the L*ORD *had charged them, that they should not do like them. And they left all the commandments of the L*ORD *their God, and made them molten images, even two calves, and made a grove, and worshiped all the host of heaven, and served Baal. And they caused their sons and their daughters to pass through the fire,* *and used divination and enchantments, and sold themselves to do evil in the sight of the* L%%ORD%%, *to provoke him to anger. Therefore the* L%%ORD%% *was very angry with Israel, and removed them out of his sight: there was none left but the tribe of Judah only. Also Judah kept not the commandments of the* L%%ORD%% *their God, but walked in the statutes of Israel which they made. And the* L%%ORD%% *rejected all the seed of Israel, and afflicted them, and delivered them into the hand of spoilers, until he had cast them out of his sight. For he rent Israel from the house of David; and they made Jeroboam the son of Nebat king: and Jeroboam drove Israel from following the* L%%ORD%%*, and made them sin a great sin. For the children of Israel walked in all the sins of Jeroboam which he did; they departed not from them; Until the* L%%ORD%% *removed Israel out of his sight, as he had said by all his servants the prophets. So was Israel carried away out of their own land to Assyria unto this day."*

The Southern Kingdom Is Taken Captive into Babylon

The Southern Kingdom also departed from the marriage contract (obedience to the Torah) of the G-d of Israel. Therefore, the Southern Kingdom, the *house of Judah*, was taken captive into Babylon. The rejection of following the Torah of the G-d of Israel is given in II Kings *(Melachim)* 17:19-20 as it is written:

> *"And* **Judah** *kept not the commandments of the* L%%ORD%% *their God, but walked in the statutes of Israel which they made. And the* L%%ORD%% *rejected all the*

Ephraim and Judah Become One House

seed of Israel, and afflicted them, and delivered them into the hand of spoilers, until he had cast them out of his sight."

The G-d of Israel's anger upon the Southern Kingdom, the *house of Judah*, for forsaking the Torah of the G-d of Israel can be found in Jeremiah *(Yermiyahu)* 44:2-6, 10, 22-23 as it is written:

*"Thus says the L*ORD *of hosts, the God of Israel; You have seen all the evil that I have brought upon Jerusalem, and upon all the cities of Judah; and, behold, this day they are a desolation, and no man dwelleth therein, Because of their wickedness which they have committed to provoke me to anger, in that they went to burn incense, and to serve other gods, whom they knew not, neither they, ye, nor your fathers. Howbeit I sent unto you all my servants the prophets, rising early and sending them, saying, Oh, do not this abominable thing that I hate. But they hearkened not, nor inclined their ear to turn from their wickedness, to burn no incense unto other gods. Wherefore my fury and mine anger was poured forth, and was kindled in the cities of Judah and in the streets of Jerusalem; and they are wasted and desolate, as at this day ... They are not humbled even unto this day, neither have they feared, nor walked in my law* [TORAH], *nor in my statutes, that I set before you and before your fathers ... So that the L*ORD *could no longer bear, because of the evil of your doings, and because of the abominations which ye have committed; therefore is your land a desolation, and an astonishment, and a curse, without an inhabitant, as at*

> *this day. Because you have burned incense, and because you have sinned against the* LORD, *and have not obeyed the voice of the* LORD, *nor walked in his law* [TORAH], *nor in his statutes, nor in his testimonies; therefore this evil is happened unto you, as at this day."*

Because the Southern Kingdom, the *house of Judah*, broke their marriage contract (obedience to the Torah), they were taken captive to Babylon. In Jeremiah (*Yermiyahu*) 25:2-10 it is written:

> *"The which Jeremiah the prophet spake unto all the people of Judah, and to all the inhabitants of Jerusalem, saying ... the word of the* LORD *has come unto me, and I have spoken unto you, rising early and speaking; but you have not hearkened. And the* LORD *has sent unto you all his servants the prophets, rising early and sending them; but you have not hearkened, nor inclined your ears to hear. They said, Turn you again now everyone from his evil ways, and from the evil of your doings, and dwell in the land that the* LORD *has given unto you and to your fathers forever and ever: And go not after other gods to serve them, and to worship them, and provoke me not to anger with the works of your hands; and I will do you no hurt. Yet you have not hearkened unto me, says the* LORD; *that you might provoke me to anger with the works of your hands to your own hurt. Therefore thus says the* LORD *of hosts; Because you have not heard my words, Behold, I will send and take all the families of the north, saith the* LORD, *and Nebuchadnezzar the king of Babylon, my servant, and will bring*

Ephraim and Judah Become One House

> *them against this land, and against the inhabitants thereof, and against all these nations round about, and will utterly destroy them, and make them an astonishment, and a hissing, and perpetual desolations. Moreover I will take from them the voice of mirth, and the voice of gladness, the voice of the bridegroom, and the voice of the bride, the sound of the millstones, and the light of the candle."*

Therefore, we can see that the G-d of Israel judged both the Northern Kingdom and the Southern Kingdom **because** they did **NOT** follow **His Torah** and the **covenant** that He made with **Abraham**.

G-d's Judgment Upon the Northern Kingdom of Israel

The book of Hosea was written to prophesy of the judgment of the Northern Kingdom for breaking their marriage contract (obedience to the Torah) and mixing paganism with the worship of the G-d of Israel. The Northern Kingdom of Israel desired to assimilate with the nations around them. At mount Sinai, the G-d of Israel instructed the seed of Abraham *(Avraham)* in their marriage contract that they were to be a holy people (separate from the nations around them). They were not to assimilate themselves with other nations and follow after their ways. Because the Northern Kingdom of Israel desired to assimilate with the other nations, their judgment for breaking their marriage contract (to not assimilate) was assimilation into the nations of the world. In other words, what they sowed, they reaped.

Restoring the Two Houses of Israel

In order to prophesy of this judgment of assimilation, the G-d of Israel instructed Hosea to marry a whore named Gomer. The children born in the marriage between Hosea and Gomer were prophetic of what would happen to the Northern Kingdom because they committed spiritual whoredom with the nations around them and followed after their gods and their ways. Whoredom in the Bible is symbolic of spiritual idolatry and forsaking the Torah and the true worship of the G-d of Israel. In Deuteronomy *(Devarim)* 31:16 it is written:

> *"And the* LORD *said unto Moses, Behold, thou shall sleep with thy fathers; and this people will rise up, and go a whoring after the gods of the strangers of the land, whither they go to be among them, and will forsake me, and break my covenant which I have made with them."*

In Judges *(Shoftim)* 2:17 it is written:

> *"And yet they would not hearken unto their judges, but they went a whoring after other gods, and bowed themselves unto them: they turned quickly out of the way which their fathers walked in, obeying the commandments of the* LORD*; but they did not so."*

Therefore, in order to symbolize this spiritual whoredom committed by the Northern Kingdom of Israel for forsaking the Torah and breaking their marriage contract, the G-d of Israel told Hosea to marry a whore. From this marriage, three children were conceived. In Hosea *(Hoshea)* 1:2-9 it is written:

Ephraim and Judah Become One House

"The beginning of the word of the Lord *by Hosea. And the* Lord *said to Hosea, Go, take unto thee a wife of whoredoms and children of whoredoms: for the land has committed great whoredom, departing from the* Lord*. So he went and took Gomer the daughter of Diblaim; which conceived, and bare him a son. And the* Lord *said unto him, Call his name Jezreel; for yet a little while, and I will avenge the blood of Jezreel upon the house of Jehu, and will cause to cease the kingdom of the house of Israel. And it shall come to pass at that day, that I will break the bow of Israel in the valley of Jezreel. And she conceived again, and bare a daughter. And God said unto him, Call her name Lo-ruhamah: for I will no more have mercy upon the house of Israel; but I will utterly take them away. But I will have mercy upon the house of Judah, and will save them by the* Lord *their God, and will not save them by bow, nor by sword, nor by battle, by horses, nor by horsemen. Now when she had weaned Lo-ruhamah, she conceived, and bare a son. Then said God, Call his name Lo-ammi: for ye are not my people, and I will not be your God."*

The three children that Hosea had by Gomer in Hosea chapter 1 were the following:

1. *Jezreel,* which means "G-d will sow or scatter."
2. *Lo-ruhamah,* which means "no mercy."
3. *Lo-ammi,* which means "not my people."

When the G-d of Israel speaks to the Northern Kingdom saying to them that He will have "no mercy" and they are "not my people", this is the Biblical way of saying that the G-d of Israel will cut off his covenant relationship with them and divorce the Northern Kingdom of Israel. In Jeremiah *(Yermiyahu)* 3:8 it is written:

> *"And I saw, when for all the causes whereby* **backsliding Israel** [Northern Kingdom] **committed adultery** *I had put her away, and given her a* **bill of divorce** ..."

G-d Promises to Fulfill His Covenant with Abraham

Even though the G-d of Israel divorced the Northern Kingdom *(house of Israel)*, He also promised that when this judgment is complete that He would fulfill His covenant with Abraham *(Avraham)* through this judgment. Furthermore, even though the G-d of Israel told the Northern Kingdom *(house of Israel)* that they were "not His people" (Hosea *[Hoshea]* 1:9) and He would show them "no mercy" (Hosea *[Hoshea]* 1:6), He also prophesied that the future descendents of the Northern Kingdom *(house of Israel)* would later be called "my people" after the G-d of Israel showed "mercy" toward them through the Jewish Messiah *(Mashiach) Yeshua*/Jesus. In Hosea *(Hoshea)* 1:10 it is written:

> *"Yet the number of the children of Israel shall be as the sand of the sea, which cannot be measured nor numbered; and it shall come to pass, that in the place where it was said unto them, You are not my people, there it shall be said unto them, You are the sons of the living God."*

Ephraim and Judah Become One House

WOW! After declaring to the Northern Kingdom that they were "not his people" (Hosea *[Hoshea]* 1:9) and they would be showed "no mercy" (Hosea *[Hoshea]* 1:6) because they broke their marriage contract and forsook His Torah, the G-d of Israel prophesied that He will fulfill His covenant that He made with Abraham *(Avraham)* through this judgment (Hosea *[Hoshea]* 1:10) !!!

The Northern Kingdom Is Prophetic of Christianity

In the book of Hosea, the G-d of Israel's judgment upon the Northern Kingdom for breaking their marriage contract and forsaking the Torah was divorce and cutting them off from His covenant. In doing so, the G-d of Israel would show them "no mercy" and they would be "not my people." These are the **EXACT** words used to describe the non-Jews who have accepted *Yeshua*/Jesus as the Jewish Messiah *(Mashiach)*. In I Peter *(Kefa)* 2:5, 9-10 it is written:

> *"You also, as lively stones, are built up a spiritual house, a holy priesthood, to offer up spiritual sacrifices, acceptable to God by Jesus Christ* [Yeshua HaMashiach] *... But you are a chosen generation, a royal priesthood, a holy nation, a peculiar people; that you should show forth the praises of him who has called you out of darkness into his marvelous light: Which is time past were not a people* [Hosea 1:9] *but are now the people of God* [Hosea 1:10]; *which had not obtained mercy,* [Hosea 1:6], *but now have obtained mercy* [Hosea 2:23]"

Restoring the Two Houses of Israel

The Role of the Kinsman Redeemer to Save G-d's People

The G-d of Israel made a provision in the Torah that a near kinsman could redeem his brother's possession if it was sold away. When the Northern Kingdom *(house of Israel)* was at mount Sinai and entered into a marriage contract with the G-d of Israel, they were entitled to an inheritance by being a member of the family of the G-d of Israel. When the G-d of Israel divorced the Northern Kingdom *(house of Israel)*, their inheritance was lost because they "sold it away" when they committed idolatry against the G-d of Israel. However, in Leviticus *(Vayikra)* 25:25, it is written:

> *"If thy brother be waxen poor, and has sold away some of his possession, and if any of his kin come to redeem it, then shall he redeem that which his brother sold."*

Therefore, the G-d of Israel made provision in the Torah that one of his brothers (a member of the Southern Kingdom, the *house of Judah*, the Jewish people) could redeem those from the Northern Kingdom *(house of Israel)* who "sold away" their inheritance. For this reason, the Jewish Messiah *(Mashiach)* Yeshua/Jesus was born from the tribe of Judah to be a kinsman redeemer *(go'el)* to the descendents of the Northern Kingdom *(house of Israel)* as well as all those who would repent *(teshuvah)* of their sins and accept *Yeshua*/Jesus as their personal Messiah *(Mashiach)*.

In order for the descendents of the Northern Kingdom *(house of Israel)* to become members again of the

Ephraim and Judah Become One House

family of the G-d of Israel, they needed to be **grafted** into the olive tree of the G-d of Israel. In doing this, the G-d of Israel would (renew) the original covenant (marriage contract) at mount Sinai because the original covenant (marriage contract) was broken. This (renewed) covenant would be the original covenant written upon the hearts of all those who would accept the Jewish Messiah *(Mashiach) Yeshua*/Jesus through the indwelling Holy Spirit *(Ruach HaKodesh)*. The role of the indwelling Holy Spirit *(Ruach HaKodesh)* is to write the Torah of the G-d of Israel upon the hearts of His people so that they could worship the G-d of Israel in Spirit and in truth. (Jeremiah *[Yermiyahu]* 31:31-33, John *(Yochanan)* 4:24, 16:13, Hebrews 10:15-16).

In Jeremiah *(Yermiyahu)* 31:31, the Hebrew word translated into English as "new" can mean RENEW. In Jeremiah *(Yermiyahu)* 31:31-33 it is written:

> *"Behold, the days come, saith the* LORD, *that I will make a new* [renewed] *covenant with the house of Israel and with the house of Judah: Not according to the covenant that I made with their fathers in the day that I took them by the hand to bring them out of the land of Egypt; which my covenant they broke, although I was a husband unto them, saith the* LORD: *But this shall be the covenant that I will make with the house of Israel; After those days, says the* LORD, *I will put my law* [TORAH] *in their inward parts, and write it in their hearts; and will be their God, and they shall be my people."*

The Jewish Messiah *(Mashiach) Yeshua*/Jesus is to be a kinsman redeemer *(go'el)* to His people. By being a kinsman redeemer, He would bring restoration to both houses of Israel. He would do this by being a suffering Messiah known as *Messiah ben Yosef*/Joseph at His first coming and by being the Kingly Messiah known as *Messiah ben David* at His second coming. By the Jewish Messiah *(Mashiach) Yeshua*/Jesus being a kinsman redeemer *(go'el)* to His people, the G-d of Israel could fulfill the covenant that He made with Abraham *(Avraham)*.

In His role as the Kingly Messiah *(Mashiach)* known as *Messiah ben David* through the outpouring of the Holy Spirit *(Ruach HaKodesh)*, the G-d of Israel would redeem and restore both houses of Israel and gather them from all the nations and bring them back to the land of Israel in the end of days at the advent of the Messianic Age *(Athid Lavo)*. (Isaiah *[Yeshayahu]* 49:5-6, Ezekiel *(Yechezekel)* 36:24-28, 37:15-28, Acts 1:6-8).

The Role of the Messiah to Fulfill God's Covenant with Abraham

The Jewish Messiah *(Mashiach) Yeshua*/Jesus came from the tribe of Judah to play the role of the kinsman redeemer *(go'el)* in order to fulfill G-d's promise to Abraham *(Avraham)* through His mercy to David and his seed (Romans 1:3, Hebrews 7:14, Revelation 5:5).

The Jewish Messiah *(Mashiach) Yeshua*/Jesus came to reign over the house of Jacob forever. The house of Jacob refers to a united Northern Kingdom (the *house of Israel, Ephraim, the house of Joseph*/Christianity) AND the Southern Kingdom (the *house of Judah*/Judaism). In Luke 1:31-33 it is written:

> *"And, behold, thou shalt conceive in thy womb, and bring forth a son, and shalt call his name JESUS*

Ephraim and Judah Become One House

[YESHUA]. *He shall be great, and shall be called the Son of the Highest: and the* LORD *God shall give unto him the throne of his father David: And* **he shall reign over the house of Jacob forever:** *and of his kingdom there shall be no end."*

In Luke 1:67-73, Zacharias prophesied by the Holy Spirit *(Ruach HaKodesh)* that the G-d of Israel would redeem His people by bringing a deliverer *(go'el)* from the house of David to fulfill His covenant with Abraham *(Avraham)* as it is written:

"And his father Zacharias, was filled with the Holy Spirit, and prophesied, saying, Blessed be the LORD *God of Israel; for he hath visited and redeemed his people, And hath raised up a horn of salvation for us in the house of his servant David; As he spake by the mouth of his holy prophets, which have been since the world began: That we should be saved from our enemies, and from the hand of all that hate us; To perform the mercy promised to our fathers, and to remember his holy covenant; The oath which he sware to our father Abraham."*

Through the words given to him by the Holy Spirit *(Ruach HaKodesh)*, Zacharias is relating how the redemptive plan of the G-d of Israel would be accomplished by the Jewish Messiah *(Mashiach) Yeshua*/Jesus being a kinsman redeemer *(go'el)* to His people through the mercy that He promised David to fulfill the covenant that He made with Abraham *(Avraham)*. When this redemption is complete, the Jewish Messiah *(Mashiach) Yeshua*/Jesus will rule over a united Israel, the **house of Jacob**, forever (Luke 1:31-33).

Restoring the Two Houses of Israel

The Role of the Messiah as Messiah Ben David

The Jewish Messiah *(Mashiach) Yeshua*/Jesus is likened unto David. One of the titles of the Jewish Messiah *(Mashiach)* is *Messiah ben David*. How is the Jewish Messiah *(Mashiach) Yeshua*/Jesus associated with David? Let us examine how this is so.

1. David was from Bethlehem in the land of Judah (I Samuel *[Sh'muel]* 17:12).
    a) Bethlehem is called the city of David (Luke 2:4).
    b) *Yeshua* was born in Bethlehem (Matthew 2:1).

2. G-d called David, "*His Son*" (II Samuel 7:14).
    a) *Yeshua* is called G-d's son (Matthew 3:16-17).

3. *Yeshua* is called the "*Son of David*" (Luke 18:38-39).

4. G-d promised David that his throne would be forever (Psalm *[Tehillim]* 89:3-4).
    a) *Yeshua*/Jesus came to sit on the throne of David (Luke 1:31-32).

5. David desired to build a house for the name of G-d (I Chronicles 28:2).
    a) *Yeshua*/Jesus was faithful to build the house of G-d (Hebrews 3:4-6).

6. G-d made a covenant of mercy with David (Psalm *(Tehillim)* 89:1-3, 31-34).
    a) *Yeshua*/Jesus extends mercy upon all those who believe on His name (Luke 18:38-39).

Ephraim and Judah Become One House

7. David went from being a shepherd to a king (II Samuel *[Sh'muel]* 7:8).
    a) *Yeshua*/Jesus came at His first coming as a shepherd (John *[Yochanan]* 10:11)
    b) *Yeshua*/Jesus will come during His second coming as a King (Zechariah *[Zecharyah]* 14:4, 9)

8. a) *Yeshua* has the key of David (Revelation 3:7).
    b) *Yeshua* is the root and offspring of David (Revelation 22:16).

The Fullness of G-d's Covenant with Abraham

The fullness of the covenant that the G-d of Israel made with Abraham *(Avraham)* has not yet been fulfilled. Let's reexamine several scriptures again so that we can understand the fullness of the covenant that the G-d of Israel made with Abraham *(Avraham)*. In Genesis *(Bereishit)* 17:7-8 it is written:

> *"And I will establish my covenant between me and thee and thy seed after thee in their generations for an* **everlasting covenant**, *to be a God unto thee, and to thy seed after thee. And I will give unto thee, and to thy seed after thee, the land wherein you are a stranger,* **ALL** *the land of Canaan, for an* **everlasting possession;** *and I will be their God."*

While the covenant is unconditional and everlasting, the fulfillment of the covenant is conditional upon the family of the G-d of Israel being obedient to His Torah, commandments and statutes.

Restoring the Two Houses of Israel

In Leviticus *(Vayikra)* 26:3, 11-12 it is written:

> "**IF** *you walk in my statutes, and keep my commandments, and do them ... And I will set my tabernacle among you: and my soul shall not abhor you. And I will walk among you, and will be your God, and you shall be my people.*"

The fullness of the G-d of Israel's covenant with Abraham *(Avraham)* consists of the following:

1. The family of the G-d of Israel keeping His Torah (because it is written upon their heart).

2. The family of the G-d of Israel living in the land of Israel (after being scattered in the nations of the earth).

3. The G-d of Israel setting up His tabernacle and dwelling with His people (through the Jewish Messiah *(Mashiach)* during the Messianic Age).

The Role of the Messiah to Unite Both Houses of Israel

Two primary functions of the Jewish Messiah *(Mashiach)* is to bring salvation to the Gentiles (non-Jews who would be **grafted** into the olive tree of the G-d of Israel) and to gather **both** houses of Israel, the Northern Kingdom (*house of Israel* / Christianity) and the Southern Kingdom (*house of Judah*/Judaism) back to the land of Israel in the end of days. These two things can be seen in Isaiah *(Yeshayahu)* 49:5-6 as it is written:

Ephraim and Judah Become One House

*"And now, saith the L*ORD *that formed me from the womb to be his servant, to bring Jacob* [all twelve tribes] *again to him, Though Israel be not gathered, yet shall I be glorious in the eyes of the L*ORD*, and my God shall be my strength. And he said, It is a light thing that thou shouldest be my servant to raise up the tribes of Jacob, and to restore the preserved of Israel: I will also give thee for a light to the Gentiles, that thou mayest be my salvation unto the end of the earth."*

During the first coming of the Jewish Messiah (*Mashiach*) *Yeshua* / Jesus as the suffering Messiah known as *Messiah ben Yosef*/Joseph, He brought salvation to the Gentiles (non-Jews who would be **grafted** into the olive tree of the G-d of Israel). During the second coming of the Jewish Messiah (*Mashiach*) *Yeshua*/Jesus as the Kingly Messiah known as *Messiah ben David*, He will restore the preserved (remnant) from **both** houses of Israel and bring them back to the land of Israel through the outpouring of the G-d of Israel's Holy Spirit (*Ruach HaKodesh*).

The Gathering of the Exiles Back to the Land of Israel

In Acts 1:6-8, the disciples *(talmidim)* asked the Jewish Messiah *(Mashiach) Yeshua*/Jesus if He was going to "restore the kingdom to Israel" (redeem, restore and gather all twelve tribes from exile and bring them back to the land of Israel) during His first coming as the suffering Messiah known as *Messiah ben Yosef*/Joseph. The Jewish Messiah *(Mashiach) Yeshua*/Jesus answered by saying that this event would happen through the outpouring of the Holy Spirit *(Ruach HaKodesh)* upon those who would be witnesses of this restoration at a later time. In Acts 1:6-9 it is written:

> *"When they therefore were come together, they asked of him, saying,* LORD, *will thou* **at this time** *restore again the kingdom to Israel? And he said unto them, It is not for you to know the times or the seasons, which the Father has put in his own power. But ye shall* **receive power** *after that the* **Holy Ghost [Ruach HaKadesh]** *is come upon you: and ye shall be* **witnesses** *[of the restoration of all twelve tribes back to the land of Israel] unto me both in Jerusalem, and in all Judea, and in Samaria, and unto the uttermost part of the earth. And when he had spoken these things, while they beheld, he was taken up; and a cloud received him out of their sight."*

From a Jewish *(house of Judah)* perspective, the very last words of a person can be prophetic and very significant. For example, Jacob *(Ya'acov)* blessed his twelve sons and told them their prophetic destiny on his deathbed (Genesis *[Bereishit]* 49). Therefore, the last words of the Jewish Messiah *(Mashiach) Yeshua*/Jesus before He ascended into the heavenlies are **very** significant. **THE EVENT** which He reminded His followers to understand is the restoration and gathering of the exiles from **both** the Northern Kingdom *(house of Israel/*Christianity) and the Southern Kingdom *(house of Judah/*Judaism) back to the land of Israel from all the nations of the world through the outpouring of the G-d of Israel's Holy Spirit *(Ruach HaKodesh)*. This event is associated to His second coming as the Kingly Messiah *(Mashiach)*

Ephraim and Judah Become One House

known as *Messiah ben David*. This is the fulfillment of the prophecy in Ezekiel *[Yechezekel]* 37:15-28).

Ephraim (Christianity) and Judah (Judaism) Become One House

In Ezekiel *(Yechezekel)* 37:15-27, the G-d of Israel promised that He would unite the two houses of Israel, Ephraim (*house of Israel* / Christianity) and Judah (*house of Judah*/Judaism), and bring them back to the land of Israel in the end of days. When they return to the land of Israel after being scattered in all the nations of the world, they will return in repentance *(teshuvah)* and keep the Torah of the G-d of Israel. After this event, the G-d of Israel promised to set up His tabernacle *(Mishkan)* and dwell with His people through His servant David (the Jewish Messiah *[Mashiach] Yeshua*/Jesus) and usher in the Messianic Age *(Athid Lavo)*. In Ezekiel *(Yechezekel)* 37:15-27 it is written:

> *"The word of the* Lord *came again unto me, saying, Moreover, thou son of man, take thee one stick, and write upon it, For Judah, and for the children of Israel his companions: then take another stick, and write upon it, For Joseph, the stick of Ephraim, and for all the house of Israel his companions: And join them one to another into one stick; and they shall become one in thine hand. And when the children of thy people shall speak unto thee, saying, Wilt thou not show us what thou meanest by these? Say unto them, Thus saith the* Lord *God; Behold, I will take the stick of Joseph* [CHRISTIANITY], *which is in the hand of Ephraim, and the tribes of Israel his fellows, and*

will put them with him, even with the stick of Judah [JUDAISM], *and make them one stick, and they shall be one in mine hand. And the sticks whereon thou writest shall be in thine hand before their eyes. And say unto them, Thus saith the* Lord *God; Behold, I will take the children of Israel from among the heathen, whither they be gone, and will gather them on every side, and bring them into their own land: And I will make them one nation in the land upon the* **mountains of Israel** [WEST BANK]; *and one king shall be king to them all: and they shall be no more two nations, neither shall they be divided into two kingdoms any more at all: Neither shall they defile themselves any more with their idols, nor with their detestable things, nor with any of their transgressions* [TESHUVAH]: *but I will save them out of all their dwelling places, wherein they have sinned, and will cleanse them: so shall they be my people, and I will be their God. And David my servant* [THE JEWISH MESSIAH] *shall be king over them; and they all shall have one shepherd: they shall also walk in my judgments, and observe my statutes, and do them. And they shall dwell in the land that I have given unto Jacob my servant, wherein your fathers have dwelt* [THE LAND OF ISRAEL]; *and they shall dwell therein, even they, and their children, and their children's children forever: and my servant David shall be their prince forever. Moreover I will make a covenant of peace with them; it shall be an everlasting covenant with them: and I will place them, and multiply them, and will set my sanctuary in the midst of them forevermore* [THE MESSIANIC AGE]. *My tab-*

Ephraim and Judah Become One House

ernacle also shall be with them: yea, I will be their God, and they shall be my people."

In Ezekiel *(Yechezekel)* 37:15-27, we see the fulfillment of the G-d of Israel's covenant with Abraham *(Avraham)* based upon the following:

1. The family of the G-d of Israel living in the land of Israel (after being scattered in all the nations of the earth) (Ezekiel *[Yechezekel]* 37:21-22, 25).
2. The family of the G-d of Israel (Christianity and Judaism) repenting *(teshuvah)* and keeping His Torah (because it is written upon their heart) (Ezekiel *[Yechezekel]* 37:23-24).
3. The G-d of Israel setting up His tabernacle *(mishkan)* so that He could dwell with His people (during the Messianic Age) (Ezekiel *[Yechezekel]* 37:23, 26-27).
4. The Kingly Messiah known as *Messiah ben David*, ruling over the family of the G-d of Israel *(Yeshua*/Jesus) (Ezekiel *[Yechezekel]* 37:22, 24).

Ephraim (Christianity): The Prodigal Son

In Luke 15:11-32, the Jewish Messiah *(Mashiach) Yeshua*/Jesus tells a parable about a prodigal son.

When the Jewish Messiah *(Mashiach) Yeshua*/Jesus came to the earth at His first coming as the suffering Messiah *(Mashiach)* known as *Messiah ben Yosef*/Joseph, the Northern *Kingdom (house of Israel)* had already been scattered and assimilated into the nations of the world for over 700 years because they had broken the marriage contract at mount Sinai and rebelled against the

Restoring the Two Houses of Israel

Torah of the G-d of Israel. The two sons in the parable refer to the two houses of Israel, the *house of Israel* (the Northern Kingdom) and the *house of Judah* (the Southern Kingdom). In Jeremiah *(Yermiyahu)* 31:20, Ephraim *(house of Israel)* is called a son of the G-d of Israel who has rebelled against the G-d of Israel and His Torah and has a desire to repent *(teshuvah)*. Therefore, Ephraim *(house of Israel)* is the prodigal son in the parable.

The Northern Kingdom, Ephraim/*house of Israel*, is also a spiritual picture of future Christianity. Following the death and resurrection of the Jewish Messiah *(Mashiach) Yeshua*/Jesus, the early believers in *Yeshua*/Jesus as the Jewish Messiah *(Mashiach)* were considered a sect of Judaism (Acts 28:22). At this time, they kept the Biblical Sabbath (from Friday sundown to Saturday sundown) and the Biblical festivals (Leviticus *[Vayikra]* 23.

As the body of believers in the Jewish Messiah *(Mashiach) Yeshua*/Jesus became more and more non-Jewish, some of the leaders of the movement became anti-Semitic and encouraged the people to not obey the Torah of the G-d of Israel. Eventually, this ushered in the dark ages and brought unfathomable hardship to the Jewish people *(house of Judah)*.

In modern days, more and more members of the *house of Israel*/Christianity are repenting *(teshuvah)* of the sins of their fathers and embracing the Hebraic/Jewish roots of their faith in Messiah. In doing so, there is an increased desire among a remnant in the *house of Israel*/Christianity to keep the Torah and the commandments of the G-d of Israel. The love of the Torah and keeping the commandments of the G-d of Israel is the

Ephraim and Judah Become One House

key of David. The Jewish Messiah *(Mashiach) Yeshua/* Jesus has the key of David (Revelation 3:7).

In Luke 15:11-32 is the parable of the prodigal son as it is written:

> *"And he said, A certain man had two sons: And the younger of them said to his father, Father, give me the portion of goods that falleth to me. And he divided unto them his living. And not many days after the younger son gathered all together, and took his journey into a far country, and there wasted his substance with riotous living. And when he had spent all, there arose a mighty famine in that land: and he began to be in want. And he went and joined himself to a citizen of that country; and he sent him into his fields to feed swine. And he would fain have filled his belly with the husks that the swine did eat: and no man gave unto him. And when he came to himself, he said, How many hired servants of my father's have bread enough and to spare, and I perish with hunger! I will arise and go to my father, and will say unto him, Father, I have sinned against heaven, and before thee, And am no more worthy to be called thy son: make me as one of thy hired servants. And he arose, and came to his father. But when he was yet a great way off, his father saw him, and had compassion, and ran, and fell on his neck, and kissed him. And the son said unto him, Father, I have sinned against heaven, and in thy sight, and am no more worthy to be called thy son. But the father said to his servants, Bring forth the best robe, and put it on him; and put a ring on his hand, and shoes on his feet: And bring hither the*

fatted calf, and kill it; and let us eat, and be merry: For this my son was dead, and is alive again; he was lost, and is found. And they began to be merry. Now his elder son was in the field: and as he came and drew nigh to the house, he heard music and dancing. And he called one of the servants, and asked what these things meant. And he said unto him, Thy brother is come: and thy father hath killed the fatted calf, because he hath received him safe and sound. And he was angry, and would not go in: therefore came his father out, and entreated him. And he answering said to his father, Lo, these many years do I serve thee, neither transgressed I at any time thy commandment: and yet thou never gavest me a kid, that I might make merry with my friends: But as soon as this thy son was come, which hath devoured thy living with harlots, thou hast killed for him the fatted calf. And he said unto him, Son, thou art ever with me, and all that I have is thine. It was meet that we should make merry, and be glad: for this thy brother was dead, and is alive again: and was lost and is found."

Let us examine the details of this parable closer so that we can understand how the prodigal son is a reference to Ephraim who is a spiritual picture of future Christianity.

1. A certain man (G-d the Father) had two sons (Luke 15:11).

2. The elder son is Judah (*house of Judah* /Judaism) and the younger son is Ephraim (*house of Israel*/ Christianity). Judaism dates back to the original

Ephraim and Judah Become One House

marriage contract given at mount Sinai. Christianity dates back to the (renewed) marriage contract (Jeremiah *[Yermiyahu]* 31:31-33, Hebrew 10:15-16) through the death and resurrection of *Yeshua*/Jesus.

3. The younger son (the Northern Kingdom, Ephraim/Christianity) spent his inheritance on riotous living (by departing from the Torah of the G-d of Israel) and went to a far country (the nations of the world) and was feeding on swine (a reference to not obeying the Torah) (Luke 15:12-15).

4. There was a famine in the land (a famine of the hearing and teaching G-d's Torah/Word — Amos 8:11) and he (younger son/Ephraim/Christianity) decided to return to his Father and repent before Him (for departing from Torah) (Luke 15:14-21).

5. The Father was waiting for his younger son (Ephraim/Christianity) to return to Torah. When he repented, G-d the Father extended mercy to Him (Jeremiah *[Yermiyahu]* 31:18-20) (because of G-d's promise to David) and forgave him (Luke 15:21-24).

6. The joy of the Father was so great when the younger son (Ephraim/Christianity) returned (back to Torah) that the Father (the G-d of Israel) decided to fit him with the best robe (wedding garment) and put a ring on his hand (wedding terminology) (Jeremiah *[Yermiyahu]* 31:18-22,

Luke 15:21-24) which is a reference to the Messianic Age *[Athid Lavo]*.

7. The elder son (Judah/Judaism) was in the field and inquired about the celebration that the father was giving the younger son (Luke 15:25-26).

8. It was told to the elder son (Judah/Judaism) that the younger son (Ephraim/Christianity) had repented (returned to Torah) and the Father was waiting for the younger son's (Ephraim/Christianity) return and now that he has returned, there will be a wedding party (the advent of the Messianic Age/*Athid Lavo*) (Luke 15:27).

9. The older son (Judah/Judaism) was upset because he told his Father that he had never departed from the commandments (Torah) and the Father never had a wedding party (ushered in the Messianic Age/*Athid Lavo*) for him. But now after the younger son (Ephraim/Christianity) had departed from Torah and repented, the Father was having a wedding party (usher in the Messianic Age/*Athid Lavo*) for the younger son. (Luke 15:28-30).

10. It was told the older son (Judah/Judaism) that he was forever with the Father (Luke 15:31-32).

Therefore, when the prodigal son (Ephraim/*house of Israel*/Christianity) repents *(teshuvah)* for departing from the Torah of the G-d of Israel, the G-d of Israel will celebrate with the greatest family reunion party that

Ephraim and Judah Become One House

you can ever imagine — the ushering in of the Messianic Age!!!

G-d's People Fleeing From the Land of Babylon

Today, the greatest number of members from the *house of Israel*/Christianity and the *house of Judah*/Judaism live in the United States. When the two houses of Israel become united (Ezekiel *[Yechezekel]* 37:15-28), the *house of Israel*/Christianity and *the house of Judah*/Judaism will need to leave the USA and go to the land of Israel when the USA (Babylon) comes under the judgment of the G-d of Israel (Jeremiah *[Yermiyahu]* 50/51 and Revelation 18).

Spiritually (*sod*/deeper meaning), the USA is the land of Babylon. The word Babylon means *"confusion."* Babylon is a generic term in the Bible that refers to the ways of the adversary *(HaSatan)* and his kingdom of darkness. The Bible talks about a financial Babylon, a political Babylon, a religious Babylon and a land of Babylon. Literally *(Peshat)*, the land of Babylon is the area of Iran and Iraq. However, today, very few members of the *house of Israel*/Christianity and the *house of Judah*/Judaism live in Iran and Iraq. Therefore, there must also be a spiritual (*sod*/deeper meaning) land of Babylon.

Today, the USA is the spiritual land of Babylon. The G-d of Israel's greatest judgment of any nation on the earth will fall upon the USA because she has encouraged Israel to part the land (Joel *[Yoel]* 3:2) that the G-d of Israel promised Abraham *(Avraham)* (Genesis

Restoring the Two Houses of Israel

[Bereishit] 17:7-8) through UN Resolutions 242 and 338 and because the USA does not recognize Jerusalem (*Yerushalayim*) as being the capital of the nation of Israel but rather desires for it to be an international city. Furthermore, there is great immorality in the USA because of abortion, homosexuality, drugs, gambling and pornography etc.

The USA is the modern day Sodom and Gomorrah. In Jeremiah (*Yermiyahu*) 50:4-6, 17-18, 51:50 it is written:

> *"In those days and in that time* [a reference to the day of the LORD and the advent of the Messianic Age], *saith the LORD, the children of Israel shall come* [the assimilated Northern Kingdom/house of Israel/Christianity], *they and the children of Judah together* [the Southern Kingdom/house of Judah/Judaism] *going and weeping: they shall go, and seek the LORD their God. They shall ask the way to Zion* [the land of Israel] *with their faces thitherward, saying, Come, and let us join ourselves to the LORD in a perpetual covenant that shall not be forgotten. My people hath been lost sheep: their shepherds have caused them to go astray* [pastors in the church and rabbi's in the synagogues], *they have turned them away on the mountains: they have gone from mountain to hill, they have forgotten their resting place ...Israel is a scattered sheep; the lions have driven him away: first the king of Assyria hath devoured him* [the Northern Kingdom/house of Israel] *and last this Nebuchadnezzar king of Babylon hath broken his bones* [the Southern Kingdom/house of Judah]. *Therefore thus saith*

Ephraim and Judah Become One House

the LORD of hosts, the God of Israel; Behold, I will punish the king of Babylon and his land, as I have punished the king of Assyria ... Ye that have escaped the sword, [the war in Babylon/the USA] *go away, stand not still: remember the LORD afar off, and let Jerusalem come into your mind* [return to the land of Israel]"

In these verses in Jeremiah, we see the following:

1. The children of Israel (the Northern Kingdom/ Christianity) AND the children of Judah (the Southern Kingdom/Judaism) fleeing Babylon (the USA) and seeking their way to the land of Zion (the land of Israel) (Jeremiah *[Yermiyahu]* 50:4-5).

2. Their shepherds (religious leaders) in Christianity and Judaism have led the family of the G-d of Israel astray (Jeremiah *[Yermiyahu]* 50:6).

3. Those who have escaped the sword (war and judgment in the USA) are seeking the way to Jerusalem (Jeremiah *[Yermiyahu]* 51:50).

When Will the Two Houses of Israel Be United ???

In Hosea *(Hoshea)* 5:15, 6:1-4, it gives us a time reference **when** the two houses of Israel will be united as it is written:

"I will go and return to my place, till they acknowledge their offence, and seek my face: in their

affliction [the tribulation/Jacob's trouble/the birth pangs of the Messiah/*Chevlai shel Mashiach*] *they will seek me early. Come, and let us return unto the* LORD: *for he has torn, and he will heal us; he has smitten, and he will bind us up. After two days* [2,000 years] *will he revive us: in the third day* [1,000-year Messianic Age/ *Athid Lavo*] *he will raise us up, and we shall live in his sight. Then shall we know, if we follow on to know the* LORD: *his going forth is prepared as the morning; and he shall come unto us as the rain, as the latter and former rain unto the earth. O* **Ephraim** [house of Israel/Christianity] *what shall I do unto thee? O* **Judah** [house of Judah/ Judaism] *what shall I do unto thee? for your goodness is as a morning cloud, and as the early dew it goeth away."*

Highlighting these verses, it says:

"I will go and return to my place, till they **acknowledge their offence** *... in their* **affliction** *they will seek me early ...after* **two days** *... his going forth is prepared as the morning ... O* **Ephraim** *what shall I do unto thee? O* **Judah** *what shall I do unto thee?..."*

In this scripture, it tells us that the Jewish Messiah *(Mashiach) Yeshua*/Jesus will not return to the earth as the Kingly Messiah known as *Messiah ben David* until **THEY**, **Ephraim** (*the house of Israel*/Christianity) and **Judah** (*house of Judah*/Judaism), acknowledge their offence. What offence does Ephraim (*house of Israel*/ Christianity) have to acknowledge? What offence does

Ephraim and Judah Become One House

Judah (*house of Judah*/Judaism) have to acknowledge? Ephraim (*house of Israel*/Christianity) has to acknowledge that they have departed from the Torah of the G-d of Israel and have called it a "strange thing" (Hosea *[Hoshea]* 8:12). Judah (*house of Judah*/Judaism) has to acknowledge that *Yeshua*/Jesus is the Jewish Messiah *(Mashiach)*.

This will happen after two days (2,000 years) from the first coming of the Jewish Messiah *(Mashiach) Yeshua*/Jesus as the suffering Messiah known as *Messiah ben Yosef*/Joseph during their "affliction" which is a Jewish idiomatic phrase for the tribulation/*Chevlai shel Mashiach*/birth pangs of the Messiah/Jacob's trouble.

The Reunification of Ephraim and Judah During Jacob's Trouble

In Ezekiel *(Yechezekel)* 37:21-22 it tells us that when the two houses of Israel are united that they will return to the *"mountains of Israel."* The mountains of Israel are called in the Bible the mountains of Judea and Samaria. In the Western world, the mountains of Judea and Samaria are called the *"West Bank."* This is the land that the world wants Israel to give to the PLO so that they can have their PLO state.

By comparing Ezekiel *(Yechezekel)* 37:21-22 with Ezekiel *(Yechezekel)* 34:11-13, we can understand that the two houses will return to the *"mountains of Israel"* in a *"dark and cloudy day."* In Ezekiel *(Yechezekel)* 34:11-12 it is written:

Restoring the Two Houses of Israel

> *"For thus says the* L<small>ORD</small> *God; Behold, I, even I, will both search my sheep, and seek them out. As a shepherd seeks out his flock in the day that he is among his sheep that are scattered; so will I seek out my sheep, and will deliver them out of all places where they have been scattered in the* **CLOUDY AND DARK DAY.***"*

The *"dark and cloudy day"* is a Jewish idiom for the *"day of the* L<small>ORD</small>.*"* In Joel *(Yoel)* 2:1-2 it is written:

> *"Blow ye the trumpet in Zion, and sound an alarm in my holy mountain: let all the inhabitants of the land tremble: for the* **DAY OF THE LORD** *cometh, for it is nigh at hand; A day of darkness and of gloominess, a* **DAY OF CLOUDS AND OF THICK DARKNESS**…*"*

As we learned earlier in this book, the *"day of the* L<small>ORD</small>*"* is a Jewish idiom for the 1,000-year Messianic Age *(Athid Lavo)*. Furthermore, every Biblical day begins in the evening and ends in the morning (Genesis *[Bereishit]* 1. The "evening" part of the "day of the L<small>ORD</small>" is the tribulation/*Chevlai shel Mashiach*/Jacob's trouble. In Jeremiah *(Yermiyahu)* 30:1-7 it tells us that the two houses of Israel *(Ephraim* and *Judah)* will return to the land of Israel during Jacob's trouble as it is written:

> *"The word that came to Jeremiah from the* L<small>ORD</small>, *saying … For, lo, the days come says the* L<small>ORD</small>, *that I will bring again the captivity of my people* **Israel AND Judah** *says the* L<small>ORD</small>: *and I will cause them to* **return to the land** *that I gave to their fathers, and they shall possess it. And these*

Ephraim and Judah Become One House

are the words that the L ORD *spake concerning* **Israel AND** *concerning* **Judah**. *For thus says the* L ORD; *We have heard a voice of trembling, of fear, and not of peace. Ask ye now, and see whether a man does travail with child? Wherefore do I see every man with his hands on his loins, as a woman in travail,* [tribulation/birth pangs of the Messiah] *and all faces are turned into paleness? Alas! for that day is great, so that none is like it: it is even the time of Jacob's trouble* [Israel AND Judah]; *but he shall be saved out of it."*

In Jeremiah *(Yermiyahu)* 31:15-22, we also see Ephraim *(house of Israel/*Christianity) repenting for departing from the Torah of the G-d of Israel and returning to the land of Israel when "a woman shall compass a man" (which is a reference to the Messianic Age/*Athid Lavo*) as it is written:

"Thus saith the L ORD; *A voice was heard in Ramah, lamentation, and bitter weeping;* **Rachel weeping for her children** *refused to be comforted for her children, because they were not. Thus saith the* L ORD; *Refrain thy voice from weeping, and thine eyes from tears: for thy work shall be rewarded, saith the* L ORD; *and they shall come again from the land of the enemy. And there is hope in thine end, saith the* L ORD, *that* **thy children shall come again to their own border**. *I have surely heard* **Ephraim** *bemoaning himself thus; Thou hast chastised me, and I was chastised, as a bullock unaccustomed to the yoke: turn thou me, and I shall be turned; for thou art the* L ORD *my God. Surely after that I was turned, I* **repented;**

> *and after that I was instructed, I smote upon my thigh: I was ashamed yea, even confounded, because I did bear the reproach of my youth. Is* **Ephraim** *my dear son? Is he a pleasant child? for since I spake against him, I do earnestly remember him still: therefore my bowels are troubled for him; I will surely have mercy upon him, saith the* LORD. *Set thee up waymarks, make thee high heaps: set thine heart toward the highway, even the way which thou wentest: turn again, O virgin daughter, turn again to these thy cities. How long wilt thou go about, O thou backsliding daughter? for the* LORD *hath created a new thing in the earth,* **A woman shall compass a man.**"

This period of time when Ephraim and Judah will be restored and reunited with each other (Ezekiel [Yechezekel] 37:15-28) is also called *"the day of Jezreel."* In Hosea *(Hoshea)* 1:10-11, it tells us that when the G-d of Israel fulfills His covenant with Abraham *(Avraham)* and the two houses of Israel are reunited that the children of Israel AND the children of Judah shall walk together as it is written:

> *"Yet the number of the children of Israel shall be as the sand of the sea, which cannot be measured nor numbered;* [the words of G-d's covenant with Abraham] *and it shall come to pass, that in the place where it was said unto them, You are not my people, there it shall be said unto them, You are the sons of the living God. Then shall the children of* **Judah AND** *the children of* **Israel** *be gathered together, and appoint themselves one head* [Ezek-

Ephraim and Judah Become One House

iel 34:11-13, 23, 37:24-25] *and they shall come up out of the land: for* **great** *shall be the* **day of Jezreel**.*"*

In Jeremiah *(Yermiyahu)* 3:14, 17-18 it tells us that when the children of Israel and the children of Judah return to Zion (the land of Israel) and walk together that all nations will be gathered against Jerusalem *(Yerushalayim)* as it is written:

> *"Turn, O backsliding children says the* LORD; *for I am married unto you: and I will take you one of a city, and two of a family and* **I will bring you to Zion** ... *At that time they shall call* **Jerusalem** *the throne of the* LORD; *and* **all the nations shall be gathered unto i**t [Zechariah 14:2] ... *in those days the* **house of Judah** *shall* **walk with** *the* **house of Israel**, *and they shall come* **TOGETHER** *out of the land of the north* **to the land** *that I have given for an inheritance unto your fathers."*

Therefore, the two houses of Israel will be restored and reunited (Ezekiel 37:15-28) during Jacob's trouble (Jeremiah 30:7) in their affliction (Hosea 5:15) in the *"day of Jezreel"* (Hosea 1:11) when they return to the mountains of Israel (West Bank) (Ezekiel 34:11-13, 37:21-22) and walk together with each other (Hosea 1:11, Jeremiah 3:18) prior to the Jewish Messiah *(Mashiach) Yeshua*/Jesus setting His feet down upon the mount of Olives (Zechariah 14:4) and teaching the Torah to the nations from the city of Jerusalem *(Yerushalayim)* during the Messianic Age *(Athid Lavo)* (Isaiah 2:2-3).

Restoring the Two Houses of Israel

A Prayer For the Messianic Age

When the G-d of Israel made a covenant with Abraham, it was an eternal and everlasting covenant. The fulfillment of this covenant was dependent upon the seed of Abraham being obedient to the Torah of the G-d of Israel. By being obedient to the Torah of the G-d of Israel, the seed of Abraham was promised a land and the G-d of Israel would tabernacle with His people in this land. However, by being disobedient to the Torah of the G-d of Israel, the seed of Abraham would be exiled into all the nations of the earth.

After they were exiled, if the seed of Abraham repented and confessed their sins to the G-d of Israel, He promised to redeem them from all the nations where they have been scattered and bring them back to the land of Israel. The reunification of the seed of Abraham (the *house of Israel* and the *house of Judah*) would take place in the end of days prior to the coming of the Jewish Messiah and the establishment of the Messianic Age on the earth. During the Messianic Age, the G-d of Israel promised to tabernacle with His people through the Jewish Messiah.

This is the fullness of the covenant that the G-d of Israel made with Abraham. This is the Gospel according to Torah !!!

May the G-d of Israel redeem and restore the two houses of Israel and return them to the land of Israel and bring forth the Messianic age speedily in our Days.

NEXT YEAR IN JERUSALEM !!!

From the Author

I pray that this book has been a source of inspiration and rich blessing to you. If so, I would encourage you to read the other two books that I have written. They are entitled, *The Seven Festivals of the Messiah* and *Who is the Bride of Christ?*

The book, *The Seven Festivals of the Messiah,* teaches how the G-d of Israel gave the Biblical Festivals in Leviticus *(Vayikra)* 23 to teach about the first and second coming of the Jewish Messiah *(Mashiach) Yeshua*/Jesus and our personal relationship with Him. The price of this book is $12.00 (US), postage paid.

The book, *Who is the Bride of Christ?* examines the Biblical characteristics of the Bride of Messiah. It also shows how the future role and destiny of the Bride of Messiah in the Kingdom of G-d is related and associated with embracing our rich Hebraic heritage in Messiah. This book is $25.00 (US), also postage paid.

If you order the *Seven Festivals of the Messiah* and *Who is the Bride of Christ?* the cost is $32.00 (US), postage paid, for both books.

If you have a greater interest in studying the Hebraic roots of faith in the Jewish Messiah *(Mashiach) Yeshua*/ Jesus, I would encourage you to visit the *Hebraic Heri-*

Restoring the Two Houses of Israel

tage Ministries International website and join the GLOBAL network of ministries and individuals who are doing so by filling out the ministry guest book located at the website. Furthermore, at the website you will find MANY articles that will help you in studying the Hebraic roots of faith in Messiah. For more information about *Hebraic Heritage Ministries International*, please see the following page.

From the Author

Hebraic Heritage Ministries International

- Teaching the Hebraic Roots of faith in Messiah

- Networking Groups who are studying the Hebraic Roots of faith in Messiah

- Standing with the Jewish people and Fighting Anti-Semitism

- Christian Zionists who have a Loving Heart for the Land of Israel

Please visit our Web Site and Join our Network ! ! !

http://www.geocities.com/Heartland/2175/index.html

OR

http://www.hebroots.org/

Mailing Address:

Hebraic Heritage Ministries International
P.O. Box 81
Strasburg, Ohio, USA 44680

Endnotes

Forward

1. Adapted from Raphael Patai, *The Messiah Texts* (Detroit, Michigan: Wayne State University Press, 1988), p. 181.
2. Ibid., p. 321.
3. Ibid., p. 181.
4. Ibid., p. 144.

Chapter 4 — The Sabbath: Our Rest is in Messiah

1. Adapted from Theodor Gastor. *Festivals of the Jewish Year* (New York, New York: William Morrow Co., 1952), p. 282.
2. Pesikta Rabbathi, 117b.
3. Adapted from Rabbi Aryeh Kaplan. *Made in Heaven: A Jewish Wedding Guide.* (New York, New York: New York, New York: Moznaim Publishing, 1983), p. 194.
4. Gastor, *Festivals of the Jewish Year*, pp. 282-283.
5. Kaplan. *Made in Heaven: A Jewish Wedding Guide.* pp. 74, 77.
6. Ibid., p. 144.
7. Gastor, *Festivals of the Jewish Year*, p. 271.
8. Adapted from Isidor Margolis and Rabbi Sydney Markowitz. *The Jewish Holidays and Festivals.*

(New York, New York: Carol Publishing Group, 1962), p. 14.
9. Gastor, *Festivals of the Jewish Year*, p. 275.
10. Kaplan. *Made in Heaven: A Jewish Wedding Guide.* p. 173.
11. Adapted from Central Conference of American Rabbis. *Gates of the Seasons: A Guide to the Jewish Year.* (New York, New York, 1983), p. 19.

Chapter 7 — Is the Messiah G-d?

1. Adapted from Dr. James Trimm. "Let's Get Truthful: A Response to the Anti-Missionaries" (Tape series and Study Guide) (Hurst, Texas, 1999). Tape #9, "The Diety of the Messiah" and study notes.

   This tape series and study guide can be ordered from the Society for the Advancement of Nazarene Judaism (SANJ) at the following address:

   SANJ
   P.O. Box 471
   Hurst, Texas 76053

   Web address: **http://www.nazarene.net/**

2-27. Ibid.

Chapter 8 — Israel: The Fig Tree Blossoms

1. Adapted from Mike Evans, *Jerusalem Betrayed* (Nashville, Tennessee: Word Publishing, 1997), p. 143.

Endnotes

2.. Adapted from Stanley Ellisen, *Who Owns the Land?* (Portland, Oregon: Multnomah Press), p. 60.
3. Adapted from James Rudin, *Israel for Christians* (Philadelphia, Pennsylvania: Fortress Press, 1983), p. 24.
4. Ellisen, *Who Owns the Land?* p. 60.
5. Evans, *Jerusalem Betrayed*, p. 144.
6. Ellisen, *Who Owns the Land?* p. 62.
7. Adapted from Howard Sachar, *A History of Israel: From the Rise of Zionism to Our Time* (New York, New York: Alfred A. Knopf, Inc., 1976), p. 354.
8. Ellisen, *Who Owns the Land?* p. 63.
9. Ibid., p. 63.
10. Adapted from Alan Taylor, *Prelude to Israel* (New York, New York: Philosophical Library, 1959), p. 15.
11. Ellisen, *Who Owns the Land?* p. 67.
12. Adapted from William Hull, *The Fall and Rise of Israel* (Grand Rapids, Michigan: Zondervan Publishing Co., 1954), p. 129.
13. Adapted from Louis Finkelstein, *The Jews, Their History, Culture and Religion*. 2 Vols. (New York, New York: Harper and Bros., 1949), p. 691.
14. Sachar, *A History of Israel: From the Rise of Zionism to Our Time*, pp. 128-129.
15. Adapted from Michael Cohen, *Palestine and the Great Powers, 1945-1948* (Princeton, New Jersey: Princeton Univ. Press, 1982), p. 184.
16. Evans, *Jerusalem Betrayed*, p. 163.
17. Hull, *The Fall and Rise of Israel*, p. 142.
18. Ibid., p. 204.
19. Ellisen, *Who Owns the Land?* p. 71.

20. Evans, *Jerusalem Betrayed*, p. 171.
21. Hull, *The Fall and Rise of Israel*, p. 205.
22. Evans, *Jerusalem Betrayed*, p. 171.
23. Hull, *The Fall and Rise of Israel*, p. 205.
24. Ellisen, *Who Owns the Land?* p. 72.
25. Ibid., p. 75.
26. Dimont, *Jews, God and History* pp. 378-379.
27. Ellisen, *Who Owns the Land?* pp. 82-83.
28. Rudin, *Israel for Christians*, p. 45.
29. Adapted from Dennis Prager and Joseph Telushkin *Why the Jews?* (New York, New York: Simon and Schuster, Inc., 1983), p. 155.
30. Finkelstein, *The Jews, Their History, Culture and Religion*, p. 1532.
31. Ellisen, *Who Owns the Land?* p. 91.
32. Adapted from Michael Pragai, *Faith and Fulfillment* (London, England: Vallentine, Michell and Co., 1985), p. 232
33. Ibid.
34. Taylor, *Prelude to Israel*, p. 56-57.
35. Cohen, *Palestine and the Great Powers, 1945-1948*, p. 20.
36. Ellisen, *Who Owns the Land?* p. 92.
37. Hull, *The Fall and Rise of Israel*, p. 235.
38. Taylor, *Prelude to Israel*, pp. 94-95.
39. Ellisen, *Who Owns the Land?* p. 93.
40. Cohen, *Palestine and the Great Powers, 1945-1948*, p. 186.
41. Ellisen, *Who Owns the Land?* p. 93.
42. Evans, *Jerusalem Betrayed*, p. 174.
43. Sachar, *A History of Israel: From the Rise of Zionism to Our Time*, p. 278.
44. Cohen, *Palestine and the Great Powers, 1945-1948*, p. 274.

Endnotes

45. Taylor, *Prelude to Israel*, p. 102.
46. Ellisen, *Who Owns the Land?* pp. 99, 101.
47. Ibid. p. 99.
48. Sachar, *A History of Israel: From the Rise of Zionism to Our Time*, p. 289.
49. Ibid. p. 291.
50. Pragai, *Faith and Fulfillment*, p. 224.
51. Cohen, *Palestine and the Great Powers, 1945-1948*, pp. 305-306.
52. Ellisen, *Who Owns the Land?* p. 103.
53. Sachar, *A History of Israel: From the Rise of Zionism to Our Time*, p. 444.
54. Hull, *The Fall and Rise of Israel*, pp. 333, 340.
55. Sachar, *A History of Israel: From the Rise of Zionism to Our Time*, p. 444.
56. Hull, *The Fall and Rise of Israel*, p. 342.
57. Ibid.
58. Ellisen, *Who Owns the Land?* p. 107.
59. Ibid., p. 111.
60. Ibid., p. 112.
61. Ibid., p. 113.
62. Evans, *Jerusalem Betrayed*, p. 213.
63. Ellisen, *Who Owns the Land?* p. 114.
64. Sachar, *A History of Israel: From the Rise of Zionism to Our Time*, p. 640.
65. Ibid.
66. Sachar, *A History of Israel: From the Rise of Zionism to Our Time*, p. 656.
67. Ellisen, *Who Owns the Land?* p. 115.
68. Cecil Roth, *Encyclopedia Judaica* (Jerusalem, Israel: Keter Publishing House, 1972), p. 493.
69. Sachar, *A History of Israel: From the Rise of Zionism to Our Time*, p. 667.
70. Ellisen, *Who Owns the Land?* p. 115.

Restoring the Two Houses of Israel

71. Sachar, *A History of Israel: From the Rise of Zionism to Our Time*, p. 750.
72. Ibid., p. 759.
73. Ibid.
74. Ibid., p. 812.
75. Ibid., p. 791.
76. Ellisen, *Who Owns the Land?* p. 122.
77. Ibid., p. 127
78. Adapted from Thomas Kiernan, *Arafat: The Man and the Myth* (New York, New York: W.W. Norton and Co., 1976), p. 114.
79. Adapted from Amos Perlmutter, *Israel: The Partitioned State, A Political History Since 1900* (New York, New York: Charles Scribner's Sons, 1985), p. 34.
80. Kiernan, *Arafat: The Man and the Myth*, pp. 114, 116.
81. Ibid., p. 14.
82. Ellisen, *Who Owns the Land?* p. 129.
83. Kiernan, *Arafat: The Man and the Myth*, pp. 113.
84. Ibid., pp. 160-161, 235.
85. Evans, *Jerusalem Betrayed*, p. 64.
86. Adapted from Alan Hart, *Arafat: Terrorist or Peacemaker* (London, England: Sidgwick and Jackson, 1984), p. 163.
87. Ibid., p. 118.
88. Evans, *Jerusalem Betrayed*, pp. 64-65.
89. Ibid., p. 127.
90. Kiernan, *Arafat: The Man and the Myth*, p. 80.
91. Ibid., p. 25.
92. Ibid., p. 202.
93. Evans, *Jerusalem Betrayed*, p. 65.
94. Kiernan, *Arafat: The Man and the Myth*, p. 231.
95. Ellisen, *Who Owns the Land?* p. 132.

Endnotes

96. Adapted from Yehoshafat, Harkabi, *Israel's Fateful Hour* (New York, New York: Harper and Row, 1988), p. 14-22.
97. Ellisen, *Who Owns the Land?* pp. 135-136.
98. Adapted from David Grossman, *The Yellow Wind* (New York, New York: Farrar, Straus, and Giroux, 1988), pp. 151.
99. Adapted from David Shipler, *Arab and Jew* (New York, New York: Times Book (Random House), 1986), p. 144.
100. Ibid., p. 110.
101. Ellisen, *Who Owns the Land?* p. 143.
102. Evans, *Jerusalem Betrayed*, pp. 72-73.
103. Ibid., pp. 73-75.
104. Ibid., p. 78.
105. Ibid., p. 80.
106. Ibid., pp. 80-81.

Chapter 11 — The Judgment of the Nations

1. Evans, *Jerusalem Betrayed*, p. 92.
2. Ibid., pp. 92-93.
3. Ibid., p. 100.
4. Ibid., p. 50.
5. Ibid., p. 51.

Bibliography

American-Israeli Cooperative Enterprise (AICE), Jewish Student Online Research Center (JSOURCE) Internet Web site: http://www.us-israel.org/jsource/index.html.

Central Conference of American Rabbis. *Gates of the Seasons: A Guide to the Jewish Year.* New York, New York, 1983.

Cohen, Michael. *Palestine and the Great Powers, 1945-1948.* Princeton, New Jersey: Princeton Univ. Press, 1982.

Dimont, Max. *Jews, God and History.* New York, New York: Simon and Schuster, 1962.

Ellisen, Stanley. *Who Owns the Land?* Portland, Oregon: Multnomah Press, 1991.

Evans, Mike. *Jerusalem Betrayed.* Nashville, Tennessee: Word Publishing, 1997.

Finkelstein, Louis. *The Jews, Their History, Culture and Religion.* 2 Volumes. New York, New York: Harper and Bros., 1949.

Gastor, Theodor. *Festivals of the Jewish Year*. New York, New York: William Morrow Co., 1952.

Good, Joseph. "Rosh HaShanah and the Messianic Kingdom to Come." Port Arthur, Texas: Hatikva Ministries, 1989.

Grossman, David. *The Yellow Wind*. New York, New York: Farrar, Straus, and Giroux, 1988.

Harkabi, Yehoshafat. *Israel's Fateful Hour*. New York, New York: Harper and Row Publishers, 1988.

Hart, Alan. *Arafat: Terrorist or Peacemaker*. London, England: Sidgwick and Jackson, 1984.

Hull, William. *The Fall and Rise of Israel*. Grand Rapids, Michigan: Zondervan Publishing Co., 1954.

Israel Ministry of Foreign Affairs Internet Web site: http://www.mfa.gov.il/mfa/home.asp.

Jeffrey, Grant R. *Armageddon Appointment with Destiny*. Toronto, Ontario: Frontier Research Publications, 1988.

Kaplan, Rabbi Aryeh. *Made in Heaven: A Jewish Wedding Guide*. New York, New York: Moznaim Publishing, 1983.

_____ . *The Aryeh Kaplan Anthology II*. New York, New York: Noble Book Press Corp., 1991.

Bibliography

Kiernan, Thomas. *Arafat: The Man and the Myth.* New York, New York: W.W. Norton and Co., 1976.

Lapin, Rabbi Daniel. "America's Biblical Blueprint." Mercer Island, Washington: Cascadia Tapes, Inc., 1997.

Margolis, Isidor and Rabbi Sydney Markowitz. *The Jewish Holidays and Festivals.* New York, New York: Carol Publishing Group, 1962.

Patai, Raphael. *The Messiah Texts.* Detroit, Michigan: Wayne State University Press, 1988.

Perlmutter, Amos. *Israel: The Partitioned State, A Political History Since 1900.* New York, New York: Charles Scribner's Sons, 1985.

Pragai, Michael. *Faith and Fulfillment.* London, England: Vallentine, Michell and Co., 1985.

Prager, Dennis and Joseph Telushkin. *Why the Jews?* New York, New York: Simon and Schuster, Inc., 1983.

Roth, Cecil. *Encyclopaedia Judaica.* Jerusalem, Israel: Keter Publishing House, 1972.

Routtenberg, Lilly and Ruth Seldin, *The Jewish Wedding Book.* New York, New York: Harper and Row Publishers, 1967.

Rudin, James. *Israel for Christians.* Philadelphia, Pennsylvania: Fortress Press, 1983.

Sachar, Howard. *A History of Israel: From the Rise of Zionism to Our Time.* New York, New York: Alfred A. Knopf, Inc, 1976.

Shipler, David. *Arab and Jew.* New York, New York: Times Book (Random House), 1986.

Taylor, Alan. *Prelude to Israel.* New York, New York: Philosophical Library, 1959.

Trimm, James Dr. "Let's Get Truthful: A Response to the Anti-Missionaries." Hurst, Texas: Society for the Advancement of Nazarene Judaism (SANJ), 1999.

Notes

Notes

Notes

Od Yishama

Od Yishama B'aray Yehuda
Uv'chutzot, Uv'chutzot
Yerushalayim

Od Yishama B'aray Yehuda
Uv'chutzot, Uv'chutzot
Yerushalayim

Kol Sasson V'kol Simcha
Kol Chatan V'kol Kalah

Kol Sasson V'kol Simcha
Kol Chatan V'kol Kalah

A Song Shall Be Heard

"Thus saith the Lord; Again there shall be heard in this place, which ye say shall be desolate without man and without beast, even in the cities of Judah, and in the streets of Jerusalem ... the voice of joy, and the voice of gladness, the **voice of the bridegroom***, and the* **voice of the bride***..."*
(Jeremiah *[Yermiyahu]* 33:10-11)

Shaloo, Shalom, Yerushalayim!!!

Pray for the peace of Jerusalem!!!

Shalom in Messiah!!!